The Great Road

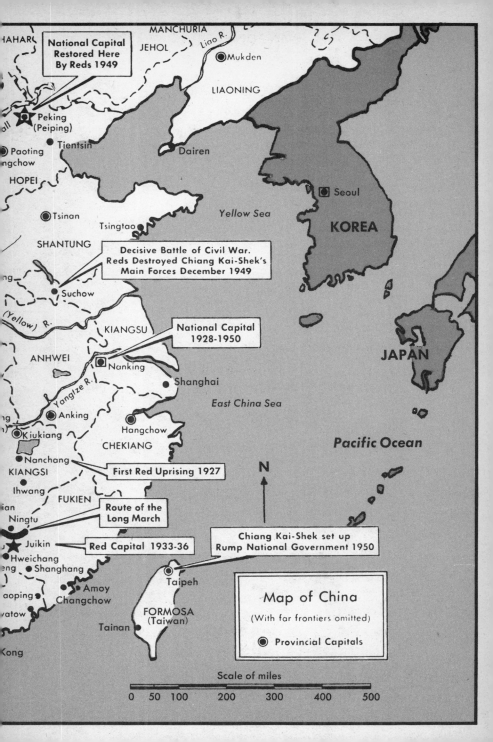

CHAHAR

MANCHURIA

JEHOL

Liao R.

National Capital Restored Here By Reds 1949

Mukden

LIAONING

Peking (Peiping)

Tientsin

Dairen

Paoting

ngchow

HOPEI

Seoul

Tsinan

Yellow Sea

KOREA

SHANTUNG

Tsingtao

Decisive Battle of Civil War. Reds Destroyed Chiang Kai-Shek's Main Forces December 1949

Suchow

(Yellow) R.

KIANGSU

National Capital 1928-1950

ANHWEI

Nanking

Shanghai

JAPAN

Yangtze R.

Anking

East China Sea

Kiukiang

Hangchow

CHEKIANG

Pacific Ocean

Nanchang

First Red Uprising 1927

KIANGSI

Ihwang

N

FUKIEN

Route of the Long March

Ningtu

Chiang Kai-Shek set up Rump National Government 1950

Juikin

Red Capital 1933-36

Hweichang

eng Shanghang

aoping   Amoy

Changchow

vatow

Taipeh

Kong

FORMOSA
(Taiwan)

Tainan

Map of China

(With far frontiers omitted)

◉ Provincial Capitals

Scale of miles

0   50 100   200   300   400   500

CHU TEH, 1937

The Great Road

The Life and Times
of Chu Teh

by Agnes Smedley

New York and London

Publisher's Foreword

HISTORIANS of the present are peculiarly fallible. They are circumscribed not only by the unavailability of many facts of varying degrees of relevance but also by the difficulties in the way of achieving a three-dimensional stereoscopic view of the facts falling within their field of vision. Yet it is already safe to assert that the Chinese Revolution of 1949 is one of the crucial turning points of the twentieth century, ranking with the October Revolution and the defeat of fascism in World War II in world-historical importance. It has profoundly if not decisively affected the balance of forces between the socialist and nonsocialist parts of the world. It has dealt a mortal blow to imperialism in Asia and probably in Africa. It has conclusively shown that a social revolution can be successfully carried through in an economically backward country with only a small modern industrial base and urban proletariat.

Life is richer than any theory, however subtle and complex. The Chinese Communists are Marxists, not Hegelians. When it became clear that the Chinese Revolution could not be contained in the accepted Marxist formulas, they did not say, "So much the worse for the Chinese facts." In the midst of their struggle for survival they proceeded to evolve a more flexible and sophisticated theory which enriched Marxism by reflecting and absorbing the stubborn realities of the Chinese scene.

We do not have to await the verdict of future historians to decide that, as far as China was concerned, the Chinese Communists were better Marxists than their foreign mentors, whether Russian, German, French, or Anglo-Saxon. It was one of the paradoxical legacies of imperialism that, because of the prestige attaching to anything foreign—including foreign revolutionaries—in an economically backward country, the Chinese Communist Party had time and again to pay for mistakes for which its foreign advisers were to a considerable, if still undetermined extent responsible. Some of these mistakes, as in the periods immediately preceding the counter-revolutions in Shanghai and Hankow in 1927 and during the Fifth Kuomintang Extermination Campaign in 1933-1934, were almost suicidal in their consequences and entailed great suffering and loss of life. The wheel was to turn full circle, for the Chinese Communists, having thoroughly digested the lessons of the past, showed themselves far less dependent on foreign advice and aid in acquiring power than did the Kuomintang in losing it. There is no need to point the moral for progressives everywhere, whether in the industrially advanced but often politically backward countries or in the colonial and semi-colonial countries still struggling toward national emancipation.

The fallibility of contemporary historians does not reduce their responsibility either to the present generation or to posterity. Like the course of the Chinese Revolution itself, American works on China in the last thirty years have been extremely uneven. It is sad but true that there is still no reasonably comprehensive and dependable book in English on the background and course of the Great Revolution of 1925–1927. Yet the events of those fateful years, in which scores of millions of Chinese began for the first time to take an active part in molding their own lives, are no less fascinating, no less packed with drama and melodrama, no less fraught with historical significance, than the French Revolution from 1789 to 1793. Much Western writing on the subject is dominated by issues often bearing as much on Russian Communist Party history as on China, and its angle of vision tends to suffer from the same kind, if not the same degree, of Europo-centrism as the reminiscences of Old China Hands. For the rest, to this day many Westerners are dependent on Malraux's *Man's Fate* for their impressions of the Great Revolution. Whatever its literary merits—and they are no doubt substantial—*Man's Fate* is primarily a story about foreigners in China, or rather in Treaty Port China, and is, moreover, chronologically unreliable. In any case, no conscientious intellectual would want to rely on *A Tale of Two Cities* or *The Gods Are Athirst* for his impressions of the French Revolution.

With the 1930s, the record of contemporary historical writing on China began to be much more creditable. A number of Americans have written excellent books either directly on China or with a predominantly China background, although it must be confessed that with one or two exceptions professional historians are not to be found in their ranks and that the stream has been drying up of late. Such outstanding works as Edgar Snow's *Red Star Over China*, Jack Belden's *China Shakes the World*, *The Stilwell Diaries*, and Carlson's *The Chinese Army*—the list is not intended to be exhaustive—immediately come to mind.

Agnes Smedley's works must stand high on any such list. Together they constitute a valuable contribution to the history of the Chinese Revolution. In her own words, she was "neither brave nor learned, just historically curious." It says much for her untutored historical curiosity that it was sufficiently strong to enable her to identify herself and grow with the Chinese Revolution.

She has told us something of her own background in *Daughter of Earth* and *Battle Hymn of China*. She was born in a north Missouri village in 1893. When she was still quite small, her family moved to a Rockefeller mining camp in Colorado where she acquired a hatred of capitalism with the air she breathed.

She became and remained an aggressive feminist throughout her life. There are few more touching passages in her writings than her description in *China Fights Back* of her reaction to Chu Teh's refusal to let her go to the Eighth Route Army anti-Japanese battlefront at Wutaishan in the winter of 1937. Evans Carlson's diary gives an independent eye-witness account, which is worth quoting in full:

I told Agnes about my trip to the front, and at dinner tonight at 4 p.m. (our usual hour) Agnes asked Chu Teh for permission to go to Wu T'ai Shan with me. Both Chu Teh and Jen Peh-hsi demurred. They offered various excuses, said that those who went to the front had to be prepared to shoot.

"I'll shoot!" said Agnes. "I was raised in the West."

"But you are a woman," they objected.

Well, that raised Agnes' ire. She went for them with all the fire she possesses which is considerable.

"I'm not a woman because I want to be," she said. And as an afterthought, she flung out with biting sarcasm, "God made me this way!"

Well, that brought down the house, for, of course, they were all atheists. (Michael Blankfort, *The Big Yankee*, Boston, 1947, p. 209.)

But, unlike other less socially minded feminists, she disdained to make a career out of her feminism. The "daughter of earth" was a working-class mixture of Harriet Beecher Stowe and Florence Nightingale as well as Susan B. Anthony. When, during her endeavors to make up for the stunted education of her childhood (she did not even complete grade school), she came into contact with Indian nationalists in New York City, she threw herself into the Indian independence movement. As this occurred during World War I and as she was wholehearted in whatever she did, she landed in solitary confinement in the Tombs. The

British accusation that she was a German agent was as baseless as the charge, rifled from Japanese police files thirty years later, that she was a Chinese Communist agent. In fact, Agnes Smedley never was a Communist. To quote the *Battle Hymn of China:* "For years I listened to Communists with sympathy and in later years in China I gave them my active support, but I could never place my mind and life unquestioningly at the disposal of their leaders. I never believed that I myself was especially wise, but I could not become a mere instrument in the hands of men who believed that they held the one and only key to truth."

It is quickly apparent from her writings that her beliefs and conduct were not the products of complex reasoning processes. She was content to follow her heart, and if her political analyses and judgments of individuals were sometimes unsophisticated, her class instinct, which according to Lenin is the beginning though not the end of political wisdom, stood her in good stead in most situations.

Her eight years in Germany she spent in learning German, studying Indian history and Chinese nationalism, and teaching English for a living. Although much of her energy was taken up by personal problems, she found time to help organize the first German state birth control clinic and to participate in the political life of Indian and Chinese residents in Germany.

Agnes Smedley first went to China at the end of 1928 as the special correspondent of the *Frankfurter Zeitung.* (Perhaps one should not read too much into the fact that Agnes Smedley and Edgar Snow, two of the outstanding American journalists reporting on China, were employed for many years by German and English newspapers.) The Chinese people never had a better American friend. "I always forgot I was not a Chinese myself" was no mere literary pose but the simple expression of the depth of her emotional identification.

Her very first reaction was characteristic. When she saw a policeman kicking a coolie in a street in Harbin, she said to her interpreter, "This is the Middle Ages," which is not very different in substance from Tawney's more deliberate verdict. She traveled south and, making Shanghai her headquarters, became a close friend of the great Chinese author Lu Hsun and of Mao Tun, now the President of the Association of Chinese Writers. Undeterred by threats of physical violence and by numerous attempts at intimidation, she fearlessly reported on Japanese aggression and on the Kuomintang terror. One of her notable successes was her contribution to obtaining the release of the Chinese woman novelist, Ting Ling, from jail after the latter had been kidnapped by the Blue Shirts. Her newspaper articles and early books on China pro-

vide a much-needed corrective to the stereotyped picture to be found in
so many American textbooks on the Far East, a picture of steady social
and economic progress in Kuomintang China in the decade between
Chiang Kai-shek's betrayal of the revolution in 1927 and the outbreak
of the Sino-Japanese War in 1937. *China's Red Army Marches* was one
of the first books in English to give an account of the growth of the
Red Army and of the Soviet Republic in Kiangsi, and it still remains
a vivid human document.

Agnes Smedley was never constitutionally strong and she was prone
to overtax her reserves of nervous energy. Her health broke down in
1933, and she spent nearly a year recuperating in the Soviet Union. But
she could not stay away from China. On revisiting America in 1934
after being away some fifteen years, she found it "like a strange planet."
Nor could she reconcile herself to staying in Russia, where she could
have lived comfortably on the royalties from translations of her writings, and where "life . . . would have been free and easy compared
with China." Still far from recovered, she returned to China and was
soon advised to convalesce in Sian. The climate there was physically
and, towards the end of 1936, politically more salubrious than that of
Shanghai. She thus had a ringside seat at the Sian Incident, surely one
of the most fantastically complicated and tortuous episodes of recent
times. Yet it has an underlying simplicity which saves it from being
merely bizarre. Chiang Kai-shek wanted to wipe out the Chinese Communists. The Chinese people wanted to resist the Japanese invaders—and
something had to give.

It so transpired that Agnes Smedley was one of the minor casualties
at Sian. She was hounded by a Blue Shirt officer and held up by trigger-
happy marauding soldiers. But she was as unaffected by such personal
mishaps as was Rayna Prohme before her. Needless to say, she was
persona non gratissima with the Kuomintang government, and as government troops moved towards Sian early in 1937, she availed herself
of the opportunity to spend some time in Yenan, where she met many
Chinese Communist leaders. She found the personality of Chu Teh
particularly sympathetic and decided to write his biography. In March
of 1937, she began the regular series of conversations with him which
were to furnish the raw material for *The Great Road*.

These conversations were never finished. The Sino-Japanese War
started in July, and Chu Teh had to leave for the front. Despite her
chronic gastric ulcers and a serious back injury, Miss Smedley toured
the base hospitals and saw more of Chu Teh in action on the Shansi
front towards the end of 1937. Most of 1938 she spent in Hankow

where she participated in the drive for international medical aid to the Chinese Army and to the Chinese Red Cross Medical Corps. She was appalled by the scale on which America was providing Japan with the sinews of war and was one of the few who tried to rouse world public opinion against this abominable traffic in death. She also helped in enlisting foreign doctors, including Norman Bethune and a number of Indian and refugee European doctors, for the Eighth Route and other Armies.

Leaving Hankow just before it fell in October 1938, she wore herself out traveling with armies at the front and tirelessly inspecting their hospitals. Her account of the New Fourth Army is justly celebrated. The story of the "little devil," Shen Kuo-hua, who was assigned to her as an orderly by the Storm Guerrilla Detachment (its commander, Li Hsien-nien, is now Minister of Finance in the People's Government at Peking), was included by Hemingway in his anthology of war literature under the title "After Final Victory." Perhaps the tribute she cherished most was the one Kuo-hua himself paid her in a little market town the inhabitants of which had never seen a foreigner:

"She is a woman and our American friend! She helps our wounded. In Tingjiachun she found a wounded man and fed him and gave him a bath. She even helped him do all his business." . . . "Look at her bandaged hand!" he demanded, taking my hand in his. "She got this when she picked up a pan of hot water while she was bathing a wounded soldier. She is both my father and my mother. If any of you are sick, she will cure you."

Only when hospitalization had become imperative did she consent to go to Hongkong where she soon resumed her propaganda activities despite local red tape.

Agnes Smedley's flaming sincerity attracted a wide variety of people. The friendships with Madame Sun Yat-sen, Evans Carlson, and General Stilwell are easily understandable, but her circle also included Major (now General) Dorn, J. B. Powell, and a number of other American correspondents in China, the British Ministry of Information representative in Hongkong, Donald MacDougall, and the British Ambassador to China, Sir Archibald Clark Kerr. Clark Kerr was a minor Scottish laird, an intellectual, a brilliant diplomat, and entirely human. It is hard to fathom why he was transferred from Chungking, where he was doing a superb job in most difficult circumstances, to Moscow, where his special talents found no outlet. Foreign Offices move in mysterious ways their wonders to perform.

The New Fourth Army episode in December 1940–January 1941 brought about a sharp deterioration in the internal situation and heightened the danger of civil war. To return to Kuomintang China and remain ineffectual under the surveillance of Tai Li's police was impossible for a person of Miss Smedley's temperament. Accordingly, in the summer of 1941 she decided to go back to the United States, where in *Battle Hymn of China* she faithfully carried out the testament of the Kwangsi general, Chung Yi: "Tell your countrymen. . . . Tell your countrymen." After 1945, she longed to return to China, but with the outbreak of civil war her journey had to be deferred. She hoped to resume her conversations with Chu Teh where they had broken off in 1937. But it was not to be. An incurable illness protracted her stay in England, where she died early in 1950, an exile from her native land and from the country whose cause she had so faithfully served for over twenty years.

Unfortunately, her failing health prevented her from doing much work on her manuscript of *The Great Road*. What she left was all in first draft which she intended to revise as well as supplement. The reader will notice that there is a complete blank between the end of the Second Kuomintang Extermination Campaign in 1931 and the beginning of the Long March in October 1934, and that the story after the end of 1937, when she stopped seeing Chu Teh (though she continued to receive letters from him), is skimpish and is really only a preliminary sketch. This is easy to understand since her plan to return to China was never fulfilled. Moreover, an adequate post-1937 narrative would have required a summary of Communist-Kuomintang relations, the fluctuating tide of the Sino-Japanese and Civil Wars, and the role of America in Chinese affairs up to the triumph of the People's Liberation Army; for Chu Teh's life after 1937 was inseparable from the unfolding national drama. This would have been a major undertaking transcending her original intentions and could only have been carried out in much more propitious circumstances.

The blank between 1931 and 1934 is less comprehensible. In *Battle Hymn of China* Miss Smedley states that between March and early July, 1937, she had taken down the record of Chu Teh's life up to 1934 and that she stored her notebooks before departing for the front. It must be inferred either that the notebooks for 1931-1934 were subsequently lost or that she never had a chance to make even a first draft of the material they contained. The former seems more likely, since in the text she has many highly enlightening details on the course of the Long March itself. Perhaps her executors will some day be able to remove any doubts as to the notebooks, which should certainly be pre-

served if they are ever located. As it is, it is necessary to give a minimum
indispensable background to the immediate antecedents of the Long
March.*

The Red Army had decisively rebuffed the Fourth Extermination
Campaign launched by Chiang Kai-shek in the spring of 1933. In two
battles, three Kuomintang divisions had been annihilated and more
than 10,000 rifles captured. Accordingly, Chiang made the most thor-
oughgoing preparations for the Fifth Campaign which started in
October, 1933, and ended with the departure of the Red Army from
Kiangsi in October, 1934, on its epic Long March of 8,000 miles. He
mobilized nearly a million men, an air force of nearly 400 planes, and
vast supplies for the project. The international situation was very
favorable from Chiang's point of view. He had just received a $50
million Wheat Loan from the RFC, and he enjoyed at least the moral
support of all the major powers except the Soviet Union. The strategy
of the campaign was planned by his German military advisers, headed
by Von Seeckt, former Chief of Staff of the German Army. It was
designed to derive the maximum advantage from the Kuomintang
Armies' overwhelming superiority in manpower and in matériel and
gradually to throttle the Red Army by a tight economic blockade and
by a system of ever-narrowing circles of blockhouses. (A similar system
was later adopted by the Japanese but with much less success, partly
because they were operating over much larger areas, but mainly because
the Communists had learned their lesson in Kiangsi and responded in
accordance with the basic Chu-Mao military doctrine.)

What was the situation in the Communist camp in October of 1933?
This was precisely the period in which the so-called third "Left" line
associated with Wang Ming and Po Ku was exerting its greatest influence. The provisional Central Committee headed by Po Ku had recently moved its headquarters from Shanghai to the Kiangsi base area
and intervened disastrously in military affairs. As a result of its erro-
neous diagnosis of the overall situation ("the situation for an immediate
revolution now exists in China"; the Fifth Campaign would determine "which is the victor and which the vanquished in the contest
between the revolutionary way and the colonial way"; and so on), it
rejected an alliance with the Fukien rebellion led by the patriotic Tsai
Ting-kai, whose Nineteenth Route Army had distinguished itself in the

* For further detail, see Mao Tse-tung, "Strategic Problems of China's Revolutionary War," *Selected Works*, Vol. I, pp. 175-253; "Resolution on Some Questions
in the History of Our Party," *Selected Works*, Vol. IV, pp. 171-218; and Edgar
Snow, *Red Star Over China*, pp. 179-188 and 389-392.

fighting at Shanghai in 1932. Much worse, the Committee fell right into the trap set by the German generals and persisted in fighting a passive positional warfare to which the base area's resources were simply not adapted.

The course of the campaign is described by Mao as follows:

> . . . the enemy advanced by means of the new strategy of building blockhouses, and first occupied Lichwan. However, in the hope of recovering it and halting the enemy beyond the border of the base area, we attacked Siaoshih, which was a strong enemy position in the White area southeast of Lichwan, but again we gained no ground. Then we moved back and forth seeking battle between the enemy's main forces and his blockhouses and were reduced to a completely passive position. All through the fifth counter-campaign, which lasted a year, we did not show the slightest initiative or dynamic force. . . . We lost the initiative in our first move—certainly the stupidest and worst way of fighting. (*Selected Works*, Vol. I, pp. 232 and 234.)

The Communists simply could not survive in their base area after the losses they endured. They suffered 60,000 casualties in one siege, and the Kuomintang itself admitted that "about 1,000,000 people (almost entirely peasants) were killed or starved to death in the process of recovering Soviet Kiangsi" (Snow, *op. cit.*, p. 186). Whoever was responsible for the mistakes,* there was no alternative but to abandon Kiangsi in order to save the Red Army. The sequel was the famous Long March.

The history of Agnes Smedley's repeatedly thwarted attempts to com-

---

* Snow suggests that a Comintern advisory committee in Shanghai must share this responsibility together with Li Teh, the German Communist military adviser, who arrived in Kiangsi in 1933 (*op. cit.*, pp. 389-392). But Snow's account of their role is obscure, not altogether consistent, and admittedly conjectural. There is no reason to doubt that the Chinese Communists utilized Li Teh's professional knowledge of German General Staff strategy and tactics. Whether his military recommendations were adopted, and, if so, whether it was because of his prestige as a Comintern emissary or because they were supported by the temporarily dominant Po Ku group, is not known. The guess may be hazarded that the Po Ku group exploited Li Teh's prestige as a *foreign* military expert to get their own military policy adopted. In any case, the official "Resolution on Some Questions in the History of Our Party" attaches the blame to the dominance of the third "Left" line and does not even contain a hint of the subordinate Snow hypothesis that the foreigner, Li Teh, was a convenient scapegoat. Perhaps here too there is a lesson for foreign progressives.

plete her biography of Chu Teh is a sufficient explanation of *The Great Road's* unevenness in quality and coverage. This unevenness is somehow in keeping with the biographer's character and may therefore be aesthetically appropriate.

What is more relevant for students of contemporary history, it does not seriously detract from the book's importance as a social and historical document of the highest value. Together with Tretiakov's *Chinese Testament* and Mao's "autobiography" in Snow's *Red Star*, it immediately takes its place as a sociological classic. These works are worth more than all the polysyllabic outpourings of the academic sociologists who impose their Max-Weberian abstractions on the void of their ignorance of China. They plunge readers into Chinese society with its vivid diversity and its howling contradictions, and at the same time introduce them to flesh-and-blood individuals who, precisely because of their individuality, typify large social groups. It would be absurd to pretend that Chu Teh is merely a "typical" Chinese peasant. Yet where can one find a better example of typical, if conflicting, peasant attitudes than in his desire to help on the farm after passing his first— and last—imperial examination and his family's horror at the blasphemous spectacle of a scholar degrading himself, and therefore his economic value to them, by manual labor?

It would be instructive to compare *The Great Road* with *Chinese Testament* in some detail. The latter is the biography of a student in the turbulent years encompassing the 1911 Revolution, the May 4th Movement, and the first Kuomintang-Communist United Front. Like the Tans, the Chus were Szechwanese. Like Tan Shih-hua's father, Chu Teh was a member of the Ko Lao Hui, the Tung Men Hui, and the Kuomintang, and a participant in the 1911 Revolution and in the defeat of Yuan Shih-kai's attempted restoration of the monarchy. Both risked their lives many times for the abortive bourgeois-democratic revolution. Like Tan Shih-hua himself, Chu Teh was deeply affected by the nationalist upsurge following the May 4th Movement. Tan, a left-wing Kuomintang student in Peking, decided to complete his education in Moscow. Chu Teh, a minor militarist only recently cured of opium addiction, a rejected applicant for membership in the Communist Party and nearly twenty years Tan's senior, went to Berlin to find the Great Road.

If *Chinese Testament* is the biography not merely of Tan Shih-hua but of a whole generation of Chinese students, the early part of *The Great Road* is the biography not of one but of innumerable Chinese peasant families. There is a striking contrast between Tan's early years in a lower-gentry household and Chu's in a peasant family. And the contrast is heightened, not diminished, by the fact that the Tan household's fortunes were exposed to the vagaries of the father's clandestine revolutionary activities and that Chu Teh was favored above all other members of his family. The "King of Hell's" exactions left Chu Teh with an indelible hatred of landlords for which there was no equivalent in Tan Shih-hua's upbringing.

Chu's mother was nameless and "face"-less, the daughter of a member of a theatrical group. The family was ruled by his grandmother, a matriarch obsessed by the desire to recover the land they had lost; and Chu's education was planned as a move in the long-term strategy of recovery. Chu was thus able to become an official—true, only a military official, much to his family's disgust. But he never lost his peasant roots.

It is now generally recognized that one of the main sources of the Chinese Communists' strength is their capacity to reflect and anticipate the peasant's elemental aspirations. Agnes Smedley was guided by a wise instinct in her choice of Chu Teh as a sitter, if only because of his gift for projecting the peasant's point of view to the nth degree. It was this gift, plus political insight of a very high order, which led him to the conclusion that "the peasants of China are the most revolutionary people on earth." It was this gift which enabled him to identify himself so completely with his troops and to organize them for the first time in Chinese history on the basis of what Evans Carlson called Christian principles or "ethical indoctrination." Surely there has never been another commander in chief who, during his years of service, spun, wove, set type, grew and cooked his own food, wrote poetry and lectured not only to his troops on military strategy and tactics but to women's classes on how to preserve vegetables.

If *The Great Road* belongs to the same genus as *Chinese Testament* as a social document, as a historical document it bears comparison with *Red Star Over China*. The two books overlap only at certain points, and even here they are complementary rather than competitive.* Snow's book is unquestionably a classic, and Agnes Smedley's deserves to become one. There is space here for only a brief mention of some of *The Great Road's* historical highlights.

* Snow's chapter "Concerning Chu Teh" (pp. 354-363) is the exception to this statement. Here he was at the disadvantage of having to rely on second-hand and unchecked information; hence the description of Chu as "this scion of a family of landlords" and a number of other inaccuracies.

Foreigners who visited Yenan and who now come back from People's China astonished by the Communists' moral earnestness are unfamiliar with the strong puritan strain in the Chinese intellectual tradition. This tradition was never entirely submerged. It is apparent in the formation of numerous small groups of young intellectuals, such as the one Chu Teh joined with his fellow-teachers at the Ilunghsien school, who solemnly dedicated their lives to their country: such groups—often almost private secret societies—were a common phenomenon in the two decades before political life had crystallized around the two major, parties. It is strongly apparent in Chu Teh's remarkable mentor and patron, Tsai Ao, about whom one cannot help asking for more. As it is, the details on the 1911 Revolution and the anti-Yuan Shih-kai movement in Szechwan and Yunnan help to fill in a rather vague chapter in modern Chinese history.

Chu Teh's description of Southwestern warlordism is most useful and it is to be regretted that Miss Smedley did not repeat his account in full. For not only were such warlords as Liu Hsiang, Chang Chun, Teng Hsi-ho, and Yang Sen national as well as provincial figures; but the period 1911-1949, throughout which political power depended on naked force, is unintelligible without a grasp of the nature and roots of warlordism. The theme of unity and division runs like a red thread throughout Chinese history. From 1842 to 1949, under the double stress of foreign encroachments and internal disintegration, it was the theme of division which prevailed. Warlordism, a malignant variation on the theme of division "sired and fed by foreign money, was Yuan Shih-kai's legacy to China." The warlords were militarist politicians, semi-feudal *condottieri*, who played power politics with their armies and combinations of armies just as the imperialists played power politics with the warlords themselves. However intricate the interplay of these two games, they invariably had one result—the Chinese people got kicked around.

Chiang Kai-shek, like Yuan Shih-kai before him, aspired to become the supreme warlord with all China as his bailiwick—note his reiterated identification of China with himself. The fact that Yuan's antecedents were in the decadent Manchu Army and Chiang's in the Shanghai stock market and underworld in no way vitiates the comparison. Many of Chiang's moves made no sense except in terms of the crazy quilt of warlord intrigues and ambitions, and even his approach to international politics was that of a warlord.

Chu Teh's first assignment from the Kuomintang on his return from Germany in 1926 was to win over his old associate, the Szechwanese warlord Yang Sen, to the cause of the Northern Expedition, or at least to neutralize him—an assignment which was greatly facilitated by the brazen British bombardment of Wanhsien in eastern Szechwan. But the Kuomintang established a symbiotic relationship with warlordism, which penetrated the Communist ranks when Chang Kuo-tao tried and failed to convert the New Fourth Army into his own private army.

Agnes Smedley's account of the Civil War from the Nanchang uprising to the end of the Second Extermination Campaign and of the Long March provides a wealth of material for the political as well as for the military historian. The importance of Chu Teh's contribution to the development of the classical Communist methods of warfare needs no underlining. But there are many other details of absorbing interest. To mention only one or two: There is the strange episode of the Tungku Communist leaders of landlord origin who did everything for the revolution except divide up their own land! To this day, agricultural cooperatives are careful in admitting ex-landlords. There is the story of 'ne Committee to Combat the Counter-Revolution, which from its inception was rooted in the people. This goes far towards explaining why the Chinese security organization has been relatively free from the bureaucratism and abuses which have afflicted its Russian counterpart.

The Long March was the climax of *Red Star Over China*, and we found ourselves reading and re-reading Snow's version. We are confident that many people will have the same reaction to *The Great Road*. The Long March is unique in military annals. Compared to it, Hannibal's march across the Alps fades into "the small theater of the antique"; and whilst Napoleon's retreat from Moscow was a disastrous fiasco, the Long March was the prelude to final victory. For sheer drama, the scene when the Red Army emerged from the lethal Grass Lands and first came into contact with Chinese peasants on the Kansu border—"we touched their houses and the earth, embraced them, and we danced and sang and cried"—can only be compared with Xenophon's "Thalassa! Thalassa!"

Perhaps the most valuable single contribution of *The Great Road* from a political point of view is the history of the Chang Kuo-tao deviation. To the best of our knowledge, this is the first full account in the English language and for this reason alone the book is required reading. Chang, a foundation member of the Chinese Communist Party and commander of the New Fourth Army, refused to cooperate with the New First Army and wished to stay in Western Szechwan and Sikang, where the Communists would have been cut off from the anti-Japanese struggle and the main stream of political life. To further his plans, he kidnapped and detained Chu Teh and members of his staff for a year. The fate of the Chinese Communist Party hung by a hair. The course of events after 1937 might have been very different if, first, Chang had not been defeated by the Mohammedan warlords of Chinghai as a consequence of his misguided political and military strategy; and if, second, the Communists had not succeeded in winning over the rank and file of the New Fourth Army by their policy of "patiently to explain."

The Great Road is not an official biography in any sense. Chu Teh himself provided most of the data for events up to 1937, but the narrative, comments, and interpretation are Agnes Smedley's and Agnes Smedley's alone. If she obviously had a great admiration for her subject, it is an admiration shared by many others who have come into contact with him. Evans Carlson said of Chu Teh that he was the only *practicing* Christian he had ever known besides Carlson's father, who was a Congregationalist minister. The Belgian Catholic priest, Father Vincent Lebbe, also testified to Chu Teh's "Christian principles." In *Twin Stars of China,* Carlson wrote that "Chu Teh has the kindliness of a Robert E. Lee, the tenacity of a Grant and the humility of a Lincoln." One of General Stilwell's last private acts in China, in October 1944, was to send Chu Teh his lined jacket. Eighteen months later, when General Marshall was on his mission in China, Stilwell wrote: "General Marshall can't walk on water. It makes me itch to throw down my shovel and get over there and shoulder a rifle with Chu Teh."

After Agnes Smedley's death, several attempts were made to have *The Great Road* published in English. But none succeeded. It first saw the light in a Japanese translation in serial, then in book, form. It is our pleasure as well as our privilege to make *The Great Road* available to the English-speaking public for the first time.

The manuscript has been edited in consultation with Miss Smedley's executors. In addition to imposing consistency in matters of styling and the spelling of Chinese names, we have made the kind of minor corrections which we feel sure the author herself would have made before sending the manuscript to the printer. But nothing basic has been added to or changed in the text as Miss Smedley left it. A Chronology to assist the reader is appended beginning on page 445 below, and a map showing the main localities which figure in Miss Smedley's narrative will be found in the end papers at the front and back of the book.

LEO HUBERMAN
PAUL M. SWEEZY

New York City
June 1956

Prelude

THIS is the story of the first sixty years of the life of General Chu Teh, commander in chief of the People's Liberation Army of China. Though General Chu authorized me to write it, it is not an official biography. Time, distance, and the world-shaking work of the Chinese revolution of which he is one of the chief leaders have precluded any final check by him of my facts and interpretations.

This book was first conceived in January 1937, when I arrived in the ancient town of Yenan, northwestern China, where the old Chinese Workers and Peasants Red Army, and the Central Committee of the Chinese Communist Party which guided that army's destiny, had just established headquarters. Throughout the seven years which I had lived in China up to that time, the official Chinese press, echoed by the foreign press both in China and abroad, had described General Chu Teh variously as a "Red bandit chieftain," a "Communist bandit," a murderer, thief and arsonist. They had, however, never attempted to explain why millions of honorable and hard-working peasants, workers, idealistic students and intellectuals had been willing to fight or die for the cause which he espoused.

A thousand legends had been woven about his name, so that I expected, upon arriving in Yenan, to find a fiercely heroic and fire-eating figure, an iron revolutionary whose eloquent tongue could set forests afire. Consumed with curiosity, I went with two friends to his headquarters on the first evening of my arrival in Yenan, and stepped inside the door to his private room.

The first thing I saw was an unpainted table lit by candlelight and piled with books, documents and papers, and the dim outline of a figure in blue-gray cotton uniform who had arisen as we entered.

First, we stood appraising each other. I knew already that he was fifty-one, but I now saw that his face was heavily lined, his cheeks sunken, and that he looked at least ten years older. He had but recently completed the epic Long March of the Red Army and the marks of undernourishment and suffering were on him.

In height he was perhaps five feet eight inches. He was neither ugly nor handsome, and there was nothing whatever heroic or fire-eating about him. His head was round and was covered with a short stubble of black hair touched with gray, his forehead was broad and rather high, his cheekbones prominent. A strong, stubborn jaw and chin supported a wide mouth and a perfect set of white teeth which gleamed when he smiled his welcome. His nose was broad and short and his skin rather dark. He was such a commonplace man in appearance that, had it not been for his uniform, he could have passed for almost any peasant in any village in China.

Men had told me that he was a simple, kindly and very commonplace man, hard-working, and without any interest in making himself a personal hero. All that they said seemed true, yet that term "simple" seemed true only after a fashion. His eyes, gazing at me, were very watchful and appraising. Unlike the eyes of most Chinese, which are black, his were a deep and soft brown, large, and gleaming with intelligence and awareness. I knew that a revolutionary leader of such long and bitter experience as his could not have remained so very simple and yet survive.

One thing I sensed at once: every inch of him was masculine, from his voice and movements to the flat-footed way in which he stood. As my eyes became accustomed to the murkiness of the room I saw that his uniform was worn and faded from long wear and much washing, and I noted that his face was not immobile, but exceedingly expressive of every emotion that passed through him.

Still recalling the many tales circulated about him I told him of the charges of banditry against him, and expected him to laugh as I did. Instead of laughing, he fell suddenly silent, lowered his head and stared at the earthen floor, and his face became drawn and stark as if from tragedy. In that brief moment I caught a glimpse of some deep and tragic emotion seldom seen by his friends and comrades who spoke of him as a perennially optimistic man. The moment passed, he raised his head and looked at me with level eyes and said:

"Banditry is a class question."

I thought of one line in a Western American folk ballad, "Some rob with a gun, some with a fountain pen," but held my peace and was soon asking him something about his life. No, he replied to one question, he was not a rich landlord by origin but, instead, the son of a poor peasant family of Szechwan Province. I was to learn later that few or none of his own comrades knew much about his life and that none of them had had time to sit down and write books about him or anyone else.

It was while he was speaking that I conceived the idea of writing his

biography, and when he asked me what I wished to do in Yenan I replied:
"I would like you to tell me the story of your whole life."

"Why?" he asked, curiously, and I answered:

"Because you are a peasant. Eight out of every ten living Chinese are peasants. Not one has ever told his story to the world. If you would tell me your life story, a peasant would be speaking for the first time."

"My life is only a small part of the life of the Chinese peasants and soldiers," he remarked. "Wait a little, look about and meet others before you decide."

I did as he suggested, and indeed met many men of more dramatic character than General Chu, men whose lives are the stuff from which great literature is made. Chinese peasants, however, are not dramatic, and I clung to my original idea, and in March 1937 we set to work.

As the weeks and months passed, with two or three evenings a week spent writing down what General Chu told me, I sometimes despaired of my task. He came of obscure, illiterate people and there were no letters, books, documents, or diaries to consult. He could not always remember exact dates and, until he was past forty, there was almost no public mention of his existence. He was a very busy man and often seemed to think the details of his childhood unimportant. Chinese family life, his military career, and, finally, his Communist Party discipline and life, had moulded him into a collectivist until it was sometimes difficult to know just what he as an individual had thought or done, or just where he left off and the revolution began.

The anti-Japanese war began while we were in the midst of his life story and he went to the front. I therefore put the book aside, but soon left for the front, not only to write a different book but also to observe him in action in so far as this was possible. Therefore, for one year I was able to watch him at work, at play, and at war with Japanese imperialism.

Apart from his multifarious military and political duties, it seemed to me that I had never known any human being with such a tenacious lust for life, nor one so basically democratic. There seemed no aspect of human existence that he did not long to explore and understand. Apart from the evenings of regular work with me in Yenan, he would some-times drop in to talk with me and with other people who gathered to drink tea in the sunny courtyard of the place where I lived, to eat peanuts, tell tales, sing songs and, as he sometimes said, "to boast."

During such idle, friendly moments I would often line everyone up and teach them the Virginia reel. Nothing on earth could keep General Chu from taking part in such dances, and he would swing his partner, *do-si-do,* and kick up the dust with a gust as great as that of the youngest guard in the line. When I had taught him all I could of folk dancing, he asked me to teach him Western social dancing, which I did.

He danced as he worked—plugging at it patiently, convinced that it was just another means of breaking down old Chinese feudal customs. He liked it, too, but he was not the sort of which great dancers are made, as was one of his generals, the colorful Ho Lung.

Prowling around to see what General Chu was doing, I sometimes found him lecturing in the Red Army Academy, renamed Kangta—the Anti-Japanese Resistance University—or playing basketball with the cadets in the courtyard of the academy. At the front later I often sat on the sidelines as a critic and watched him and his staff officers compete in basketball with some of their headquarters guards. General Chu would often shake his head a little wistfully and remark that the young guards never liked him to play on their side because he wasn't a very good player.

He loved the theaters and he loved singing, and only necessary work kept him from theatrical performances in Yenan or at the front. In the last years of the Second World War, when the American Military Observer Group in Yenan gave showings of American movies, he was seen at almost every showing, howling at Abbott and Costello who, incidentally, are in the tradition of Chinese clowns and slapstick artists.

On the first evening that he was to work with me I stood with Lily Chang, a young actress who was my Chinese teacher and secretary-interpreter, and waited for him on the terrace before the loess cave rooms which we occupied. Lily was to interpret when I failed to understand Chinese or when the German which both General Chu and I spoke, to some extent, broke down—which was often. As we waited we looked down on the small town of Yenan in the valley below with the Yen River flowing beyond its ancient walls and, beyond the river, the high pagoda on the loess cliff and the broad flat in the valley where the Yen flowed eastward to join the Yellow River, China's Sorrow. The broad flat, now a drill ground soon to become an airfield, had but recently been turned into a race course. That was when a party of hard-riding, tough Mongols came riding down from the north for a conference with the Red Army, an occasion which caused General Chu to issue warning advice to all women and girls to make themselves scarce or to become very formal lest the guests misunderstand their welcome.

Yet the women and girls, I among them, turned up on that broad flat to watch the horse races between the Mongols and the Red Army cavalry and we wondered at the Mongol riders who had trained their shaggy mounts in swift trotting while they bent far back in the saddles until they were all but lying down on the backs of their horses. A Red Army rider had borrowed my swift pony, given me by General Chu, for the races, and Lily and I had yelled ourselves hoarse as we watched the little pony, like an Arabian steed, falling behind the tank-like Mongolian pony with his flying mane and long tail. The Mongols had now returned to Inner Mongolia, taking Red Army military and political advisers with them. War with Japan was being prepared and the revolution was lapping over into Inner Mongolia.

On the hour set, for he was a punctual man, we saw General Chu coming through the streets of the little town in the valley below. His guard was behind his undistinguished figure and General Chu was turning his head as if in conversation. He walked bent forward a little from the waist and his legs moved in a pumping gait that had carried him over untold thousands of miles of the paths and roads of China. He came up the loess cliff, coughing the hoarse bronchial cough that he had contracted in the mountains of eternal snow of Sikang Province. He halted once and he and the young guard with the automatic at his hip stood looking up the Yen River valley, pointing as they spoke. There was talk in the town of building a dam up the valley to prevent floods and provide irrigation, and to reforest the naked hills and valleys. Their voices came up to us, his deeper and a little hoarse, mingling with the higher and fresh voice of the tall and handsome youth by his side. It occurred to me that three generations were involved in this vast Chinese revolution: General Chu's, the young guard's, and the young generation below the teen age.

General Chu and the young guard came on up the hill to our terrace. The peasant family that shared the terrace with us, hearing his voice, came out and greeted him with a loud welcome, peasant to peasant; and he went among them, patting the head of a little boy and taking the baby from the arms of the mother to lift it in the air above him and laugh with it.

In such a manner, and in such a setting, this book began.

Book I

The Road's Beginning

Chapter 1

SITTING across the little table between us, with the candlelight playing on his lined face, General Chu's eyes gleamed and he seemed consumed with curiosity to hear what questions I would ask about his life.

"Begin at the beginning," I said.

He was born, he began, on a Chinese date which is the equivalent of December 12, 1886, new calendar, near Ilunghsien in Szechwan Province, just twenty-two years after the Taiping Rebellion was crushed by the Manchu court and its foreign allies. He gave the date by the old lunar calendar which the Chinese Communist press later said was November 30th, and which a Chinese writer who started to write his biography—but fell by the wayside—said was December 18th. It may be that General Chu did not know the exact date of his birth; but that he was born, there can be no doubt.

Though he had a regular name in childhood, he said, he was nicknamed "Little Dog" at birth because boy babies were given animal names to deceive the evil spirits which lie in wait for sons. Girls were so insignificant that even the evil spirits did not molest them.

"What do you remember first in life?" I asked, and General Chu said, "Nothing very important."

"Tell me the unimportant things," I urged.

He lowered his head and sat in silence for some time, staring at his clasped hands. He then began speaking falteringly—of light, color, sound, high mountains and forests, fragrant wild flowers "as big as my outstretched hand," flowers that "scented the land for miles around"; of sunshine, a running river, and a little lullaby.

His mother sang the lullaby and, to his delight, acted it out with her eyebrows as she sang:

> The moon is like an eyebrow,
> The moon is curved with two ends dangling.
> The moon is like an eyebrow,

9

> The moon is like a sickle.
> It's not like an eyebrow that's forever frowning.

This lullaby aroused both pleasure and pain in him—pleasure because his mother sang it to him; and, later, pain because she sang it to his baby brother. He had thought it belonged to him alone.

He remembered that his infancy and childhood were almost barren of love, and that he grew up "wild," forced to depend on himself for all but food, clothing and shelter. He knew that his mother loved him and he could never recall one harsh word from her. She was so hard-worked that she found time to caress only the baby she was suckling at the moment. There was always a baby.

"I loved my mother, but I feared and hated my father," Chu Teh remarked calmly and naturally. "I could never understand why my father was so cruel."

As soon as he could hold a spoon he fed himself, and later came the rough chopsticks. When hurt he cried alone or not at all because no one had time to comfort him. He ran about all but naked in warm weather, but in winter was sewn into a little padded jacket and trousers. The trousers were open in the back to enable him to squat by himself when necessary. Was he ever sick? No, he had never been sick in his life.

With strange wonder he remembered his playing. "I played so hard that I would fall down on the ground and sleep anywhere, then get up and start all over again until I fell down and slept again."

He smiled a little as he remembered the shafts of sunlight through the shade trees and which eluded him when he tried to capture them in his dirty little hands. There were some fruit trees at a distance from his home, and when they were in blossom he would shake the branches to make the petals fall in a shower about him. There were wild flowers everywhere, a rustling bamboo grove behind the house, a long swing slung from the high branches of a shade tree, and a seesaw across a log. There was a nearby river, narrow and swift, bathing the foot of the mountain that arose beyond, with red pebbles on the bank, and a bridge, small boats and bamboo rafts, and flashing fish.

To the west of the house was a long low hill, Sleeping Dog Hill, and just beyond it the Big Road, wide enough for a cart to pass—an adventurous road stretching into misty distances, coming up from the south and disappearing into the northern mountains.

As General Chu talked there emerged the picture of a chubby little child with a shaved head, a small bellyband about his middle or a little apron as his only clothing in summer—a gay and tough little fellow like a tiny, sturdy boat launched on a stormy sea.

One of his earliest memories was a feeling of injustice; he and his brothers liked to fish in the river or pond, but they had to fish secretly lest a steward of their landlord catch them—because all the fish in the river, and even in the pond on their small farm, belonged to landlord Ting who sent men to sweep them up in nets and carry them away. Little Dog and his brothers would scream in protest, but his elders watched in sullen silence, and his father cursed when the men were gone. The same men were sent to pick the fruit from the fruit trees in autumn, and sometimes they cursed the Chu family as thieves who had stolen some of it. All the fish in the ponds and rivers, all the fruit on the land of the tenants, all the forests on the mountains, were claimed by landlord Ting—for China, for all the talk of its basic democracy, was a feudal country.

Chu Teh remembered how he used to play the game of jacks such as American children play, except that he and his brothers played it with little stones and a ball of paper rolled very tight. In the autumn he and his older brothers made kites and flew them from the mountainside as they sang the ancient daisy song of escape from disaster:

> The daisy is yellow, we are strong,
> The daisy is fragrant, we are healthy,
> On the double ninth we drink daisy wine.
> Men and daisy drank on the double ninth.

That song was to run through his life like the leitmotif in a symphony. In ancient times, ran a legend, a magician warned his disciples of a flood which they and their families could escape provided they fled to the mountains, which they did. Ever since that time the people of China had flown kites on that day and sung the daisy song.

Chu Teh's elder brother, Tai-li, four years older than himself, had a flute and a *hu-chin*, or two-stringed violin, and Little Dog would squat by his side and listen rapturously to the playing. When his own hands were big enough, he also played, and after he grew to manhood he bought and learned to play many musical instruments.

His second brother, Tai-feng, two years his senior, filled him with distress because he snared birds and, when old enough, shot them with the family bird-gun. Little Dog would run to the dying birds, gather them up in his hands and cry over them. His mother forbade Tai-feng to kill them but the boy shot them anyway.

When talking of his mother, General Chu's face became suffused with tenderness and pain. His mother was in her early twenties when he was born. She was taller and stronger than most women and her trousers and jacket were patched and threadbare, her hands big-veined and almost black from work, her tousled hair rolled in a knot at the nape of her neck, and her large brown eyes kind and melancholy.

"I look like my mother," he said. "She bore thirteen children in all. Only six boys and two girls lived. The last five children were drowned at birth because we were too poor to feed so many mouths."

The eldest child was a girl, Cho-hsiang, who cried for months when her feet were being bound and crippled, and at the age of fifteen she was married. After Cho-hsiang came Tai-li, the eldest son, called "Little Horse" in infancy, and after him Tai-feng, nicknamed "Little Calf." Chu Teh, the fourth child and third son, was named Tai-chen. All the boys bore the generation name Tai, just as their father and uncles bore the generation name Shih.

As the fourth child and third son, General Chu said he was "caught in the middle of a large family so that I was not only a son of the oppressed, but even within the family I was oppressed—forced to run errands and help my elder brother, or act as a nursemaid for the younger children. I have heard that as I was ready to be born my mother was cooking rice. Before the rice was done I was born. Then she got up and resumed cooking. I remember no birthday celebrations—we never celebrated such things. We were very poor but I never knew it because everyone else except the landlord was also poor."

His mother, he said, "was so humble that she had no name of her own." As a girl she had had a name, but after marriage she was known only by her position in the family: as "Mother" to her children, as "Second Daughter-in-law" to her husband's parents, and as "You" or "Mother of our First-born" to her husband. She was always pregnant, always cooking, washing, sewing, cleaning, or carrying water, and she took her turn in the fields, working like a man. Peasant women were chosen as wives because of their ability to work. Love played no role. Before marriage a woman was under the rule of her father, after marriage under her husband and his parents and, if her husband died, subordinate to her eldest son. She could not remarry. For such were the ancient feudal concepts laid down by Confucius.

A woman's duty was to work and bear sons to carry on the family line and provide labor power for the family. She had no individual rights whatever. If she failed in the traditional duties, her husband could divorce her. She could not divorce her husband for any reason, but he could "put her away" for many—such as disobedience to him or his parents, showing disrespect for his parents, or talking too much. It was a male's prerogative to talk as much as he liked.

Officials and men of well-to-do families always took concubines, but peasants could not afford such luxury. Concubines enhanced a man's prestige—they were a part of the old feudal social system. The women and girls of the Chu family, like all peasant women and girls, were foot-bound and oppressed, and to educate a girl was considered as foolish as watering another man's garden.

Chu Teh's elder uncle, Chu Shih-nien, was an unusual man who never mistreated his wife nor "put her away" because she bore him no child. Because their marriage was barren, sometime in his early childhood Little Dog was given to them as their son, and they adopted him by binding rites. Why he was selected he did not know and so long as the family lived under one roof the changed relationship made no difference. In later years, however, this adoption explained why he, alone of all the sons of the Chu family, was chosen to receive an education, to enable him to protect the family from tax collectors and other officials.

General Chu's mother came from the Chung family, and the Chungs were wandering theatrical people who hired themselves out as musicians and players for marriages, funerals, or birthday celebrations, or who set up a rude platform and performed rough comedy skits or ancient traditional plays at county fairs or on market days. Such theatrical people were social outcasts, they were desperately poor and were often politically suspect.

"But they were very gay and happy people and the peasants loved such folk artists very much," Chu Teh said, smiling with affection as he recalled them.

The Chu children grew up singing peasant songs and playing every type of musical instrument that fell into their hands—the Chungs were perhaps responsible for that. Some of the folk melodies were melancholy, some gay and rowdy and humorous, a few were love lyrics, and others were slyly political. There was one particular song critical of the ruling Ch'ing, or Manchu, dynasty:

> Recalling the history of Szechwan,
> It is a heavenly country,
> Capital of kings and emperors from ancient times.
> It was a good country and the strength
> Of its eight fronts threatened Wu.
> The cypress before the Ministers' Hall,

The ancient trunks of trees,
The powerful beams of old supported us.
But how is it now!

The Chus were one of the thousands of "guest families," which meant
that they were immigrants from other provinces who had not yet lived
eight generations in the province and thereby won the right to be considered natives, or Founding Fathers. The first group of the Chu family
came from Kwangtung Province in the far south shortly after the great
White Lotus Rebellion at the end of the eighteenth and beginning of the
nineteenth centuries. This rebellion, and its crushing by the Manchus,
depopulated the province so that poor peasant families from Kwangtung
and Kwangsi moved in to Szechwan and became "guest families."
Though the Chus had lived in Szechwan for some eighty years, they still
spoke the Kwangtung dialect and preserved Kwangtung customs, and
only Chu Teh's generation grew up speaking both the Kwangtung and
Szechwan dialects.

The first group of Chus saved enough money to buy a little land and
build a house near the market town of Ta Wan, which was not far from
Ma An Chang in Ilung district, or county, but with time the depreda-
tions of landlords, officials and usurers had compelled them to mortgage
the place, move out and become tenants of this or that landlord. When
Chu Teh was born his family was one of some sixty tenant families who
cultivated the estate of landlord Ting, who was simply referred to as the
"King of Hell."

The three acres of land which the Chus rented from the King of Hell
consisted of terraced mountain and valley land, almost every inch of
which was carefully cultivated by hand. The family home stood near the
foot of a forested mountain that arose on the east just beyond the small,
swift river. Three or four other tenant families lived nearby and, together
with the Chus, constituted the village known as Linglungtsai. The market
town, Ma An Chang, lay some two miles to the north. A little farther
on stood Ta Wan and near it the ancestral home for which the Chus
sighed. Another twenty-five miles or so to the north stood the walled
town of Ilunghsien which, to the peasants, was a great metropolis which
only a few had ever visited. A few miles to the west of the Chu home
flowed the Chialing, one of the four rivers from which the province takes
its name: Szechwan means "Four Rivers."

Three generations lived in the Chu family home: Grandfather and
Grandmother Chu; their four sons whose generation name was Shih,

with their wives and children; and the third generation of whom Chu Teh was one and whose generation name was Tai.

Of the second generation, the eldest son and titular head of the joint family was Chu Shih-nien, or Chu the First—Little Dog's foster father—who was about thirty-seven years of age when Little Dog was born. The second son, Chu Shih-lin, or Chu the Second, was Little Dog's dreaded father, a violent and passionate man. Of the two younger uncles General Chu seldom made mention. Nor did he do more than mention his younger brothers. Chu the First, Little Dog's foster father, was a serious-minded, ambitious man, who worked hard, skimped, squeezed every cash until it screamed, and planned for the entire family.

Like all peasant families, the Chus were an economic unit organized for hard, disciplined labor to stave off starvation.

"My grandmother organized and directed the entire household economy," General Chu explained. "She allotted each member his or her task, the heavy field work to the men, the lighter field work and household tasks to the women and children. Each of her four daughters-in-law took their turn, a year at a time, as cook for the entire family, with the younger children as helpers. The other women spun, sewed, washed, cleaned, or worked in the field. At dawn each morning the daughter-in-law who was cook for that year arose, lit the fire, and started breakfast. When we heard my grandfather moving about, all the rest of us also got up and went immediately about our chores, such as carrying water from the well, chopping wood, feeding the ducks, pigs and chickens, or cleaning up.

"All the meals were the same the year round. The men all ate together, for such was the custom, and after them the women and children. We were too poor to eat rice except on rare occasions. Breakfast was a gruel of kaoliang (sorghum), with perhaps a little rice or some beans mixed in, and with a common bowl of vegetables. We also had tea, but without sugar, of course. Dinner and supper consisted of about the same things. Instead of gruel, the kaoliang mixed with rice was cooked dry and there was a common bowl, or perhaps two, of boiled vegetables. When my brothers and I managed to fish without being caught—we loved to fish—we might have a bowl of rice. Meat or other special food was served only at the lunar New Year celebration, if at all.

"Though Szechwan was a salt-producing province, salt was so expensive that poor people bought as little as possible. There were three kinds of salt: the refined white grain salt for the rich, a brown salt for people in medium circumstances, and a blackish, unclean salt, sold in solid cakes to poor people like ourselves. This salt was so precious that it was not cooked with the food. It was either dissolved in hot water and a bowl of the liquid placed in the center of the table into which we dipped our vegetables, or a solid piece of salt was placed in a bowl in the center of the table and we wiped our wet vegetables on it.

"My grandmother apportioned not only the work, but she also rationed the food according to age, need, and the work being done. Even in eating we did not know the meaning of individual freedom, and we always left the table hungry. I grew up hungry, so that later, in the revolutionary movement, it did not bother me so much as if I had never known it. It was the same with work. I grew up working so that, later, I never felt that I lost face when I did physical labor. It was the same with walking: after I reached manhood I sometimes had a horse to ride, but I have walked most of my life, and long distances, months and years at a time, side by side with the soldiers I commanded.

"After our revolution is victorious we will develop our country and our people will have enough to eat and wear, and they will ride in trains and motor cars, and have time and energy to develop themselves culturally—though we develop ourselves culturally even under the hardest circumstances.

"My grandmother was an unusually capable woman and a good administrator, and like all the other members of my family she worked according to her strength until she was laid in her coffin. She saw to it that the landlord was paid his annual rent, which was over half the grain crop together with feudal dues such as extra presents—eggs, a chicken here and there, and sometimes a pig. We all hated these ancient feudal dues—I call them feudal despite differences of definition of the word, because the landed gentry imposed all sorts of obligations and duties of a servile character on us and other peasants.

"For example: when our landlord moved his big joint family to their cool mountain home each summer, the men of all his tenant families were obliged to drop everything and transport them, without cost. In the autumn they had to bring them back. Also, in times of social unrest, such as during bandit activities or peasant uprisings, his tenants were obliged to assemble at his home where they were handed weapons and ordered to fight for their lord and master. The peasants accepted these ancient feudal customs with fatalistic despair. They saw no way out."

Like other families, the Chus were expected to settle all accounts before dawn of the lunar New Year. At the end of each old year the Chu family gathered in the general living room where Grandmother Chu, aided by her eldest son—Chu Teh's foster father—apportioned each member his share of the year's income and decided what clothing was needed by each. The women, who knew each strip of cloth in the household, knew just whose trousers could be patched again and who should have a new pair. Every piece of clothing was worn and patched until there was nothing of it left. Each jacket and pair of trousers was carefully taken care of, while cloth shoes—made by the women—were worn only on the rarest of occasions, and could therefore last a long time. After everything was settled in these family councils, the frugal old grandmother took possession of the family savings and buried them in a jar in her bedroom floor.

The work began immediately after breakfast and, except for the noonday meal and supper, lasted until darkness drove everyone to bed. It would have been condemned as rank extravagance to have a light when darkness fell, just as it was considered extravagance for any man of the family to smoke the tobacco which they grew in the fields and dried and prepared for market. Now and then the Chu men would fill the bowl of one pipe with tobacco and pass it from one to another, each taking a puff. Chu Teh's father sometimes declared openly that each man should have the right to a whole pipe of tobacco. But he was a resentful and violent man who had to be held in check by the others.

There was no laziness, no slackness, no weekly day of rest for the Chu family, or for other peasants either. Well-situated people enjoyed themselves for a week or two during the lunar New Year celebrations, but for tenants and poor peasants there was no rest even during that period. Peasants could slacken a little during the winter months, but even then the soil had to be prepared for the spring crops, or winter crops put in. Pigs and chickens, grown through the summer, were taken to the market town for salt. After the cotton from the fields was picked and cleaned, the women spun it into yarn, but they did not weave. Weaving was done by wandering weavers, all of whom were men. During the winter also, oil was pressed from the rape grown in the fields and either used for cooking or sold, or, on the most exceptional occasions, placed in a bowl with a twisted cotton wick and used for a light in the evening. Chu Teh was twenty years of age before he had a light in the evening, and it was only after he returned home as a student that he slept in a bed by himself, and had a room to himself, and that was only for a few days.

There was also an old, unwritten feudal law that tenants, both men and women, had to work for their landlords, free of charge, during the New Year or other national festivals, or on special occasions such as when the landlord's wife or one of his concubines bore another son, or when a banquet was prepared for some visiting official. On such occasions the tenants were also expected to make special gifts of food to the landlord.

"It did not matter to the landlord that the peasants did not have enough food for themselves, or that they were needed at home for plowing or harvesting," General Chu remarked bitterly. "The men of my family had to go, and my mother or foster mother had to work in the King of Hell's kitchen. When they returned home they sometimes brought out some choice bit of food which they had hidden in their clothing, and gave us children each a bite; and they told us tales that sounded like fairy stories."

Sometimes, when General Chu talked like this, I would be unable to go on and he would regard me with curious and questioning eyes.

"Sometimes," I would explain, "you seem to be describing my own mother. We did not work for a feudal landlord, but my mother washed clothing for rich people and worked in their kitchens during holidays. She would sometimes sneak out food for us children, give us each a bite, and tell us of the fine food in the home of her employer. Her hands, too, were almost black from work, and she wore her hair in a knot at the nape of her neck. Her hair was black and disheveled."

"And your father?" he asked in wonderment.

"In my early childhood he was a poor farmer who plowed the fields in his bare feet, but wore leather shoes most of the time. He ran away periodically because he hated our life, and left my mother alone. He was not so disciplined as the men of your family. Then he became an unskilled day laborer, and we never had enough to eat. But we did have salt enough."

"The poor of the world are one big family," he said in his hoarse voice, and we sat for a long time in silence.

Chapter 2

GENERAL CHU never mentioned Szechwan without recalling its magnificent beauty. The mountains about his home were a part of the high range that juts eastward from the towering Great Snow Mountains which stretch along the western borders. The Great Snow Mountains and the jutting northern range shelter the whole province and the great enclosed plains known as the Red Basin and give the province its mild, crisp climate in which rich vegetation of both a temperate and subtropical variety flourishes in abandon. The Red Basin, with the provincial capital of Chengtu lying in its heart, is one of the richest regions of China, producing crops the year round. The province is also rich in salt and minerals and, General Chu reminded me, "Szechwan was always coveted by both French and British imperialists who conspired to add it to their empires."

"Have you ever seen the flowers of Szechwan?" he asked suddenly. "They are very big and beautiful and so fragrant that they scent the air for miles around."

His home, a dark old building crumbling from decades of rain, wind, and snow, stood in the midst of natural grandeur. Its long east-west section faced south, the roof was of gray tiles, and roughhewn unpainted doors hung on wooden pivots and, like most doors in China's interior, could be lifted off and used as beds. Two shorter wings, roofed with straw, jutted off from the main section at right angles. There were no windows, the doors alone admitted light, and the floors were of earth packed smooth and hard. The house was plastered with mud and unpainted. In warm weather the family ate outside in the half-courtyard which, at harvest time, was also used as a threshing floor.

Except for the kitchen—on the left as you entered—and the central room in the main section, the building consisted of bedrooms. There was a lean-to for pigs and poultry. The central room in the main section was the family gathering room where visitors were received or special ceremonies performed. A roughhewn square table surrounded by benches stood in the center of the room, and directly behind it against the wall was the cabinet in which the family kept its ancestral tablets—small polished strips of wood each bearing the name of an ancestor. A small clay figure of Kwan Yin, Goddess of Mercy, stood on a shelf before the cabinet.

The family made simple sacrifices before this ancestral shrine a few times each year, including the lunar New Year and the feast of the dead on the fifteenth day of the seventh month. As the lunar New Year approached they took down the grimy drawing of the Kitchen God from the wall behind the kitchen stove, smeared its lips with wild honey that it might give a good report to heaven about the family, and burned it in the courtyard. On New Year's Day a fresh drawing of the god was pasted on the wall with rice paste.

The Chus believed in such ancient ceremonies, and they believed in the Earth God that watched over the crops, and in an array of good and evil spirits. The ubiquitous spirit of the fox was a particular nuisance that could engage in a lot of mischief or even assume many disguises,

such as that of an old man with a beard or, in the case of hermits and
lonely scholars, that of a beautiful young woman. "The purest supersti-
tion, of course," General Chu remarked, laughing a little, "and quite
convenient for lonely scholars."

His family believed that their poverty and hard life was due to an
unlucky fate, caused by an unpropitious constellation of the stars. They
were illiterate, pessimistic, sighing at their unhappy lot. They knew nothing except hard work. In childhood Little Dog accepted all the current
superstitions, including a belief in ghosts. Once he heard a traveler
along the Big Road tell about a man who had studied in America where,
it seemed, people did not believe in ghosts as a rule and where there were,
therefore, no ghosts. That remark made such an impression that General
Chu remembered it fifty years later.

The Big Road—as he thought of the single-track road that ran past his
home—was one of the most important influences of his childhood. It
was a branch of the ancient courier routes that formed a loose network
across the face of the Empire. It came up from the south, ran northward
to Ilunghsien, and on through the mountains where it joined one of the
main courier routes that led to Sian and northeastward to Peking,
the capital.

Much of his childhood was spent watching travelers pass along the
Big Road. There were merchants transporting goods from Chungking
far to the south, and there were itinerant artisans, an occasional scholar
in a long gown, or sometimes even the King of Hell himself, riding in a
fine sedan chair and fanning himself with a fan while servants ran by his
side. As the lunar New Year approached, officials sometimes passed in
fine green chairs, with retainers and servants running by the side or in
advance to clear the way of vulgar people. Funerals passed, the coffin
followed by mourners in coarse white cloth and white headbands, some
of them clearly enjoying the occasion. There were bridal processions,
the red-dressed bride hiding shyly behind the curtains of her red bridal
chair and preceded and followed by men with banners and clanging
cymbals and other men bearing litters loaded with her household furniture and clothing and all that she brought as a dowry to her husband's
family home. These marriages were often gay and bawdy affairs, as is
the custom of peasants around the world, with experienced married
women giving the bride advice that caused her cheeks to burn, and boys
and men tying bells to the rope network that serves as springs beneath
the bridal bed.

Little Dog would squat on Sleeping Dog Hill and watch the world go
by: ladies of the gentry, who seldom left their homes, passing in sedan

chairs, and peasant women jogging by on a donkey on their way to pray for sons at some temple, to consult a fortune teller, or to pay the annual visit to their families. On market days theatrical troupes, such as Little Dog's mother's family, might go by, and also peasants with produce for sale. Columns of transport coolies would pass carrying salt in long baskets slung from their shoulders. These salt coolies were unhappy creatures clad in rags, their bodies were gaunt, their feet and legs sometimes covered with running sores, and many had tubercular coughs.

Sometimes the men of the Chu family would leave the fields to talk with some traveler who stopped for a rest and a drink of boiled water under the shade trees before the house. From such men Little Dog learned that China was bigger even than Szechwan, which was an empire in itself. He heard them talk easily of Chungking, Sian, and of Peking where "The High," as they called the old Empress Dowager, sat on the Dragon Throne. Sometimes they even mentioned Kwangtung, the native land of his forefathers. Chengtu, the provincial capital, was said to have a high, long wall as old as time and with five gates: the Gate of Clear Distance opened toward the Great Snow Mountains, Tibet and Central Asia; the Gate of Bright Welcome opened eastward; but the gate nearest the Chu family home was only named the Northern Gate, which seemed unfair.

Merchants from every part of the Empire traveled to Chengtu to buy furs, musk, jade, tea, and the medicinal herbs and fine silks for which Szechwan is famous. They could also buy tiger bones and deer antlers to cure certain diseases, and the precious herb, ginseng, worth its weight in silver.

As time passed, Little Dog heard of more distant cities and places: of Yunnanfu, far to the southwest, capital of Yunnan Province, the land South of the Clouds, and of Burma, beyond it, which the British barbarians seized from China the year before Little Dog was born, and of Annam, south of Kwangtung, which the French seized in a war with China in the same year. Peking paid for that war by increasing the price of salt, and the people rioted.

From travelers along the Big Road the child also heard that foreign barbarians always defeated Chinese armies in battle, that the Ch'ing dynasty was rotten, ignorant and tyrannical and its armies useless, and that the people's long-brewing anger was growing with each year. Times were becoming harder, too, and the cost of city goods had doubled within a few years.

"I used to follow some of the travelers along the Big Road until they ordered me to go back," General Chu said. "I wanted to travel."

From time to time during the year, itinerant artisans left the big towns and cities and came along the Big Road, wandering from village to village to work for such families as needed their special skills. Carpenters, metalsmiths, mat weavers, cloth weavers and others, all were skilled artisans who owned and carried their own tools of trade. Each autumn the mat weavers appeared at the Chu home to repair old mats or weave new ones when required. These mats were very important because they served as mattresses against the winter's cold. They were as big as a double bed, tightly woven, and were two, four, or more inches thick and woven in beautiful designs. When new and fresh they were fragrant and a golden yellow.

An old weaver, whom General Chu referred to simply as the Old Weaver, came each winter to weave cloth from the cotton thread spun by the women of the Chu family. The coarse woven cloth was then dyed an indigo blue, hung on long bamboo poles to dry, after which the women cut and sewed it into garments for the family, into quilt coverings or other uses of the household.

"These itinerant artisans were a part of the peasant economy," General Chu explained. "Coming from the big towns or cities, they were much more advanced and independent than the peasants, to whom they brought new ideas. They were even folk historians and some of them could read and write. They lived in the homes where they worked, and each evening the family gathered about to listen to their talk. They told us that the Ch'ing dynasty was selling us to foreign barbarians who wanted to make us slaves; that the numberless taxes which we and other peasants paid were given to foreigners to pay for loans or for indemnities imposed on China following defeats in wars started by the foreigners. They said we were poor not because of our bad fate but because the gentry and the nobles lived luxurious lives and unloaded all taxes on the people. I did not know what a luxurious life meant, but I thought it meant people could eat everything they wanted, wear fine clothing and live in fine houses with slaves to do all the work—like our landlord."

The wandering artisans knew a great deal about Chinese history and sometimes mentioned the British opium and other foreign wars earlier in the century which had destroyed Chinese sovereignty and imposed indemnities which were appalling for the times. The Ch'ing "trembled and obeyed the foreign devils." And now machine-made foreign goods entered China virtually duty-free so that they were destroying Chinese goods and the livelihood of the artisans. Also, they said, foreign missionaries in Szechwan were arrogant and proud, and they and their converts despised the Chinese people and called them by a word "heathen" because they did not believe in the foreign gods.

The Chu family already knew about the French Catholic missionaries who had caused a rebellion in central Szechwan in the year Little Dog was born. The French Catholic priests claimed extraterritorial rights for their Chinese converts, and if converts were brought before the magistrate in disputes with non-Christian Chinese, the French priests threatened the magistrate until he rendered decisions in favor of the converts. A Szechwan landlord, infuriated by such abuses, raised an army of peasants who burned Catholic churches and attacked converts, and when the government captured, imprisoned and killed him by torture, his son took his place and fought until he, too, was captured and killed and the rebellion put down with fearful bloodshed.

Of the wandering artisans who came to his family home each year, General Chu said:

"They were the advance guard of the later industrial proletariat, and as such were more enlightened, independent, and alert than the peasants."

Some of the artisans told tales about the great Taiping Revolution in the mid-nineteenth century, the greatest Chinese peasant rebellion up to that time and one which was strikingly similar, even in its Christian coloring, to the German Peasants' War three centuries earlier. In fact, one of the artisans who came to the Chu home each winter, the Old Weaver, had himself been a soldier in the Taiping Army under Shih Ta-kai, one of the most beloved of the Taiping leaders, a Hakka and a scholar who had sold all he owned, including his land, and turned the proceeds over to the Taiping Army. There were many Hakkas in the Taiping Army, for the army started in the south and the Hakkas live in many coastal and southern regions of south China. Where the Hakkas came from no one knew exactly, but it is said they were perhaps descendants of immigrants who came from north China thousands of years before. They have still a distinctive dialect and customs of their own, and the feet of their women have never been bound. General Chu Teh's chief of staff, General Yeh Chien-ying, was himself a Hakka, as were many of his troops and a number of his commanders.

The Old Weaver who wove cloth for the Chu family each winter seems to have been a Hakka also. He was a grim old fellow with a scalding tongue who would set up his long narrow loom in the courtyard or, if it was too cold, in the kitchen, and begin his weaving. Little Dog would watch in fascination because the old man's long brown hands worked as swift as light. He could weave twenty *chih,* some twenty to thirty feet of cloth, a day, for which he charged two or three cash a *chih,* with food and a place to sleep as was the custom. That was a lot of money for a man to earn; he could live for a week on one day's labor.

Despite the Old Weaver's caustic tongue, the Chu family never wearied of listening to him, and Little Dog would often squat by his side and plead:

"Honorable Old Weaver, please tell me a story."

The grim old man with the long brown hands and lined face would begin:

The Tartars knew how to squeeze the people, but we taught them that the people were no longer big beans out of which fat could be squeezed whenever they wanted to build themselves a new palace. Everyone is poorer now than when I fought under the red banners. Today anyone can pay twenty thousand in silver and become a magistrate and call himself the father and mother of the people. Ilunghsien has to send fifty thousand taels in silver to Chengtu each year, but the magistrate squeezes ten times that from the people. In my youth myriads of men, and women too, followed Li Hsiu-cheng, the Faithful Prince, who commanded all the Taiping Armies and who never submitted to the Ch'ing and the scurvy gentry and foreign barbarians. Shih Ta-kai was my chief and though a learned man and a prince he allowed no man to kowtow to him. But today people kowtow, and the longer the pigtail the more virtuous they feel, seeds of piss that they are!

When Shih Ta-kai led our army westward through all the south, we scattered the Tartars like chaff before us. In Tungtze in Kweichow we came in through the south gate and the slave troops fled out through the north. The people welcomed us and called Shih Ta-kai *I-Wang*, or Prince, and Prince Shih called the people to the Drum Tower and told them that we were dividing the land among those who labored on it and that it no longer belonged to the tiger gentry.

The people prepared a great banquet and pleaded with us to stay with them. They presented silver to Prince Shih, but he told them to distribute it to us soldiers instead. And that was done, though we did not fight for money.

We could not stay in Tungtze because we planned to drive the Tartars from Szechwan and from all China forever. Shih Ta-kai explained this many times, but when we started on the road the people clung to his saddle and wept and we turned back and stayed another night, and had another banquet, and Prince Shih agreed to leave a hundred troops behind to train young men to fight. When we left Tungtze the people still wept and followed for a great distance. It was the same everywhere. The enemy called us robbers and bandits, the people called us saviors.

There was a town where a landlord as rich as the King of Hell brought a box of silver and a slave girl to Shih Ta-kai, but Prince Shih stood up in mighty anger and said:

"Do you take me for an official? I order you to divide your land among your tenants, free your slaves and distribute all your silver among them. Do this before the sun sets."

The landlord ran to the river and drowned himself, and it was no loss.

Yes, our army perished at the Ta Tu River. I was not there. I was with the column that drove through Szechwan to encircle Chengtu from the east while Shih Ta-kai led forty thousand to attack it from the west. Prince Shih's troops died by the thousands at the Ta Tu River, and some in the river because they were starving and preferred death in the river to surrender to the Tartars. They had no food and they ate all their horses and mules. The spears of Prince Shih's army were broken at the Ta Tu River.

The chief Chinese slave of the Tartars was Viceroy Lo Ping-chang of Chengtu, whose aide was the Tartar, Liu Jung. These two devils bribed the savage Lolos and armed them with foreign guns to attack Shih from the rear and cut off his food supply. Lo's army of robbers and thieves had rifles and cannons from the foreign barbarians. They built defenses along the Ta Tu River and Shih Ta-kai could not cross, for we Taipings had only bows and arrows.

The enemy lifted banners on the north bank of the river, bearing the characters: "Those who submit will have their lives spared." Shih Ta-kai read the words, for he was a learned man, and he said to his soldiers:

"If we fight we die, and if we do not fight we die. So we will fight!"

They made rafts, and five thousand boarded them and held their leather shields before them and their spears in their hands. Their chieftains, in their red jackets, stood up fearlessly and the soldiers rowed and everyone shouted fiercely, and they kept their faces on the enemy beyond. But the foreign cannon blazed, the rafts were destroyed, and the Ta Tu River was clogged with the bodies of the dead.

Bitter gall filled the heart of Prince Shih, and he went alone to a rocky field where he knelt and prayed to the Christian God which he and many of us believed in at that time. But God gave no sign and Shih Ta-kai wept. When he stood up there was a poor peasant digging the field with a mattock and he went up to him and said:

"Old countryman, I am Shih Ta-kai. The Tartars offer a big reward for my head. Take my sword, cut off my head, and you will be poor no longer."

The poor man knelt and said he could not, but Shih Ta-kai lifted him and told him to kowtow to no man.

Today there are storytellers who tell you that that poor man took the sword and chopped off Shih Ta-kai's head and delivered it to the Tartars. That is a lie. Prince Shih was not killed, nor was he put to death by the slicing process in Chengtu as Viceroy Lo boasted.

Instead, Shih Ta-kai returned to his camp from the rocky field, and there his Fourth Daughter stood up before him. This Fourth Daughter was not his natural daughter. He had rescued her after the Tartars had murdered all her scholarly family. Her family had educated her as if she were a son, and she was learned. When Shih Ta-kai rescued her, she offered to become his concubine from gratitude, but he adopted her instead and she copied his reports and letters for him.

This Fourth Girl once saw a Taiping officer who resembled Prince Shih so closely that she asked her foster father to give her to the officer as wife. And this was done.

Now, when Prince Shih returned to his camp on the day God deserted him, the Fourth Girl said she feared that all the army would soon die of hunger, for there were no horses or mules to eat, five thousand men had drowned in the Ta Tu River and others had thrown themselves in rather than surrender.

The Fourth Girl pleaded with Prince Shih, saying that the banners across the river offered life to all Taipings who surrendered. She begged Prince Shih to escape and lead our army to victory while her husband, who looked like him, surrendered.

Now this was done, and it was the Fourth Daughter's husband who surrendered to the Tartars and was sliced to death in Chengtu by Viceroy Lo Ping-chang who thought he was Shih Ta-kai.

Prince Shih shaved his head and burned scars in his scalp as monks do, and in a saffron robe went forth as a Buddhist monk. He never reached our column in central Szechwan because by then our spears were also broken, our army had withered away, and I returned to my weaver's trade. One year later our capital at Nanking fell to the Tartars and foreigners and our commander in chief, Li Hsiu-cheng, the Faithful Prince, fell into the hands of Tseng Kuo-fan and was murdered by him at midnight. The Faithful Prince was true and honorable and knew no fear of death. He was a hero beyond compare. When the Tartars and foreign devils captured Nanking they slaughtered people for three days and three nights, but not one Taiping surrendered to them.

The Old Weaver sighed and fell silent.

"What happened to Shih Ta-kai?" a voice asked, though all knew well the story because they had heard it a thousand times; and the Old Weaver said:

Official scholars boast that Tseng Kuo-fan who served the Tartars was a great general and scholar, and that he defeated us. The victors write the histories. Foreign guns in Tartar and gentry hands defeated us. Tseng feared the foreign barbarians, but he feared the Chinese people more. He commanded the combined armies of the Tartars, the Chinese tiger gentry, and the foreign barbarians who massacred the people of captured cities and villages. We treated the conquered with respect, we shared our food with the hungry and we gave loans without interest to people in need, but our enemies helped no man. When Viceroy Lo's armies at the Ta Tu River raised that banner that promised liberty to all who surrendered, Shih Ta-kai's army surrendered. His soldiers were disarmed and taken to Ta Shu Pu where the enemy slaughtered them all. The Tartars are strangers to honor.

On dark nights, when there is no moon, you can still hear the spirits of our Taiping dead wailing at the Ta Tu River crossing and over the town where they were slaughtered. They will wail until they are avenged. Then their spirits will rest.

The Old Weaver looked at the stark faces of his listeners, for by then there were many who had gathered, and continued:

Many men have seen Shih Ta-kai since that time. Two men saw him at the Min River crossing at Chiating not so long ago. One was a boatman and one was Mr. Li, a merchant from Chekiang on his way to buy musk and herbs in Chengtu. The boatman was preparing to cast off when an old man with a long white beard and carrying a paper umbrella appeared and asked to be taken across the river without pay. When the boatman said money was of no consequence, the old man said:

"If you cross at this moment, a storm will sink your boat."

The boatman was surprised, for there had been no cloud in the sky. He looked at the heavens and was surprised to see black clouds rolling up over the mountains. He tied up his boat and went with the merchant and the old man to a wine restaurant for wayfarers. The storm broke before they were seated and lashed boats on the river to pieces. In wonder the boatman asked the honorable old man who he was, but the old man answered:

"I am no longer of this world, so why should I tell you? If I spoke the truth you would be afraid."

Then he said:

"The wind and moon are still here,
   But where are our rivers and mountains?"

The boatman and the merchant were frightened by these warning words about the fate of China, and when the old man politely refused the wine they offered him, they were more astonished.

The storm passed and the three men crossed the river, but the old man walked quickly away and forgot his umbrella on the ferry boat. The merchant picked it up and read the name "*I-Wang*," and the name of a Buddhist temple written on it. There had been only one *I-Wang* in China, and that was Shih Ta-kai. They went in search of him, calling his name everywhere, but he had disappeared and no one except themselves had ever seen such an old man as they described. The merchant kept the umbrella, and many men have seen it since.

"Honorable Old Weaver," quavered Little Dog's scared voice, "was that Shih Ta-kai or was it his ghost?"

"It is all the same!" replied the Old Weaver, and began chanting one of the best-loved poems of Shih Ta-kai:

> My whip swings,
> In sorrowing triumph
> I cross the central plains
> Moved neither by enmity nor gratitude.
> When Heaven is deaf to all judgment or feeling,
> How can I save the people with my bare hands?
> Three armies grip the reins,
> Pitying their exhausted horses,
> Ten thousand climb the mountains
> Like sick monkeys.
> Though millions have suffered,
> My aim remains unachieved.
> The face of all the southeast
> Is streaked with tears.

Such tales Chu Teh was to hear told and retold through all the years of his life, and Shih Ta-kai's poems were impressed on the memory of his own and succeeding generations.

"The peasants dared not admit that Shih Ta-kai had been killed,"

General Chu remarked sadly. "To admit that would have meant to give up hope. Yet Shih did surrender himself and his army to the Ch'ing, and he was really sliced to death in Chengtu. His disarmed troops, promised liberty, were massacred. Such would have been the fate of myself and other men of the Red Army had we ever surrendered to Chiang Kai-shek in the past."

Consulting the memoirs written by Viceroy Lo Ping-chang of Szechwan in the '60s of the nineteenth century, I found this laconic passage about Shih Ta-kai:

On the 13th he came into camp leading his child, four years of age, by the hand, and gave himself up with his chiefs and followers. Shih Ta-kai and three others were conveyed to Chengtu on the 25th and put to death by the slicing process; the child was reserved until the age prescribed by regulations for the treatment of such cases.

Of Shih Ta-kai's army, only four thousand were still capable of fighting. The rest, dying of starvation, were set free to die at leisure. The four thousand were herded into the town of Ta Shu Pu where, Viceroy Lo's memoirs complacently state, "on the night of June 18, 1863, at a rocket signal," they were "dispatched." One year later at Nanking the main Taiping Army, led by the indomitable peasant commander in chief, Li Hsiu-cheng, met a still more gruesome fate.

The generations which followed were nurtured on two schools of literature about the Taipings. The ruling classes, fed on official literature, believed that Tseng Kuo-fan was the great hero-statesman who conquered the wild and lawless Taipings who had slaughtered twenty million people and left China a waste. The common people, or over eighty percent of the Chinese population, were nurtured on folk tales and underground folk literature which pictured the Taipings as heroes and saviors of the poor and oppressed who were crushed by the hated Manchus and foreign devils. Sun Yat-sen, who became the father of the later Chinese Republic, born of a poor peasant family of the south just after the rebellion was crushed, was nurtured on the latter school of literature, as was Chu Teh's generation in the far west.

It was no accident that the Chinese Red Army, founded by Chu Teh and Mao Tse-tung sixty-four years later, not only assiduously studied the Taiping Revolution in order to learn from its mistakes, but even adopted many of its rules and tactics. When the Chinese People's Liberation Army, successor to the Red Army, marched triumphantly into Peking eighty-five years after the Taiping Revolution went down to defeat, its

steel guards on its captured American tanks and fieldpieces were em-
blazoned with its eight military disciplines, some of which were lifted
bodily from the disciplines of the great Taiping Army. This new army
was taught that the Taipings had started China's bourgeois democratic
revolution and that it was its own historic task to complete what the
Taipings had begun.

One approaches the tragic majesty of the Taiping Revolution with
something like awe. Long before it began in 1847, conditions in China
had been shaping up into an uprising against Manchu despotism. The
First British Opium War of 1839, ending in disastrous defeat and the
Nanking Treaty of 1842, reduced China to a semi-colony and added fuel
to the smouldering flames of revolt. In the wake of this war came the
great south China famine with its consequent banditry and piracy and
its mass starvation, for which the Manchus had no solution but the
naked sword.

Into this amorphous stream of torment there now entered a new
element, Protestant Christianity. The Chinese read and reinterpreted the
Gospels with their teachings of equality and the brotherhood of the poor
and oppressed. This Christian movement, which foreign missionaries
first hailed as the dawn of a new era in China, but which they later
denounced and betrayed when it came in conflict with the vested interests of foreign imperialism, began imperceptibly in south China. In
1847, a Chinese schoolteacher, Hung Hsiu-ch'uan, returned to his native
village after a period of study in the American Baptist Mission in Canton.
After converting and baptizing his family and neighbors, Hung and his
new converts formed pious congregations of God Worshippers which,
within a few years, spread among the peasants of all of south China.
The Manchus immediately branded the God Worshippers as a subversive
secret society, and in reply the Christians organized their own militia
which was soon in armed conflict with government troops sent to exterminate them.

As the struggle grew, many old anti-Manchu secret societies flocked
to the rebel banners, while educated and gifted men, moved both by the
new faith and by hatred of Manchu tyranny, also joined. One such man
was Shih Ta-kai, a young Hakka landowner of wealth and education,
who sold all his property and turned the proceeds into the common funds
to organize the Christian militia into an army which was named the
Army of Great Peace, or the Taipings. The banners of this army were
red and the jackets of its officers were red. Two years after it was
organized in 1851, this army swept like a flood over all south China,
established the Taiping Tien Kuo, or Kingdom of Great Peace, in
Nanking, and threatened Peking.

Because they existed and struggled in ignorance of and isolated from the great streams of human endeavor of the Western world, the Taipings cast a flood of light on the high intelligence and spiritual grandeur of a people which the Western world regarded both then and for the next hundred years as reactionary, ignorant, benighted and inferior.

It was an age when great discoveries were being made in the West, many of which were used to subject China and other countries which had not yet learned to make modern weapons of war. The middle classes were struggling against feudalism and for more advanced social forms. British progressives had already succeeded in abolishing Negro slavery, Western women were demanding sex equality, and the working class was claiming the right to organize labor and political associations.

Just as the Taiping Rebellion was beginning, Karl Marx and Friedrich Engels published the *Communist Manifesto*. During its course, Darwin also published his *Origin of Species*, the 1848 revolutions erupted, simmered and succumbed; India's Great Rebellion of 1857 went down in blood; and the American industrial North fought the feudal South, founded on human slavery.

The progressive forces of Europe and America drew strength and comfort one from the other, but the Taipings in far-off, isolated China fought the same battles against feudalism—and imperialism—and would have triumphed had not the reactionary West gone to the rescue of reactionary China.

The Taipings confiscated and divided the land, abolished slavery and emancipated women, thus striking deadly blows at feudalism. They made the sale and use of opium a capital crime. Prostitution, and the use of wine and tobacco, were forbidden. Each Sabbath morning all Taipings gathered to hear sermons, sing hymns, and repeat the Ten Heavenly Laws—the Ten Commandments.

The Taiping Kingdom of Great Peace existed for fifteen years, but as the years passed its leaders became enmeshed in fratricidal strife and corruption. However, it was the Second Opium War of 1858, waged by the British and their French allies against Peking, which really spelled the doom of the Taipings. This war, ending in the Treaty of Tientsin, legalized the import and sale of British opium, imposed new and heavy indemnities, and delivered China's Maritime Customs to British control. The Manchu court agreed to carry out the terms of this treaty, but the Taipings condemned it as another link in the chain of China's subjection. The foreign imperialist powers, which until then had more or less remained neutral, now turned their guns on the Taipings and, jointly with the Manchu armies and the armed forces of the landed gentry, set to work to destroy the Christian power which refused to be their instrument. Simultaneously, the Christian missionaries suddenly discovered that the Taipings were not real Christians, that their forms of baptism were false, their Christianity corrupted by Confucianism and that they were, on the whole, fakes. The Christian Western powers and the Christian missionaries therefore supported the Manchus and landed Chinese gentry who were "heathens," rigid adherents of the feudal ethical system, Confucianism, and inveterate enemies of Christianity in any form.

In July 1864, a year after Shih Ta-kai and his army perished at the Ta Tu River in far western China, the combined Manchu and Chinese armed forces, together with the mercenary foreign army, the Ever Victorious Army commanded by the Englishman, Charles Gordon, under the supreme command of Tseng Kuo-fan, breached the walls of Nanking, and for three days and three nights slaughtered Taiping men, women and children until three hundred thousand of them lay in their own blood. The body of Hung Hsiu-ch'uan, chief Taiping leader who had committed suicide shortly before, was dug up and thrown to the dogs. Captured Taiping leaders were beheaded, and Li Hsiu-cheng, the commander in chief whose loyalty and tenacity had won him the title "The Faithful Prince," was captured and delivered to Tseng Kuo-fan, who had him murdered at midnight.

One foreigner and one alone, the Englishman A. L. Lindley, served the Taiping cause and was sent by the Faithful Prince to England to tell the British people the truth about the rebellion. In his two-volume history, published in London in 1866, Lindley bitterly accused the Christian powers of "the blackest treason to their faith" and declared that he could only pray that England would not have "to answer for the sin of crushing the first Christian movement in modern Asia." Cast down but not destroyed, he prophesied, the Taipings would yet arise "phoenix-like from the ashes of their glory."

Like other Communist leaders, General Chu Teh had made an intensive study of the Taiping Revolution—he called it a "revolution," rather than a "rebellion" against the dynasty, because it sought basic changes in society and "spearheaded the first Chinese bourgeois democratic revolution"—the revolution against feudalism or semi-feudalism, and for national independence. Unlike the British author, Lindley, he regarded the religious content of the revolution as incidental only. Almost all social upheavals in China, he said, had taken on a religious coloring, much as had similar upheavals in Europe of the past. The Taipings divided the land, in part, and in part introduced communal distribution of food, clothing, and other essentials. They forbade the use of opium, wine, tobacco, and they went as far in the emancipation of women as they knew how: they forbade foot-binding—a reflection of the Hakka origin of many Taiping leaders—allowed widows to remarry, and gave women the right to compete with men in the official examinations. Women served in separate regiments in the Taiping Army and, like the men soldiers, were highly disciplined and moral in conduct.

The revolution failed because it failed to organize the peasants completely and carry the agrarian revolution to its ultimate conclusion; because its leaders became involved in internecine strife; and because it made many serious tactical mistakes and failed to develop a revolutionary political party to lead it. The God Worshippers Society was not a political party, but a Christian ethical organization which advanced, but did not carry out, many of its social revolutionary ideas.

Inspired in part by Christian principles, the Taipings also came out against feudal Confucianism, idol worship, and ancestor worship, thus enabling their enemies—the nobility and merchants, the scholar class, and the landed gentry—to mobilize the superstitious against them. Despite their mistakes and weaknesses, they wrote a heroic chapter in the revolutionary history of the Chinese people and lit the flame of hope, never extinguished, in the hearts of the masses.

Instead of the Englishman, A. L. Lindley, General Chu said the writings of Karl Marx, though fragmentary, were much more valuable in evaluating the Taiping Revolution. At the time, Marx was London correspondent for the *New York Tribune*. In one article in that daily, dated May 22, 1857, he declared that the Taiping uprising was "a popular war for the maintenance of Chinese nationality," and that "in a popular war the means used by the insurgent nation cannot be measured by the commonly recognized rules of regular warfare, nor by any other abstract standard, but by the degree of civilization only attained by that insurgent nation."

The very fanaticism of the "southern Chinese," Marx further wrote, "in their struggle against foreigners," seemed to mark a consciousness of the supreme danger in which old China was placed. The death struggle of the oldest empire in the world was taking place, he declared, and a new era was opening in all Asia.

In still another article, Marx made the startling statement, not even thought of by the Taipings, that the Taiping Revolution was "the first cry in the creation of a Chinese Republic," and that it had already begun to write the words "Freedom, Equality and Love of Others" over the doors of that republic!

The Taipings failed, General Chu said, but the Chinese Communists had learned from their mistakes and would never repeat them. When the Taipings were crushed, China was hurled back into medievalism and into new depths of poverty and national subjection. Peasant uprisings flared up here and there in the following decades, but each was drowned in its own blood. By the time Chu Teh was born, opium, the use of and traffic in which the Taipings had made a capital offense, was taken for granted and had become one of the foreign weapons in the subjection of the people.

"Our people existed in darkness," General Chu said. "They hated their lot but knew no way out. They arose time and again, and time and again were beaten down. The intellectuals who might have given leadership to such uprisings kept themselves aloof, contemptuous of the baseborn. To the peasants, all officials were like a plague of locusts. Any rich man, be he deaf and dumb, feeble-minded or a criminal, could buy title and office. When I was a child, and throughout my life, officials could come as lean as tigers to office, but leave it fat. 'Official' and 'tax collector' were words of ill omen.

"Our people have struggled for liberation for a hundred years, and the first and greatest of these struggles was the Taiping Revolution. Millions of Chinese peasants are still slaves. Our revolution today is against human slavery. We will yet complete the bourgeois democratic revolution begun by the Taipings."

Chapter 3

ONCE the habit of recalling his childhood memories and impressions was established, all sorts of little memory-pictures began floating up out of General Chu's past. He thought so little of them that he would have passed them by had I not sprung upon them like a cat and asked him to elaborate. He would do so readily enough but he was a very busy man and, at times, seemed to think it a waste of time.

One such memory-picture was this:

How old he was he could not remember. He was very small and he was standing on the hill before his home, watching that Big Road as usual, when a wild weird cry, fierce and long-drawn-out, came traveling on the breeze:

"HUH-H-H-H-H-H!" it sounded first from a great distance, then more and more clearly at intervals.

Travelers had told him that tigers in the mountains gave a weird cry that froze the spotted deer in their tracks. He longed to see a tiger and a spotted deer frozen in its tracks, and now seemed his chance. He looked about but saw only his elders running across the field for cover. From the house his grandmother screamed orders, doors slammed, and his older brother Tai-li screamed at him:

"Little Dog! Quick, quick, come down!"

Something frightening was happening everywhere and Little Dog suddenly began to squawl.

"My mouth was big and my lungs were strong," General Chu said, grinning.

Then Tai-li was by his side, but was dragging him toward the bamboo grove behind the house instead of inside the house. Squawling at the top of his healthy lungs and babbling something about a tiger, Little Dog heard his brother telling him to shut his big mouth because it wasn't a tiger, but soldiers that were coming. Tai-li forced him flat on his belly and lay down beside him in the bamboo grove just as the terrible yell tore the air to shreds once more. Little Dog was now too terrified to utter another sound.

In those days, General Chu said, the soldiers of the Empire "yelled the road" to scare people away. Just where the custom had arisen he did not know, but he thought it may have originated in the early years of the Ch'ing (Manchu) conquest to prevent fraternization between the soldiers and the people.

As the two boys lay in the grove they saw first an officer on a horse ride into view along the road. This man wore a cone-shaped white hat topped with a colored button, and with a tassel hanging down the brim. His jacket was red and embroidered at the wrists and shoulders with some insignia of rank. At a respectful distance behind him swaggered a column of soldiers of the Chinese Green Standard dressed in black trousers, jackets, turbans, and rope sandals. A piece of white cloth, with the character *ping*, or soldier, in black, was stitched on the front and back of each jacket.

The soldiers carried all kinds of weapons—long-barreled muskets, lances, and broadswords—and some were fanning themselves with fans. Suddenly they all opened their mouths and gave that bloodcurdling yell again.

Only when the two little boys heard the yell coming from far away did they dare creep out and peek down the Big Road, before running into the fields where their elders were talking. Their father was cursing the soldiers as walking corpses, ill-omened turtle's eggs, the seed of

piss, and apes drawn from the whorehouses and gambling dens of
decay—which, General Chu remarked laconically, they were.

In following years Chu Teh often saw the troops of the Ch'ing
dynasty. They were slavish cowards. The lower the officer the more
airs he put on. But if he saw a superior approaching, he and his soldiers
would spring aside and give the Ch'ing salute: sinking on one knee
with one arm hanging and the head lowered. Fierce as tigers before the
peasants, they were like cringing dogs before the rich and powerful.

Chu Teh hated the very memory of the soldiers and the tax collectors, yet as he talked of them I gained the impression that he was
shrinking from such memories because they exposed the servility and
weaknesses of China to a foreigner. For General Chu had a deep sense
of pride in his nation and his people.

The peasants lived in squalid misery and sweated under swarms of
tax collectors, he continued. These tax collectors, vampires all, appeared
each month, squeezing the last copper cash from the peasants. In addition to the innumerable old taxes, they would think up new ones on
the spot and offer to "put in a good word with the magistrate" for a
"consideration." The jails were always filled with peasants and other
poor men unable to pay taxes or bribes, and even in jail their families
had to feed them. They could be released by bribery, but to get the
necessary money their families had to go to moneylenders who bled
them white.

"These conditions explain the reason that I was chosen to receive
an education," General Chu explained. "Since tax collectors, officials,
and soldiers respected or were afraid of educated men, my family
decided to send one or more sons to school. Every peasant longed to
educate his children, but in those days there were no public schools,
and private schools kept by scholars charged tuition fees that only the
well-to-do could afford. Peasants might send a son to school for a year
or two, but as soon as the boy was old enough to work in the fields, he
was taken out. In my childhood, conditions had become so bad that
education was a life necessity for the peasants. A whole clan would
pool its resources to educate one son who could talk back to the tax
collectors and soldiers, and keep accounts.

"My family was more fortunate than most. We worked very hard
and squeezed every copper cash, and we had accumulated some savings.
We had planned to use these savings to pay off the mortgage on our old
ancestral home at Ta Wan, but my elders now decided to use it to
educate my two older brothers and myself for as long as possible."

After prolonged negotiations with an old teacher who kept a private school in his home, which was some distance away, the Chu family agreed to pay tuition fees of eight hundred cash a year for Tai-li, and two hundred each for Tai-feng and Little Dog. It was a lot of money, but Little Dog's foster father was an ambitious man.

As the auspicious schoolgoing days drew near—it seems to have been in 1892—the whole family grew very solemn. Each of the three boys had to have a decent pair of trousers, a jacket, a skullcap, and a pair of sandals. Their pates were shaved and the rest of the hair washed, oiled, and braided into neat queues. Since they had now reached the "scholarly" estate, their animal nicknames were dropped and they took formal school names. Their neighbors, however, respectfully called them Lao Ta, Lao Ehr, and Lao San—Old Big, Old Two, and Old Three. Chu Teh was "Old Three." The word "old," used in such connotation, was a title of honor, for the ancient respect for learning in China was engraved deeply on the hearts of the people.

Long before dawn on the first school day, the whole family was up to supervise the scrubbing and dressing of the boys, and to admonish them about unquestioned obedience to their teacher—for the relationship between teacher and pupil was second in importance only to that of parents and children. After breakfast the Three Olds, together with Chu the First, started out as if on a holy mission. The whole family watched them go until the morning mist hid them from view. General Chu could remember clearly the deep feeling of solemnity which enveloped him at the time.

There were sixteen other boys of various ages in the school, all of them sons of small landlords. Rich boys were not there because rich landlords kept their own private schools in their homes. To the sixteen boys in the school, the spectacle of peasant children going to school seemed as ridiculous as if three water buffaloes had entered the schoolroom to study the classics. Peasants, coolies and workers worked with their hands and were not expected to use their minds. Confused and humble, the "three buffaloes," as the other pupils nicknamed them, endured the torment of taunts for weeks. Finally, unable to endure the suffering any longer, Tai-li turned on one of his tormentors and knocked him down while Old Two and Old Three began fighting the others who tried to interfere. The Three Olds were small but tough, and put the sons of landlords to flight.

It was the Three Olds, not their tormentors, who were ordered to hold out their hands to be beaten, and afterwards to stand with their faces to the wall for the entire day. Old Three cried a little—but choked his sobs when he heard the other boys tittering happily, and allowed the tears to run down his face in silence. He learned early to suffer injustice, not only at school, but also at home. That night his father whipped the three boys until Chu the First told him to stop because, he insisted, the boys had done no wrong.

When the pupils taunted them for their punishment in school, the Three Olds again fought, then went straight to their teacher and held out their hands to be beaten. This time none of them cried, and when their enemies saw it they drew back and felt it wiser to leave such creatures in peace. There was a hostile truce for the rest of the school year, the Three Olds entering and leaving the school in a solid little phalanx.

In such old schools pupils began their studies with the *Three Character Classic,* a compendium of rhymed couplets of Confucian ethics and ancient history the meaning of which was never explained by the teacher. Boys were expected to practice perfect pronunciation until the characters, or words, with their various tones, were engraved on the memory. The meaning would come with the years. From early morning until noon the entire school chanted the texts aloud, over and over again, each chanting a different thing and each boy trying to hear his voice above the din. At noon they walked home for dinner—it was about two miles to the Chu home—then returned to study until evening.

After finishing the first primer, pupils went on to the *Hundred Family Names,* the *Thousand Character Essay,* the *Ode for Children,* and the *Classic of Filial Piety.* With the passage of years, those who survived were expected to finish all the *Four Books* and *Five Classics,* pass the State Examinations, and enhance the family fortune by becoming officials. The door of officialdom was the door to wealth.

General Chu said the old schools taught no modern subject—no mathematics, geography, natural science, or modern history. The theory was that the Sages had known everything worth knowing, and each succeeding generation had merely to memorize their writings. Initiative and originality were regarded as vulgar or even subversive.

Of the "Three Olds," only Tai-feng was a poor pupil, so poor in fact that his family soon took him from school and put him to work on the land. Old Three was a hard-working, obedient pupil who chanted his lessons until he fell asleep and had to be prodded awake by his elder brother. Tai-li was the smart one—a boy with such a memory that he quickly mastered his lessons and had time left to make up little melodies which he later played on his flute. Tai-li, however, had the disadvantage of age: if times grew worse, he also would be withdrawn from school and put to work in the fields.

When the first school year ended, the Chu family decided that since they had to pay heavy tuition fees their sons might as well have the very best of teachers. The King of Hell kept a family school for the sons of the Ting clan. The teacher, a member of the clan, had passed the State Examinations and become a *Hsiu Tsai*, which was equivalent to a B.A. in the Western world. Throughout the summer of 1893, therefore, Chu the First humbly entreated a steward of His Honor Ting for the privilege of sending the two boys to the Ting family school.

Chu the First went to the Ting home one day, bowed humbly before the steward, and was informed that the two Chu boys could attend the Ting school provided they helped pay the salary of the famous scholar who presided over it.

"The Tings were very rich, but they always hungered for more money," General Chu remarked with bitter contempt. "They insisted that we pay the same tuition fee as in the first school, but for this Tai-li and I could study for only half a day. We had to accept this arrangement."

The school was part of the Ting mansion, which was a huge building with many courtyards, reception and banquet rooms, and a fine ancestral hall in the center. There were sections for household slaves, and courtyards where the grain delivered by the tenants was measured, milled, and stored. How many people lived under the gargoyled roof no tenant knew, but the Tings boasted of five generations. A wall surrounded the building, the lake and gardens, and beyond the walls were other gardens, orchards, and a bamboo grove that provided delicate bamboo shoots. Some of the Ting men were opium smokers, all of them had concubines, and not one lifted a finger in work of any kind. Later, when Chu Teh studied in the first modern school in Chengtu, he noticed that "not one son of this family studied there because they had no respect for modern learning."

Tai-li and Chu Teh were scared when they first kowtowed to the Honorable Mr. Ting who taught the school, and were assigned a table in the back of the room where the light was so poor that no one had sat there before. The walls were hung with fine scrolls extolling the virtues of learning, but the thirty-six-odd Ting sons who attended the school had no use for learning. They were gentry, "boys who played and created mischief the whole day long." The teacher never punished them, but when either of the Chu boys made the slightest mistake they were scolded. They were miserable but they studied so hard that the teacher soon began treating them kindly.

The Ting boys humiliated the two peasant children by making a play on the word *"chu,"* until it sounded like "pig." Nor would they allow such peasant boys the slightest dignity, or permit them to claim anything as their own. One of General Chu's most bitter childhood memories was concerned with a pear which he picked from a tree near his home and which he took to school to eat. During a recess one of the Ting boys stepped up to him, grabbed the pear and began eating it.

"The boy said we had no right to fruit. Tai-li punched him, and when other boys ran up I kicked and scratched them. The teacher punished me a little, but ordered the other boys to leave us alone. After that incident, a crowd of the Ting boys used to go to our home and pick and eat the fruit on our trees. We drove them away with sticks. They made our lives very bitter."

Another memory-picture dated from the time Chu Teh was studying in the Ting school. There was no rain, and only a light flurry of snow that winter, so the winter crops were poor. The next spring rains failed, and the Chus watched the coppery skies with foreboding as they carried water to their fields from the river. The roads and paths turned to fine dust. In the hot summer months that followed, the grain bins of the Tings remained full from previous harvests, but the peasants began to starve. Drums rolled in the villages as the people sacrificed to the Rain God. Long processions moved along the country roads, carrying the Rain God in an open litter to soften his heart by a sight of the suffering people. Yet the King of Hell summoned his tenants as usual to transport his family to his cool mountain home.

Throughout the first year all members of the Chu family carried water to their kaoliang and vegetable patches, and Grandmother Chu rationed food to two lean meals a day. Tai-li and Chu Teh would come home from school at noon and spend the rest of the time until nightfall carrying water.

Merchants in the towns hoarded rice until people exchanged farm tools, cattle, clothing, household furniture, and, finally, their daughters, for it. Strangers from the big cities bought peasant girls, the beautiful ones for brothels or concubines, the ugly ones for household slaves. When winter came, the Chu family still had enough money to pay tuition for their two sons.

Peasants less fortunate than the hard-working, parsimonious Chus wandered off to become contract laborers in the salt wells at Nanpu or coolies in Chungking or other cities. The more desperate became soldiers or bandits. There were charity kitchens in the big cities where the starving could get one bowl of gruel a day, but in the villages there was nothing.

The Chu men took turns standing guard over their crops at night and in the autumn harvested their kaoliang, squash, and turnips and the children gathered wild greens and herbs from the mountains. The Ting family returned from their mountain home and their stewards brought back foreign-style rifles and ammunition from Chengtu against brewing trouble.

Old Big and Old Three were now thin and humble, grave and adult beyond their years. The last of the family savings were delivered to the King of Hell for tuition. The family began to sell their few possessions, even their precious mats from their beds, but not their agricultural implements or their daughters.

In the second summer of the drought the people lost all faith in the Rain God, and haggard members of the ancient Ko Lao Hui, or Elder Brother secret society, began whispering in the villages. Peasants arose from their beds at night to mutter at the merciless skies and the blank moon.

One early summer day, just as the Chu men had been summoned to the Ting mansion to help transport the family to the mountains, someone lifted his head and cried out: "Listen!"

Old Three heard a strange sound. At first he thought it was his mother, who was again giving birth inside the house. A horseman galloped wildly down the road and on toward the Ting home, and the strange sound grew louder, coming from the north where a cloud of dust was rising along the Big Road.

From the dust cloud there soon emerged a mass of human skeletons, the men armed with every kind of weapon, foot-bound women carrying babies on their backs, and naked children with enormous stomachs and cavernous red eyes plodding wearily behind. Through a vast confusion of muttering voices Old Three heard the urgent clanging of cymbals and the roll of drums from the Ting mansion. The King of Hell was summoning his tenants to fight for him.

The Chu men heard the summons but did not move. The avalanche of starving people poured down the Big Road, hundreds of them eddying into the Chu courtyard, saying: "Come and eat off the big houses!"

Grandfather and Grandmother Chu laid restraining hands on their sons, and through the din came the faint cry of Chu Teh's mother: another baby had been born.

Then the "hunger marchers" were gone. The Chu family was not yet desperate enough to join them.

The next day the Chu family heard that wild, weird yell of ruffian soldiers. "HUH-H-H-H-H-H-H!" it sounded savagely, and the family

barred the doors of the house and fled to the mountains. But the
soldiers swept by without halting. A few nights later desperate peasants
took refuge in the Chu home and talked in whispers of a wild battle in
which hundreds of the starving people had been killed, wounded or
taken prisoner. They had fought fiercely, and had taken many soldiers
with them into the shadows. Before the soldiers caught up with them
they had besieged the Ting estate and other big family homes, and though
some had been killed they had entered and eaten.

How the Chu family managed to live that last terrible summer
General Chu could not remember, but he could remember that now and
then food was brought into the house by someone during the night;
and that his father and one of his younger uncles sometimes disappeared
and were gone for days. Many peasants had turned bandit and went on
raids of distant places. Whether any of the Chu men joined them
General Chu never knew.

Blessed rain fell during late summer and autumn that year and the
famine ended. By then many landowning peasants had sold everything
and sunk into the ranks of tenants. Tenants had become coolies or
soldiers or laborers on the landed estates. And all were in debt to moneylenders. Their sons and sons' sons would inherit those debts.

Though the Chu family had taken no loan, they now had nothing
left. One day a steward of the Tings appeared and informed them that
since they had paid no rent during the famine, and since His Honor
"had also suffered," henceforth their rent would be increased. Chu the
First pleaded on his knees, saying his family had always been honorable
in payment, hard-working and obedient, and that not one had joined
the rice-rioters. He pleaded so hard that the steward agreed to speak to
His Honor, and indeed later informed the family that they could keep
half their land at the old rental, but would have to pay increased rent
on the remainder.

After long conferences, the family decided to split, one branch retaining half the land at the old rental, the other renting elsewhere. It was
decided that Chu the First and Chu the Fourth should move, leaving
Grandmother and Grandfather Chu with two of their sons and families
behind.

The decision that Chu the First, the titular head of the family, should
leave the old home, was taken because little Chu Teh, his adopted
son, was to continue his education. Tai-li, a big boy of twelve, would
have to leave school and henceforth work in the fields with his father,
uncle, and the women and other sons of the family. Though separated,
the family income would be pooled as in the past, and Chu Teh's

education would be the responsibility of all. Chu Teh was to part from his natural father and mother for the first time. When telling of this moment in his life, his face became drawn, and he spoke of the splitting up of the family as if it were a tragedy. It was, in truth, little less than a revolution for them all, for the family had been a closely knit unit.

A very ambitious man, Chu the First rented three acres of land on the outskirts of Ta Wan, near the old ancestral home which the family council had decided to reclaim at the earliest possible moment. Chu the First was, in a way, creeping up on the old ancestral home, but he had also selected the new location because an old scholar, Mr. Hsi Ping-an, kept a school in the neighborhood and had agreed to admit Chu Teh to it as a pupil.

Chu the First took a loan sufficient to meet the needs of both branches of the family until the next harvest, to pay the cash guarantee which all landlords demanded from tenants, and to pay for Chu Teh's tuition. On second thought, Chu the First, being ambitious, even decided to send two sons of his younger brother to school, at least for a time.

General Chu remembered that this loan was ten thousand cash, which was the equivalent of one hundred and twenty Chinese dollars in the new coins being minted in the new mint at Chengtu. It was a large sum for the times, but the family believed they could repay it after five years of hard labor and skimping.

These ambitious plans had a tragic background, General Chu explained—and this tragedy was opium. Up to that moment, though opium fields had appeared in the region, people regarded the drug as a disgrace. The Chus knew they could earn more money if they put in the opium poppy, but a sense of honor had held them back from this dire step. However, the family breakup, and the big loan, forced them to regard ethical considerations as a luxury beyond their means. Chu the First and his younger brother therefore planted part of their new land with the opium poppy. And, for a time, their condition was indeed less difficult.

General Chu always remembered Ta Wan with affection, not because its physical conveniences were superior to any he had known—they were not—but because the small town represented a step forward in the advancement of his family.

About nine thousand people lived in or near Ta Wan, he said, and it was the largest place he had ever seen until then. "It had good communications with big towns and cities, so that my family now saw more people, heard new ideas, and broadened their outlook."

To the Chu children, the little town was a big metropolis bubbling with life. There was a main street, which became a market twice a week, and there were artisans such as a blacksmith, cotton combers and cleaners, carpenters, millstone workers, menders of broken dishes, and a few weavers. The main street also boasted a butcher shop, wine and bean-curd makers, a rice-husking establishment, and a herbalist. A clean inn provided accommodations for well-to-do travelers, and there were small dark inns infested with vermin where transport coolies and their like could rent a board and a dirty quilt for a cash or two each night. A night watchman told the watches of the night, beating the hour on hollow bamboo, and kept a lookout for fires and thieves. There was also a Buddhist temple filled with gentle lohans and a kindly Buddha presided over by a saffron-robed priest. On the outskirts of Ta Wan stood a temple devoted to the Earth God.

The town had a religious society whose members, in good times, paid dues which were used for an annual feast or to make a pilgrimage to the sacred Omei mountain far to the south. Such events were more of a social than a religious occasion.

Beggars, thieves and ruffians, many of them products of the recent famine, prowled about on the weekly market day, when the main street was a din of honest peasant voices. On the market day also professional letter writers sat behind their little desks along the street, while fortune tellers, magicians and wandering actors plied their trade for a few cash. Wandering barbers, carrying a little stool, a washbasin, a towel, and a razor, would wash, oil and braid a man's queue, or even pull a tooth, for very little. It was a town to delight the hearts of country children.

From this time onward, General Chu spoke less of his family and more about his school and of public events of which he learned through the school. His family now had better food and clothing, and paid their rent and interest on time. They could have repaid the entire loan they had taken by the end of the third year, but used their savings, instead, to pay off the mortgage on the old ancestral home to which the family branch from the Ting estate moved in the beginning of the fourth year. That was a great moment. Old Grandmother and Grandfather Chu could now buy good coffins and, though still strong and healthy, would finally rest in their own earth.

This long-yearned-for achievement had not been easily won. Even the savings from three years of hard labor by both family branches had not been enough to reclaim the old home. At the end of the second year they had withdrawn Chu Teh's two cousins from school. When even this saving proved insufficient they had to take a small loan to make up the needed sum.

Other events had eaten up money. At the age of fifteen, Chu Teh's elder sister, Cho-hsiang, was married into a peasant family that owned land, and this had cost many a string of cash. The occasion had been celebrated with the customary feast of the two clans, and there had been music. Tai-li had delighted the wedding guests with his flute and *hu-chin*, and the actor family of Chu Teh's mother appeared in full force to sing and perform in return for nothing but a good meal.

General Chu barely mentioned such events in passing, but dwelt more on the new world opened to him by the school of Mr. Hsi Ping-an. It was held in the old man's home, some three miles from his home. He walked this distance each early morning and each evening.

When he and his two young cousins first entered the school, the ten other pupils made their lives miserable and for the same reasons as in the two previous schools he had attended. Peasants were supposed to work with their hands, not with their minds, and the sight of peasant boys setting out to become scholars seemed ludicrous. The memory of such bitter humiliations still rankled in General Chu's heart. Forty years had passed since then, but the majority of China's poor children were still without education. Yet when he thought of Mr. Hsi's school, his heart softened and he spoke kindly of the boys who had tormented him at first.

"Most of the other boys were merchants' sons," he said. "They were more intelligent and diligent than the sons of landlords, for they would have to work. They studied very hard and soon became my friends, because I, too, studied very hard. My closest friend was Wu Shao-pei, a boy four or five years older than I was. Shao-pei came from a bankrupt scholar's family. He was very serious-minded and occasionally studied the whole night through. I sometimes went to his home. His family had a library and he read and reread the books in it. At times, during the summer holidays, he even traveled to Chengtu to read. I worshipped Shao-pei because he studied so hard and knew so much. Our old teacher had a son about my age but he and I never became particular friends."

Mr. Hsi Ping-an was in his late sixties when Chu Teh first entered his school, and nearly eighty before he left it. Though the old man had never passed the official examination, he was respected by his contemporaries as a learned scholar with an unusual knowledge of the outside world. He loved teaching, he was courageous and enlightened and possessed a sardonic sense of humor that led him to strip ancient or modern heroes of their false trappings.

"When nearly eighty he was still a rebel and a critic filled with *chao chi* (morning air)," General Chu remarked affectionately. "He prepared me for the State Examinations."

Under the tutelage of this old man, Chu Teh finished the *Four Books* and *Five Classics*, the *Kang Chieh*, or Summary of Chinese History, and read extensively in the *History of the Twenty-four Dynasties*. When his students grew weary of the drudgery of books, the old man would invite them to stroll with him through the small fields which helped him provide a living for his family. Walking with them, he would talk satirically of emperors, generals, and officials, remarking that most of them had been rascals who had hired scholars to write tales of their learning or their virtues.

The old man urged his students to study so they could travel and study Western learning because, he said, he had heard that science had made Western countries prosperous and strong. He did not know what science was, but he was all for it. The time was coming, he would declare, when China would have to adopt Western learning or perish, and many reformers who knew this had established schools in various parts of the country.

There were a few newspapers in the port cities of China at the time, but Chu Teh and his friends had never seen one. The dynasty regarded public affairs as the exclusive concern of officials. Such news as the little school received came only from travelers or from letters.

The school did not even learn about the Sino-Japanese War of 1894-1895 until long after China had been defeated. General Chu could remember going home one evening and telling his family that the Japanese had just sunk the Chinese navy, chased the Chinese army out of Korea and south Manchuria, and was going to make China pay them a huge sum of money. His elders listened with uncomprehending eyes, for they knew nothing about Japan, Korea, south Manchuria, or the Chinese navy. Their enemies, they had assumed, were those right under their noses: the landlords, officials and tax collectors. But they were proud that one of their sons could talk of distant places and state affairs —he would make a great official some day.

General Chu also recalled the time old Mr. Hsi read out from a copy of a document signed by the constitutional monarchist reform leader, Kang Yu-wei, and by a thousand other graduates from every province in the Empire. It was a document appealing to the Throne not to ratify the Shimonoseki Treaty, but to modernize the country to prevent its enslavement by foreigners. The Throne did nothing.

The "intelligentsia of the country," General Chu said, "were terrified by the terms of the Shimonoseki Treaty. Here was the little Japanese empire, suddenly a competitor with the Western powers for the control and exploitation of China; and it was right next door to China, a vast, backward country ruled by an ignorant and decadent dynasty opposed to any change.

"From that time onward," General Chu stated with a voice level with hatred, "the Peking government became nothing but the tax collecting agency of foreign moneylenders who forced loan after loan upon it. Before another three years had passed, Peking had accepted eleven different loans from European, British, and American moneylenders. These foreigners were not content with merely drawing interest on their loans. They extorted precious railway and mining concessions, with the land attached to them, and even secured administrative and police rights to them."

Though only a child of eleven in 1897, General Chu vividly recalled the fear of the dismemberment and subjection of China by the foreign powers when the country was carved up by these powers into "spheres of influence." The Germans set the pattern by first engineering the murder of two of their own missionaries in Shantung and using the incident as an excuse for seizing the great naval base of Tsingtao, with surrounding territory, and claiming the whole province as their sphere of influence, in which they held priority in industrial development over the business interests of any other country. The Germans also exacted an indemnity from Peking for the two missionaries together with the right to open mines and build two railways in the province.

As if by common agreement, the other foreign powers followed by demanding other regions of the country as their exclusive spheres of influence. The czarist Russians took Manchuria, the British took the naval base of Weihaiwei in the north, the Yangtze River valley, and the Kowloon Peninsula across from Hongkong. The French took Kwang-chow Bay near the Indo-China border, claimed the three southern provinces bordering Indo-China as their exclusive preserve, and began surveying for the railway from Haiphong up to Yunnanfu. The French and British both claimed Yunnan and Szechwan provinces as their sphere, and the British called for British gunboats to patrol the upper reaches of the Yangtze and prepared to build a railway through Szechwan.

The Japanese laid claim to Fukien Province across from Formosa, which they had previously annexed, and Italy laid claim to a naval base south of Shanghai. "Peking rejected the Italian demand because the Italian army and navy amounted to nothing anyway," General Chu remarked caustically.

Just as all China had been parceled out "by highway robbers," America entered the imperialist arena by annexing the Philippines over the ineffective protests of an anti-imperialist movement in the United States, and looked out on a China from which its business interests had been all but excluded by the spheres of influence.

Though the British had taken the lion's share, they were worried. Since the Second Opium War, the British had controlled China's Maritime Customs, through which all imports and exports passed, and British business interests dominated the China market. Spheres of interest menaced British control of trade and even threatened war between the various rival powers. What was more, General Chu said, the mounting fear of dismemberment and subjection of the country had created a revolutionary atmosphere within the country, and the foreign powers feared something like another Taiping Rebellion.

At the time, General Chu added, there were two schools of British imperialism, one that advocated outright partition of China, and one that wanted to control the trade of the entire country behind the façade of the Ch'ing dynasty. This "peaceful" school of imperialism therefore thought up a plan by which they could eat their cake and have it too. Since every proposal advanced by the powerful British was suspect, they settled on America which, until the end of World War I, was the tail to the British kite.

The "peaceful" school of imperialism therefore sent one Alfred Hippisley, one of their customs officials in China, to Washington, to work out an "open door policy." Since the plan served American business interests also, the American government adopted it as its own, and secured the adherence of all the other powers to it. From 1900 on, this was described as the basis of America's policy and as a means of maintaining "the territorial integrity of China."

"The spheres of influence remained," General Chu added, "yet the merchants and investors of all the foreign powers had the general right to operate in every part of the country. From the Chinese viewpoint, the situation was not changed in any way. The Open Door Policy was not devised in the interests of China, but in the interests of the British in the first instance, and of the newly arrived Americans in the second. Any crumbs that fell to China were purely incidental. The collective looting of China's natural resources and industrial development began—and national fear of subjection continued to grow."

The Ch'ings were completely helpless, impotent, ignorant, and tyrannical against the people. At the time the Empire had only two or three "modern" divisions in the north. The rest of the Chinese army was equipped with only a few modern rifles, old blunderbusses, and with muzzle-loaders ten feet long which had to be laid across the shoulders of a number of men while one fired them. Some Chinese troops had only big swords, spears, and even bows and arrows. Such armed forces were impotent before the foreigners, but powerful against the unarmed people. There were twenty thousand troops in Chu Teh's native province, five thousand of them Manchus whom General Chu described as "lazy and worthless louts who, alone of all the armed forces, received their regular pay and, in addition, the annual subsidy in rice which the government gave each Manchu in the country."

Fear of foreign subjection and hatred of the Ch'ings continued to mount, and all kinds of rumors spread swiftly through the villages. Chu Teh had never seen a foreigner, but travelers declared that most of them had red faces covered with hair, legs without joints, and cats' eyes sunk deep into their heads, and that they could look at the ground and tell whether gold and silver were embedded there. Christian converts of the French Catholics, in particular, were hated, though all converts were called "foreign slaves." "Even thieves, murderers and bandits joined the Christian churches to get immunity from Chinese law," General Chu said—a statement that was borne out by history.

Chu Teh's old teacher discounted the terrifying tales of foreigners and held that there must be some good people among them—in foreign lands beyond the seas if not in China. Old Mr. Hsi called himself a follower of the great reform movement that swept the country after the Sino-Japanese War, and continued to urge his students to study and go abroad to master science. Just what the reform movement was no one knew exactly, but it embraced everything from Kang Yu-wei's constitutional monarchism to the republicanism of a Cantonese doctor, Sun Yat-sen.

It was years before Chu Teh knew just who Sun Yat-sen was and what the dread doctrine he advocated represented, but at the end of the century he learned of the word "republic" from one of its most eloquent enemies—the famous "reform viceroy," Chang Chih-tung, who was a constitutional monarchist, a Confucian, and an industrialist whose disciples were Kang Yu-wei and the brilliant scholar and writer, Liang Chi-chao.

By some means, old Mr. Hsi received a copy of the famous treatise, *Exhortation to Learning,* in which Viceroy Chang Chih-tung urged

Chinese youth to study Western learning but to beware of the dreadful thing called a "republic." The viceroy wrote:

Alas! where did they find this word that savors so much of rebellion! A Republic indeed! There is not a particle of good to be derived from it. Instead, such a system is fraught with a hundred evils. If this Republic is introduced, only the ignorant and foolish will rejoice, for rebellion and anarchy will come down upon us like night.

"Republic!" Old Mr. Hsi thought long about that word but could not make head or tail of it. Republicans were said to be a secret society of bandits who looted and murdered, or planned to do so. However, the old man was not easily scared, because every person who advocated change had been called similar names. And were not the Taipings called bandits and murderers? Yet was not the famous viceroy an advocate of the new learning, of the science that made foreigners powerful enough to overrun China?

A smile, that was half pity and half bitterness, came to General Chu's lips as he recalled the booklet which a traveler gave Mr. Hsi. It was said to be a textbook on Western science. Old Mr. Hsi suspended classes while he and his students all but memorized it, much as they had memorized the classics.

"It was nothing but a pamphlet of the most rudimentary sort, about a new soap factory in Chungking where modern machinery was used," General Chu recalled. "It had very simple outline drawings of the machinery."

Shortly after that, Chu Teh's schoolmate, Wu Shao-pei, spent a summer in Chengtu, and returned with a real textbook on Western learning —a book on mathematics, one of the first put out by the new translation bureau in Peking. A year later Shao-pei spent another summer in Chengtu to study with a friend, and this time he returned with mathematical instruments—T squares, angles, a slide rule, and what not. From the moment the textbook reached the school, old Mr. Hsi invited Shao-pei and Chu Teh to spend nights in his home to study it, together with his son. In the evenings the three students and the old man with his graying hair and scraggly beard would bend over the book under the candlelight for hours.

"I learned enough to keep accounts for my family," General Chu said, "and this weakened their prejudice against Western learning. The worship of science had begun, and I was one of its most pious devotees."

Chapter 4

THE reform movement that swept the country on the waves of fear of foreign subjection arose to a crescendo in 1898 when the young Emperor, Kwang Hsu, came of age and ascended the Dragon Throne to rule in his own right instead of through his reactionary old aunt, the Empress Dowager. The famous "reform viceroy," who later betrayed the reform movement, recommended Kang Yu-wei and his reformist followers to the Throne as advisers. The young Emperor placed the reform program in their hands and the Wu Hsu Cheng Pien, the Reform Movement of 1898, swept the country.

General Chu could still recall the passionate enthusiasm that swept through his little school near Ta Wan. The old decadent China was dying in the flames of the "Hundred Day Reforms" which embraced everything—except the land—in the country: the army, the schools, finances, and the State Examination system. The country was to be industrialized, a weekly day of rest was proclaimed, and even the queue, symbol of subjection to the Manchus, was to be discarded.

Despite reactionary opponents of change, led by the old Empress Dowager whose retainers still held great power, new schools of Western learning sprang up like mushrooms after a rain. Old Mr. Hsi cast about in desperation for modern textbooks, but it was years before these reached the country districts. The lone book on mathematics brought back from Chengtu by Chu Teh's schoolmate had to serve for the entire school, whose student body had doubled with the years. Shao-pei and Chu Teh found themselves the pioneers in introducing mathematics, spending hours each week tutoring the other boys.

There was even talk of the changed position of women, of the education of girls, and the end of foot-binding. Chu Teh's family agreed that women with natural feet would most certainly be better workers— but what man would want to marry a girl with big feet? They talked of the end of foot-binding but did nothing about it.

General Chu could remember going home from school at night to do such work as he could in the fields, and afterwards talking eagerly with his family about the wonderful reform movement. His elders listened in silence, proud of a son able to talk about such big affairs—for was he not destined for some high official position?—but they remained indifferent to the reforms.

It was not that they were merely backward and conservative, General Chu explained defensively: "It was because the reforms did not touch the land system. The 1898 reformers were trying to walk in the footsteps of Japan: that is, they planned to modernize the country on a capitalist basis while leaving the peasants in their old servitude under the landlords. They spoke of agrarian reforms, but these meant nothing but the introduction of such things as Egyptian or American long-staple cotton seeds which the landlords could buy and sell to their tenants.

"The reforms benefited merchants, landlords, industrialists, and the intelligentsia, but not the peasants who were the foundation of the country. The role of the peasants in the reforms was as taxpayers—and many new taxes were imposed to pay for the new institutions. Only basic land reforms could have won peasant support.

"The conservative reformers also labored under the illusion that the Western democratic powers would welcome a modernized, industrialized China. But the foreigners were afraid of such a China, which would merely compete with them."

Also, instead of introducing land reforms which would have won the support of the peasants and swept the reactionaries into limbo, the reform leaders tried to do away with the old Empress Dowager, whom they rightly considered the fountainhead of hostility to them. Instead of succeeding, they were betrayed by General Yuan Shih-kai, who called himself a reformer and who had pledged undying loyalty to the new Emperor by declaring that he would "faithfully perform the services of a dog or a horse" for his monarch.

The Empress Dowager thereupon swooped down and imprisoned the young Emperor, and beheaded every reform leader on whom she could lay hands. Kang Yu-wei escaped to Hongkong, and the famous scholar, Liang Chi-chao, who was to play such a great role in affairs for another decade, fled to Japan where he formed a new party and began publishing the *China Progress* monthly to keep the conservative reform movement alive. As for the famous "reform viceroy," Chang Chih-tung, who had first introduced the reform leaders to the Throne: this gentleman made a flip-flop, denounced the reformers, and, to win the Empress Dowager's favor, even penned a poem in her praise. It was not until Viceroy Chang had himself beheaded a number of young reformers who tried to assassinate him that he was reinstated in Her Majesty's favor.

Darkness descended over China once more and no one in Chu Teh's part of the country dared speak aloud about the reform movement. Depression hung over the little school and old Mr. Hsi again spoke in sardonic parables. The textbook on mathematics was studied in secrecy.

No more than a year passed when new rumors of trouble began to sweep through the villages of Szechwan like gusts of wind before an approaching hurricane. In the weekly market on the main street of Ta Wan someone mentioned something about the I Ho Chuan, or "Righteous Harmony Fists," which foreigners called the Boxers, an ancient secret society stemming back to the fourteenth century. There was hate-filled talk against foreign devils and against the "slaves of foreigners"—as the Christian converts were called.

The rumors came sporadically. There was talk of Boxer activity in north China and along the coast where foreign influence was most powerful. General Yuan Shih-kai, it was said, had become viceroy of Shantung Province—by order of his foreign masters—and proceeded to suppress the I Ho Chuan there. Here and there in eastern Szechwan, Boxer placards against foreigners and "foreign slaves" made their appearance, but were at once torn down by the authorities.

Of the Boxers, General Chu had this to say:

"They sprang from the same soil as the reform movement, but were an elemental mass movement against Ch'ing reaction and tyranny. At the same time, village economy was becoming bankrupt, there was famine in many parts of the country, and, in 1900, the Yellow River flood left millions of people homeless. The court took no measures of relief. The people held the dynasty responsible for China's humiliation and threatening destruction. The chief weaknesses of the I Ho Chuan were their poor organization and incorrect leadership, which soon left them wide open to reactionary manipulations by the court. The court turned the Boxers against the foreigners—in order to save the dynasty.

"I can remember that even small villages in Szechwan were flooded with British and Japanese cotton goods, with silks, knitted wares, sugar, umbrellas, kitchen and household goods. Even foreign nails were driving out Chinese nails, and foreign kerosene was cheaper than the seed oil which we produced on our own farms. Ancient handicraft, which had always been a part of village economy, began to disappear. The Old Weaver no longer came to our home to weave cloth each winter, and no one took his place. It was cheaper to buy British or foreign cloth in the market. People became poorer and bought cloth only when they had absolutely nothing left."

General Chu could not recall the exact date, but he remembered a day when a great crowd of starving people armed with sticks and old bird-guns surrounded the house of his old teacher and demanded food. Once more the rice-rioters were taking to the roads to "live off the big families." Mr. Hsi was not one of the "big families," but he gave all he could afford to the people and sighed heavily as he and his students watched the people move down along the Big Road, muttering as they went and casting up dust clouds.

On that same day Chu watched a column of be-queued cavalrymen, wearing black jackets and turbans and armed with modern rifles, sweep past after the "rice-rioters," and he heard of the "blood that flowed like a river" when they overtook the starving people. Conditions were such that they made some kind of mass revolt inevitable.

While the Boxer uprising was diverted against foreigners in the north, General Chu said, it assumed a social revolutionary character in southern and western China where court maneuvers were less potent. "We sympathized with the I Ho Chuan, but the people of Szechwan took little part in the rebellion. Missionaries and their converts in Chengtu were stoned a few times, and even many officials were anti-foreign.

"There was a branch of the I Ho Chuan in eastern Szechwan, where peasants flocked to the banner of Yu Tung-chen, a man who adopted the name of 'Barbarous Yu' to terrify the foreigners. Barbarous Yu and his followers harassed Christian missionaries and their converts to some extent, but their wrath was chiefly vented on landlords and tax collectors. They carried away food and quilts, and other things which they needed. Officials fled in every direction until the viceroy sent troops from Chengtu and Chungking."

During the summer of 1900, Chu Teh and his schoolmates often gathered in the home of their old teacher to talk about the Boxers and about what they should do should the uprising spread to their region.

Sitting in the midst of his students, old Mr. Hsi would say to them:

"Consider the Opium Wars, the Taiping Rebellion, the Sino-Japanese War. In these wars, one single foreign nation, or two at most, defeated China. Is China stronger today than in the past?"

"Weaker," the boys answered in chorus.

"Can the I Ho Chuan hope to win against the combined might of eight foreign armies now arrayed against them?"

"No," replied the boys sadly.

"Has The High more regard for the welfare of the country and people today than in the past?"

"Less," came the tremulous answer.

"Who ordered the I Ho Chuan to fight, then fled in safety to Sian?" asked the old man significantly and with deep bitterness.

"The High," breathed the boys.

"I have taught you the way to save China. What have I taught you?"

"We must study until we can go abroad and master Western science."

"Then, is the I Ho Chuan way the right way or the wrong way?"

"The wrong way," came the sad, and, in some cases, the tearful reply. Thus questioned an old man of China, and thus replied his disciples.

School was long since in session again when news came of the sack of Peking by the combined armies of eight nations, including the Japanese. The commander in chief was a German general, who repeated to his troops the command of the German Kaiser—that they should strike such terror to Chinese hearts that no Chinese would ever dare lift his head again.

The order had been obeyed, or so the foreigners thought. The foreign troops, ably assisted by foreign civilians, had looted Chinese homes and palaces in Peking, seizing precious paintings, rugs, vases, furniture and clothing—before burning the buildings to ashes. People of every age and both sexes were murdered by the thousands. The wells and lakes of the ancient city were filled with the bodies of women and girls who preferred death to outrage, or who had been outraged.

A smile that was not a smile formed about General Chu's mouth as he recalled the fate of Peking.

"The news almost paralyzed our school for days," he said. "The final reckoning showed that some two hundred foreigners and a few thousand converts had been killed in the uprising. The number of Chinese killed were a hundredfold greater, but the foreigners never mentioned that, for a Chinese life was cheaper than grass. When we heard the peace terms we were unable to speak. A new and heavy indemnity had been imposed on China—the peasants would have to pay it. The victors thought up many ways of humiliating our people. Every Chinese convert or his family who had suffered was to be indemnified; the State Examinations were suspended for five years in cities where foreigners had been killed; the Taku forts near Tientsin were razed and foreigners got the right to garrison the Peking-Tientsin railway and the Legation Quarter in Peking; and a number of new cities, including two in Szechwan, were opened to foreign trade. Peking also gave foreign warships the right to navigate China's coastal and inland waters at will."

Chu Teh and his schoolmates went among the peasants on market days in Ta Wan and other towns and villages, speaking of the danger to Szechwan, and of the staggering indemnity which the people would now have to pay in new taxes. The United States, General Chu said, returned a small part of its share in the Boxer indemnity for the purpose of building Tsinghwa University near Peking, but this was no philanthropy. Tsinghwa was set up for the purpose of training students to be sent to the United States for advanced studies, after which they were expected to serve American interests. After the Russian Revolution of 1917, the new Soviet government returned its share of the Boxer indemnity unconditionally, and simultaneously repudiated all treaties and agreements previously concluded between the old czarist and Peking governments—or about China with any other power. Germany and Austria were forced to relinquish their share of the Boxer indemnity after World War I, but thirty years passed before the other powers returned their share of the indemnity, and then on terms that were in their own selfish interests.

Three years after General Chu talked with me in this harsh manner about the interested motives behind the founding of such institutions as Tsinghwa University, I heard a French diplomat in Chungking bemoan the ingratitude of the Chinese who had been educated in French schools in China. Instead of serving French interests, he declared with amazing frankness, they acted just like men who had been educated in Chinese institutions. The Americans had more success, he complained, but even many of their "products" had bit the hand that fed them. Consequently, the French would have to make revisions in their educational institutions in China—or close them down altogether as a failure. His entire approach to the question of French schools in China was their usefulness to France.

In talking about the Boxer Rebellion, General Chu seemed to possess little or no knowledge of the foreign interpretation of that uprising. He was so completely Chinese, so completely one of the people, that he viewed it entirely from that angle. Despite its weaknesses and "the reactionary uses to which it had been put," he said, "the rebellion nevertheless demonstrated the tremendous strength, bravery, and fearlessness of the Chinese people"; and he recalled a story that even captured Boxer mules in north China had refused to obey the invading foreign armies. They had sat back on their haunches and refused to move even when mauled by foreigners.

General Chu clearly had more respect for the Boxer mules than for the Manchu court which the victorious foreigners finally permitted to return to Peking from Sian, to which city it had fled. The old Empress Dowager fawned upon the victors and presented precious jewels to the wives of foreign ministers whom she invited to tea in her palace. Her jewels alone, Chu said, would have been sufficient to pay the entire indemnity, but the government thought up new taxes on the people instead, driving them deeper into poverty and despair.

After the rebellion, he continued, every Chinese was afraid of the dread foreigners, "but foreigners in the interior, where foreign armies and navies could not penetrate, were also scared of the Chinese." Missionaries in Szechwan were now less "loudmouthed" in their contempt for the "heathen." Afraid of losing their influence over Chinese youths, they even introduced more scientific subjects into their schools.

When I asked him if he had ever thought of going to a missionary school to study Western science, General Chu stared at me in amazement. "How could I?" he exclaimed. "I was a patriot! The missionaries turned Chinese into political and cultural eunuchs who despised their own history and culture. Chinese Christian converts could speak Chinese but hardly write a letter in their own language. They thought America, Britain, or France was the paradise to which the souls of all good Chinese went when they died."

Hatred of the Manchus deepened and hardened after the Boxer Rebellion, he continued, and the republicans under Sun Yat-sen's leadership grew stronger and bolder. A new republican newspaper, the *Min Pao*, founded in Hongkong, called for the extermination of the dynasty. This paper was smuggled into the interior but it took some five or six years before Chu Teh saw a copy of any republican publication. The conservative reformers also became bolder and began publishing a small clandestine newspaper in Chengtu. Chu Teh's little school saw one copy of the latter newspaper—it was the first newspaper they had ever seen. It published nothing but news, but "news in those days was revolutionary." People made copies of it and sent them to their friends.

After the rebellion, the court proclaimed a number of new but cautious reforms, but after proclaiming them did nothing. However, intellectuals again took hope and began founding new schools in which Western learning was taught. There were still no modern textbooks and the teachers had to teach from memory or from notes. The students in Chu Teh's school watched for every traveler in the hope of falling heir to some book, and every time an intellectual from Chengtu passed through, old Mr. Hsi would suspend classes and invite the travelers to tell everything they knew about Chengtu and Peking or other places. The students could sit for hours, their eyes on the speaker's face or following every movement of his hands, missing not one shade of expression or meaning. Chu Teh was a youth in his middle teens, with large brown eyes, a shaved pate and a long queue down his back. He had reached an age when he could fully comprehend the extent, if not the solution, of China's problems.

The tragedy of the Boxer Rebellion was carved deeply upon his memory, and as he talked about it he seemed oblivious of time, and was like a man talking to himself.

"When I studied in Germany in later years," he said, his voice as cold and hard as packed ice, "I was sometimes a guest in homes where I saw Chinese rugs, vases, paintings, carved furniture, or other art treasures. When I asked about them, my hosts became embarrassed and I knew they were loot from the homes and palaces of Peking. I also saw Boxer banners hanging in a Berlin military museum. Had I sought for them, I could have found similar things in the homes of Frenchmen, Britons, Americans and Japanese."

Pausing, he suddenly asked me if I had ever read the Kaiser's orders to his troops in China during the Boxer Rebellion—orders which were followed by all the invading foreign troops. Since I had but a vague memory of that order, I searched among the books in the library for it. Instead of the order itself, I found the letter which Mark Twain had written to the *New York Sun* on Christmas Eve, 1900, describing foreign atrocities against the Chinese after the rebellion. The letter was based on a report made by a certain Rev. Ament, of the American Board of Missions, about the indemnities which he had collected from Chinese villages in which converts had been killed by the Boxers. Mr. Ament had collected three hundred taels in silver for each convert killed, and "also assessed fines amounting to thirteen times the amount of the indemnity"—money which, the reverend gentleman said, "will be used for the propagation of the Gospel." Mark Twain quoted a report from Mr. Ament from Peking:

Mr. Ament declares that the compensation he has collected is moderate when compared with the amount secured by the Catholics, who demand, in addition to money, *head for head*. They collect 500 taels for each murder of a Catholic. In the Wenchiu country, 680 Catholics were killed, and for this the European Catholics here demand 750,000 strings of cash and 680 heads.

Mark Twain added:

Our Reverend Ament is justifiably jealous of those enterprising Catholics who not only get big money for each lost convert but get "head for head" besides.

Had the Kaiser's orders to German troops in China during the rebellion been applied under similar circumstances to America, he wrote, they would have read like this:

March through America and slay, giving no quarter: make the German face there . . . a terror for a thousand years; march through the Great Republic and slay, slay, slay, carving a road for our offended religion through its heart and bowels.

Midnight came and passed as my secretary, Lily, read out and translated this article. General Chu listened, his eyes narrowed to small points, and when it was finished he asked:

"Who was Mark Twain?"

It took another hour to explain this, for we got down an encyclopedia from the library and Lily translated the entire section on the great American writer. Until that moment General Chu had never known that there had been any foreign sympathy for the Chinese during and after the Boxer Rebellion. The knowledge that there had been seemed to give him comfort and fortify his conviction that the heart of "the common people" everywhere was sound.

Book II

The Road to Revolution

Chapter 5

GENERAL CHU, when he next came to talk to me, recalled at length the mass misery that followed the Boxer Rebellion. A famine swept Kwangsi Province, where government troops slaughtered the starving and rebelling people, destroyed villages and left mounds of the unburied dead on which dogs fed at leisure.

In many provinces the annual land tax was collected six or seven times each year, the prisons were filled with peasants unable to pay the taxes or the bribes demanded by the officials. The Chu family was more fortunate than most, yet even they were now caught in the net of official extortion. After seven years of hard labor they had liquidated their old debt of ten thousand cash, but the new taxes and extortions ate up everything they earned. Rents had gone up and the interest on loans increased. In previous years the Chus had taken two small loans to pay Chu Teh's tuition fees, but times were so bad after the Boxer Rebellion that they could neither pay the tuition nor take a loan at the exorbitant interest rate.

Unwilling to allow Chu Teh to drop out of school, old Mr. Hsi took him into his home, merely asking that the family deliver a hundred-weight of rice, in installments, to feed the boy. Chu Teh now returned to his own home during the holidays and vacations only, when he took his place in the fields with the others.

Living in his old teacher's home, he listened to intellectual travelers who spent the night and sat under the candlelight until midnight talking of dire warnings of revolt. These travelers, General Chu said, often had official connections in Chengtu, and were therefore well informed. The school year of 1904-1905 passed, and still he lived as a disciple in the home of his master, studying and listening to travelers, gaining a vast amount of knowledge that otherwise would have been denied him. He heard talk of the Anglo-Japanese alliance, and in 1904 came rumors of a new war, this time between Japan and czarist Russia over Manchuria. It was weeks before the news of Japan's victory, in 1905, reached Szechwan villages.

After this war, he said, Japanese influence spread swiftly throughout China, and Japanese advisers were attached to every branch of the government, to industries, and to schools and colleges. "A Japanese teacher even began teaching in a new school not far from my home. Frightened by the rapid rise of Japanese imperialism, Peking sent thousands of students to Japan. In addition a stream of private students poured to Japan—most of them to study military science, administration and international law.

"Many Chinese students went to Japan to study because the cost of living there was about the same as in China. Some went to America on Boxer indemnity scholarships, but America was not popular in China in 1905 because the final step in the Chinese Exclusion Act had just been taken and because news circulated in China of maltreatment, and even murder, of Chinese in the United States. A nationwide boycott of American goods began and even in Ta Wan people looked carefully at all goods before they bought anything, fearful of buying something made in America.

"We heard rumors of some trouble in Russia in 1905," General Chu said, "but we in Szechwan heard nothing beyond this of the 1905 Russian Revolution. Russia was far away. The defeat of a white imperialist power by Japan, an Asian nation, lit the fires of hope in subjugated countries, from Egypt to China, and nationalist struggles for independence began to break out."

Yet Japan's victory over Russia, General Chu said, had a very different reception in China than it had in India, Persia, and elsewhere because it had been fought on Chinese soil and for Chinese territory. Not all Chinese shared the opinion of Dr. Sun Yat-sen that Japan's victory was the opening shot in the struggle of Asian peoples against their white rulers. Dr. Sun hoped to use Japan, but Japanese imperialists intended to use the nationalist movement of China to fish in troubled waters.

In 1905 Dr. Sun was in Japan, still an exile with a heavy price on his head, and it was there that he founded, in 1907, the Tung Meng Hui, an alliance of secret revolutionary societies whose goal was the armed overthrow of the Manchu dynasty and the establishment of a Chinese republic on the Western model. Large numbers of Chinese students in Japan joined the society and later returned to China to found branches in every part of the country.

The rise of Japan to a power capable of defeating a white power in battle and taking possession of Chinese territory exposed the progressive impotence of the Ch'ing dynasty which now found it necessary to fight for its life against the hostile Chinese people. And this, General Chu declared, was the reason the court, still in the hands of the old Empress Dowager, decided to introduce reforms and allow the industrialization and modernization of the country—on the Japanese model. Of course, General Chu said, she placed the reforms in the hands of high officials whom the people called "foreign slaves," and, of course, foreign money-lenders again descended on Peking like wolves on the fold.

Again it was the British and Americans who were in the forefront of a group of powers allied with them and who began negotiating for great loans to Peking in return for which they demanded railway concessions. Since Chinese industrialists themselves were planning to build railways with Chinese money, and thus keep such developments in Chinese hands, the foreign bankers insisted that the government should centralize all railway construction in its own hands and allot all new projects to them. Chinese opposition to this "railway conspiracy," led by the British and American bankers, soon became the very heart of the national independence movement and, eventually, precipitated the 1911 Revolution.

As hatred of Manchu oppression of the people and subservience to foreigners grew, an anti-tax movement spread throughout the south and echoed through Szechwan; a mass movement against forced labor spread through Shantung, and the Tung Meng Hui, under General Hwang Hsing's leadership, arose and fought in Hunan Province where Hunan industrialists planned new railways and the opening of new mines. The miners from the Pinghsiang mines of Hunan took an active part in the uprising and, General Chu added, "the Chinese working class began to step out onto the battlefield of national liberation." The armed uprising was crushed with fearful bloodshed and its chief leaders fled into exile once more.

Immediately after the new educational reforms were proclaimed in 1905, Chu Teh visited his family and urged them to allow him to study in the modern school which had just been established at Shunching, not far from his home. When they argued that they had no money, he told them the school was a government institution where everything was free, and that he would need only a little pocket money, which would be but a fraction of the cost of rice which they were delivering to his old teacher. His family still refused, saying that they had made heavy sacrifices to educate one son to become an official and that they did not now intend to allow him to run off to a newfangled school which might be closed down any day, as had the new schools in the past. They had no faith whatever in the permanence of the reforms.

Unable to move them, Chu Teh returned to the home of his old teacher and pleaded with him to intercede on his behalf. The old man, who

believed in the "new learning," and whose word was law with the parents
of his students, therefore invited the heads of the Chu family to his home
for a long conference. When it ended, Chu Teh's elders consented to
allow him to attend the new school, but upon condition that he continue
his studies for the State Examinations in which he was scheduled to
appear in 1906. For the new school taught not only modern subjects, but
also prepared youth for the official examinations.

A few days before the autumn school term of 1905 opened, Chu Teh,
then nineteen years of age, knelt in gratitude before his old teacher,
and then before his foster parents, and set out by foot to join the new
school. That was a great moment in his life—as great as the first day he
had entered school when his family lived on the Ting estate. He would
study everything—natural science, foreign languages, world history,
geography—and carry on his old studies at the same time. A new world
was opening to him and he was a part of the new, reformed China.

Arriving at the new school, he registered, as was the custom, under a
school name—Chu Chien-teh—which he selected for himself. The Chinese
often changed their names in those days, and this was his second school
name. Then came the terrible announcement of his teacher-adviser, who
informed him that he would not have time to prepare for the official
examinations and take more than one modern subject. The adviser proposed that he take the Japanese language, which was taught by the
Japanese teacher who had just been sent to the school. Physics and
chemistry were taught, but there were no textbooks and no laboratory,
and the teachers had to depend on memory and on such notes as they
had made while studying the subjects themselves. The new learning was
in its infancy in Szechwan.

"I was so miserable that I wept," General Chu said, "but the word of
a teacher was law, and I obeyed. After that I continued to study for the
examinations, and though I studied Japanese I learned very little. I am
a poor linguist, and anyway I disliked the teacher because he was a
Japanese and the Japanese had just occupied Chinese territory. I dis-
trusted everything he tried to teach, even if it was only the words for
dog and cat.

"Though I could not study the subjects I wanted to study, I learned
a lot by association with the eight hundred other students and from the
teachers in the school. I often gathered with other students in the homes
of teachers at night. Most of these teachers were reformers—one was a
man named Chang Lan who, I learned later, was a secret member of the
Tung Meng Hui. Old Dr. Chang Lan is now a democratic leader in China.
All such teachers mingled their teaching and their private talks with us

with indirect political propaganda against the dynasty. They never mentioned the dynasty by name, but merely spoke against the 'old system.' We knew what they meant, but never said so. We didn't dare attack the dynasty openly."

When the school year ended, Chu Teh returned to Mr. Hsi's home and, together with the old man's son, spent the summer in drudgery over the classics in preparation for the official examinations. In late August 1906, he and the son of Mr. Hsi left Ta Wan for Ilunghsien, in company with a party of older men who were also to appear for the district State Examinations. Ilunghsien was only some twenty-five miles away, yet no member of the Chu family had ever traveled so far from home. It was a small city which they regarded as so large and dangerous that his foster father had asked Mr. Hsi to arrange for the two youths to travel with older men who could protect them from the city slickers of the big metropolis, and caution them against falling victim to thieves.

"My family need have had no worry about my parting with money," General Chu laughed. "They had taken a loan sufficient to pay for my examination expenses and my living for a month in Ilunghsien, but, except for the very small pocket money which I had had the year before, I had never had money in my life. I didn't know how to spend money, and before buying anything I squeezed each cash until it screamed. I was a peasant with a peasant's attitude toward money."

In Ilunghsien Chu Teh found nearly a thousand candidates of all ages registering and paying their examination fees in the old Confucian temple. He was the only peasant. Most of the others were from landlord families—gentlemen in formal silk gowns and caps who had traveled by sedan chairs with servants attending them. Again, following an immemorial custom, Chu Teh took a new name—Chu Tsung-men—which was to be his official name throughout his life, if he became an official. This name, as was the custom, had been chosen for him by the teacher who had prepared him for the examinations—old Mr. Hsi.

He and his young friend then rented a small room, bought charcoal and food in the market, and prepared to cook their own meals during the period of the examinations. Neither of the youths had ever been in a restaurant in their lives, and the cost of such meals staggered them. Each day they went to the market and haggled and bargained, and finally reluctantly paid what was necessary.

Despite the proclaimed reforms, no changes had been made in the examination system. The examiners were the same as in the past, they knew only the old system and, as from immemorial times, selected examination topics from the classics. General Chu recalled them with bitter contempt, saying that only one subject was of any value because it required extensive knowledge of past Chinese history. One of the essays was a theme taken from a military treatise by old Sun Tze, from before the time of Christ.

The examinations lasted for one month. At the end of each fifth day there was a two-day recess during which time the candidates waited to see if they had passed and would be entitled to tackle the next group of subjects. Hundreds of men fell by the wayside, but Chu Teh and his friend passed each group and appeared for the finals.

During the recess periods, Chu would hover about, listening respectfully to candidates who were planning to leave for Japan, or for the new Higher Normal College in Chengtu. Strangely enough he remembered one candidate who had studied for one year in Japan already. He remembered him in connection with some electrical machine the student claimed to have bought there and which, he said, made a buzzing sound and could cure rheumatism. This candidate was most vociferous in his patriotic determination to destroy the old order and introduce the new, but just why he had returned to China to take the examinations remained a mystery to Chu Teh. The fellow, however, was planning to set up as a doctor of medicine in Chengtu, and put his magical machine to use.

"I'll cure your rheumatism, or any aches and pains you have," the fellow argued with Chu Teh, who replied:

"But I haven't got rheumatism! I have no aches or pains. I've never been sick a day in my life!"

"It doesn't matter," the student urged, seeing that he was dealing with a country bumpkin. "My machine will give you the strength to master anything you want to do." And he mentioned his price which, he insisted, was dirt cheap and was less than he would charge anyone else.

When Chu Teh escaped from the insistent "modern doctor," he carefully counted his money to see if any of it had disappeared. It had not. The fellow had met his match.

Of all the conversations that he heard, the one that attracted Chu Teh the most was about the new government Normal College in Chengtu which was said to have a special physical training department where men could study athletics and graduate as teachers of the subject at the end of one year. In addition to such subjects, the department also taught mathematics, geography, and military drill. Physical training was a new subject in China and one of which Chu Teh had never heard, but the thought of being able to graduate at the end of one year and begin earning his own living as a teacher seemed to solve all his problems.

He detested the idea of becoming an official under the dynasty because, even if he passed this district examination, and the later provincial one, his family would never have enough money to buy an official position for him. No one could get an official position without paying for it. The sums were very high, even if he did not continue until he had passed the still higher examinations, where the bribe money would be prohibitive. Of course, if he passed the present examinations, his family could get money by marrying him off to some well-to-do girl who would most certainly be illiterate and foot-bound. The subject had already been proposed to him, but the new winds of freedom were blowing through China and young men were saying that they would never marry until China was free; and that, even then, they would marry only educated girls. In the previous year he had heard many noble sentiments from modern students and had taken them seriously. Even if his family considered him selfish or unfilial, still he had rejected all idea of marriage.

By the time the month was out in Ilunghsien he had made up his mind to study physical training in the Higher Normal College in Chengtu. He had never lied to his family in his life, but he now wrote them a letter in which he lied. He told them that he was certain to pass the examinations, after which he could study for the provincial examinations, at state expense, in Chengtu. All he would need would be just a little pocket money. He pleaded with them to take another small loan to last him for a year, after which he would appear for the higher examinations.

While waiting for a reply to this letter, and for the final results of the examinations, he went on an excursion to the Nanpu salt wells, some twenty or more miles away where, it was said, there was some new Western machinery. He had never seen a modern machine and this was his chance.

With a group of candidates he therefore walked to Nanpu. They saw no modern machinery, but they saw thousands of sick and diseased salt workers toiling from dawn to darkness under the old indentured serf labor system. Except for the loincloth about their middle, they worked entirely naked. Their bodies were yellow from malaria or jaundice, there were big running sores on their feet and legs, and many coughed hollow, tubercular coughs. They had sold themselves for a period of years to labor contractors, who fed them just enough to keep them working, and housed them in dark, verminous hovels. Medical care for workers was unheard of in those days—and General Chu added "as in these days"— and labor organizations, had they even been dreamed of, would have been banned as criminally subversive.

The experience that brought the lot of these men right to Chu Teh's own doorstep was when he met a peasant youth with whom he had played in childhood on the Ting estate. This young man was now an indentured salt laborer, slowly dying of tuberculosis. When Chu recognized him and tried to talk with him, the youth turned away in silence, as if ashamed of his misery. The shadow of all the men of his family seemed to rise up before Chu. What the future of his brothers, nephews and cousins would be, he did not know, but he became afraid. He realized how he carried the heavy burden of responsibility for his family. Fear began to torment him and he wondered if he should have written that lying letter to his foster father. On the way back to Ilunghsien he argued with himself and finally convinced himself that, after studying in Chengtu for one year, he could become a teacher and start sending money to his family.

Back in Ilunghsien he found his name posted on the boards among the successful candidates. He had passed and was now a *Hsiu Tsai*—the equivalent of a B.A. in Western countries.

A merchant arrived from Ta Wan on the following day and presented a letter from his family and a loan which they had taken for his year's pocket money in Chengtu. He replied, enclosing in his letter a "victory proclamation"—a red sheet of paper announcing success in the examinations. This proclamation, he knew, would be posted in Ta Wan, his family would have "face," and townspeople would come to congratulate them and present small sums of money to help pay for his examination expenses. His heart was now more at ease.

At daybreak next morning he was on the road to Chengtu, his one good set of clothing and his good pair of cloth shoes wrapped in the quilt about his shoulders. Travelers usually took eleven days to reach Chengtu, but he decided to cut the time in half. Being a peasant who had walked long distances to and from school most of his life, and had done his share of labor in the fields, he could walk rapidly for long distances.

"I was young and I walked alone," General Chu said.

Chapter 6

NO LAND on earth was so beautiful as Szechwan, Chu Teh told himself, as he swung rapidly toward Chengtu: no mountains so majestic, no rivers so swift, no fruits or flowers so gorgeous or fragrant. Making short cuts through valleys, and around mountains glowing in autumn colors, he was on the road each dawn with old peasant songs on his lips.

At night, worn and dust-covered, he sheltered in peasant homes where hospitality was taken for granted and the offer of payment an insult. For food there were street vendors.

In the late afternoon of the fifth day, less than half the usual time taken to reach the provincial capital, he saw the massive medieval walls of Chengtu across the red-soiled plain and, far beyond, the hazy outline of towering mountains.

Halting at a running stream, he bathed, drew on his good shoes, and one hour later reached out and touched the walls of the outer Northern Gate as if fulfilling some sacred pledge. Then on he went into the maze of city streets bordered by a thousand magnificent shops and ancient buildings said to rival the splendor of Peking. Exulting in an ecstasy of achievement, forgetful of weariness, he knew only that he was at last in the literary, educational, political and commercial center of western China.

It was here that the Big Road of his childhood fantasy met and mingled with the great trade routes from the east and north, from Yunnan to the south, and from far-away Tibet. Never had his imagination conjured up such grandeur as he saw in the broad, clean streets, the gold-emblazoned shop signs, the myriad restaurants, wine and herb shops, or the great shops filled with precious Szechwan silks and foreign goods.

Next morning, the sixth after leaving Ilunghsien, he registered in the physical training section of the Higher Normal College where some one thousand young men were enrolled. The first thing he noted, he said, was that some of his teachers wore false queues which were kept in place by skull caps. These men had cut off their queues while studying in Japan, and upon returning home had bought false ones.

"I admired them tremendously," General Chu said. "They were revolutionary, and I admired everything revolutionary."

The next most startling sight was a group of girl students with natural feet. These girls were in private schools in Chengtu, and either traveled in sedan chairs or walked in small clusters through the streets. He longed to talk with them, but dared not because friendly contact between men and women did not exist in those days. The only respectable relationship was marriage, and marriages were arranged by the two families. Marriage cost money, he had no money, nor did he intend to marry—at least not until he could marry an educated girl with natural feet like one of those in Chengtu.

"I was a very emotional person and I idealized girls, but from a respectable distance," General Chu remarked nervously, as if treading on forbidden ground. Or was he fearful of talking of such things to a

foreign woman? From what I had already observed of him, he was a
lusty man with a ribald sense of humor whose remarks often set a table
of men rocking with laughter. Thirty years and more had passed since
he was a shy youth watching girls from a respectable distance in Chengtu.

Quickly dropping the subject, he talked of his life in the provincial
capital. In 1906, he said, there were two large government schools in
Chengtu, one the Higher Normal College, and the other the new Military
Academy which trained officers for the Reform Army, and had a branch
for the training of non-commissioned officers. He thought of transferring
to the Military Academy but feared to break entirely with his family
who still shared the ancient contempt for soldiers. Yet the "new militarism" was in the air and the Manchu viceroy, Sze Liang, was building
up a new army of which the later viceroy, Chao Erh-feng, was commander in chief. Handsomely clad army officers strode proudly through
the streets, mingling with the uniformed students of the Normal College,
all of them conscious of the role they were to play in the new China.

Though a disciplined student, Chu Teh soon became more interested
in national developments than in his academic studies. Yet he studied
hard, particularly under teachers with false queues who peppered their
lectures with propaganda about "freedom and equality" and the iniqui-
ties of the "old system." While criticizing the new reforms as too limited,
too cautious, these teachers still dared say nothing against the dynasty.

The teachers who were constitutional monarchists enjoyed greater
freedom of expression than republicans, and therefore had many disciples among the students, and could even speak somewhat freely of their
newspaper, the *Szechwan Jih Pao* which was, however, still semi-secret.

The republicans, members of the Tung Meng Hui, had to work in the
darkest secrecy. Rumors ran through the Normal College that three of
the teachers were members of the Tung Meng Hui and that one of them
was Dr. Chang Lan, who had previously taught at the modern school at
Shunching where Chu Teh had spent one year. This same Chang Lan
later played a leading role in the 1911 Revolution and, during the Second
World War, when he was already an old man, became one of the founders
and the President of the Chinese Democratic League.

Candidates for the secret Tung Meng Hui had to be guaranteed by
two members and pass through an initiation ceremony during which they
drank the blood oath of loyalty to the cause. Chu Teh tried to ferret out
members of the society who could guarantee him for membership, but
the nearest he got was finding a copy of its little newspaper, the *Min Pao*,
which someone slipped under his pillow in the dormitory. The paper had
passed through so many hands that much of its print was obliterated.
The little paper attacked the constitutional monarchists and called the

new reforms a "vile deception designed to preserve the corrupt monarchy." Chu read and reread the little sheet, then slipped it in the bed of another student.

There were a number of Christian mission schools in Chengtu, also, but Chu Teh and his student colleagues despised their students as "foreign slaves." Missionary students lived in a small isolated world, had no interest in national problems, worried about their souls and an after life, and were trained to work as clerks in foreign banks, business houses, and missionary institutions—all of which kept a sharp eye out for the fleshpots of this earthly existence. These missionary students were men and women without a country, taught to turn the other cheek to the aggressive foreign imperialists who themselves never even dreamed of practicing what they preached.

One of the first things Chu Teh did upon entering the Normal College was to visit the laboratory, which was the proud possessor of one microscope and of a human skeleton which was regarded with interested equanimity because it was said to be a foreign skeleton sent from abroad. The college also had wall maps and a big colored globe of the world which attracted great attention. One lecture hall in the physical training department was hung with large colored prints depicting battle scenes between foreign armies and navies. Chu Teh studied these prints so intently and so often that, thirty-two years later, he could describe every detail of them. But the college had no modern textbooks, and the teachers still had to teach from memory or from notes taken while abroad.

Chengtu seethed with new life. The new officials were encouraging native manufacture and promoting home industries and handicraft. A modern silk filature, a cotton spinning and weaving mill, a mint, and the arsenal, were all operated by modern machinery. Together with a group of four friends from his native district, Chu Teh went from one to another of these institutions in the hope of seeing foreign machinery. In each case they were turned away, and the most they could do was stand outside the walls, listening to the hum of the machines.

While the city flourished, General Chu said, the peasants in the countryside lived the same dark lives as in the past, burdened with taxes to pay for the new reform institutions. The landlord gentry, always lazy and opposed to progress, had now become more aggressive and had bought official titles and positions which enabled them to levy all kinds of taxes on the people. Walking through the streets, Chu Teh would sometimes hear a shout:

"Make way! Big man coming!" and a fine sedan chair, bearing one of the new official gentry, would sweep past in grand style.

Then there was the master race, the Manchus, who lived in the special

Manchu city in the northwestern corner of Chengtu. No Chinese dared visit this section of the city unless he wished to be beaten. The Chinese worked very hard, but the Manchus received a cash allowance, as well as free rice, from the government, throughout their lives. There were a few Manchu officials who did some work, but the majority of the master race did no work whatever and did not even keep their section of the city clean. Manchu men sat in the teahouses of the Chinese city all day long, and everyone hated their guts.

The glorious year passed and Chu Teh graduated. He had made five close friends: one, Ching Kun, was the son of a Chengtu intellectual family; the other four were sons of progressive families in Ilunghsien, his native district. These four young men from Ilunghsien had just graduated from the regular college courses and were planning to open the first modern school in their native town. They asked Chu Teh to join them as teacher of physical education and as business manager of the school, at an annual salary of twelve thousand cash, or about one hundred and twenty dollars in Chinese money. Chu accepted with enthusiasm and made arrangements to be in Ilunghsien before the school opened.

After two years away from home, Chu Teh did not realize how much he had become a part of the new China, nor how much his family had remained a part of the old. As he trudged back toward Ta Wan, he felt certain his family would understand why he had lied about the Chengtu school. He would have only to explain for them to approve his new profession—especially since he would be earning good money and could begin repaying not only the loans taken for his education, but the family debts.

He had written in advance that he would spend the summer at home helping in the fields, and they were expecting him. One of his nephews saw him coming from afar, waving and shouting, but instead of waving back the boy fled across the fields toward the house, and then everything was in motion, with everyone running. By the time Chu reached the house, his whole family was lined up in two rows, and as he came up they all bowed respectfully before him. Instead of treating him as a son, his foster father bowed him into the house and forced him to take the seat of honor in the general family assembly room. About him were his family, their eyes gleaming with pride, and everyone addressing him in the formal and humble language which the poor used with the rich and powerful.

General Chu's voice, as he talked of this home-coming, became low with pity and sorrow. The whole house had been cleaned, and special food prepared, in his honor, and though no member of his family had ever had a room to himself, a special room had been set aside for his private use, and it had been furnished with the best bed, table and chair from the whole house. They had even given him their one good bed mat and an open lamp fed by seed oil that he might have the luxury of a light at night.

He was allowed to do no work whatever and each time he tried they protested and forced him to sit down and do nothing. They served him special food, but ate only poor food themselves. They said nothing but their eyes lingered in amazement at his hands. Instead of allowing his fingernails to grow long, as did officials and the gentry, his were cut as short as theirs. Realizing with growing shock that they thought he was a big official, or would soon become one, he kept postponing the moment when he would have to tell them that he had lied to them and that he would henceforth teach an undignified subject, physical training.

In the two years he had been away, his family's poverty had deepened. The change was not so obvious from the outside, but all too clear from within. Clothing had been washed and patched in honor of his homecoming, but it was threadbare and faded—the same clothing that had been worn for years. He learned that the family was heavily in debt and that a haunting anxiety hung over everyone. They expected him to rescue them at last. Both branches of the family had worked and waited for this moment.

"I knew they felt obliged to offer me a wife," General Chu said, "and I knew that I could command a dowry big enough to pay our debts. But they were so awed by what they considered my greatness and my learning that they did not dare hint at marriage. They hung on every word I spoke as if jewels were falling from my lips. Only when I talked enthusiastically about the new reforms did my foster father remark that reforms were good for 'nobles,' but meant nothing to peasants. The peasants were paying for the reforms in high rents, innumerable taxes, and in every conceivable way the government could think up. Most cloth in the market was now of foreign make and cheaper than the native cloth, yet peasants could afford to buy cloth only when they were half-naked. Tax collectors came around every two or three months to demand the yearly taxes again—taxes for the new schools, for uniforms for the new army, for the local troops, for a new road that was never built, for the repair of irrigation canals, or to pay the local official salaries. The landlords unloaded all taxes off on their tenants by raising the rents. To pay the taxes peasants had to go in debt to usurers at high interest rates. Against this gnawing uncertainty and poverty, my eager talk of the reform movement sounded thin and empty."

After a few days in his foster father's home, Chu Teh visited his natural father and mother and his grandfather and grandmother in the old ancestral home, then paid visits to other relatives. Everywhere he met the same reception, and he realized with each passing day that he was a burden and that they hoped he would leave.

It was while he was visiting his ancestral home that he finally confessed his lie and told them that he would henceforth be a teacher of physical training in Ilunghsien. He hurried on to explain that he would earn money and could start paying off the family debts.

"The effect of my confession was terrifying," General Chu said. "First there was a long, shocked silence, then my father asked what physical training meant. When I explained, he shouted out, saying that the whole family had worked for twelve long years to educate one son to save them from starvation, only to be told that he intended to teach boys how to throw their arms and legs around. Coolies could do that, he shouted in violent bitterness, then turned and ran from the house and did not return while I was there. That night I heard my mother sobbing.

"Next morning I announced that I was leaving for Ilunghsien to help my friends organize the new school. They tried not to show the relief they felt, but I sensed it, and my mother's eyes were red and swollen from weeping.

"I returned to my foster father's home. My father had already been there and told them of the disgrace that I had brought upon them all. My foster father sat in total silence while I defended myself, telling him just why I had lied and acted as I had. The official examination system had now been changed, I explained. Henceforth all candidates would require modern knowledge which I did not have—including natural sciences, international law, history, and other subjects. Most of what I had learned in the old schools was now useless. In any case, I argued, even had I passed the higher examinations, I would have had to pay heavy bribes before receiving a government post. Our family could never raise so much money. Even if they succeeded, I would have to become a corrupt official and loot the people as did other officials, to pay it back— and the new China should be honest. I talked of the great changes taking place in China and of the new education in which physical training was a part.

"My foster father was a very kind man and he was willing to listen even if he did not understand. This in itself tormented me and that night I did not sleep at all, but lay in my solitary room trying to re-evaluate my entire life. I had betrayed the ancient virtue of filial piety, yet I argued with myself that family loyalty must give way to broader loyalties

—to the country and all the people. A man could not serve his family by serving it alone. Though the son of a peasant, I now knew that I was no longer a peasant with one foot in the field and one in school, but that I had become a member of another class. It was too late to turn back, nor did I intend to turn back. I had chosen my road.

"I did not blame my family. I had always hated my father's violence and cruelty, but I now knew that the merciless realities of peasant life were responsible for them. Nor did I blame my family for servile conduct toward me when I came home. I recognized it as one of the harsh products of the old system. When they repulsed my efforts to bridge the gulf between them and me, and to work in the fields that summer, they were merely trying to prevent me from sinking back into the darkness of peasant life.

"That last night was a torment, and next morning I left for Ilunghsien. My foster father, who had always loved me, walked with me for many miles before turning back. He finally stopped to turn back, and then he said:

" 'We are simple country people and do not understand many things. What is unclear today may be clear later on. Care for your health and write us.'

"He would be sixty that year, and he was old and worked-out. He wore threadbare clothes and a pair of old rope sandals. When he turned back I wept."

Then on and on along the road that he, a man of the new China, had chosen to tread, he came to Ilunghsien where, as he expressed it, "I fought my first real battles against feudalism."

He and his four teacher friends—Li, Liu, Tien, and Chang—had expected some opposition from the old scholars who kept the old-style schools, but had not even dreamed of the open warfare in which they soon found themselves enmeshed.

In the great cities like Chengtu, General Chu explained, feudal forces were in retreat, but in the countryside the landed gentry and their allies still ruled like kings, setting all standards of thought and conduct and controlling the courts, the police, and the local armed forces. The old scholars sprang from such families and, in common with them, condemned the new learning as a barbaric invasion threatening the "national essence." In reality, said General Chu, the new learning merely threatened their livelihood.

Despite the old feudal forces, there were a few progressive families— intellectuals and merchants—who realized that China must change or die, and to such families Chu Teh's teacher friends belonged. Such forces were in a minority, so much so in fact that only twelve boys enrolled in the new school when it first opened. Even these twelve alarmed the conservatives who began warning that "when one dog barks, all the dogs within a hundred li will answer."

The battle for the new learning began with skirmishes of this kind, followed by rumors that the new teachers were "fake foreigners" who had cut off their fingernails, wore false queues, and were teaching barbarian thought. They were said to be contemptuous of filial piety, righteousness, and even of the virtues of womanhood. Why, ran the question, had none of these new teachers married as did respectable young men?

Despite the rumors, a few students from the old schools began joining the new—a development which led the conservatives to move up their heavier guns. One of the new teachers, ran the charge, was a man named Chu, from the meanest classes, who was teaching something called "body training," which called for boys to strip naked and go through contortions before this teacher! The use of the body was quite proper for peasants and coolies, but the sons of gentlemen used their minds!

General Chu said that the battle line soon ran "from the old schools into the homes, the streets, shops, teahouses, and temples. We were called racial scum, men who remained unmarried for unnatural reasons. Servant girls and other women in the streets ran from us, men would stop and stare after us, and boys threw stones.

"The families of our students defended us with great courage and vigor, and fathers and grandfathers took turns sitting in my physical training classes. They told the public that my students were not stripped, but wore their trousers and jackets, and that all students should strengthen their bodies so they would not fall victim to disease and to foreign enemies of the country. They also proclaimed that the college from which we teachers had graduated had been founded by the provincial viceroy.

"Nothing helped. Before the year 1907 was out, our school was temporarily closed while we teachers were hauled before the magistrate where I was accused of teaching an indecent subject. All the teachers, and all the men of the families of our students, appeared in my defense.

"I made my first public speech at that time. What I said I cannot remember, but I gave an account of my education and of the meaning of physical education and athletics as I had learned them in the Chengtu college. I also explained that physical training was being introduced in all new schools as a means of preserving the health and strengthening the bodies of students. Foreign armies had defeated China in many wars,

I explained, and China would have to become as strong as foreign countries or become like India.

"We won the case and reopened our school, but the feudal forces soon brought us to court again, accusing us of corruption of school funds. The progressives again rallied to our defense and again we won. Next we were accused of having shaved off our queues and of wearing false ones. This would be equivalent to treason to the dynasty. We proved this charge false.

"By that time we had become so popular and our supporters so numerous that we had about seventy students in our school. As the old forces lost ground legally, and as public opinion turned against them, they adopted all kinds of dirty tricks. They hired ruffians to dump buckets of night soil before our school and, when this failed to stop us, they hired gangsters to attack us in the streets.

"I began training my students to fight in self-defense—by jujitsu, with their fists, and with sticks. We carried sticks and fought pitched battles with gangsters in the streets. We even captured some of the ruffians and hauled them to court, where they betrayed their paymasters to protect themselves."

General Chu said that the same kind of struggle was going on throughout China. Except in the big port cities, students had to fight for the right to study the new education and they spent half their time in self-defense.

The new school in Ilunghsien was also a center of new political thought which percolated through the small city and into neighboring towns and villages. Soon people were declaring that the dynasty was the most corrupt and oppressive of any in Chinese history and that the reforms had been proclaimed, not because the court wanted a modernized China, but in an effort to preserve itself from the Chinese people. The old Empress Dowager died in November 1908, but the day before her death the young Emperor, whom she had held prisoner since 1898, was poisoned. As he lay dying, the young Emperor asked his brother, the Prince Regent, to avenge his death. He accused General Yuan Shih-kai, henchman of the Empress Dowager and betrayer of the reform movement of 1898, as his murderer.

The first act of the Prince Regent, therefore, was to strip General Yuan Shih-kai of all official position and banish him from Peking—an act of great courage because General Yuan was a favorite of the British and Americans, and it was they who later, in 1911, maneuvered this man into the Presidency of the Chinese Republic over the elected President, Dr. Sun Yat-sen.

General Chu said that his experiences in Ilunghsien were among the most important in his life because they gave him knowledge of feudal forces in action, and also self-confidence in active struggle. As his knowledge and vision broadened, and as the national situation grew more critical, he said, he realized that teaching was not "the living road for me." Throughout that year in Ilunghsien he had been corresponding with his Chengtu student friend, Ching Kun, whose family had forbidden him to study in the new Military Academy in the capital. Chu had also heard that his old schoolmate, Wu Shao-pei, who had also graduated from the Normal College, had gone to Yunnan Province to enter the new Military Academy there. He had done this because his family also refused to allow him to adopt a military career.

Ching Kun kept urging Chu Teh to join him in Chengtu and run away to join the Yunnan Military Academy, thus sparing their families the shame of having to admit that their sons had adopted a military career. Though the new school term of 1908 had opened, Chu Teh's friends urged him to go. Until then Chu had begun repaying his family debts and had kept only enough to pay for his living in Ilunghsien. He did not have enough money to go to Yunnan, but his teacher friends solved this problem by taking up a collection among themselves.

Before leaving Ilunghsien, Chu Teh and his four teacher friends met in solemn conclave and took a pledge that not one of them would ever seek or accept an official position, nor marry, until China was liberated from Manchu and foreign control. Solemnly they declared that Chinese youth would learn the meaning of dedication by watching Li, Liu, Tien, Chang, and Chu!

Since his family could no longer depend on him for money, Chu Teh decided to go home before proceeding to Chengtu and to tell them the truth. To spare themselves disgrace, he knew they would never let it be known that their son had joined the army. He would also assure them that as soon as he graduated from the Yunnan Military Academy and began earning money he would again help pay the family debts.

In early December 1908, he therefore left for his home. "I spent but one night at home, but that one night was enough," General Chu said. "When I told my family that I was leaving to join the new army, they thought I had gone insane." To become a teacher of such an outrageous subject as physical training was one thing, but to join the scum of the earth was more than they could take. They had tried to be very kind at first, and cautiously urged him to stay home and rest his brain for a time; they were convinced that too much book learning had affected his mind. When he assured them that he was perfectly sane and that he had dedicated his life to the liberation of China from Manchu and foreign rule, "the reaction was terrible, terrible!" This was the last straw even for his foster father, and when he left for Chengtu no one appeared even to bid him farewell. He left his home, an outcast, with all doors and hearts closed against him.

"It was terrible, terrible," said General Chu. "Yet I had chosen my road and I could not turn back."

Chapter 7

THE youth who trudged into Chengtu in mid-December 1908 was not the gawky, shy peasant boy who had entered it two years before. He was now twenty-two, more experienced and self-confident, yet by no means a man of the world. And he was sorely troubled. His attitude and actions, both then and for years thereafter, revealed much of the innocence and simplicity of a village boy.

Nor for that matter did he, at any time in his life, develop anything approaching the sophisticated cynicism that characterizes so many men of his generation. Even after he turned fifty, his first impulse was to believe in the inherent goodness of human beings, of youth in particular. In 1944, in the midst of the Second World War, a young American correspondent with a sophisticated New York background visited Yenan. He wrote that General Chu and his comrades were totally lacking in cynicism—and that cynicism was one of the first essentials in politics. Without this quality, the young man implied, a political movement such as that led by the Chinese Communists could not succeed. . . .

Arriving in Chengtu, Chu Teh found his friend Ching Kun, who had secretly rented a junk to take them down the Min River to the Yangtze, after which they were to make their way by foot over the mighty mountain range into Yunnan Province, the land "South of the Clouds." Another passenger, a cook on his way to Yunnanfu to hunt for a job in some French home, would help pay for the boat.

Before daybreak next morning, the two youths slipped out of Ching Kun's home and made their way to the river where the cook and the boatmen were awaiting them. The junk was a shallow bark open at both ends and with a mat cabin in the center where they could take shelter and sleep at night to avoid the expense of inns. Seven boatmen were

required to navigate the treacherous rapids of the river as it plunged
south and southeastward toward the Great River, the Yangtze.

When the Min began sweeping downward past the mighty Omei mountain, the boatmen struggled to keep their junk afloat. On either hand
towered sheer cliffs, dense primeval forests of pine and blue cedar,
flowery bamboo, thick underbrush and vines; and beyond towered the
queer-shaped peaks of the sacred mountain about which time had woven
a thousand legends.

Eager to see something of their country, the travelers halted in the
main cities for a few hours, and finally disembarked at Suifu on the
Yangtze. Next morning, with their bedding and clothing roll over their
shoulders, they crossed the Great River and began climbing. The narrow
paths clung to the mountainsides like silken threads, with sheer cliffs of
solid stone on one hand and black chasms yawning on the other.

The road was divided into stages to enable travelers to take shelter
before darkness fell each night. Above and about rolled a wilderness of
snow-clad mountains shot through with jagged black peaks, as if an
angry sea had been suddenly turned to stone. Some peaks were 11,000
or more feet above sea level, with rivers crashing through dark chasms
at their base or appearing from underground and then disappearing
again with a roar.

Chu Teh had heard of "eating Yunnan bitterness," but only now did
he realize its full meaning. There were villages along the path where the
houses were nothing but low, mean hovels where opium-sodden people,
with huge goiters hanging from their necks, lived with many goats,
sheep, dogs, and an endless variety of vermin. There were small patches
of cultivated ground about the hovels, most of the area planted to the
opium poppy. The Imperial Anti-Opium Edicts had been proclaimed
three years previously, but the major part of Yunnan's revenues still
came from opium, and three quarters of its population smoked the drug.

In late February 1909, eleven weeks after leaving Chengtu, the three
travelers stood on a ridge and looked across the long funnel-like plain
at ancient Kunming, then called Yunnanfu, lying at the northern tip of
the jade-green Kunming Lake at an altitude of 6000 feet. Far to the west,
mountains of eternal snow scraped the skies.

That evening, in Yunnanfu, the cook bade the two youths farewell and
went forth to seek his fortune in French kitchens. Chu and his friend
put up at a tiny inn that boasted fewer bedbugs than others, and Ching
sent off a letter to a Chengtu friend in the Military Academy at Wuchiaba,
five miles beyond the city walls. In those days, General Chu explained,
natives of other provinces were not admitted to the Yunnan Military

Academy unless sponsored and guaranteed by old residents, or by respectable Yunnan families.

While awaiting a reply to the letter, the two friends eagerly explored the city and its environs, visiting the markets teeming with Chinese peasants and with Lolo and Shan tribespeople from the mountains. They thought of themselves as modern, emancipated youths, yet they were products of the age—and of the learning of the age—who therefore accepted many superstitions, prejudices, and historical myths. Like other Chinese, they regarded the Lolos as savages, and accepted without question the myth that Yunnan had been "civilized" by General Wu San-kwei in the seventeenth century. It was years before Chu Teh realized that Wu San-kwei had been a traitor who let the Manchu armies into China in 1644 to help him crush a peasant rebellion in the north. Once inside the Great Wall, the Manchus rejected General Wu's money and his requests that they withdraw back into the northeast whence they had come. Instead, they remained and conquered all China and appointed Wu San-kwei the viceroy of Yunnan and the neighboring Kweichow Province. From Yunnanfu, General Wu hunted down the last member of the Ming dynasty and put him to death on a hill inside Yunnanfu's walls, a hill still called "Compel to Die." In 1909, Chu Teh and Ching Kun moved admiringly among the relics of Wu San-kwei's barbaric reign.

Ching's friend soon arrived and took them with him to Wuchiaba, where they set to work to make friends with Szechwan army officers who for years had lived in the province and whose sponsorship could gain them admission to the Military Academy.

The Yunnan military situation was very complicated at the time, General Chu said. Apart from the old feudal provincial army, regiments and divisions of the new army were being organized in a few cities. There had been one regiment of Szechwan troops in the province for many years, and the new Reform 19th Division, the core of the new Reform Army, had been built up around it at Wuchiaba. As this regiment was retrained and rearmed, many of its officers and men were transferred to new regiments of Yunnan natives for training purposes.

The new 19th Division was armed with Krupp rifles, machine guns, and fieldpieces. The Manchu viceroy regarded it as an instrument to protect the dynasty from the rising revolutionary movement. Peking had sent a number of high northern Chinese officers, who were monarchists, to hold commanding positions and act as super spies against suspected subversive elements. Many of the young officers, who were simultaneously instructors in the Military Academy, had studied in

Japan. Some of them were under suspicion as members of the secret republican society, the Tung Meng Hui.

The monarchist officers suspected all young officers on general principle, but the viceroy trusted, and confided in, two or three of them. Of these confidants of the viceroy one was the President of the Military Academy, and another was Tsai Tung-pei—generally known by the name of Tsai Ao—who was commander of the 37th Brigade of the new army and also an instructor in the academy. One officer, in his middle thirties, whom the viceroy soon had cause to suspect, was named Lo Pei-chin, commander of the Szechwan Regiment.

Chu Teh and his young friend soon made friends with a young Szechwan commander, to whose provincial patriotism they appealed on their behalf and who agreed to sponsor their admission to the academy. The young commander, however, warned them that they might be rejected because they were Szechwanese. They both appeared for the entrance examinations, and, though both passed, Ching Kun was accepted while Chu Teh was rejected.

Flabbergasted that he alone had been rejected, Chu asked his friend the meaning of such treatment. A little embarrassed, Ching explained that, at the last moment, he had been so afraid that he would be rejected that he had lied about his native province, and had registered as the son of a landlord family of a Yunnan city.

"That taught me a lesson," said General Chu, "and I decided not to be so truthful in future. By that time almost all my money was gone and I had to find a way to live until I could think up some new way to get into the academy. Though no educated man in those days ever became a common soldier, I volunteered as a private in the Szechwan Regiment. The young Szechwan commander supported my action and said he would help me enter the academy.

"It was at this time that I dropped my old name and simply registered under the name Chu Teh, which I had never used until then. I also gave a Yunnan city as my birthplace, which accounts for the tale that I am a Yunnan native. I served as a regular soldier for a short time, completing my basic training and doing all the labor required of a soldier. During this time I made friends with three other soldiers whom I suspected of being members of the old peasant secret society, the Ko Lao Hui. There were many members of this society in the old armies, and they were always on the lookout for new members. However, they did not have time to invite me to join before other things intervened.

"Shortly after finishing my basic training I was promoted to company clerk, and a few weeks later my company commander recommended me for officer training in the academy. Lo Pei-chin, our regimental commander, approved the recommendation and I appeared once more for the entrance examinations, this time as Chu Teh, a Yunnan native. I passed, and found myself one of five hundred cadets, with everything, including pocket money, provided. That was another great moment in my life."

The Yunnan Military Academy was modeled on similar institutions in Japan, and the courses and discipline, therefore, were very strict. There were no summer vacations, but Sunday was a day of rest during which cadets and instructors were at liberty. There were six hours of classes, and two of drill, each day. Apart from stiff military courses, geography, mathematics, history, and international affairs were also taught. In addition, the cadets had their clubs where men gathered of an evening to discuss everything on earth.

"I made friends with cadets who later made history," General Chu said, smiling strangely, "some of them as self-sacrificing patriots, but others as corrupt officials or treacherous warlords. I also renewed my friendship with my old friend, Wu Shao-pei, from Ta Wan, who was now a history instructor in the academy. I plunged into the work and life of the academy, studying as never before in my life. I knew I was at last traveling the road that would save China from subjection and I was so enthusiastic that I felt that the youth of China could move mountains and change the course of rivers."

One of his teachers was Brigadier General Tsai Ao, the young officer trusted by the viceroy of the province and a man without whom the course of Chinese history might have taken a very different turn. Tsai Ao was only twenty-seven at the time, just four years older than Chu Teh, yet a man who had achieved things of which Chu had only dreamed.

Tsai was a native of Hunan Province, son of a poor scholar's family, where he, in previous years, had become a disciple of Liang Chi-chao, a famous scholar and leader in the Reform Movement of 1898. Liang Chi-chao, one of the most brilliant writers of the age, had founded one of the first modern schools in Changsha, Hunan, where Tsai Ao had studied and become noted for his brilliancy. Tsai had then gone on to Japan to study military science, after which he returned to China and helped build up the Reform Army in Yunnan Province.

General Chu described Tsai Ao as "a typical intellectual—frail and fair-skinned," with far-spaced eyes in a thin face, a rather feminine chin, but with a grim, stubborn mouth. Tsai was reserved and distant in manner, and very severe with himself and with all his students. Time was to prove this thin, frail man as one of the most brilliant and dynamic

leaders of the age, with a natural genius for organization and administration—and a leader capable of outwitting the most cunning and cynical
of officials.

The headquarters of Tsai's brigade was in the academy compound,
where he worked late every night and where Chu Teh sometimes went
to talk about his studies. Tsai's wife was an educated woman, but the
cadets never caught sight of her. The walls of Tsai's office were lined
with books in both the Chinese and Japanese languages, some of which
Chu was permitted to take out and read. It was here that he found a
Chinese volume that had a section on the life of George Washington,
which he read and reread. He read Montesquieu's *Spirit of Laws,* one of
the first foreign books translated into Chinese which had greatly influenced Chinese reformers. He also read the works of the brilliant Liang
Chi-chao and Kang Yu-wei on the reforms in modern Italy, on Russia
of Peter the Great, and one volume on the Meiji Emperor.

Tsai Ao also had newspapers, some from his native province as well
as occasional copies of secret republican publications, some of which
came from Hongkong and Tokyo. These fiercely attacked monarchists of
every brand and called for the armed overthrow of the Ch'ing dynasty.
Tsai allowed Chu Teh to read these newspapers in his office, but voiced
no opinion about them. Nor did Tsai ever speak a word against the
dynasty. Unlike many other instructors, he injected no revolutionary
idea in any of his lectures. Month in and month out he drove himself and
his students like a slave driver for part of the day; the rest of the time
he lived a life apart, cool, reserved, withdrawn. Chu Teh adored the man,
worshipping his brilliant mind and his capacity for work. Tsai seemed to
represent all that he wished to be but was not and never could be. All
that he ever accomplished was due to hard and methodical study and
work, whereas Tsai's mind seemed to work in lightning flashes of genius.
Despite the differences between this peasant and his intellectual teacher,
an unspoken sympathy and friendship developed between them, ripening
with the passing years.

Chu Teh had been in the academy for no more than a few weeks when
a cadet who belonged to his club asked him to join the Tung Meng Hui.
Chu accepted and was immediately initiated, taking the blood oath of
loyalty.

This secret republican organization had two branches in the academy.
Instructors had their own groups, while cadets had a parallel organization divided into isolated cells of seven or eight men each. Only one man
in each cell had contact with the center, and none of the cells were con-

nected—a device against betrayal from within any one cell. A member knew only those in his own cell.

Over a decade later, foreign and Chinese reactionaries charged that the cell system of the Chinese Communist Party was an alien idea imported by the Russian Bolsheviks. When I mentioned this, General Chu dismissed it as stupid if not a deliberate fabrication. Or, he added, it was based on the foreign imperialist assumption that the Chinese people were a subhuman race without intelligence. The cell system, he said, was as old as Chinese secret societies, and the Tung Meng Hui had taken it over from the ancient Ko Lao Hui.

With no publication of its own in Yunnan, the Tung Meng Hui smuggled literature into the interior from the coast. Cadets made copies and circulated important articles further.

"In our secret cell meetings we talked eternally about military uprisings. Theoretical political discussions were either feeble or nonexistent. We were followers of the God of War. We were forced only by national developments to broaden our ideas.

"Those were times of great suffering for our people. There were floods, droughts, and famine, and of all calamities the dynasty was the greatest. Struggles of desperation began to break out. Starving peasants arose under the leadership of the Ko Lao Hui in many places, attacked landlords, tax collectors, government institutions, and seized food. The uprisings were mercilessly crushed by the government and the heads of the leaders stuck on high poles before towns and villages. The Tung Meng Hui led sporadic revolutionary uprisings.

"The two streams of struggle never mingled. The peasants fought their desperate battles alone, the Tung Meng Hui did the same. The Tung Meng Hui membership consisted primarily of intellectuals, with a sprinkling of merchants and other middle-class elements, whom class prejudices kept from uniting with the peasants. The result was that everyone was crushed. What was worst of all—the Reform Armies in the various provinces, under control of the dynasty, crushed them.

"Up to then, the soldiers of the Reform Army had been given modern military training, weapons, and uniforms, but nothing had been done to change their minds. No changes had been made in their treatment as men, and they were still subjected to the same brutalizing and humiliating beatings and cursings as in past ages. Not even the revolutionary intellectuals could think of the common soldier as anything but a ruffian who had to be treated like an animal."

Chu Teh was the first man in the Yunnan Military Academy to raise the question of the humane treatment of the common soldier. Supported by a number of other cadets, he led a movement for the abolition of corporal punishment of soldiers. Some of the young officers agreed with them, but could do nothing because army rules were made by the highest officers sent from Peking to prevent just such "subversive" activities. It was not until after the 1911 Revolution that Dr. Sun Yat-sen abolished the corporal punishment of soldiers in the armies loyal to him but, General Chu stated, Chiang Kai-shek again introduced the old feudal practices after establishing his dictatorship in Nanking in 1927.

"Chiang Kai-shek's officers still curse, beat, or even kill soldiers at will," General Chu declared, as he talked with me of this evil, which he called one of the greatest in modern China.

Up to the 1911 Revolution, General Chu resumed, few revolutionary leaders, not to mention the middle and upper classes, could conceive of civil rights for the common people, least of all for soldiers. The bulk of Tung Meng Hui members thought of themselves as future benevolent rulers who would give the people what was good for them. To them, soldiers were mere expendable flesh in the hands of enlightened young officers. "Without any revolutionary theory to guide us, we had to learn only from bloody experience."

It was the use of the Reform Armies against the revolutionary movement which forced the Tung Meng Hui, under orders from Dr. Sun Yat-sen, to begin secret political work among the troops of the Reform Armies. Chu Teh learned about the orders when he was assigned work by the Tung Meng Hui, in the Szechwan Regiment. This was dangerous work because the new viceroy of Yunnan, Li Ching-hsi, had organized an extensive espionage network against revolutionaries.

Chu Teh began his new task by looking up the three soldiers with whom he had been friendly while serving as a private in the Szechwan Regiment, and whom he had suspected of being members of the Ko Lao Hui. The system of work which he developed became the pattern which the Chinese Communists used in later years. Sitting with these men in an isolated spot, he talked with them about their personal and economic problems and wrote letters for them to their families. From this, he went on to discuss national problems.

It wasn't long before they invited him to join the old Ko Lao Hui. He accepted and his initiation took place before many soldier members who gathered in an isolated temple in the hills. There he went through the ancient ritual, which included much kowtowing and drinking the blood oath of brotherhood. This oath was carried out in the following manner: first, Chu Teh and the members giving the oath cut a vein in their wrists and allowed a few drops of their blood to fall into a bowl of wine. The bowl was then passed around and each of the principals in the ceremony drank a little. As this was done, Chu pledged deathless loyalty to the society's principles of brotherhood, equality, and mutual aid. He then learned the signs and passwords by which society members can, to the present day, identify one another anywhere.

Political work with the Szechwan Regiment became less dangerous thereafter. The soldiers depended on him for knowledge, while he depended on them for protection. He could talk freely with small groups of men who would continue the work with other soldiers.

"The soldiers were illiterate men who had lived the hardest and most brutalized life," said General Chu, "yet many of them were very intelligent men and had a hunger for knowledge and new ideas that was very moving. I had great respect for them, and after I began commanding troops I never permitted any officer to mistreat a soldier under my command. After all, most of the soldiers came from the poor peasantry."

I interrupted his narrative to remark: "So you could say, 'There, but for the grace of God, go I.'"

"It would be more truthful to say, 'There, but for the chance that my elder uncle adopted me, go I,'" he amended.

Because "times were dangerous and disasters afflicted the country," he found no difficulty in talking with the soldiers about national events. At the time the soldiers were talking about an uprising, led by the Tung Meng Hui, at the frontier town of Hokow. The Szechwan Regiment had been sent to Hokow to reinforce the border garrison and put down the uprising, but by the time it arrived hundreds of soldiers of the garrison had joined the rebels. Told that they were being sent to put down a bandit uprising, the Szechwan Regiment found, not bandits, but scholars and even some merchants with "Dare to Die" badges on their sleeves and guns in their hands, fighting from door to door and calling to the soldiers: "Death to the alien Ch'ings! Ten thousand years to the Chinese!" and other such things.

The regiment had put down the uprising, but hundreds of soldiers from the border garrison had retreated into Indo-China with the revolutionaries. Who could understand such a fearful thing, which clearly meant that another Boxer Rebellion was brewing!

The soldiers were also amazed at the fearlessness of the rebels, who had fought to kill! Up to that time Chinese troops seldom fought to kill—unless sent against a poorly armed enemy such as a peasant uprising. When faced with a strong enemy they had always retreated. The Hokow rebels, though poorly armed, had fought fiercely, and the Szechwan

Regiment had, for the first time, fought to kill. Ai-ya! What was going to happen to China!

The soldiers clustered around Chu Teh, who explained the program of the Tung Meng Hui, which had led the Hokow uprising. He went on to explain the servile impotence and ignorance of the alien dynasty which sold the country to foreigners and taxed the people to pay the foreigners, reducing the peasants to beggary.

Just how was the government selling the country to foreigners? Well, take the railway loans which British, American, German, and French bankers were forcing on Peking. In return they demanded the right to build railways through the country. Railways would be good for the country, but not on the terms set by the foreign moneylenders. The whole country was agitating against the railway loans which would further destroy the country's independence. These loans were also connected with a currency loan from the foreigners, who demanded the right to appoint a foreigner to sit in high position in Peking to supervise the expenditure. Other countries had lost their independence by such methods, and now China was on the butcher's block.

The railways planned by these foreign moneylenders ran from Canton in the south to Hankow on the Yangtze, with a branch line running westward to Chengtu in Szechwan. Chinese industrialists in Hunan had raised money to build a railway with Chinese money, and Chinese industrialists in Szechwan had already floated provincial bonds and raised money for the Szechwan railway. A part of the railway in Szechwan was already being built, but the foreign moneylenders demanded that it be turned over to them, instead, for construction. In order to hide their plot, the foreigners insisted that Peking centralize all railway projects in its own hands—and turn them over to the foreigners.

Chu Teh further explained the projected railway loans by telling about the railway which the French were thrusting from Indo-China to Yunnanfu. This French railway concession had been wrung from Peking some ten years previously, when the French had staked out Yunnan Province as a part of their sphere of influence. When the last spike was driven, the entire Yunnan Military Academy marched into Yunnan to watch the first train arrive. Chu Teh stood with the cadets, and when the first train rolled in, one of the academy instructors suddenly wept. Then everyone wept.

Agitation against the projected railway and currency loans to Peking precipitated the greatest tragedy suffered by the Tung Meng Hui up to that time. When it became clear that the hated loans would be signed, Dr. Sun Yat-sen and other Tung Meng Hui leaders called for a great

armed uprising at Canton, which was to be the signal for the final struggle to overthrow the Ch'ing dynasty and establish a republic.

"The Canton uprising was the final effort to prevent the hated railway
loans from being signed," General Chu explained. "It was to take place
around the end of March or in early April 1911. Hundreds of trained
Tung Meng Hui leaders from every part of the world began gathering in
Canton in March, and Sun Yat-sen used all the money he had collected
from Chinese abroad, to buy arms and ammunition for this final struggle.
The plan was discovered before everything was ready, and the revolutionaries in Canton were forced to fight before they were ready. The
Reform Army at Canton was called out against them, and after a few
hours of fierce fighting our men were disastrously defeated. Seventy-two
of the chief leaders were killed outright, hundreds of others were
wounded, and the rest had to flee for their lives.

"It was a terrible defeat, a tragedy that shocked the revolutionary
forces of the entire country. Only then did the Tung Meng Hui realize,
deeply, that serious political work should be carried on among the soldiers of the Reform Armies. Only after this tragedy was such political
work begun throughout the country.

"Though we had suffered this great defeat, national hostility to the
railway loans was so fierce that Peking and the foreigners signed them
secretly six weeks later. The chief negotiator of the loans was an American, Willard Straight, who represented four big American banking cor-
porations. The chief Chinese negotiator was Sheng Hsuan-huai, Minister
of Communications, one of the most notorious officials of the country
whom the Chinese people simply called 'the father of deceit and corruption.' Not only were the loans signed secretly, but the government announced the centralization of all railways—which meant that no Chinese
could build railways without the permission of the government. The government was completely subservient to foreign moneylenders."

Chu Teh held long talks with the soldiers of the Szechwan Regiment
about these hated loans. The dynasty, he said, had signed its own death
warrant. By July 1911, Szechwan Province was in revolt. Merchants,
industrialists, students and intellectuals gathered before the viceroy's
yamen in Chengtu to protest the loans, and the viceroy turned the soldiers loose on them, killing and wounding many. Peasants, led by the
Ko Lao Hui, then marched to Chengtu to protest, and were told that they
could enter the city if they stacked their arms outside. They stacked the
arms and entered—and were also massacred. After that, the viceroy,
Chao Erh-feng, was simply referred to as "the Butcher."

After these massacres, Chu Teh continued, Szechwan's economic life was paralyzed. People refused to pay taxes, merchants closed their doors, and students and teachers organized and aroused the province. Unable to depend on the Reform Army, "the Butcher" called in Tibetan troops who shot people on sight. Preceded by these troops, officials went from shop to shop and significantly asked merchants why they had closed their doors. The merchants hurriedly opened their doors once more: business would now proceed as usual, proclaimed the Butcher. Yet the streets remained as empty as a graveyard. No person appeared to buy.

Tibetan troops were sent against rebelling villages but the peasants ambushed and exterminated them. As during all periods of struggle, the peasants struck at their ancient enemies—the tax collectors, money-lenders and feudal landlord officials.

Missionaries began to squawl "Boxers! Boxers!" and they and other foreigners throughout the country advised the government to crush the rebellion before it was too late, simultaneously calling for international armed intervention. Dr. Sun Yat-sen and other republicans were referred to in the foreign press as "crackbrained theorists, visionaries, disappointed office seekers, and soreheads." These and other terms of opprobrium were heaped upon Dr. Sun's head by some foreigners until the day he died in 1925.

General Chu could remember the hope which the foreigners placed in the Manchu general, Tuan Fang. Peking ordered Tuan Fang to leave the Wuhan cities on the Yangtze, where he was in charge of railway affairs, and lead troops to subdue Szechwan. Upon reaching the eastern borders of Szechwan, General Chu said, Tuan issued a proclamation in which he stated that the troops he commanded were for the purpose of suppressing bandits. The Szechwan people, he said, should have been grateful to the Throne, yet they were raising disturbances, closing down schools and markets, refusing to pay taxes, "and in every way behaving like rebels."

"Let there be no more trouble," the big general ordered. "Let business proceed as before. Let the taxes be paid. Let all be peaceful. Then can the railway be built, the Throne will be gratified, I will be gratified, and all the people of Szechwan reap the benefit."

Instead of obeying this noble Manchu, one missionary in Szechwan indignantly wrote, agitators increased their agitation and were even sending despicable "river telegrams." A "river telegram" was a piece of wood on which patriots wrote news, messages and calls to revolt, after which the wood was tossed in the river, to be washed ashore and read in isolated places.

Tuan Fang, with his troops, reached Chungking on October 10, 1911, just in time to hear that the Reform Army in Wuchang behind him had arisen, chased the viceroy to a gunboat in the Yangtze, and established the first Republican Military Government. The Manchu general dilly-dallied after that, reluctant to venture further on the road to Chengtu, while high officials in Peking ran themselves ragged in an effort to force him to march by double stages.

By some means unknown to Chu Teh at the time, all the men in the Yunnan Military Academy learned of the telegraphic news which poured into the viceroy's headquarters in Yunnanfu. Foreign ministers in Peking, they learned, had demanded that the government recall General Yuan Shih-kai from banishment and place him in supreme command of all the armed forces of the country and, in fact, of the government. Peking obeyed a week later, and General Yuan's "gray wolves" were soon moving against the rebel stronghold, Wuhan. They captured Hankow and burned most of it to the ground.

The sinister figure of the "foreign slave," Yuan Shih-kai, whose very name aroused Chu Teh to hatred, had returned to the stage of national affairs.

Chapter 8

W<small>HEN</small> he next came to resume the story of his life, General Chu told a story of frustration and danger. By July 1911, when he graduated from the Military Academy with the rank of second lieutenant, the monarchists were so afraid of young officers that the new graduates were not given command of troops, but merely sprinkled around in the Reform Army as "trainees," or were given odd jobs to do for higher officers. For a time Chu served as adjutant to a company commander who used him as his personal servant, sending him out to shop for anything he needed, or ordering him to prepare and serve tea. A few weeks later Chu was transferred to General Tsai Ao's brigade and given charge of company supplies—a job which he particularly welcomed because it enabled him to work directly with the soldiers.

As soon as Yunnan received news of the Wuhan revolt on October 10th, the viceroy canceled the annual autumn maneuvers of the new army, withdrew all ammunition from it, and banished Lo Pei-chin, commander of the Szechwan Regiment, to a distant part of the province.

Troops of the old army were transferred to the capital and issued modern rifles and ammunition. Defense works, swiftly thrown up around the viceroy's yamen, were manned by two companies of machine gunners, one of them commanded by Captain Li Feng-lo, a secret republican who soon warned the Tung Meng Hui that the viceroy was planning to massacre all revolutionary suspects.

"The viceroy thought he had us sewed up in a bag," General Chu said. "Our academy president—a secret republican—and Tsai Ao, whom the viceroy trusted as a constitutional monarchist, cautioned him against hasty actions, warning that the execution of a few republicans had precipitated the Wuchang revolt. They advised that ammunition be issued to the Reform troops as usual, and that the annual autumn maneuvers be held to avoid an impression that the government was weak and afraid."

Immediately after the Wuchang uprising, Chu Teh received a new assignment from the Tung Meng Hui: to carry on political agitation among the bodyguard of a divisional general of the old Yunnan Army whose headquarters was located in a nearby village. The job was dangerous but Chu again made contact with Ko Lao Hui soldiers among the bodyguard, who, being blood brothers, could not betray him.

"All I had to do was just tell them the news," General Chu said. "Province after province was rolling over to the revolution, and two expressions—*kwang-fu* and *fan shen*—were on everybody's lips. *Kwang-fu* means 'restored to light' and *fan shen* literally means 'to turn over the body' or 'stand up.' Politically it really meant to overturn the dynasty and to adopt a new way of life. The general's bodyguard listened to my news and explanations with a faraway expression on their faces. Later, they shot their officers and joined the revolution."

The viceroy finally consented to the autumn maneuvers and issued ammunition to the Reform Army. A whisper ran through the ranks: "Save ammunition!" Too lazy to go into the hills with the troops, the high monarchist officers from Peking went into Yunnanfu to feast, smoke opium, and plot.

By October 30th, the maneuvers were finished and the troops back in their barracks, two of them at Wuchiaba and the other, the Szechwan Regiment, stationed a mile north of the capital where its commander, Lo Pei-chin, was in hiding after returning secretly from banishment. The troops had saved enough ammunition to last until Yunnan fell to them.

Midnight of October 30th had been set for the uprising, but at eight o'clock that evening news reached the Tung Meng Hui leaders that someone had betrayed the plans to the viceroy. Suspicion pointed to a regimental commander, Lu Shao-chen, but there was no proof. Terrified, the viceroy personally telephoned the new army headquarters at Wuchiaba. Tsai Ao answered and declared that everything was quiet and that the commanding general and his chief of staff had gone home to dinner, though in reality they had already been arrested. The viceroy ordered Tsai Ao to arrest every revolutionary suspect in the new army and deliver them to him in chains.

Tsai Ao replied: "I'll be coming with them within an hour."

Since the plans had been betrayed, new orders were sent out to all units of the Reform Army to begin marching on the capital at nine o'clock.

"We didn't know exactly what was happening," General Chu said, "but the atmosphere was very tense and we were all watchful. Suddenly we heard firing from a village. My company commander, who was a monarchist, took two platoons of troops and ran away in the dark. I took command of another platoon and went after them. We rounded up and brought back most of the soldiers, but the commander and a number of troops escaped."

By nine o'clock all the troops had cut off their queues, the symbol of subjection to the Ch'ings, raised a red banner with the character for Han in the center (Han means the Chinese), and had gathered at the designated concentration point. Punctually on the hour of nine, Chu Teh saw, to his amazement, that Brigadier General Tsai Ao was coming up with other Tung Meng Hui leaders, and had been placed in supreme command.

Tsai made a short, terse speech in his cool, sharp voice, stating that he had been elected supreme commander by the Tung Meng Hui, and that the Reform Army would now overthrow Ch'ing rule in Yunnan and join the thirteen provinces which had already declared their independence of Peking and established Republican Military Governments.

Reviewing the troops to see that everything was in order, Tsai asked if anyone had anything to report. Chu Teh stepped forward, saluted, and reported that his company commander had fled with two platoons, but that he had taken another platoon and brought back most of the troops. Tsai ordered Chu to assume command of the company.

"We began marching on the capital at once," General Chu said. "Troops of the old army, billeted in villages along the way, began joining us, though some fled. We had gone only a couple of miles when we met a cavalry regiment sent out by the viceroy with orders to report to

Tsai Ao to 'suppress bandits.' When Tsai asked them where they were going, and their commander said they were under orders to report to Tsai Ao, Tsai said:

" 'I am Brigadier General Tsai Ao.'

" 'Where are you going?' the cavalry commander asked in amazement.

" 'We are going to Yunnanfu to overthrow the Manchus and reestablish Chinese rule,' Tsai replied. 'You are Chinese—join us!'

"There was the most terrible confusion! Horsemen began dashing about shooting at nothing, with our own cavalry trying to round them up. Men were running and shouting, and our Ko Lao Hui yelling to their blood brothers in the cavalry regiment to join us. Some joined us, then deserted, then turned back and joined us again. Others rode off wildly into the night, shooting into the air. In the midst of the confusion we heard the roar of guns from the north of the capital and realized that our Szechwan Regiment was already attacking. In giving final orders, our leaders had forgotten that the Szechwan Regiment was only a mile from the North Gate, while we were five miles away. The attack was therefore not coordinated. We had also sent a group of academy cadets, with concealed guns, inside the city, but under orders to wait near the Southern Gate until we came up, and then to fight and open the gate for our entry."

The revolutionary troops now began swift-marching toward Yunnanfu, and as they approached the city they saw the black figures of large numbers of troops of the old army on the city wall above. Instead of firing, these troops bent over the wall and shouted:

"What's up?"

Just then pistol shots from inside the Southern Gate were heard—the cadets concealed inside had attacked. Still the troops on the walls above fired not one shot, but just waited curiously. Suddenly the heavy old city gates swung open and the revolutionary troops poured through, each unit under orders to occupy a specific strategic point in the city. And still the old troops on the city walls did not fire, but allowed themselves to be disarmed. Soon all the public buildings and other strategic points were occupied. There was serious fighting only at the arsenal, but revolutionary gunners blasted in the doors and began distributing ammunition to their comrades.

It was so dark that no one could distinguish friend from enemy, and General Tsai Ao ordered all units to hold their positions until dawn.

Dawn found Chu, with his company, drawn up before the defense works surrounding the viceroy's yamen, where the old order made its last stand. Captain Li Feng-lo, commander of one of the machine-gun companies manning the defenses, ordered his troops not to fight. Chu Teh's company was one of the two that went over the walls surrounding the yamen, but they were no sooner over than one of their own artillery units opened up on the yamen, endangering them all. Only after the unit was called off could they open the gates.

There was little fighting from that time onward. The chief job of the revolutionaries was dragging the old soldiers out from hiding places inside the compound. In the residential mansion they found the viceroy hiding under a bed, "all dressed up in coolie clothes." The revolutionary soldiers dragged the fellow out by his queue, which they lopped off with a sword, and hustled him off to Tsai Ao's command post, where he collapsed at the sight of one of the officers whom he had most trusted.

Most of the old monarchist officers and officials were rounded up and shot, but the viceroy was later allowed to leave for Peking. His experience and terror made such a lasting impression on him that, six years later, he rejected a high position in the Peking warlord government.

Reform units in other parts of Yunnan had also arisen on the night of October 30th, and within a few days the whole province had overthrown Manchu rule. The revolutionaries suffered only some forty dead and one hundred wounded.

"The dynasty was so rotten that when we blew on it, it collapsed," General Chu remarked.

On the afternoon of October 31st, Tsai Ao and other leaders addressed a huge mass meeting of civilians and soldiers and Tsai was proclaimed Military Governor of the Yunnan Republic. Chu Teh and his company were patrolling the streets of the city, "vigilant against reactionaries and protecting revolutionaries." As they marched they sang old ballads and composed new ones on the spot. They made up new words to the ancient daisy song which generations of men had sung on the ninth day of the ninth moon—the song of escape from disaster. In the long years that followed, Chu Teh's troops always sang that song of victory.

The Yunnan revolutionaries had little time for rejoicing. Weeks before the uprising, their leaders had made plans to send an expeditionary force into Szechwan where the revolutionary forces were still unable to overthrow Manchu power. Cadets from the Military Academy who came from other provinces had long since slipped away to their native provinces to take part in the revolution. The natives from Szechwan left under orders to report to Tung Meng Hui leaders in Chengtu and Chungking and inform them of plans for the expeditionary force. When the Yunnan

Army reached the city of Suifu in south Szechwan, the people of Chengtu and Chungking were to arise and establish Revolutionary Military Governments similar to those in other revolting provinces.

Immediately after the uprising, General Tsai Ao personally led eight battalions—two of them from the Szechwan Regiment—up over the ancient trade route toward Szechwan. Chu Teh, now commissioned captain, marched with his company in this expedition. The expeditionary force was small, yet thought sufficient to tip the scales in Szechwan.

Three weeks later the expedition contacted the first two enemy battalions before the walls of Suifu. The enemy let out bloodcurdling yells and fired one volley from their old muzzle-loaders . . . The very memory of this aroused hatred in General Chu's mind because it epitomized the feudal backwardness and impotence of the old China which "made a big noise like a few peas in an empty gourd."

Without missing a step, the Yunnan revolutionaries continued advancing, one platoon returning the fire with its model rifles. The enemy battalions broke and fled wildly in every direction, many of them "taking to the hills to join the bandits with whom they had always been connected."

Suifu welcomed the revolutionaries with banners and demonstrations, and a Republican Military Government, composed of merchants, Tung Meng Hui intellectuals—of whom there were a few in the city—and representatives of the Yunnan Army, was established.

Though the Yunnan expeditionary force had operated by plan, still no news came of the expected uprisings in Chengtu and Chungking. The army therefore pushed on toward Chengtu, entering the great Tzeliuching salt well region and beyond to get astride all routes of communication along which the army led by the Manchu general, Tuan Fang, was advancing.

It was in this region that the revolutionaries first heard that Tuan Fang, together with his brother, had just been beheaded by their own troops and that Tuan's head had been sent in an American kerosene can to the authorities in Chungking. They also heard that Viceroy Chao, "the Butcher," upon learning of the advance of the Yunnan forces and the beheading of Tuan Fang, surrendered power to a Chengtu committee made up of businessmen, industrialists, and landlord gentry which immediately called on both sides to "lay down your arms because our aims have been achieved."

General Chu's face was a study in contempt as he recalled the "committee of time-serving property owners" that wanted to step into the boots of the old officials. The Yunnan Army continued marching on Chengtu until news reached it that the expected uprisings, led by the Tung Meng

Hui and the Ko Lao Hui, had taken place in Chengtu and Chungking and that Republican Military Governments had been established. Only then did the army halt and hold its positions in south Szechwan.

Chu Teh, with his company, spent the next three months patrolling the salt well city, Tzeliuching, and now and then taking part in short campaigns against bandit raids. The salt wells, which had previously closed down due to bandit raids and other disturbances, had now resumed operations, but under the old conditions. Both the peasants and the workers had sympathized with the 1911 Revolution and had hoped for reforms to better their sad lot. They were bitterly disappointed, General Chu said. None were undertaken because, "within a short period of time, the 1911 Revolution was aborted by republican compromise with foreign imperialism."

What happened during that period made a deep impression on his mind and influenced his thinking for the rest of his life. He explained it in these terms:

The Republican National Assembly met in Nanking in December 1911, and elected Dr. Sun Yat-sen the first provisional President of the Republic. It appointed a committee which drew up a democratic constitution, the first in Chinese history to grant civil rights to the people. Dr. Sun was abroad at the time, rushing between Washington, London and Paris in a futile effort to hold up a new foreign loan, the "Reorganization Loan," which the International Banking Consortium was planning to grant General Yuan Shih-kai, who was now in complete control of the Peking government. Dr. Sun hoped this loan could be given to the new Republic and on terms that would not further destroy China's sovereignty. The foreign governments and the consortium, however, informed him that they dealt only with "recognized governments" which, in this instance, meant Peking. Still believing that these Western democratic governments would welcome a new Chinese Republic that emulated them in many respects, Dr. Sun therefore rushed back to China in late December 1911, and a few days later took the oath of office as China's first provisional President.

In an article published abroad and later in China, Dr. Sun expressed his hopes for the reconstruction of China. While adopting a republican constitutional government, he wrote, the new China should not allow capitalism to be established because such a system would result in "a despotism a hundred times more frightful" than that of the Manchus, and "rivers of blood will be required to liberate ourselves from it." In America, Britain and France, he warned, "the gulf between the rich and the poor is far too great," and unless China had a "social revolution, our people will be deprived forever of joy and happiness."

Such plans were not shared by Dr. Sun's comrades in Nanking, many of whom even aped foreign imperialists by calling him an "impractical visionary." From this point they went on to urge disastrous compromises about the new Reorganization Loan and about the Republic itself. The foreign powers and the International Banking Consortium were debating the possible recognition of the Republic, but only on condition that Dr. Sun Yat-sen resign as President in favor of their own "strong man," General Yuan Shih-kai, whom they called a "liberal and great administrator and the only man capable of holding China together."

The American minister to China at the time cabled Washington repeatedly, urging that the Reorganization Loan be given Yuan Shih-kai at once lest the monarchy collapse. If given to Yuan, he cabled, the "rebels might be forced to submit to reasonable terms"; and, unless this were done, foreign armed intervention might become "necessary."

The American minister to China, General Chu repeated time and again, was among the first to demand international armed intervention against the 1911 Revolution. China was saved this tragedy, not because the foreign powers believed in the independence and integrity of China, but because the European powers were in conflict over African colonies, and war was threatening. Only America and Japan could have intervened in China, but the British and other imperialist powers did not want that.

The foreign powers and their bankers, however, took steps just as disastrous, and the new Republic fell into the trap. At foreign insistence, Dr. Sun Yat-sen was forced to withdraw as President in favor of General Yuan Shih-kai. In preparation for this move, Yuan himself drew up the edict of abdication of the boy Emperor. This edict stated that Yuan Shih-kai was empowered to form a republican form of government. The republicans swallowed this insult though it clearly implied that the monarchy, and not the Chinese people, was the source of all power.

Dr. Sun resigned from the Presidency in the belief that General Yuan could be more easily controlled if he were President of the Republic, and because he wanted peace. He believed that Yuan would not dare take the Reorganization Loan on terms dictated by the Banking Consortium.

Chu Teh and his comrades, doing small but necessary jobs in Szechwan, at first did not believe the rumors that Dr. Sun had resigned in favor of General Yuan, who was a known monarchist and a treacherous man who had betrayed the Reform Movement of 1898. If this man could not even honor his oath of allegiance to the Emperor, what would he do to the Republic, they asked one another. Yet the rumor became a fact and the fact spread confusion and demoralization in republican ranks.

Looking back over the years, General Chu could see that the 1911 revolutionaries went from mistake to mistake, while Yuan and the foreigners played with them as a cat plays with a mouse, at one time slapping them down, and at another enticing them with promises of recognition and money. Instead of dallying in Szechwan, General Chu said, the Yunnan revolutionary army should have marched at once on the Wuhan cities in central China and smashed Yuan's armies there. Instead of this, the republicans compromised with their mortal enemies.

The urban population of the times "had progressed beyond mere reformism to realizing the necessity of setting up a new governmental power," General Chu said, yet they now allowed themselves to be sucked down into the morass of feudalism and imperialist intrigues. They also allowed feudal elements to remain in the army and in official positions. In the years that followed, Yunnan was one of the very few provinces that made political and military progress—though this also did not last long.

"We could blame foreign imperialism for the abortion of the 1911 Revolution," General Chu stated with harsh conviction, "yet the foreigners could have done nothing whatever had there not been Chinese willing to sell themselves and their country. On the revolutionary side we failed because we did not introduce democracy. Also, the desire for profit and promotion was very great in our own ranks so that, after the first selfless burst of revolutionary fervor, it was easy for men to lose their character."

He felt certain, he said, that there were citizens in foreign countries who sympathized with the Chinese Republic and had supported Sun Yat-sen, but he had read only of the stand taken by V. I. Lenin, the exiled Russian revolutionary leader, in an article published in Geneva while Dr. Sun was still President.

Lenin wrote that Dr. Sun could not be compared with the presidents of republics in Europe and America "who are business men, agents, or tools in the hands of the bourgeoisie" which had long since "renounced all the ideals of its youth." Dr. Sun, he wrote, was "a great revolutionary democrat of nobility and courage" whose program of reconstruction breathed a militant, sincere spirit of democracy and frankly raised the problem of the Chinese masses. General Chu could quote the exact words in which Lenin analyzed Yuan Shih-kai whom the imperialist powers called a "liberal" and the only "strong man capable of holding China together." Lenin's words were:

Such liberals are above all capable of treachery. Yesterday they feared the emperor, cringed before him; then, when they saw the strength and sensed the victory of revolutionary democracy, they betrayed the emperor; tomorrow they will betray the democrats in order to strike a bargain with some old or new "constitutional emperor."

Still speaking of that era and its aftermath, General Chu said:

Thirty years of revolutionary experience have taught me that a revolution must have a revolutionary party founded on scientific principles. It must have a revolutionary army which not only fights, but sees to it that a democratic system, with the masses as its source of strength, is carried out. Revolutionary phrases are not enough. Many men today mouth Sun Yat-sen's words while betraying them in practice, but the real disciples of Sun Yat-sen were never afraid of democracy.

Book III

Scourge and Pestilence

Chapter 9

IT WAS a troubled and confused army that left Szechwan in March 1912 and marched southward to its home base in Yunnan over the same route it had come with such wild hopes four months before.

The two battalions of Szechwan troops in the Yunnan Army had been left behind in Szechwan. Yunnan was one of the poorest provinces in the country and would now have to draw in its belt to put through the modernization program planned by Tsai Ao and other republican leaders.

Chu Teh and his comrades were somber as they trudged along over the ancient trade route. Instead of having moved mountains and changed the course of rivers, as they had believed themselves capable of doing in October, they could not help feeling that they were retreating. Perennially optimistic, Chu tried to keep up his courage by arguing that even a monarchist would never dare betray the Republic, and that Yunnan could become the model province which its leaders planned.

In May, back in Yunnan, during a military ceremony, he was promoted to the rank of major, and was humbly grateful when General Tsai Ao singled him out as one of the men to receive both the "Support Szechwan" medal and the "Recovery" medal—the latter meaning the recovery of Chinese rule from the Manchus. The unspoken friendship between the two men, established in previous years, remained unbroken, and General Tsai had taken time off occasionally to ask Chu not only about himself but about his family. Chu had heard from his family again and had been sending them most of his salary.

"You do not look well," Chu had said to Tsai. "We worry about your health." Tsai had smiled a strange little smile in reply, as if he were thinking of something far away.

In a speech to the troops, Tsai reported on the problems of Yunnan and on the need for each man to make sacrifices far greater than the struggle against the Manchus had called for. The troops had not been paid for two months, and sweeping economies would have to be made. Maimed soldiers, and the families of men killed in battle, were to receive life pensions. Old soldiers were being retired and young servicemen who wished to leave the army could do so. Henceforth, no officer of any rank, and no official, could receive more than a maintenance allowance for himself and his family.

The provincial administration was being reformed and simplified, and the young graduates of a new school for administrators would soon replace all the old and corrupt officials who had been left in their positions. New schools were being founded, new industries established, and modern roads and buildings would be built. A new normal school was training both men and women teachers. The Military Academy, which had been closed since the Revolution, would reopen in the autumn.

Chu Teh spent the rest of that spring and summer of 1912 training troops. In the autumn he was transferred to the Military Academy and placed in charge of one of the five companies into which the cadets were organized. By then, great changes had taken place in the country, as well as in his private life.

"I was married that autumn," General Chu remarked rather indifferently. "My wife's name was Hsiao Chu-fen. She was a girl of eighteen, a student in the Normal School, and the daughter of an intellectual family that had played an active role in the reform movement and the Revolution. She was a sincere and fairly progressive girl, and her feet had never been bound. Her brother, who was one of my army friends, arranged the marriage. I was twenty-six, old enough for a normal man to be married; and I was a normal man and needed a wife."

Whether or not General Chu loved this girl he never said, nor was it necessary for him to say anything for me to understand that he did not. The most he ever said about his relationship was that he and his wife were friends and had more than enough to talk about when they met. He was proud that the marriage was not bourgeois, and that the two of them had even met and talked, in the presence of Chu-fen's family, before they made up their minds. This was a revolutionary step in those days: respectable girls, even after the Revolution, still did not talk with their husbands before marriage.

Furthermore, Chu-fen continued her studies in the Normal School and lived in the school dormitories, while Chu Teh stayed at the Military Academy. They met only on Sundays, the one day in the week when he was at liberty. "We were both revolutionaries with serious work to do," General Chu added, and turned again to problems that seemed of greater importance to him than his marriage.

When the Military Academy reopened he found himself closely associated with a large number of cadets from other provinces, many of them

young men who had left the academy in the previous year to take part in
the Revolution in their native provinces. Some had gone as far away as
Shanghai and Canton. Returning to complete their subjects, they were
much more experienced and less naive than Chu Teh and his friends
had been. Cadets from other provinces were refugees, as were a number
of the instructors, for Yuan Shih-kai had begun a reign of terror against
republicans. Yunnan, one of the few provinces in which republicans held
supreme power, was filling up with refugees.

"They enriched the life of Yunnan by becoming teachers, officials,
army officers, and workers on the two newspapers which we now published in Yunnanfu," General Chu said. "I spent most of my leisure hours
listening to the refugee cadets and instructors tell of the arrest, imprisonment, and assassination of republicans by Yuan Shih-kai's paid
henchmen."

The chief national problem was the Reorganization Loan which the
International Banking Consortium was negotiating with Yuan Shih-kai.
Its terms were so dangerous to China that it was condemned by the entire
country. Dr. Sun Yat-sen warned the foreign bankers that the Chinese
people would repudiate the Reorganization Loan if it were made on their
stipulated terms. Yuan replied to the opposition by arrests, imprison-
ments, and assassinations and by removing all republicans from office.
He appointed only officials loyal to himself.

Among the refugees who became instructors in the Yunnan Military
Academy were two or three who had studied in France. Hoping to learn
how the French had completed their great revolution, whereas China
seemed to be failing, Chu spent hours questioning these men about
French parliamentary institutions.

In the autumn of 1912, the famous revolutionary leader, Sung Chiao-
jen, tried to save the Republic by absorbing all revolutionary organizations into a new federated political party, the Kuomintang, or Nationalist
Party. Chu Teh was one of the first men in Yunnan to transfer his old
Tung Meng Hui membership to the new organization. The Kuomintang
members acted secretly, as in the past, because Yuan's spies and assassins
were prowling the land exactly as they had done under the Manchus.

General Chu's account of what happened thereafter took on the quality
of a nightmare in which the leading characters seemed like specters
doomed by blindness forever to repeat historical mistakes over and over
again.

The first parliamentary elections, held in the winter of 1912, were
fought on the issue of the Reorganization Loan. Fearless of death,
Kuomintang leaders waged their campaign against the loan both in

China and abroad, declaring that for China to take this loan would be like a thirsty man drinking poison.

The Kuomintang won a majority of seats in the new Parliament, which was to meet in Peking in April 1913. In March of that year a ray of light momentarily shone on the scene. The new American President, Woodrow Wilson, electrified revolutionary elements by announcing that his government could not approve of the participation of American bankers in the loan. It threatened, he said, the administrative integrity of China. The American banking groups thereupon withdrew, only to reappear later as individual entities instead of members of the International Consortium.

Almost simultaneously with the American President's announcement, Sung Chiao-jen, organizer of the Kuomintang and leader of the national campaign against the loan, was assassinated by one of Yuan Shih-kai's henchmen. It happened while he was on his way to Peking to take his seat in Parliament. Despite this new outrage, the five remaining banking groups in the consortium met with Yuan Shih-kai in the Peking branch of the British Hongkong & Shanghai Banking Corporation. There they secretly signed the contract for the Reorganization Loan—on terms dictated by the foreigners. The vice-chairman of Parliament broke into the room and denounced the loan as unconstitutional, but at a wave of hands guards threw him out.

In a desperate effort to prevent the loan contract from being carried out, Dr. Sun Yat-sen appealed to the London president of the consortium, warning that blood would flow if the bankers persisted. Dr. Sun was ignored, as if he did not exist—as indeed he did not for the leading characters in the tragedy.

By June 1913, six southern provinces of China arose against Yuan Shih-kai who had secretly signed the hated Reorganization Loan. The rebels were defeated almost before they could take to the battlefield because Yuan used the loan to equip, feed, and finance his armies and to build up his personal dictatorship thereafter. Again Sun Yat-sen and other republican leaders fled into exile, with prices on their heads. Dr. Sun hid in the home of Japanese friends in Tokyo where Yuan's agents searched for him. In November 1913, Yuan outlawed the Kuomintang and ordered its members shot on sight. In December he proclaimed Confucianism the state religion and revived the worship of heaven, an ancient rite reserved only to emperors.

He next dissolved Parliament and gathered together an advisory council of old militarists and monarchists to help him rule the country. And soon a new character stepped out on the stage in the form of Dr. Frank

Goodnow, a citizen of the American Republic who had been sent to Peking as Yuan's "constitutional" adviser. By mid-1914, Dr. Goodnow had produced a weird document called the "Constitutional Compact" which Yuan proclaimed as the law of the land and which General Chu subsequently described as "the first fascist constitution in the world." This "Compact" made Yuan Shih-kai the supreme dictator of all China, with the right to appoint or dismiss every official or army officer in the land; to determine the official system and official regulations; to declare war, conclude peace, make treaties, and confer titles of nobility.

A few weeks later Dr. Goodnow drew up another document giving Yuan the right to appoint his successor. A few months later again, he produced the notorious "Memorandum" in which he argued that a monarchy was more suitable to China than a republic but that it should be carefully engineered to prevent too much public opposition. Yuan used the Memorandum as propaganda in his nationwide monarchist campaign. To achieve a semblance of public support, he instructed officials throughout the country to cable him petitions to restore the monarchy with himself as emperor. "Bowing to public demands," Yuan proclaimed January 1, 1916, as the date of his coronation.

Yunnan was so isolated from national affairs, General Chu explained, that it was not until December 1913 that someone warned Yuan Shih-kai that a "dangerous genius" named Tsai Ao was still loose in that province, and that his prestige and cunning were such that he could best be controlled in Peking. Instead of assassinating Tsai, Yuan therefore ordered him to Peking to become, of all things, chief of the Land Demarcation Bureau and one of his military advisers.

All secret republicans in Yunnan went into little huddles, after which Tsai wired that he would proceed to Peking at once. Had he refused, General Chu said, Yunnan would have been overrun by Yuan's armies and Tsai would have had to choose between assassination and exile. Tsai's old teacher, Liang Chi-chao, was an official in the Peking government, and might protect his life. Tsai's plan was to maintain the Yunnan revolutionary regime intact and keep the province in Kuomintang control until the republicans could reorganize their shattered ranks.

Before leaving Yunnan, Tsai deployed the 1st Division, in which Chu Teh was an officer, along the length of the French railway and along the border. Encouraged by Yuan's rise to power, all the imperialists were again riding high, and the French were arming bandits and tribesmen to make raids into Indo-China so as to give French troops the excuse of chasing them back into Yunnan and holding such territory. Chu Teh spent the next two years of his life fighting bandits and tribesmen armed with good French rifles and preventing their paymasters from extending their occupation of Chinese territory.

Those two years on the border were dark and miserable for him. South Yunnan, he said, is a sweltering tropical region of high mountains and malarial valleys shrouded in dense fogs that breed lung diseases, and with water so bad that everyone suffered from intestinal disorders. Now and then he would make a trip to Mengtzu, where he would find letters, newspapers, and an occasional book from his wife awaiting him. The newspapers were no help. They made depressing reading. No ray of light shone in China, and the Western powers were slaughtering one another in the First World War.

In an effort to relieve the dreary monotony of his existence he would sometimes call on a French businessman in Mengtzu whom he had met and who delighted in answering his questions about French life and institutions and who introduced him to the writings of Voltaire. He could also talk to a few young republican officers who, with him, cursed their divisional commander and the divisional chief of staff, Lu Shao-chen. Lu had been suspected of having betrayed the 1911 Revolution in Yunnan. After the Revolution was victorious, both these high officers had pledged allegiance to the Republic. After Tsai Ao left for Peking and Yuan began his monarchist movement, they reverted to their old beliefs. Fifteen years later, when General Chu commanded the Chinese Red Army in Kiangsi, Chief of Staff Lu turned up as one of Chiang Kai-shek's divisional commanders. The two men fought each other on the battlefield.

When the First World War began, General Chu continued, China was completely shrouded in darkness. Japan, which was one of the Allied Powers, seized and held the great naval base of Tsingtao which German imperialism had wrested from China in 1897. In early 1915 also, the Japanese made their notorious secret Twenty-one Demands on China which were intended to turn China into a Japanese protectorate. After a few months of bickering, Yuan signed them in a slightly revised form, and thereby signed his death warrant.

Tsai Ao later informed the country that Yuan Shih-kai signed the Japanese Twenty-one Demands on condition that Japan recognize his new dynasty. Yuan had also offered the other foreign powers sweeping rights and privileges in return for recognition.

During his two years on the border, Chu Teh was twice promoted. In December 1915 he became full colonel and was given command of the

10th Yunnan Regiment of which his battalion had been a part. This second promotion, he later learned, had been the work of General Tsai Ao who had just returned secretly from Peking.

Tsai had escaped from Peking under the most dramatic circumstances. Evading Yuan's secret police, who had followed him night and day for two years, he reached Tientsin and took a ship for Japan. After conferring with exiled Kuomintang leaders, he had gone from there to Indo-China and secretly returned to Yunnan by way of the French railway.

Two incidents had led Chu Teh to suspect that the clouds over China were lifting. One of them was his own promotion in rank. The other incident was the announcement in a press report that the famous writer Liang Chi-chao, who had been an official in Peking, had resigned on grounds of ill health. In a letter of resignation to Yuan Shih-kai, Liang had argued that, though he looked strong and healthy, he suffered from "swollen pulses, dizziness, coughs and cold and wind on the stomach," and a long list of other ailments. They compelled him to leave, so he claimed, for medical treatment in the beneficial climate of the United States.

Upon reaching a foreign concession in Tientsin, a few hours by train from Peking, all Liang's ailments vanished. Instead of going to America, he sat down and began pouring out vitriolic articles against Yuan Shih-kai and his dynasty, articles that enraged Yuan all the more because Liang was a constitutional monarchist. Liang was soon on the jump, a few steps ahead of Yuan's assassins, and eventually turned up in south China to continue his campaign in a more salubrious atmosphere.

Upon reading that Liang had resigned and was attacking Yuan, Chu Teh and his young republican officer friends put their heads together. If Liang had escaped, they speculated, Tsai Ao had also fled, or he had been arrested and perhaps killed. For Liang was Tsai's old teacher and had been his protector in Peking.

In mid-December 1915, while in Mengtzu, Chu Teh met an old Kuomintang friend in the streets. The man bowed very formally, as if meeting a chance acquaintance, but while bowing he hurriedly asked him to bring his most trusted republican officer friends and meet him that night in a temple on the outskirts of the town.

That evening a small group of men met at the arranged place, where Chu's old friend produced a small piece of cloth. It was a letter signed by Tsai Ao, which ordered them to obey the instructions his emissary would give them.

At dawn on December 25th, ran the instructions, Tsai Ao would lead

the troops in the Yunnanfu region in revolt, take the oath of allegiance
to the Republic, and issue a call to the country to arise in revolt and
destroy Yuan Shih-kai. Simultaneously, the republicans at Mengtzu and
other main cities were to do the same. The troops at Mengtzu were to
move by train to Yunnanfu. Eight regiments of the Yunnan Army were to
march from there into Szechwan Province to overthrow Yuan Shih-kai's
rule. The uprising was to take place before January 1st, when Yuan's
coronation as emperor was to take place, and before the foreign powers
could recognize the new dynasty.

Chu Teh and other Republican officers spent the rest of the month
training new recruits to be left behind as border guards. Before dawn on
the morning of December 25th, Colonel Chu led a picked body of troops
to divisional headquarters to arrest the monarchist officers, only to find
that they had fled.

At dawn all the troops in the Mengtzu region were assembled. Chu
and his comrades reported on the state of the nation, and administered
and took the oath of allegiance to the Republic. Commandeering trains,
they loaded their troops and left at once for Yunnanfu.

At the same time Tsai Ao and other leaders appeared before a great
mass meeting of troops and civilians in Yunnanfu where they all took the
oath of allegiance to the Republic. Simultaneously they released a telegraphic manifesto to the nation. It called for the destruction of Yuan
Shih-kai as a traitor to the nation who had turned his sword against the
Chinese people while kowtowing to his foreign imperialist paymasters.

Chu Teh and his officer friends soon swung from the train in Yunnanfu and rushed to Tsai Ao's headquarters, where they found him in
conference with his staff.

"When Tsai Ao arose and came toward us," General Chu said, "I was
so shocked that I could not speak. He was as thin as a ghost, his cheeks
were sunken, and his eyes were like burning lights in his head. He was
dying of tuberculosis and his voice was so low and weak that we had to
listen closely to everything he said. When he came up to me I bent down
and wept and could not say a word.

"Though he was dying, his mind functioned like a sword, as in the
past. We sat down and he explained plans for the uprisings throughout
the country, but said that Yunnan would have to carry the burden until
republican forces could organize in the other provinces. Three days later
we were to leave for Szechwan where some of Yuan's strongest armed
forces were stationed. He felt certain others were already being moved
from surrounding provinces into Szechwan, and he warned us that this
would be a very different campaign from that of 1911. Szechwan was

filled with northern troops, all of them excellently armed and fed by foreign loans which Yuan kept taking from the foreign powers. We could not blow Yuan's armies over as we had blown over the Ch'ings. He had four brigades in south Szechwan alone, commanded by one of his personal henchmen, while another of his friends, the strutting little war-lord Tsao Kun, was commander in chief in Chengtu. This Tsao Kun was the same little rascal whom we later called the 'Bribe President' because in 1923 he paid each member of Parliament five thousand dollars to vote for him as President.

"Our 2nd Division, Tsai told us, was leaving at once for Kweichow Province to clean out Yuan's forces there, then for Kwangsi, and then on to Kwangtung on the coast. The 1st Division, with additional troops, was to go on the Szechwan expedition, and additional reinforcements would follow as soon as they were trained.

"Tsai was to command the Szechwan expedition in person and, in addition, to be supreme commander of the republican forces in three other southern provinces. The Yunnan Army was now renamed the Hu Kuo Chun, or Army for the Defense of the Republic."

When Tsai finished his report, Colonel Chu spoke up, saying:

"But you can't go on this expedition! You are sick. It would kill you!"

Tsai looked at and beyond him, saying: "There is no other way. In any case I have little time left. I will give it to the Republic."

Chu Teh saw his young wife only late at night when he returned from staff conferences or from the hectic preparations for the Szechwan expedition in which his 10th Regiment was to take part. At dawn on the third morning after he had reached Yunnanfu, eight regiments of the Hu Kuo Chun were marching toward southern Szechwan. Because his 10th Regiment had had two years' experience in guerrilla fighting with bandits and tribesmen on the frontier, it was chosen to spearhead the attack on Yuan's armies which knew nothing but positional warfare.

The news of the Yunnan uprising and the manifesto calling for the destruction of Yuan Shih-kai spread terror and confusion among the foreigners in China. Diplomats, missionaries, and the foreign press began a violent campaign attacking the revolutionaries; one American correspondent wailed in a report to the *New York Tribune*:

"Alas! What manner of men are these who have dared raise the banner of revolt against their King! A rabble of ruffians and half-grown boys!"

The Hu Kuo Chun continued marching. On the Szechwan-Yunnan border it met two battalions of Szechwan troops who, instead of firing, raised their rifles in the air and ran toward them with wild shouts of joy. Enemy headquarters, they said, was in the small city of Nachi south of the Yangtze. There also was a telegraph office which Tsai Ao needed to communicate with the revolutionary forces in the southern provinces.

Fighting began almost at once against four enemy brigades south of the Yangtze. This initial battle, spearheaded by Colonel Chu Teh's 10th Regiment, lasted for three days and three nights without a pause. The entire Hu Kuo Chun was engaged and Chu Teh's troops became famous for their night fighting and hand-to-hand encounters. On the second day, Tsai Ao placed two more regiments under Chu's command, and by daybreak of the fourth morning the enemy had been clawed to pieces and the revolutionaries were in enemy headquarters in Nachi. Colonel Chu stood with his troops on the southern bank of the Yangtze and looked across at Luchow, the fortified enemy stronghold in south Szechwan.

"We did our first mass work among the peasants during this war against the monarchy," Chu Teh said. "Led by the Ko Lao Hui, the peasants arose in arms, attacked enemy transports, and delivered food and ammunition to us. Boatmen moved up and down the river with supplies for us, ferried our troops across the river, and carried our wounded from the battlefield."

The republicans had now found new allies. The famous writer Liang Chi-chao, who had organized his "Progress Party" in previous years, rallied his followers to support the revolution. Revolutionaries from Szechwan and other provinces, and exiles returned from abroad, made their way to the Hu Kuo Chun. One of these exiles, Sung Ping-wen, soon became one of Chu Teh's closest associates and exercised decisive influence upon him in the next seven years.

Losses in the first three-day battle forced the Hu Kuo Chun to halt for reorganization, the distribution of ammunition, and the deployment of troops. In this reorganization, General Tsai Ao raised Chu to the rank of brigadier general in command of a brigade, and assigned him the returned exile, Sung Ping-wen, as his brigade secretary, a position which in those days—at least with Chu Teh—was something like a political commissarship.

General Chu described Sung Ping-wen as a veteran revolutionary in his middle thirties, of medium height, and dark-skinned "like a peasant." Sung had graduated from a Peking university where, in 1911, he had taken part in a plot to assassinate the Prince Regent. When the plot failed, he was one of the men who escaped to Japan where he worked on Sun Yat-sen's republican newspaper until the 1915-1916 Revolution began. Sung came from a scholarly family of Szechwan which had taken part in the 1898 Reform Movement and in every revolutionary struggle thereafter. Sung's sister had broken all old feudal concepts and had taken an active part in the 1911 Revolution as an underground worker.

During the period of reorganization following the first three-day battle, General Chu was ordered to hold all territory south of the Yangtze while the rest of the Hu Kuo Chun crossed the great river to launch an attack on the main enemy strongholds to the north. Some of Yuan Shih-kai's troops were already wavering, one of them a brigade commanded by General Feng Yu-hsiang, later known as the "Christian General." General Feng sent a representative to General Tsai Ao to arrange a truce and to inform Tsai that he did not believe in the monarchy. The commander in chief of Yuan Shih-kai's armies in Szechwan had also sent a representative to Tsai to feel out the situation so that he might be on the winning side at the most propitious moment.

The Hu Kuo Chun brought up reinforcements from Yunnan and Kweichow provinces until it had twenty-six regiments in the field against eighty thousand of Yuan's well-equipped northerners. By mid-March 1916, all south Szechwan was a battlefield, and for the next forty-five days and forty-five nights the fighting raged without cessation. By April, Chu Teh's brigade had grown to six thousand men engaged in hand-to-hand battles with three times that number of fresh enemy troops hurled against them.

"We had the Ko Lao Hui peasants behind us," General Chu stated proudly, "and they were like the sands of the sea. North of the river, cities changed hands a dozen times, but our troops finally captured and held Suifu and other cities and laid siege to the fortified enemy stronghold, Luchow. Tsai Ao's headquarters moved with my brigade, shifting with the tide of battle. Nachi changed hands three times. Tsai's voice grew weaker, his eyes more feverish, and his uniform hung like a shroud about his gaunt body. I had such heavy losses that my 10th Regiment had to be replenished three different times. It was in this battle that the Yunnan Army won the renown that is still associated with it."

It was in this struggle also that Chu Teh won his reputation for fierce tenacity and loyalty. Men who saw him in action said that he seemed to be able to do with three or four hours' sleep at night and that his physical strength seemed limitless. His troops knew him as a peasant like themselves, a man who treated them like men and would allow no officer to curse or strike them. His soldiers loved him, even the wounded continued to fight, and it was impossible to keep his wounded men in the hospitals long enough for them to recover.

During this Szechwan campaign, General Chu said, Yuan Shih-kai tried many mangy tricks. In February he postponed his coronation in the belief that this would prevent the revolution from spreading. In early March, while republicans of the whole country were gathering their forces, he turned on Peking and slaughtered hundreds of people, many of them his own officials whom he accused of plotting against him. On March 18th he sent gunmen to Shanghai where they assassinated the chief Kuomintang leader. By the end of March, when the whole country was on the verge of revolt and while the Hu Kuo Chun was clawing his armies in Szechwan to pieces, he tried to gain time by renouncing the monarchy completely and called on the old national Parliament, which he had destroyed in 1913, to reconvene.

"The 'Turtle's Egg' was scared to death," General Chu remarked, his voice hard with hatred at the memory. "We paid no attention to his tricks, but fought on, and by the end of the first week in April six southern provinces had taken the field against him and eight others rejected all his orders. A new Revolutionary Military Government was established at Canton and elected Li Yuan-hung, the Vice-president of the Republic whom Yuan had held prisoner in Peking for years, as President. Yuan's only friends were the foreign imperialists, militarists and monarchists. When two of his chief generals, his personal friends, one in Szechwan and one in Nanking, refused to obey his orders and urged him to resign, he grabbed a sword, rushed into the room where one of his concubines lay in bed with her newborn baby, and hacked them both to pieces. He was that kind of man.

"By June we had shattered his armies in Szechwan and the whole country was in revolt. On June 6th, while Sung Ping-wen and I were working in our headquarters in Nachi, the telegraphic news came that Yuan had just died in Peking. I sent men out to spread the news. Li Yuan-hung, whom Yuan had held prisoner until the day of his death, now became President, and General Feng Kuo-chang of Nanking became Vice-president. General Tuan Chi-jui, chief henchman of Japanese imperialism, who had a powerful military machine of his own, remained Premier. The government which replaced Yuan's was again a compromise with militarism and imperialism. Only in name was it a republic."

An obituary notice in the British *North China Herald* expressed the hope that Chinese, as well as foreigners, would mourn the death of a "great man," and added:

Yuan Shih-kai's death will be deeply lamented by all foreigners and especially by the British nation. . . . A great man is dead. . . . Errors

he may have committed . . . but they were errors of a large nature.
. . . Had he not been ready to catch up the reins of Government when
they dropped from the nerveless hands of Sun Yat-sen, the history of
China during the past five years would have been very different.

General Chu Teh turned pale when he was reminded of such opinions
as this. Yuan Shih-kai, he said, was nothing but the instrument of foreign imperialism, a man who sold himself to the highest bidder which,
at the time, happened to be Anglo-American imperialism, just as his
successor, Tuan Chi-jui, was "the running dog of Japanese imperialism."

So far as he could see, he said, the only hopeful thing that came out of
the new Peking setup in 1916 was the appointment of General Tsai Ao
as Governor General of Szechwan—yet Tsai was a dying man. On June
7th, the day following Yuan Shih-kai's death, Tsai ordered Chu to occupy
the enemy stronghold Luchow, and garrison the surrounding territory,
including the great Tzeliuching salt well region.

"By then, my brigade was so dirty and ragged that it looked like a
band of beggars," he said. "My veteran 10th Regiment received the
honor of entering Luchow first. More than half of its original forces had
been killed in action, and even the replenishments were now veterans.
We cleaned ourselves up and entered Luchow. The people welcomed us
with firecrackers, waving banners, and with shouts and songs. As we
entered, the northern garrison troops withdrew from the opposite gate,
stealing and looting as they went. They had come to Szechwan like
conquerors and were leaving like bandits."

General Tsai Ao was carried into the living quarters connected with
Chu Teh's military headquarters. The doctor attending him ordered him
to stay in bed and see no one until he was strong enough to travel to
Chengtu. Tsai stayed in bed, but he had brought his secretary and chief
of staff with him. And he worked on plans for the reconstruction of
Szechwan. When Chu Teh protested, Tsai replied in his weak voice that
he had little time left and that what he did would determine the fate of
west and southwest China and, perhaps, the country.

After no more than two weeks in bed, Tsai insisted on leaving for
Chengtu. He traveled overland by sedan chair, taking five regiments of
troops with him.

"They literally had to fight their way to the capital," General Chu said.
"Local militarist armies swarmed everywhere, ruling territory as their
private property. Warlordism, sired and fed by foreign money, was
Yuan Shih-kai's legacy to China."

After Yuan's death, Dr. Paul Reinsch, American minister to Peking at the time, called on the Russian minister. He asked him if he thought the Chinese regarded Russians as half-Asiatic and therefore brothers. The Russian minister replied wearily:

"No—they count us with you and other Europeans, as a scourge and a pestilence."

Chapter 10

WHEN General Chu talked of the era of warlordism, he made no effort to paint himself as a hero. Instead, the picture he painted of himself and his environment had a nightmarish quality. His figure seemed to move through a miasma of chaos, at first confident and hopeful, then confused and stumbling until he was finally sucked down into the very militarism which he thought he was fighting.

Just ten days after Tsai Ao had taken office in Chengtu, General Chu related, he had to surrender his position of governor general to Lo Pei-chin, his chief of staff and right-hand man, and leave for Japan in a last but futile effort to save his life. Tsai came down the river in a boat, with a doctor and nurse as attendants, and was carried to Chu Teh's home in Luchow for a few days' rest before proceeding further. When Chu caught sight of him, he was overcome with despair. Tsai was now nothing but a shadow, he was so weak that he could walk no more than a few steps, and his voice was so soft that Chu had to bend over his bed to hear him.

This trip to Japan, Tsai whispered to Chu, was a waste of time and money because he knew he was dying. He was not afraid of death, but he was afraid for the future of China. Ruthless, pro-Japanese Premier Tuan Chi-jui was now the real master of Peking. Tsai had hoped to reorganize Szechwan into a firm republican base, but he had had time merely to lay the foundation for its military reorganization, which would provide a basis for the political reforms planned. The Hu Kuo Chun, linked with Dr. Sun Yat-sen's armed forces in the south, might—if Tsai's plans were executed—become powerful enough to disrupt the conspiracy of the northern warlords and their foreign masters.

As Chu Teh listened to his dying friend and leader he was filled with fear for the future. When the guiding hand of this "dangerous genius" was removed from Szechwan, ambitious men within the Hu Kuo Chun itself might break away and set up business as warlords. Tsai's genius and selflessness had commanded their allegiance in the past, and Chu doubted if even Dr. Sun Yat-sen, whom few of them had ever seen, could take Tsai's place. There was no leader of Tsai's stature in west China.

Yet there were hopeful signs that might keep the revolutionary forces united. The struggle against Yuan Shih-kai had called into being a powerful national movement for the protection of the 1912 Constitution. The Hu Kuo Chun, which now called itself the Army to Protect the Constitution—or simply, the Protection Army—was the chief arm of this movement in west and southwest China.

The fountainhead of this new national revival movement was Peking National University where a galaxy of brilliant professors had begun to emerge in 1915, in the very midst of chaos, to proclaim the "new civilization," or "new tide." In time, foreigners called this new movement the "cultural renaissance."

This "new tide," as the Chinese called it generally, and which soon began to influence the life of Chu Teh and some of his associates, increased in momentum through 1916 and 1917, particularly after the ideas of the 1917 Russian Revolution began to percolate through China. Its battle cry was democracy and modern science, and its advocates challenged everything feudal in Chinese culture, including Confucianism and the old wen-li, or dead classical language. Seldom in human history had there been a greater intellectual and spiritual upheaval in the midst of chaos than this Chinese cultural renaissance.

General Chu's voice and manner became a strange mingling of wistfulness and pride as he talked of it. He was proud of the never-ending striving and dauntless courage of the Chinese intellectual world, but he seemed filled with sadness at the memory of Tsai Ao's slow and tragic dying at the early age of thirty-four and of his own isolation from the great movement of young China that began to thunder across the country.

Only the outer ripples of this "new tide" reached him. A Peking friend of his friend and secretary, Sung Ping-wen, wrote of a new magazine, *New Youth*, one of whose editors was Professor Chen Tu-hsiu, the later secretary and one of the founders of the Chinese Communist Party. Chu Teh saw this magazine, which was reforming the Chinese written language while he still wrote in the old wen-li, only much later, when he tried to learn his own language anew. He looked back on the "new tide," with its message of mass education, democracy, and natural science, as one looks back on great and all but lost opportunities that might have changed the course of one's life. He heard but echoes of the passionate enthusiasm with which Ibsen's *Doll's House* and other plays of the Western world were received in far-away north China. As in an aside, he remarked that respectable girls still could not appear on the Chinese stage and that the role of Nora in *The Doll's House* had to be played by young men students who paved the way for modern Chinese womanhood.

He recalled Sung Ping-wen sitting by his side and bending with him over the wasted body of Tsai Ao, and that Sung had talked eagerly of the "new tide," and that he himself had tried to encourage Tsai by declaring that the old elected Parliament had again convened in Peking, had abolished Confucianism as the state religion, and had announced its determination to prevent the rise of any future dictator by making the president and the cabinet, and the appointment of high officials everywhere, responsible to it. Things were not so bad, he assured the dying man. The youth of China would prevent a repetition of history. Tsai's mind seemed to have lost none of its brilliance and he uttered whispered warnings that Premier Tuan Chi-jui was no different from Yuan Shih-kai and that his shadow was already lengthening over the land.

Then came the day when Chu and Sung and their officer friends stood sorrowfully on the pier and watched Tsai Ao's boat fade into the mists of the Yangtze, and after it was gone Sung had to comfort Chu Teh, who was like one bereft.

During this same period, Chu Teh's young wife had come up from Yunnan. Heavy with his unborn child, she had made the long overland trip by sedan chair and was now mistress of the small home which he had rented. In late September, shortly after Tsai's departure, she bore him a son whom they named Pao-chu, and they were still rejoicing over its birth when, on November 18th, the news flashed through China that General Tsai Ao had died in Japan. Stricken with grief, Chu Teh all but forgot his wife and child.

Tsai's body soon arrived in Shanghai where, after a ceremony, it was sent on to his home province, Hunan, where a monument to his memory was erected on a high hill overlooking Changsha. That was a period of much sorrow, because General Hwang Hsing, another famous revolutionary leader, also died of tuberculosis, worn out like Tsai from long years of struggle and suffering. The nation mourned two of its noblest sons, both of them still young when they died.

Yunnan Province, and all units of the Yunnan Army, held special memorial services for the young commander who had led them since 1911. Chu Teh was desolate. Tsai had been not only his supreme commander and the man on whose political leadership he had depended for years, but also his friend and teacher—two relationships which an ancient culture hallowed as second only to filial piety. And Chu was deeply rooted in the old culture. His grief was all the deeper because Tsai had represented all that he had respected, if not worshipped: brilliancy of mind, knowledge and vision, tenacity and selflessness. Tsai had been his lodestar, and now he could not see his way.

Tsai Ao's body had not yet been laid to rest when Chu Teh's young wife sickened of some mysterious fever said to be typhoid, and died. He had no more than buried her when his old boyhood schoolmate, Wu Shao-pei, who had been lying in his home, also died of that dread disease of Chinese intellectuals, tuberculosis.

Chu Teh had never known grief before, but when it visited him it was threefold, and left him prostrate. He was now left with a motherless child, who was temporarily cared for by friends. At the same time his supreme army commanders called him in for important conferences: Premier Tuan Chi-jui of Peking had sent agents to intrigue with provincial rulers and warlords throughout the country, dangling money before them. The defeated warlords of Szechwan were reorganizing their forces, and Tang Chi-yao, whom Tsai Ao had left in command in Yunnan, suddenly had money to burn and had begun building up a small personal kingdom of his own. The northern warlords began demanding the dissolution of Parliament which foreigners chose to call a "crew of callow, inexperienced youth" incapable of ruling the country.

Before 1916 was out the local Szechwan militarists attacked Chengtu, and Chu Teh was ordered to lead two brigades to relieve it. He had gone halfway when the city fell and the governor general, Lo Pei-chin, was in flight. Chu Teh drew back to his Luchow base while the Protection Army, as the Yunnan Army still called itself, established a truce with the Chengtu victors, after which both sides, while pretending to be friendly, settled down to recruiting and training new troops for the final contest of power. From that moment onward Chu Teh was caught in the net of warlordism without recognizing it as such. For, he argued, was not the Yunnan Army the one armed force in west China for the protection of the Constitution, the one army loyal to Sun Yat-sen and the Republic? It was, indeed, yet here and there some of its commanders were lending an ear to the jangle of silver in the hands of Premier Tuan's agents. They had not yet deserted, but the temptation was great.

Chu Teh's greatest personal problem was his motherless infant. He could not leave the child to the care of friends and servants forever, nor did he wish to send it to his family. By then he had liquidated his family's debts and, though they lived in easier circumstances, he did not wish his son to grow up in feudal surroundings. His son, he told himself, should become one of the modern, enlightened youth of the new China, attending modern schools in modern surroundings.

One of his old Kuomintang comrades urged him to marry again to solve this personal problem. His wife had died only a short time before, but in those days it was not at all unusual for a man to marry again shortly after his wife's death. The family, not the individual, was still the basis of Chinese society, and though Chu thought of himself as a modern man he was still in many respects a product of the old social system. Personal love was not yet the basis of marriage, though it might develop afterwards. He needed a mother for his child and he needed a wife for his home.

Before the year was out, therefore, he agreed to marry again; one of his army friends acted as the go-between. This marriage also was modern for the times, for the friend had an educated sister "with natural feet" who had taken part in the 1911 and 1916 revolutions, and had refused to marry any suitor unless she had first seen and talked with him before making up her mind.

The two army officers therefore rode off to Nanchi, a city west of Luchow, and as they rode along Chu's friend explained again that his sister, Chen Yu-chen, was very intelligent, but most "willful" in that she had reached the advanced age of twenty-one and was almost an old maid because she had rejected every suitor introduced to her by her family.

When General Chu talked of this woman who soon became his wife, his voice and manner underwent a very great change, a change of which he seemed utterly unconscious. The word "love" never passed his lips, yet it seemed to me that he had loved Chen Yu-chen almost from the moment of their first meeting.

She was not a beautiful woman, he remarked, nor was she ugly, yet there was something indefinably attractive about her. Knitting his brow in an effort to describe her, tenderness crept into his voice and became mingled with respect as he said:

"I suppose I was attracted to her because she was very serious and had such poise and dignity; and because she had been an underground worker in the 1911 and 1916 revolutions. She came from a well-to-do scholarly family that had taken an active part in the reform movement from the earliest days. We talked together and found that we both read a great deal and that we both liked music. We had many things in common but I can't remember what they were. We were married shortly afterwards and she made a home for us that was simple, modern, very clean, and kept beautiful with flowers both inside and out. We loved flowers and she made beautiful gardens. She loved my child as her own and I do not think he ever knew that she was not his own mother. When he began to toddle around, I would often come home and find the two of them in the courtyard, playing hide-and-seek among the flowers. She never bore a child, so I never had another."

As he talked of his second marriage and his Luchow home, General Chu seemed to sink back in that little lost paradise of personal happiness and lose sight of surroundings about us. His home was a haven in the chaotic sea of mounting warlordism, a little world apart. He had a good salary and his wife had money of her own, and though both were careful in expenditures, they bought the things they wished to have and entertained their friends. They built up a good library and spent considerable time reading and discussing what they read. After the ideas of the 1917 Russian Revolution, with its proclamation of racial and national equality, began to seep through China, they sought for books or pamphlets on such subjects and subscribed to magazines like the *New Youth* and the *New Tidal Wave*.

Yu-chen played the lute and Chu had his flute and *hu-chin* and with time they bought and learned to play other musical instruments, including a harmonium.

The period of his second marriage coincided with the great May 4th Movement, known as the Student Movement of 1919, when Peking students and professors led great demonstrations against the Peking warlord government's betrayal of China and against the betrayal of China at the Paris Peace Conference when the Allied Powers gave Germany's former possessions in China to Japan. This movement, which was a part of the cultural renaissance, swept the country like a forest fire, introducing the anti-Japanese boycott and drawing all patriotic elements of the population into it. The first study group in Luchow was organized in Chu Teh's home at that time and became the gathering place of the illuminati of the entire region. Books and magazines were read and discussed and great debates about the new ideas afloat in the world were held.

"Feudal social customs were still very powerful in Szechwan," General Chu explained, "but my wife and I, together with our friends, made big inroads on them. Many of us lived much as do Western intellectuals, giving dinner parties—sometimes followed by mah jong parties on a Sunday evening, where men and women met as social equals. Men brought their wives and sisters who, for the first time, learned to discuss ideas with men who were not members of their immediate families. Of course the old feudal forces called us wild and immoral though we were most respectable. The emancipation of women was one of the many aspects of the May 4th Movement. Democracy, science, national and racial equality were other aspects, while such social theories as anarchism and communism were others. All China resounded with debates on capitalism, anarchism, and communism, but not all the debaters knew what they were talking about. Our study club in Luchow could not conceive of the proletariat guiding a revolution. We had no Marxist literature other than articles in magazines and we thought of the proletariat as servants, coolies, and salt workers who could not read and write. It was confusing because Communist writers who preached Marxism were themselves high professors, students and other intellectuals and not workers. The ideas that most influenced our study club were those of racial and national equality, the right of subjected colonial peoples to independence, and the industrial and cultural development of the country."

During the five years that General Chu lived in Luchow, warlordism backed by foreign imperialist powers again gutted the Republic and he and his comrades were sucked down into it while still convinced that they were fighting warlordism and supporting the national revolutionary movement led by Sun Yat-sen.

Chapter 11

HOPING to dispose quickly of the warlord period of China, I asked General Chu to tell me just when warlordism began and when it ended.

It began with Yuan Shih-kai, he said, but has not ended to the present day. He was speaking, at the time, in the spring of 1937. There was one hopeful period, beginning with 1924, when Sun Yat-sen led the great national revolutionary movement against warlordism and foreign imperialism, but this period was also aborted in 1927 when Chiang Kai-shek turned his guns against the Chinese people and took loans from foreign and Chinese bankers to establish his own military dictatorship. As with his predecessors, Chiang's regime absorbed many of the old as well as the new-style warlords, and the chaotic and reactionary system continued.

After Tsai Ao's death in 1916, Chu explained, Szechwan became one of the chief theaters of warlordism, yet Peking was the breeding place of all national internecine strife. Within five years after 1916, Premier Tuan Chi-jui, the "strong man" of Japanese imperialism, resigned or was driven from power seven different times. Each time he returned on the backs of his own and allied warlord armies, with Japanese military and financial support. The long arm of his power found warlord allies in every province.

Tsai was hardly cold in his grave when local Szechwan militarists paid by Tuan seized Chengtu from the Yunnan "Protection Army." During the brief truce that followed, the new Chengtu rulers imposed new taxes, sold offices to the highest bidders, and seized and imprisoned rich men until they paid the bribes demanded. Peasants who could not pay the land taxes, collected for years in advance, were dispossessed and their land taken by the new rulers. The great landed estates of Szechwan which the generals built up at that time were taken from dispossessed peasants, yet this process of founding estates had continued down to the time General Chu was talking. Some of these estates were thousands of acres in extent.

After seizing power in Chengtu in 1917 and establishing a truce with the Yunnan Protection Army, the victorious warlords sent an emissary to the Protection Army to propose a military alliance against the neighboring provinces of Kweichow and Yunnan. At the same time the Chengtu warlords sent other emissaries to Kweichow and Yunnan to propose a military alliance against the Protection Army. This kind of double-dealing and double-crossing was typical of warlordism, General Chu explained. Principle played no role whatever. The emissary sent by them to the Protection Army was a young man named Liu Po-cheng, who thirty years later became known to the Western world as the Communist "one-eyed general" and one of the most brilliant revolutionary strategists China had ever produced.

"Men traveled different roads," General Chu remarked in connection with Liu Po-cheng. "Some became and remained warlords, some floundered in the swamp of militarism until they found a new revolutionary road, while some who clearly saw the new road were so poisoned by the past that they still remained warlords. Many Kuomintang military men became new warlords. Both Liu Po-cheng and I found and followed the new revolutionary road."

The story of Szechwan warlordism which General Chu told was filled with demoralization and disaster for him and others, and so long and involved that only a few of its aspects can be related. Shortly after rejecting the proposed military alliance against neighboring provinces, the Yunnan Protection Army launched an offensive against the Chengtu warlords, overthrowing them and bringing most of the province under their control. The defeated armies merely withdrew and "began feeding" on isolated parts of the province and, as General Chu expressed it, "waiting for some warlord powerful enough to lead them."

That warlord soon appeared, and he was none other than General Hsiung Keh-wu, the very man whom the Protection Army had installed in power in Chengtu as governor general.

General Chu selected Hsiung Keh-wu as something like Exhibit X to explain the evolution of a onetime revolutionary into a warlord. Subsidiary exhibits were his vice-commander, Chang Chun, and two other ambitious militarists, one named Liu Hsiang and one Yang Sen, all of whom later became Chu Teh's mortal enemies.

The story General Chu told was long and intricate, for few things in China of this nature are simple. They resemble a vast underground labyrinth with countless interlocking tunnels.

General Hsiung Keh-wu, or Exhibit X, had, like his vice-commander, Chang Chun, been a loyal Kuomintang member up to that time. Once in power, however, Exhibit X began acting exactly as had his warlord predecessor: "scraping the earth, building up a great landed estate, and sending his cash to a British bank in Shanghai until, within two years, he had a fortune in cash said to be over a million Chinese dollars." Each such warlord, fearing that his tenure of office would be short, made hay while the sun shone.

Power and wealth bred personal ambition and soon Exhibit X began, surreptitiously, absorbing the troops of the defeated warlord before him and building up his private army. In the course of such actions, he also made a military alliance with a small but most ambitious local warlord named Liu Hsiang, and by May 1920 felt himself rich and powerful enough to drive the Yunnan Protection Army from the province and take over Szechwan as his private domain. He therefore suddenly declared his allegiance to the Peking warlord government and ordered his old comrades to get out of Szechwan or be thrown out. Just how far his ambitions reached was unknown, but this was a period during which the warlords of the whole country were fighting. The one who emerged on top could capture Peking and claim the title "President of the Republic," receive foreign recognition as such without delay, and, if he were a good boy, get foreign loans.

Instead of obeying the ultimatum of their old comrade, the Yunnan Protection Army marched on Chengtu and drove Exhibit X and his ally, Liu Hsiang, out of the province. They retreated to Shensi to the north where they conscripted and trained new troops and received money from Peking, after which they drove down into Szechwan and began the longest and bloodiest civil war since the overthrow of the monarchist movement.

When the end of the year 1920 came, the Protection Army had been driven back to south Szechwan, with only half of its original forces of forty thousand men left. Chu Teh's brigade alone had been reduced to the strength of only one regiment.

In this struggle, however, Exhibit X had himself suffered heavy losses and was so weakened that his loyal ally, Liu Hsiang, simply kicked him out and installed himself in power as ruler of the province, a position which he held, with variations, for the next twenty years.

In the course of this same struggle, Yang Sen, one of the commanders in the Protection Army and an old friend of Chu Teh, also caught the warlord fever. He set himself up as an independent warlord in eastern Szechwan, with Chungking as his capital. Liu Hsiang and Yang Sen divided the province between them, the larger share going to Liu.

When General Chu Teh next heard of Exhibit X, six to seven years had passed and that frustrated gentleman had just been arrested in south China where he had engaged in a conspiracy to overthrow the new nationalist government established in Canton by Dr. Sun Yat-sen. His underground labyrinth had yet another exit. After 1927, when Chiang Kai-shek set himself up as dictator in Nanking, Exhibit X turned up as one of his generals, and his onetime vice-commander, Chang Chun, became Chiang Kai-shek's Minister of Foreign Affairs in the years immediately preceding the war with Japan, a position which he still held when General Chu told me this story in 1937. Public opinion soon forced Chang Chun to resign because of his notorious pro-Japanese policy. And somewhere along those years, both Chang Chun and Exhibit X had become members of the so-called "Political Science" clique, a group of professional politicians and militarists that had been organized in Peking during the reign of Yuan Shih-kai.

Nor does the labyrinth end there. After the Second World War, when the United States emerged as the chief foreign power in China, American spokesmen singled out the "Political Science" clique as the kind of "liberals" and "democrats" most capable of establishing a Chinese democratic government. As late as 1949 both Exhibit X and Chang Chun were back in Szechwan, now old men but still holding on to official and military power, wavering first toward Chiang Kai-shek and then toward neutrality with the People's Liberation Army of which General Chu Teh was commander in chief.

When General Chu talked of those past years in Szechwan, he time and again referred to himself and the Protection Army as an arm of Sun Yat-sen's shadowy republican government which repeatedly arose and fell in south China. During this same period Chu Teh himself was, politically, a split personality, outwardly engaged in the interminable wars of the generals, but intellectually fancying himself a follower of the May 4th Movement, the ideas of which continued to be debated in the study group in his home.

"We talked and talked, but got nowhere," General Chu remarked. "I read that workers' clubs, the seedbed of our future trade union movement, were being organized in a few places in China, but none were organized in Szechwan. Marxist study clubs had also been founded in a few places as early as 1919. The first Communist Party groups grew out of such clubs in 1920, but I knew nothing of them and we possessed no Marxist literature other than general articles in magazines. We didn't even have a copy of the *Communist Manifesto*, the first such literature to be translated into Chinese."

Though ignorant of Marxism, he added, he and his comrades were deeply impressed by news of the victories of the Russian Red Army over the armies of the czarist warlords and of the invading capitalist countries. How had Russian revolutionaries been able to defeat such powerful armies, even of the Western world, and establish their own government, whereas the Chinese had failed? His friend Sung Ping-wen and he discussed this problem many times and came to the decision that there was something fundamentally wrong with China. After all, they argued, the foreign powers could not have corrupted any Chinese had Chinese refused to sell themselves. And they talked of the Protection Army itself, some of whose officers were not different from the Peking warlords. Sung Ping-wen declared time and again that he intended to give the whole thing up and go to Peking to join the leaders of the May 4th Movement. Chu Teh declared that he would at last go abroad and study until he learned how foreign countries had managed to maintain their independence.

Time fled and still they talked and did nothing. The years passed and 1920 came with its bloody civil war and still they talked. General Chu now used his family as an excuse for lingering. In the autumn of 1919 he had brought over twenty members of his family to Luchow to live with him and his wife. He was sinking back into feudalism, proving himself a filial son and gaining face by proving that he had, and could provide for, a large family.

His foster parents remained in the old Ta Wan home where his grandparents now lay buried, while his father and mother joined him in Luchow together with his elder brother, Tai-li, and his family; his two younger married brothers with their families and one younger unmarried brother also came to Luchow.

At no time had his monthly salary as a brigadier general been less than $1000 (Chinese) a month, with the customary additional expense allowance of over half that sum. Living frugally and saving money, he was more than able to buy a house and care for his family.

Ten years had passed since he had seen his family and he was shocked to find his parents old and gray—they were nearing seventy. At last, he assured them, they could rest and spend their declining years in peace. He had made plans for all of them. All the children of school age, as well as his younger unmarried brother, were to go to modern schools, while Tai-li, as the eldest son, could remain at home and manage family affairs. His two younger married brothers were at once enrolled in the Military Training School of his brigade to receive officer training that they also might carve out brilliant careers for themselves.

It appears that he was acting like a warlord by stuffing his brigade with his own relatives while continuing to speak of the Protection Army as a republican force still loyal to Sun Yat-sen's constitutional but shadowy Republic.

His family was so awed by his power and position that they dared not utter a word against his plans. His old parents became grim, but said nothing, when he sent his two brothers to the Military Training School. They saw him only when he was surrounded by officers and officials and they sat in humble and uncomprehending silence to hear this son of theirs talk so learnedly and fluently with others in the study club.

He thought he had everything fixed up, but as the weeks passed his parents began wandering around the house like unhappy ghosts. They had always worked and did not know how to be idle. They were shy and reserved before his educated wife, and the big, crowded, noisy city of half a million souls harassed them; and there were no neighbors with whom they could gossip about crops, marriages, deaths, and local scandals. He urged them to rest and enjoy themselves, but they declared that the good food which they now had was not as healthful as the poor fare to which they had always been accustomed.

The end of the year 1919 brought a short but fierce military struggle with a local warlord in eastern Szechwan in which Chu Teh's brigade fought. He quickly commissioned his two younger brothers as lower officers in his brigade and sent them off to get their first experience in battle under his command. His parents were gray-faced with fear and misery as they bade their three sons farewell, but he laughed and reassured them. He had been in the army for many years and had not even been wounded!

"We were defeated in that short war and my brigade had heavy losses," General Chu related grimly. "Within one week both my younger brothers were killed in action! I withdrew to Luchow with my troops, taking the encoffined bodies of my brothers with me. That was a terrible homecoming. My parents were so stricken that they could not even weep. They wanted to return to their old home, but I was in such a terrible state that they remained on in Luchow for a time for my sake."

General Chu found it very difficult to talk of this period of his life, a period so filled with humiliation and a feeling of guilt that he began to smoke opium. Opium smoking was quite an ordinary thing with army officers and officials, but until then he had avoided it. Now, lying on an opium couch with a pipe and lamp by his side, he smoked and talked with his friend and secretary Sung Ping-wen, who tried in vain to win him away from the drug. Yes, he told Sung, he would stop smoking and go abroad to find a new way of life for himself and a new way for China. He talked and smoked, talked and smoked, avoiding his family and neglecting his military duties.

Then came the last big bloody war with General Hsiung Keh-wu— Exhibit X—in which Chu Teh lost all but one regiment of his brigade.

After this disaster, his family refused to remain longer with him, and insisted on returning to their old home. He did not oppose them. Giving them money, he sent them off by boat for Chungking, where they were to transfer to another boat for north Szechwan. Ten days later he received a letter from them informing him that his old father had died in Chungking and that they were taking his body with them to be buried in their ancestral fields near Ta Wan.

His whole world now lay in ruins about him and only opium gave him some relief from his confusion and misery. His wife and Sung Ping-wen argued with him, but he could not face up to reality.

Reality was this, he said: the Yunnan Protection Army now risked total extermination if it did not get out of Szechwan. All China was a chaos of warlordism, and the people were groaning in torment. A new warlord, Marshal Wu Pei-fu, now sat in power in Peking, making a temporary truce with Sun Yat-sen's southern regime as a prelude to destroying it. The first steps were being taken toward the Soviet alliance which was later made with Dr. Sun Yat-sen's government, yet of such events General Chu knew little nor did they mean much to him. He had chosen a military life as the road to his country's liberation, yet after over a decade of military struggle his dreams lay shattered like broken tiles, he had directly caused the death of his two brothers and held himself responsible for the death of his father. Opium fumes could not obscure these calamities.

He participated in the long conferences called by the Protection Army which decided to fight its way back to Yunnan Province and overthrow the regime of Tang Chi-yao who, after Tsai Ao's death in 1916, had turned that province into his small personal kingdom and won for himself the hated title of "the Little King of Yunnan."

During these conferences, General Chu came up out of the black well of his despair and began long and serious discussions with his friend Sung about the state of China and about their own future. They even organized their discussions under specific topics, dissecting each for days until they reached a conclusion. A military life, they decided, was no longer the one for them, but before choosing another they must first study political thought and institutions abroad. Sung settled his wife and children in Szechwan and left at once for Peking. Chu decided to send his wife and child to her old home in Nanchi and to leave the army to join Sung only after "the Little King of Yunnan" had been overthrown.

Chapter 12

JUST as the new year 1921 dawned, the Protection Army suddenly swooped down upon Yunnan and, after an exchange of no more than a few shots, captured the capital, Yunnanfu, and took over the province. Many of the old officials and generals in command of various cities transferred their allegiance to the new regime in order to bide their time, while the Little King, Tang Chi-yao, fled the province with as much loot as he could salvage.

The revolutionary reputation of the Protection Army was still alive so that progressive intellectuals from every part of China again streamed in to help transform the province into a republican base. Yet things were not the same as in the past and Chu Teh watched the scene with skepticism. Almost every province of the country was under the feet of marching warlord armies, crops were trampled under foot, dust clouds settled and turned to deserts, and dispossessed peasants by the millions sought a daily bowl of rice by enlisting in one or another army. Anarchy, chaos and despair had reigned for years, Peking was nothing but a market where warlords and foreign bankers traded over the prostrate body of the country. Dr. Sun Yat-sen made alliance with this or that warlord, trying to choose the lesser evil, only to be betrayed time and again.

Unable to see any way out, Chu Teh resigned from the Protection
Army and announced his intention of going abroad to study. His fellow
officers urged him to remain until the new regime was firmly established
and to become police commissioner until that time. He agreed after prolonged arguments, then sent for his wife and son who soon joined him.

He had agreed to remain, yet Yunnanfu revived tormenting memories
of the past. Wandering about the broad, clean streets, the ghost of his
youth arose to taunt him. Here, years before, he had marched and sung
in triumph at the overthrow of the Manchus. There, beyond the city
walls, lay the Military Academy where he had fervently studied how to
save the country from disaster, and here he had stormed the walls of the
viceroy's yamen. Tsai Ao had spoken in triumph from this square, and
there, in that building, had planned the overthrow of Yuan Shih-kai's
monarchy. What was it Tsai had said—something terrible that seemed
to apply to him also:

"In any case, I have little time left."

Here were the fine buildings, the broad roads, the new schools built
under the leadership of his young, dead leader, and over there his young
wife had studied and, on Sundays, walked with him and talked of the
new, peaceful and progressive China of the future. She was dead and
Tsai was dead, and now he was a man of thirty-five, an official who
smoked opium, with a fine wife but with more than one woman on the
side when it pleased him. He stood in the wreckage of his own personal
dreams and his dead hopes for his country.

Why did he remain? he asked himself, and found an excuse in Dr.
Sun Yat-sen's new proclamation to the nation. Dr. Sun had said that the
1911 Revolution had only partially realized the principle of nationalism
but had done nothing to carry out his other two principles, democracy
and the people's livelihood. Dr. Sun said that a rejuvenated Kwangtung
Province in the south would become the soil in which his three principles
of nationalism, democracy and the people's livelihood would soon take
root and spread to the Yangtze and Yellow River valleys.

Who was it who once asked him questions about the salvation of
China? Yes, his old teacher, Mr. Hsi, had asked him if China in 1900,
the year of the Boxer Rebellion, was stronger than in previous decades
when it had been repeatedly defeated by one foreign power alone, or two
at best. It was weaker in 1900 than in the previous half-century but now,
twenty-one years later, every imperialist power had a finger in the Peking
government and each had its own warlord running dog.

Could Yunnan save the Republic as it had tried to do in 1915-1916?

Could this or that general who for years had licked the boots of the "Little King of Yunnan" be trusted to remain loyal to the Republic? No, General Chu told himself.

May 1921 came, and Dr. Sun Yat-sen again gave him an excuse for malingering. At Dr. Sun's call, the extraordinary Republican Parliament assembled in Canton, established the new southern nationalist government, and elected Dr. Sun President. In a flaming declaration Dr. Sun proclaimed that the new government would uproot warlordism, unify the country by military means, and break the chains of the unequal treaties that had fettered China's sovereignty for nearly a century. Rumor had it that Dr. Sun would ally himself with the Soviet Union.

When autumn came General Chu took final steps to go abroad. He bought a Kwangtung herb said to be a cure for the opium habit and carried it in his pocket, telling himself that he would begin taking it almost any day now. Next, he transferred his life savings, $10,000 in Chinese money, to a Paris bank to help his wife and child should they require money beyond his wife's own property.

Then came the year 1922, and the Yunnan Army marched off to the east at the call of Dr. Sun Yat-sen to begin the war against the warlords and imperialism. Only a weak garrison remained behind in Yunnanfu.

Two, three weeks passed, and when the main Yunnan forces were far away panic suddenly gripped Yunnanfu. Tang Chi-yao, the Little King, was marching on the city with an army of local militiamen and bandits, and his old generals and officials were going over to him, their hands held out for the silver which he dangled before their eyes. Intellectuals fled the province or went into hiding and Chu Teh moved his wife and son to the home of friends who were preparing to flee to Szechwan.

The battle for Yunnanfu ended before it had hardly begun. The new governor led the local garrison into battle but was captured and beheaded. Chu Teh swiftly collected all the cash he had saved for his European trip, armed himself, mounted his famous horse and joined a party of nineteen other Kuomintang leaders who, with cavalry companies, were ready to crash their way out through the Western Gate and make a dash for Tzuchow to the west where the road southward into Burma would lie before them. The party of twenty leaders included General Lo Pei-chin, Tsai Ao's old comrade and a veteran revolutionary.

Riding hard, this party of refugees reached a village where they were told that General Hwa Feng-kuo, garrison commander of Tzuchow, had just proclaimed his allegiance to his old master, the Little King.

General Lo Pei-chin scoffed at this news. Hwa Feng-kuo, he said, was one of his old friends who had once been his subordinate. Hwa would remain loyal to old friendship and would allow the refugees to pass through to Burma.

No! cried the others. The old feudal virtue of friendship had long since vanished under the clink of silver, and Hwa was so corrupted that he would sell the last one of his friends to the Little King in return for higher rank and more power. Instead of trusting themselves to this treacherous man, the party should turn northward at once, take the old trade route to the Kinsha—the River of Golden Sands, as the upper Yangtze is called at that point—and pass through Sikang and western Szechwan and escape to the coast. Once in Shanghai, they could join Sun Yat-sen at Canton.

General Lo protested, saying that the northern route meant certain death. The wild mountains were inhabited by tribesmen and bandits, while Szechwan was ruled by the new warlords, Liu Hsiang and Yang Sen, whom the Yunnan army had fought.

Unable to agree, the party split. General Lo took a few of the guards and rode off to Tzuchow, while the rest rode into the wild mountains to the north. Four months later, after the northern group had reached Szechwan, they learned of the fate of their old revolutionary comrade. Instead of protecting him for old friendship's sake, Hwa Feng-kuo of Tzuchow had arrested and sold General Lo Pei-chin to the Little King, who publicly tortured him to death in the streets of Yunnanfu, together with hundreds of other captives. The Little King had offered big rewards for the capture of revolutionaries, and they were ferreted out and delivered to him. For weeks Yunnanfu was a scene of terror and carnage. So devastating was the slaughter that the cultural movement in the province was completely uprooted for decades.

After parting from their old comrade, General Chu and his companions rode hard through the wild mountains of northern Yunnan. General Lo, in asking for protection, had told of the route they had taken. Hwa Feng-kuo sent a cavalry battalion after them and offered high rewards for their capture.

The wild man hunt began. Sleeping in the open at night and riding hard from the earliest dawn until black night fell, the refugees finally reached the River of Golden Sands but could find no ferry crossing into Sikang Province where they could shake off their pursuers. The party split in two to search for a ferry crossing, riding along the high and treacherous mountains with the icy torrents of the river crashing through black chasms far below.

Chu Teh's group found the ferry first, sent guards back to guide the others, and crossed. The rest came up and began crossing. All but six leaders and a few guards had made the other bank when the enemy battalion overtook them. There was a short, desperate battle, and all of them were either killed or taken captive.

The first group were now in Sikang Province, yet the enemy also crossed the river and continued the pursuit. This territory, however, was ruled by a bandit chieftain, Lei Yung-fei, whose small kingdom reached from the river to Huili in the north, a five or six days' ride. The refugees met Lei's border guards almost at once and explained to them that they were refugees on their way to meet their chieftain. Jealous of their own territory, the guards told them to send outriders in advance to talk with Lei while the rest followed more slowly. The guards themselves would drive back the invading troops.

Two days later the refugees saw a body of armed horsemen riding down on them from the north and could distinguish their own comrades among them. They dismounted and waited. When the horsemen came up, a short, wiry man in his thirties dismounted and strode toward them. Chu Teh and his comrades waited with mingled fear and hope. The man approached, bowed and welcomed them with Old World courtesy, saying that he, Lei Yung-fei, considered them his guests.

Suspecting that this man might be a member of the ancient Ko Lao Hui secret society of which he himself was a member, General Chu, in greeting him, uttered a few words and made gestures by which such blood brothers could recognize one another anywhere. Lei's eyes gleamed as he returned the greeting and gave the awaited sign, and from that moment onward the refugees were doubly safe.

In gratitude for their reception, the refugees at once presented Lei with some of their rifles which he refused until the offer was repeated three times, thus proving that it was not merely a polite gesture. He then led them to his fortified mountain village where he ordered pigs, goats, and sheep to be slaughtered for a banquet in which hundreds of guests took part. Lei moved about among his guests in a manner that would have done credit to a nobleman.

The refugees remained with him for ten days while civilian clothing was made for them that they might thereafter travel as merchants through hostile territory.

General Chu spoke of Lei Yung-fei with deep compassion. Once an illiterate peasant, he had been nurtured on ancient tales of rebellion against tyranny such as *The One Hundred and Eight Heroes,* or the *Shui Hu Chuan*—translated into English under the title *All Men Are Brothers.* Preceding and during the 1911 Revolution he and other Ko

Lao Hui brothers had had loose connections with the republican Tung Meng Hui. During the revolution they had driven out the landlords and confiscated and divided the land. Energetic and with unusual gifts for leadership and organization, Lei had organized the peasants into an army which now, in 1922, was five thousand strong, including, strangely enough, some Lolo tribesmen. The landlords and the Szechwan warlords called him a notorious bandit chieftain.

"He was a bandit all right," General Chu admitted. "When the crops failed or food grew scarce, he raided prosperous towns beyond his territory, robbing the rich to feed the poor. Compared with the warlords, he was a righteous and honorable citizen. Banditry, after all, is a class concept. If sufficiently successful at it, you might found a kingdom and your descendants might be known as noblemen.

"In the chaos that followed the abortion of the 1911 Revolution, Lei had seen and learned many strange things. Many men had fled to him for refuge and he had protected them. He tried to emulate the great and benevolent bandit leaders of the past who stride across the pages of our folk literature and are adored by the people. In 1922 he was being hard pressed by the Szechwan warlords who were trying to conquer his territory. He had thrown them back repeatedly.

"He and I became friends and spent hours together talking about the state of China. He was an alert and intelligent man who asked me a thousand questions, and as we talked he urged me to remain with him to advise and teach him. When I said I was determined to study abroad, he became very sad. Before leaving, I presented him with my most precious possessions—my automatic pistol and my fine, beautiful horse. I accepted from him only a mountain pony to continue my journey. I also gave him my wife's address in Nanchi and invited him to make it his home if he ever visited the region or needed a refuge.

"When we left, he rode with us for many miles, then sent an armed escort up to within a mile of Huili, where his territory ended. Months later when I was in Shanghai my wife wrote me that Lei had sent a man to Nanchi with my horse and to inquire about me. A year later, while I was in Germany, my wife again wrote me. Lei Yung-fei had come in person to take me back with him. He was very disappointed to discover that I was abroad. My wife's family entertained him as an honored guest. Still another year passed and I read in the Chinese press that he had just been killed in battle with troops of the nephew of the Szechwan warlord, Liu Hsiang, and his territory overrun. I felt very badly, for Lei Yung-fei was a better man than his enemies."

After leaving Lei's territory, Chu Teh and his comrades took new names and gave their occupation as merchants traveling with an armed escort, as was necessary through such dangerous territory. Riding up over the snow-mantled mountains, they crossed the wild Ta Tu River where the Taiping Army under Shih Ta-kai had perished sixty years previously. General Chu's travel through this region stood him in good stead thirteen years later when he led the Chinese Red Army through it.

Reaching the Yachou district, the party turned due east and passed down through Szechwan. It was while in Yachou that Chu smoked his last pipe of opium. Each night and morning he began brewing the Kwangtung herb which he had bought months before to cure himself of opium addiction. He drank the brew assiduously, but it was a grueling period. Deprived of the drug he could not sleep at night and, during the day, became so weak and exhausted that he could hardly keep his saddle. It was the hardest battle he had ever fought, for it was against himself and the craving that tormented him. By mid-May, when the party reached his wife's home in Nanchi, he still suffered from insomnia and would arise from his bed at night to wander about or read. Yet he was on the way to victory.

The refugees were surprised that they were not molested by the Szechwan warlords, whose agents were everywhere and had learned of their arrival. His wife and old friends, who told them the tragic fate of their captured comrades in Yunnanfu, also explained that the Szechwan warlords were now so firmly entrenched that they were even trying to enlist experienced military men. The rest of the party took ship at once and left for the coast, but General Chu remained for a few days to be with his wife and child. His son was now a dark-skinned little chatterbox, six years old, a pocket edition of himself and a gay little fellow who adored sitting on his father's lap to read what his mother had taught him.

"*Koo-li* (coolie)," the child would read proudly. "That means bitter strength. *Koo*—look! It looks like the face of a little old man—it's screwed up. He's in pain. He has a hard life."

Just as he was preparing to leave for the coast, Chu received a telegram from General Yang Sen, the warlord who ruled eastern Szechwan. Yang invited him, "in the name of old friendship," to come to Chungking as his guest.

Chu wired his acceptance and bade his wife and child farewell. He never saw them again. Thirteen years later they were murdered by the warlords of the west.

In early June 1922, during the Dragon Boat Festival, General Chu's boat docked at Chungking and General Yang Sen stepped out from among his armed bodyguard and greeted him effusively as if no shadow

had ever crossed their friendship. General Liu Hsiang had just come
from Chengtu for a secret military conference the nature of which Chu
was too wise to ask. He knew without asking. Wars had been raging in
other parts of the country for months. Dr. Sun Yat-sen's expedition
against the warlords had failed. The Yunnan Army had taken part in
that expedition. The governor of Kwangtung Province, left behind in
Canton while Dr. Sun was at the front, had sold out to British bankers
of Hongkong and staged a *coup d'état*. Soong Ching-ling, Dr. Sun's wife,
had escaped to Shanghai where Dr. Sun soon joined her.

With this new abortion of the revolutionary movement General Wu
Pei-fu, strong man of British imperialism, was now master of Peking
and of most of China. General Chu did not have to be told that the
Szechwan warlords had allied themselves with Wu and that they knew
no allegiance except to themselves. He also knew that either of them
would betray the other and usurp all Szechwan when he felt himself
strong enough to do so.

The brief description which General Chu reluctantly gave of his week
in Chungking sounded like some scene lifted from the page of a medieval
tale. There was a continuous round of banquets and mah jong gambling
parties replete with sing-song girls, shrieking *hu-chins*, and flowing wine,
everything enveloped in the fumes of opium. Neither of the warlords
smoked, yet they offered Chu the customary opium pipe and expressed
surprise that he had given up the habit.

Over their cups the three men talked as feudal lords once talked.
Reviewing past battles, they recalled just what each had done at such
and such a time, praising one another's brilliant maneuvers while
belittling their own. Not one word was uttered about the soldiers who
had fallen like leaves in autumn, not a word about the suffering peasants
or the crops trampled under the feet and hoofs of the opposing armies.
Above all, nothing was said about Sun Yat-sen and the fate of the
Chinese Republic.

As Chu Teh had anticipated, Yang Sen invited him to join his staff,
and was unable to understand how a defeated general thirty-six years of
age, without a fortune and apparently without a future, could refuse.

"Why did you refuse?" I asked General Chu.

"I was not that old or corrupt!" he retorted.

"Why did you go to Chungking at all?" I insisted, for I still could
not comprehend the spider's web of feudal relations and influences that
had surrounded him all his life. Nor could I fully fathom the confused
gropings of a man, once a poor peasant, who had tasted power and
prestige and at least some of the fleshpots of life.

General Chu's mouth was twisted wryly as he explained that it would have been dangerous for himself and his family had he refused Yang Sen's invitation. He had also been curious to see what had happened to a onetime revolutionary. Still another reason was undeniable: he still had one foot in the old order while the other was searching for a foothold in the future.

When he explained to his hosts that he was leaving for Europe to study and find a new way of life, they smiled a little and Liu asked him why he wasted so much time and money when he could merely retire for a time to Omeishan.

General Chu's sardonic wit bubbled up at the memory.

"As you must know, defeated warlords and politicians often retire to some sacred mountain like Omeishan where they live for a time in a temple to build up a reputation for piety and scholarship before making a comeback. They always let it be widely known that they are composing poetry, communing with their souls, and seeking a virtuous way of life. If unable to write poetry themselves, they hire some degenerate intellectual to do it for them. Some of them also make long trips to sweep the graves of their ancestors and thereby prove their filial piety. For a time they drop the butcher's knife and become a saint.

"When I still assured General Yang that I intended to study abroad, he assured me that there would always be a place waiting for me on his staff when I returned. One week later I was in Shanghai."

Book IV

The Quest

Chapter 13

BEFORE leaving for Europe, General Chu had decided to achieve three things. These three things were planned as he traveled down the Yangtze to Shanghai, for he had a lifelong habit of methodical planning before he acted.

First, he would enter the French Hospital in Shanghai to cure himself of the insomnia that had tormented him since he gave up opium smoking. He had all but cured himself of the opium craving, but insomnia was a misery and a temptation to return to the drug.

Second, he would see something of the coastal regions and the north because he was, in a way, a country greenhorn who had seen nothing of his country except the far west and southwest. The names of the great cities, Nanking, Shanghai, and Peking, were woven into his being but he had only imagined what they were like. He knew that Shanghai was the bastion of Far Eastern imperialism, but legends in west China claimed that it was a city founded on modern science where gold all but grew on trees.

Third, he hoped that his old friend, Sung Ping-wen, now working on a newspaper in Peking, could introduce him to leaders of the May 4th Movement, to Sun Yat-sen and other national revolutionary leaders with whom Sung had worked in Japan in former years. Among the national revolutionary leaders whom he wished to meet was Professor Chen Tu-hsiu, professor in Peking National University, leader of the great cultural renaissance, a founder and the secretary of the infant Chinese Communist Party.

Upon reaching Shanghai, General Chu took a ricksha and went at once to the French Hospital where he reported that he had cured himself of opium smoking, but that he still could not sleep at night. Could they cure him?

The influence which the French exercised on General Chu's plans was something of which he seemed unconscious even when he told me the story of his life fifteen years later. He had transferred his money to Paris

143

banks, he had the address of the French Hospital when he landed in Shanghai, and he soon went to a French steamship line and reserved two third-class passages on a French steamer, the *Algiers,* which would sail for Marseilles in early September. One passage was for himself, one for his friend Sung Ping-wen, to whom he had written even before reaching Shanghai. Sung had asked him to make the reservations and then come on to Peking.

When Chu Teh left the hospital, after a week there, he went with a Yunnan refugee friend, a member of the old Tung Meng Hui, with whom he lived for another week while he explored the city of which he had heard such fabulous tales.

While in the hospital his friend had brought him books and newspapers and he had read them with methodical thoroughness. A new wind had begun blowing through China, and the press he read was filled with reports of the new labor movement and the Communist Party which guided it. From what he read Chu Teh decided to join the new Communist Party. Just what its principles were he did not know, fully, but one thing had become more than clear: the foreign imperialists attacked the party with everything ugly in their vocabulary. If this party was regarded by the foreign enemies of China as a menace to them, it was the party for Chu Teh.

The Communist Party had been formed on July 1, 1921, just one year before Chu reached Shanghai. It was still small and weak but it was an offspring of the May 4th Movement and was anti-feudal, anti-militarist and anti-imperialist. Its leaders were primarily students, professors, and other intellectuals, yet it was a party based on the workers and peasants, and it was the organizer of the new labor movement which had just won a great victory over British imperialism.

This victory, the first victory over foreign imperialism in Chinese history, had stirred the whole country. In January 1922, while Chu Teh and his comrades were riding hard through the mountains of Yunnan, the Chinese seamen of British Hongkong had demanded an increase in wages and the recognition of their underground seamen's union. British seamen had unions and had just won a big increase in wages, but the Chinese had had no increase in wages for eight years, years during which the cost of living had gone up by more than 200 percent.

The British of Hongkong rejected all the Chinese demands and arrested and imprisoned the seamen union leaders who made them. These leaders were beaten up in prison and one of them killed. At the call of the union leader, Su Chao-jen, who had escaped arrest, the seamen struck work to a man; and within twenty-four hours every Chinese worker in the great port of Hongkong, including even the servants in the homes of their white and Chinese masters, also walked out. Hongkong, proud bastion of British power, was paralyzed for fifty days. The strike ended with the recognition of the seamen's union, a small increase in wages and an apology to the arrested and beaten-up men.

General Chu's voice trembled when he spoke of this first Chinese victory over foreign imperialism which aroused wild enthusiasm in all China. Sun Yat-sen's government at Canton had contributed $200,000 to the strike fund, Chinese generals had sent heavy contributions, and workers of the whole country had given their pennies. Workers of the Soviet Union had taken up collections for them, and the British Labor Party had raised the Hongkong strike issue in the House of Commons.

The victory of the Hongkong workers, General Chu declared, was the opening shot of the Chinese working class in the liberation movement of the Chinese people and nation. It inspired all Chinese workers. During the strike the railway workers on the Peking-Hankow railway walked out. Two days later the railway strike ended with an increase of one dollar a month in wages and the right of the workers to organize workers' clubs, the seedbed of the trade union movement. The leaders of the railway strike and some of the key leaders of the Hongkong strike were Communists.

"As with India and other colonial countries," General Chu said, "our Chinese labor movement was never narrowed down to mere economic gains. Of course it fought for higher wages, shorter hours, and human conditions for workers, but it was also political from its inception. It was also directed against militarism and imperialism. This was because it was led by the Communist Party."

On May 1, 1922, one month before General Chu reached Shanghai, the railway workers—fathers of the Chinese labor movement—called the first National Labor Congress. This congress, held secretly in Shanghai, elected a committee whose task it was to begin the immediate organization of workers of the entire country. It also issued a historic proclamation which called for industrial, as opposed to trade, unions, an eight-hour day, civil rights and educational opportunities for workers, and demanded the end of the whipping and other cruel treatment of workers in factories.

General Chu emphasized the fact that it was not uncommon for both foreign and Chinese factory owners and foremen to walk around in their factories with whips in their hands, hitting anyone who worked too slowly or who fell asleep from exhaustion at his machine. Before 1927 the killing of workers was not at all unusual. The work day ranged from twelve to fourteen or more hours, wages were barely enough to keep workers alive for a few years, and the workers' quarters were dark, insanitary tenements that resembled rabbit warrens where sickness and disease lurked. There was no protection for workers either then or when General Chu talked with me in 1937.

"No one has ever estimated the cost in human lives of the vast foreign and Chinese fortunes wrung from the workers of Shanghai alone," General Chu said. "To the present day death wagons go about Shanghai each day to pick up dead bodies from the streets. Thirty to fifty thousand such bodies are picked up and buried in paupers' graves each year in Shanghai. Other thousands are buried by their relatives and friends. Others are not counted at all but thousands of exhausted workers are dismissed from factories each year and told to go back to their native villages to die."

General Chu had set out to explore Shanghai—this fabulous city of wealth and privilege of which he had heard and read. He tramped up and down, around and about, through the fine foreign business and residential sections with their great buildings, paved streets, light and water systems; then into the "dark hell" of the workers' districts where men, women, and little children labored for their meager bowl of rice. He looked into the thousands of small Chinese workshops where small boys, bought from famine- or war-torn regions, worked as slaves until they fell dead at their primitive machines. A pall of poverty, sickness, and misery hung over all working-class Shanghai. The city, he said, was a "hell of limitless luxury and corruption for the few, and limitless work and suffering for the many." At night he saw homeless workers sleeping on the hard pavements in the shadow of great modern buildings which their hands had built, and "their bodies were as thin and flat as if something had rolled over them."

Modern science in the service of capitalism had brought no good to China, he told himself in despair, but from what he had heard in the far interior, the British and Dutch colonies of Nanyang (the South Seas) were very different. For legendary tales had circulated everywhere of the wealth amassed by Chinese emigrants to Nanyang. As for Western countries, he knew that they must be paradises of modern science.

"Of one thing I was certain," said General Chu, "no country on earth was as miserable as China."

As he tramped through the streets of Shanghai, and, later, of Nanking and Peking, all his frustrations came out in fantastic daydreams. When he saw exhausted men sleeping on the pavement, or the dark turgid rivers of men, women, and little children pouring from factories; when he saw a foreigner shove a Chinese off the pavement, phantom armies arose behind him and followed him into battle. Advancing in mighty waves, they slew phantom foreigners or washed them into the sea by the thousands.

The memory of such fantasies depressed him. Unlike most people, he showed not the slightest hesitancy in speaking of his daydreams. He explained them by saying:

"I suppose I had been a military man for so long that my mind could function only in military terms."

From Shanghai his pilgrimage took him to Nanking, where he made a trip to the tomb of the founder of the Ming dynasty, a peasant whose name had been Chu and who had organized a powerful army called a Red Army that overthrew the alien Mongol dynasty. Then on to Peking where his old friend, Sung Ping-wen, gave up his job to show him the city, to travel with him into Suiyuan Province, then back to Peking and to Shanghai.

The Peking government, he remarked with contempt, was "only a shadow government shrouded in the thick smell of feudalism—a decaying cesspool where old-style officials and warlords played at government, feasted, whored, smoked opium and sold China to the highest bidder."

Sung introduced him to groups of students who had remained in the city during the summer vacations to teach night schools for workers, while other groups went to the villages to teach the peasants. He had hoped to meet Communist Party leaders, but all were away, and Chen Tu-hsiu, the party's secretary, was in Shanghai.

Back in Shanghai the two friends spent one morning with Dr. Sun Yat-sen who was then living with his wife in his home in the French Concession. General Chin Han-ting, one of Chu Teh's companions on his flight from Yunnan Province, went along.

General Chu recalled with deep emotion this first and last time he ever saw the great national leader. Fifty-six years of age at the time, Dr. Sun had spent thirty-seven years of his life in the revolutionary movement. He was still quick and vibrant in movement and, despite defeat after defeat, was still optimistic about the future.

"He was a modest and very sincere man," General Chu said. "He had been betrayed and driven from Canton by one of his own generals, but was planning to recapture Canton and re-establish his republican government. To do this he could depend on the Yunnan Army, then in Kwangsi Province, and asked us to help him. He wanted us to return to the Yunnan Army and reorganize it. He could give us an initial sum of $100,000. General Chin accepted the offer at once, but Sung and I refused.

"Dr. Sun listened carefully to the reasons for our refusal. Sung and I had lost all faith in such tactics as the alliances which Dr. Sun and his Kuomintang followers made with this or that militarist. Such tactics had always ended in defeat for the revolution and the strengthening of the warlords. We ourselves had spent eleven years of our lives in such a squirrel cage. The Chinese revolution had failed, while the Russian Revolution had succeeded, and the Russians had succeeded because they were Communists with a theory and a method of which we were ignorant.

"We told Dr. Sun that we had decided to study abroad, to meet Communists and study Communism, before re-entering national affairs in China. The great Hongkong strike victory, together with the rise of the labor movement in China, proved to us that the Communists knew something we needed to know.

"Dr. Sun had no prejudice against Communism, but he asked us why, if we wanted to study abroad, we did not go to America, which had no feudal background and where there were many progressive institutions. We replied that neither of us had enough money to study and live long in America, and that we preferred Europe where the socialist movement was said to be strongest. America might be all right for Americans, we reminded him, but it had never helped him in his struggle for the Republic. It had only helped and recognized his enemies. Yet he had looked to America for help in all the years he had spent in the revolutionary movement. European countries had done the same, of course, but now there were new social forces in Europe which would be of more help to us.

"Dr. Sun agreed with us. He talked of formulating new policies for the Kuomintang, but just what they were we did not learn at the time. Another two years passed before these became clear. He then formed an alliance between the Canton revolutionary government and the Soviet Union."

Following these talks with Sun Yat-sen, the three friends called on Hu Han-min, a right-wing Kuomintang leader, with whom they remained for a short time only. General Chu peremptorily dismissed Hu with these words: "He was a real reactionary, a typical representative of the Hongkong compradore class."

Next came a visit with Wang Ching-wei, a leftist nationalist with a great reputation as an intellectual leader, and a leader said to be closest to Sun Yat-sen. With all his inherited reverence for intellectuals, Chu Teh must have approached this man with deep respect, yet looking back across the fifteen years of characterlessness and treachery which Wang had shown since that meeting, he could remember him only with contempt. What they had talked about he either could not or did not wish to remember.

Apart from political considerations, however, Wang Ching-wei was offensive to Chu Teh as a person. A male from his head to his toes, Chu did not respect men who were neither men, women, nor good red herring.

"Wang reminded me of a concubine," he exclaimed with open disgust. "He pursed his lips and made languid gestures with his hands as he talked so that I could only watch instead of listening to the fellow. He affected all the effeminate mannerisms of decadent feudal intellectuals. He was like a female impersonator in an old Peking opera. His wife was present. She was a mannish woman and very rich. He had no money. She controlled the money and she controlled Wang through her money. People said she even told him when to go to bed with her and when he might get up!"

Next came the meeting with Chen Tu-hsiu, secretary of the Communist Party, to which Chu Teh had looked forward. At last he was meeting one of the chief leaders of the cultural renaissance, a famous professor, a brilliant writer and editor, and one of the chief organizers of the Communist Party. Chen was about forty at the time, vigorous and decisive, watchful and reserved in manner. His face was dark and pockmarked and he lived austerely in a small room in the native city of Chapei adjoining the International Settlement. From this room he directed the work of the Communist Party in organizing the underground labor unions.

The memory of this meeting clearly aroused great conflicts in Chu Teh's soul, but of these he was reluctant to speak. The great political struggle that had raged around Chen in the years that had since passed may have explained his reluctance, though only in part. Chu went to this meeting in the belief that he had only to apply for membership in the Communist Party to be accepted. Thus it had been with the Kuomintang, which anyone who applied could join. Chu had expected the same procedure with the Communist Party, after which he was convinced he would step out on a new revolutionary road.

Cool and reserved, Chen looked at his visitors, and in particular at Chu, the general with a none too savory reputation. A whole decade of militarism, with all that militarism meant in China, must have flashed through his mind. Why should a general from a far western warlord province wish to join the party of the Chinese poor? Words dried up on Chu Teh's tongue and the cloud of despair that previously shrouded him returned and enveloped him.

A man could join the Communist Party, Chen Tu-hsiu told him, provided he adopted the workers' cause as his own and was prepared to give his life to it. For a man like Chu Teh this required long study and sincere application.

Chu listened in depressed silence. He had knocked on the door of the future and it had refused to open to him.

"Those were terrible days," General Chu remarked, miserably. "I was hopeless and confused. One of my feet remained in the old order and the other could find no place in the new. At the time Shanghai was filled with refugees from Yunnan Province who could find no work and had no means of living. Each day they asked me for money and would not believe that I had not made a great fortune. I explained, but they did not believe. Each day they besieged me. I felt like a criminal."

In early September 1922, Chu and his friend boarded the French liner *Algiers,* and set their faces toward foreign lands in search of the secret of their country's liberation.

Chapter 14

THERE was nothing of the tourist in General Chu's description of his ocean voyage through south Asia to Marseilles, nor of his later trips through France and Germany. Sitting across from me, his head down, his hands clasped on the little table between us, he often seemed but half-conscious of his surroundings. His voice was filled with awe and touched with great loneliness as he recalled the limitless ocean that rolled and heaved "as it clung to the earth rolling through infinity."

First came the ports of Nanyang, the lands of the South Seas to which millions of Chinese had emigrated to seek their fortunes, to work in mines, on the great plantations, or do other hard labor in the sultry heat which few white men and often not even the native peoples would do. These were the British and Dutch colonies which he had envisaged as lands little short of paradise.

With his friend he went ashore in eagerness and returned hours later in confused hopelessness. These were half-Chinese lands where, the same as in Shanghai, his countrymen and the native inhabitants lived in humble poverty and squalor in the shadow of great buildings, palatial homes, and bridges built by their hands.

After that he saw no more Chinese, and loneliness ate at his heart. India was dark and turgid, gaunt of body and with great eyes filled with torment, with palaces on the hills and squalid hovels in dank alleyways. Then came the black men of Africa, heaving and lifting in nakedness for their white masters. Egypt was a skeleton with pus-filled eyes against a background of cold and arrogant luxury.

Chu Teh's voice was low and faraway:

"Everywhere I saw a dark world of suffering. China was not the most miserable land on earth—it was one of many. The problems of the poor and subjected are the same everywhere. After we landed in France I saw that Europe was not a paradise of modern science as I had thought. French workers were better dressed and better fed than Chinese, yet they were haunted men, and the French government was a market place where officials bargained and bought and sold. We tramped the streets of France from morning till late at night and we visited the battlefields of the great European war. France was one of the victors, yet everyone talked of the miseries of the war, and maimed veterans, widows and orphans moved liked broken shadows against a background of past greatness.

"The great European war for the redivision of the world sent three dynasties crashing in ruins and inflicted mortal wounds on the victors, yet even then I believed that the capitalist system would benefit China."

In the home of a Chinese merchant where the two friends found lodging, they heard of a group of Chinese students who had just organized a branch of the Chinese Communist Party. Chu questioned his host eagerly. The chief organizer of the group seemed to be a student named Chou En-lai, a man who with his companions later made history in China: Chen Yi, Nieh Jung-chen, Li Li-san, Li Fu-chun, and Tsai Chang, Li's wife. How to reach this group their host did not know, but someone gave them the Berlin address of Chou En-lai, who had gone to Germany to organize another group there.

Taking the train, the two friends arrived in Berlin in late October 1922, and went directly to the address of Chou En-lai. Would this man receive them as fellow countrymen, or would he treat them with cold suspicion and question them cautiously about their past careers as militarists? Chu Teh remembered his age. He was thirty-six, his youth had passed like a screaming eagle, leaving him old and disillusioned.

When Chou En-lai's door opened they saw a slender man of more than average height with gleaming eyes and a face so striking that it bordered on the beautiful. Yet it was a manly face, serious and intelligent, and Chu judged him to be in his middle twenties.

Chou was a quiet and thoughtful man, even a little shy as he welcomed his visitors, urged them to be seated and to tell how he could help them.

Ignoring the chair offered him, Chu Teh stood squarely before this youth more than ten years his junior and in a level voice told him who he was, what he had done in the past, how he had fled from Yunnan, given up opium smoking, talked with Sun Yat-sen, been repulsed by Chen Tu-hsiu in Shanghai, and had come to Europe to find a new way of life for himself and a new revolutionary road for China. He wanted to join the Chinese Communist Party group in Berlin, he would study and work hard, he would do anything he was asked to do but return to his old life, which had turned to ashes beneath his feet.

As he talked Chou En-lai stood facing him, his head a little to one side as was his habit, listening intently until the story was told, and then questioning him.

When both visitors had told their stories, Chou smiled a little, said he would help them find rooms, and arrange for them to join the Berlin Communist group as candidates until their application had been sent to China and an answer received. When the reply came a few months later they were enrolled as full members, but Chu's membership was kept a secret from outsiders.

General Chu explained this procedure as necessary because, as a general in the Yunnan Army, he had been one of the earliest Kuomintang members and he might be sent back to Yunnan by the Communist Party at some future date. Though not publicly known as a Communist, General Chu said that he broke all connections with his past, and with the old society in every way, "so that a heavy burden seemed to fall from my shoulders." There were hundreds of Chinese students in Germany at the time, most of them rich men's sons with whom he might have associated in the past. Such men he now avoided and he spent his time studying hungrily, avidly, with young men many of whom were almost young enough to be his sons.

The Berlin group of the Chinese Communist Party devoted itself almost exclusively to study. Apart from the regular university studies which its members pursued, they held three evening discussion meetings a week where they studied and discussed the problems of the Chinese revolution in the light of Marxism-Leninism. Chu Teh sat as a humble "candidate" in these meetings. When they were finished he studied with the help of one of his young comrades. Together they read and discussed such

Marxist literature as had been translated into Chinese: the *Communist Manifesto* and the *ABC of Communism*. But they devoted most time to the *Hsiang Tao*, or *Guide*, the official theoretical organ of the Communist Party in China which published study material on the history of the Chinese revolution and its problems. In the light of such material the group analyzed past revolutionary struggles in China, and Chu Teh began analyzing his own past life and activities. At the same time he began the study of the German language to qualify for entrance to some German university.

Time was a wolf pack at his heels and he studied doggedly, humbly, driving himself relentlessly and cursing his slowness in learning the German language which had no earthly connection with Chinese. Perhaps he was too old, he told himself; perhaps it was because so many years had passed since he sat on a school bench; or was it that he had been a military man for so long? He was used to an active physical life and it was a torment to sit over books for endless hours, as Chinese students, accustomed to study, could do.

He had come to Europe to study not only books, though books were the accumulated thought, if not always the wisdom, of ages. He had also come to study European civilization, which included the industrial and cultural institutions which had made it strong enough to conquer his own and other countries. The only way to do this was to go out and study it as best he could.

His manner of doing this was strikingly similar to the methodical manner in which he had once studied the classics. First he bought a map of Berlin and translated every street and institution marked on it into Chinese. Unable to speak enough German to ask directions, he decided to walk through the streets and visit every museum, school, art gallery, every beer hall and restaurant, and every factory that would admit him. He would go to the opera and attend concerts. He would visit the Reichstag and he would go through the parks, and he would try to visit the homes of the people to see how they were furnished and how the people lived. He would even go to the churches and see how they differed from Chinese temples.

He would pore over his books till his eyes ached and then go on his quest, generally alone but sometimes with his new-found friend, Teng Yen-da, a brilliant young Chinese intellectual who later became one of the most noted Chinese revolutionary leaders and who died a martyr's death. Teng would walk with him for an afternoon or an evening, then drop out, unable to endure his ceaseless tramping. When friends asked him where Chu Teh was, he would reply:

"Somewhere in the city. Yesterday it was an art museum, the day before the War Museum, last night a concert. A concert!—he sits there listening to the noise made by some fellow named Beethoven. He likes it! He says he's going to hear everything the man ever wrote!"

Another student once remarked: "He dragged me to the opera. I went to sleep. He asked me afterwards how I liked it. I said I liked the sandwiches between the acts, and he lectured me all the way home. Of course I like the songs at the mass meetings in the Sports Palace, but the rest of this German music sounds just like one big noise."

The concerts and the opera at first sounded like just one big noise to Chu Teh also, but he caught first melodies and motives and then the patterns of creative imagination that ran through the whole. He never understood the whole composition, yet he would sink to sleep at night with a vast symphony of sound like the dawn of creation, the marching of armies, or the chaotic strivings of man, sounding through his dreams.

Arising from his studies he would, day by day and night after night, go on his explorations, tramping, tramping, tramping endlessly. In the Berlin War Museum he studied weapons of wars of the past and banners captured by the German armies in battle. Before these banners he once drew up suddenly with a shock. Before him was a banner captured by the German troops in China during the Boxer Rebellion. How long he stood staring before this banner he did not know, but a phantom army of soldiers began swarming through his mind and again, as in Shanghai, Nanking and Peking, he was a general leading them in battle, slaying China's enemies and driving them into the sea. For days afterwards, as he tramped the streets, the phantom armies returned, obsessing him. Under his command they threw up barricades in the streets of Berlin, and some of them were, strangely, German soldiers who fought side by side with their shadowy Chinese comrades. And always he was victorious and his enemies vanquished.

Again General Chu shook his head as if to get rid of the phantoms as he said:

"My mind seemed to think only in military terms!"

There came a time when he thought he knew every street, every building, every institution of value in Berlin. He had visited many workers' homes, and many homes of intellectuals also, he had visited the great parks and forests about the city, had prowled through the palace and grounds of Potsdam. He had visited a camp of the Communist Youth where boys and girls sat in long orderly lines and asked him carefully formulated questions about China, many of which he found difficult to answer.

Then came the great factories, which he visited with letters of introduction from the Chinese consulate, factories that astounded and confused him by their complexities and implications. And then he began extending his explorations to other cities. With letters of introduction from the consulate, he visited factories, mines and other institutions in cities near Berlin and then farther and farther away.

"After I knew Berlin like the palm of my hand, and after I began visiting other cities and industrial establishments," General Chu said, "I began to lose my old belief that capitalism could save China. It seemed to me that if a highly organized industrial country like Germany, with a skilled, disciplined, literate and organized working class, could be defeated in war as Germany had been, then it would be foolish for China to follow in its footsteps. I remember a week that I spent in Kassel, where I saw railway locomotives created from the pig iron stage to the finished locomotive rolling out on the tracks. That made a deeper impression on me than all the cultural institutions I saw in Germany."

Before leaving Germany four years later, Chu Teh had visited almost every major city in Germany, visited the chief industrial institutions and tramped along the Rhine and through the Harz and Bavarian mountains. Every weekend and every holiday or vacation found him plodding on the road, his pockets filled with maps and with notebooks in which he methodically recorded his observations. When he finally finished he had a trunk filled with notebooks, maps and guidebooks about Germany.

He left Berlin in early 1923 and enrolled in the political science faculty of Göttingen University, where large numbers of Chinese students were studying and where the Communist branch was the strongest. In addition he took private lessons in military subjects from a baron who had once been a general in the Kaiser's army and from whom he rented a room.

General Chu's lips curled with scorn as he recalled this nobleman who insisted that he be paid for both lessons and rent in Chinese currency— these were the years of inflation—and who haggled with him for hours before settling for two dollars a lesson. Upon finishing each lesson, the baron asked for his pay, adding that it was all too little for a man of his standing and knowledge, while General Chu replied truthfully that he had learned little that he did not already know.

Though he plugged away at his German and conscientiously attended all university lectures, he felt he learned more in the three evening discussion meetings each week of the Chinese Communist branch than he learned in the university. The *Hsiang Tao,* chief theoretical organ of the Communist Party in China, continued to provide study material on problems of the Chinese revolution, past and present, while a Chinese newspaper published by the Paris Communist branch published special articles on international developments and gave a digest of the news of the world.

In early 1924 he left Göttingen and returned to Berlin to organize a branch of the reformed Kuomintang along the lines laid down by Dr. Sun Yat-sen at Canton. By then Dr. Sun had recaptured his old revolutionary base in south China and called the first national congress of the Kuomintang. This party, an amorphous body of middle-class intellectuals drawn from landlord, merchant, and capitalist families, was now transformed into a united front of various groups, including members of the infant Communist Party. The gifted student organizer, Chou En-lai, together with Chu Teh's old friend Sung Ping-wen, and a number of other Chinese students, had returned to Canton. There Chou became chairman, and Sung the vice-chairman, of the political department of the new Whampoa Military Academy which Sun Yat-sen had just established near Canton and of which Chiang Kai-shek was President. Chiang Kai-shek, an army officer about Chu Teh's own age, had played a minor role in the 1911 Revolution at Shanghai, after which he had become a stockbroker in that city and had linked up with the notorious Ching Pang, or Green Gang. This Ching Pang was an underworld organization that imposed tribute on all Chinese business institutions in Shanghai, and engaged in gambling and the white slave traffic. The chief source of income and power of the Green Gang, however, was from opium, and foreigners in China referred to its feudal leader as the "opium czar" of Shanghai.

Chiang Kai-shek was one of the officers whom Dr. Sun Yat-sen sent on a short study tour of the Soviet Union. Upon returning to China he delivered speeches in which he declared that the Communist International was the hope of the world's oppressed.

With the transformation of the Kuomintang into a national united front of all revolutionary forces, General Chu said, a new era opened in China. To his old Three People's Principles of nationalism, democracy, and the people's livelihood, Dr. Sun Yat-sen now added his Three Policies as the foundation of his new government. The Three Policies provided for cooperation with the Communist Party, the promotion of the interests of the workers and peasants, and alliance with the Soviet Union.

Through the preceding thirty-seven years of his revolutionary labors, Dr. Sun had hoped for and sought the aid of England, France and the United States. Individuals had sympathized with and helped him, but the bankers and governments of these countries, and the foreign press in China and abroad, had showered terms of opprobrium upon him, calling him a "sorehead," a "visionary," a "Cantonese theoretician" and a "disappointed office seeker."

In 1923, following long negotiations, Dr. Sun entered into an alliance with the Soviet government. The new Soviet government had proclaimed the equality of races and the right of colonial peoples to independence. It had also abrogated all unequal treaties and agreements entered into by the old czarist and Chinese governments or with any foreign power concerning China. Dr. Sun, as part of the alliance, officially asked for military and political advisers. Michael Borodin became his chief political adviser and General Galen his chief military adviser.

Foreign governments and the foreign press in China immediately branded Dr. Sun and his government as "Red" and "Bolshevik." Even many of his old followers regarded his promotion and protection of the labor and peasant movements as an alien importation as dangerous as releasing tigers and leopards. Such men, who sprang from landlord, merchant or capitalist families, soon heard the dread peasant cry: "Land to the tiller!" as Peasant Leagues formed the Peasant Self-Defense Corps to fight for a 25 percent reduction in rent and the abolition of usury. In Kwangtung Province, where the peasant movement began, the landlords and their armed retainers of the Min Tuan—the landlords' militia— together with local militarists, took up their weapons and met the peasants in battle. The Chinese peasant revolution had begun.

Until his death in March 1925, however, Sun Yat-sen held all national revolutionary forces together. Only then did many of his old followers organize open and secret cliques which demanded the abrogation of his Three Policies upon which the movement against warlordism and imperialism was founded.

The savage class warfare which later stained the soil and rivers of China with human blood was still slumbering in the womb of time when Chu Teh left Göttingen University and returned to Berlin in early 1924 to organize all Chinese in Germany behind the new Kuomintang government at Canton. General Chu remarked that it was really a waste of time for him to remain in Göttingen. He had learned enough German to carry on a conversation, but not enough fully to understand involved scholarly lectures. He was a poor linguist anyway and had no interest in securing a degree as doctor of philosophy. He had come to Europe to broaden his knowledge of the world, to secure information about Western culture, and to seek a new revolutionary road for China. In Berlin he could continue his studies of Chinese historical developments while organizing and educating Chinese students in the new principles upon which Sun Yat-sen's government was founded.

Staring into the murky darkness of the room about us as if at those far-off scenes, General Chu's voice was sometimes contemptuous, some-times bitter:

"Instead of joining the new branch of the Kuomintang, many rich Chinese students in Berlin formed a so-called Youth Party to fight us. They even sought allies among German monarchists and other similar classes, and they asked the German police to suppress our organization and the little Chinese newspaper which I founded.

"Since we had no Chinese printing press, our newspaper had to be put out in mimeographed form. I was everything on the paper from business manager to office boy and porter. I took charge of the articles, operated the mimeograph machine, addressed wrappers, licked stamps, and carried the paper to the post office to be mailed. Everywhere my comrades and I went we were followed by German detectives. We learned interesting things about those detectives—they were 'colonial experts'!—Germans who had once lived in Tsingtao, and they spoke the Chinese language.

"German imperialists were seeping into the Weimar Republic and dreaming of the day when they would again take possession of the Tsingtao naval base and former German possessions in China. They had entered the police and our own countrymen used them against us. I learned my first serious lessons in the class war in Germany when Chinese united with German imperialists against us—we have an ancient saying, 'The deer does not walk with the tiger.' "

While organizing men into the Kuomintang and doing all the necessary humble work to bring out the little Chinese newspaper, General Chu found time to speak in meetings of German workers, and from these activities he went on to broader fields—attending conferences of an in-ternational nature. He was twice arrested while attending conferences to protest the terror against the revolutionary movement in Bulgaria.

When first arrested by the German police he was released by demand of the Chinese embassy, but was kept in jail for two days when arrested the second time.

"The police kept me in jail for two days while they tried to find some law under which to hold me. Finding none, they turned me loose, but after that I was never free from detectives—'colonial experts' who spoke Chinese. During these black inflation years, rich German speculators filled the restaurants and cafés while poor men died in the streets. We allowed no event in China to pass unnoticed. We called a meeting of Chinese when the Peking government signed the new Sino-Soviet agree-ment of May 1924, when the American ambassador in Peking tried to prevent Karakhan, the Soviet ambassador, from taking possession of the old czarist legation, and when all the foreign imperialists engaged in acts of violence to prevent Chinese-Soviet friendship.

"I remember the British and American writers who campaigned against the 'yellow peril' of China and denounced the Soviet Union as 'the enemy within the gates of the white world' because it advocated the freedom and independence of China, and when they called the Canton revolutionary government a 'gang of Bolshevik anarchists' whose members practiced free love and stirred up the Chinese people."

Then came the disastrous death of Dr. Sun Yat-sen in Peking on March 12, 1925; gloom shrouded Chinese revolutionaries in every part of the world. In Berlin, Chu and his comrades called a memorial meeting and put out a special pamphlet in both Chinese and German in which they recounted Dr. Sun's forty years of heartbreaking struggle for the liberation of China. The pamphlet contained Dr. Sun's last will and testament and his final letter of friendship to the Soviet Union. In his last will and testament he exhorted his successors to ally themselves "in a common struggle with those peoples of the world who treat us on a footing of equality so that they may cooperate with us in our struggle," and in his final letter to the Soviet Union he wrote:

DEAR COMRADES:

I am going to part with you now. I wish to express my hope that the Soviet Union will find in a strong and free China a friend and ally. In the fight for the liberation of all oppressed nations throughout the world, these two allies will march toward victory hand in hand. Such a day is not far off.

Not only foreign imperialists, but many Chinese rejoiced at Sun Yat-sen's death, General Chu remarked in a heavy voice, but at the memorial meeting in Berlin many men wept. For forty years he had dominated the Chinese revolution and now that his resolute hand was removed from the wheel of national life people felt orphaned, lost, alone. Old and new leaders alike aspired for the position he had held, but none were of his stature, none possessed his selflessness, while the younger men were without the prestige which he commanded. And no sooner was he dead than cliques within the Kuomintang began gathering in dark secrecy to distort or wreck the revolutionary structure which he had built. His Chinese enemies in Germany became more courageous and renewed their attacks on his followers.

As General Chu talked of such struggles, I, who had also lived in Berlin during that same period but had known nothing of his existence, recalled one of many Chinese meetings rent with conflict. This particular meeting of perhaps five hundred people, including Germans, Indians, and Chinese, had been called by the local Kuomintang of which General Chu had been one of the chief leaders. A group of conservative Chinese students sat in a small, tight bloc, heckling and catcalling as a Chinese student spoke.

Just who the man was I did not know, but suddenly a middle-aged Chinese in a foreign business suit strode fiercely down the aisle toward the group of hecklers. Without uttering a word this man reached out, grabbed a heckler by the collar, practically lifted him into the aisle and fiercely forced him toward the door at the back. Kicking the door open with one foot, he tossed the heckler outside as if he were a sack of potatoes.

Turning, the man again strode down the aisle, this time followed by three or four Chinese students, and again he reached out and grabbed a heckler and half-lifted him toward the door while the students following him did the same with others. Man after man was hurled out of the hall until there was no heckler left, except one persistent woman, who continued to squawl at the speaker on the platform.

While the audience watched in breathless silence, the middle-aged man again strode down the aisle, reached out and dragged the woman from her seat, hustled her unceremoniously to the door and tossed her out with her men colleagues. The whole incident, which had taken little more than ten minutes, had been carried out with military precision. The middle-aged man then took up a command post in the rear of the hall while his student lieutenants distributed themselves at other strategic positions.

After telling General Chu of this scene, which I had personally witnessed, I asked:

"Did you take part in that incident? Were you that middle-aged man?"

"Perhaps!" he grinned. "We had many such meetings. The reactionaries always tried to break them up and we always tossed them out. But things changed after we received news of the May 30th massacre in Shanghai. That was in 1925 when the British police shot into a parade of workers and students who were protesting at the killing of a Chinese worker in a Japanese factory. This massacre was too much even for many conservative Chinese, and they joined in a vast German mass meeting at the Sports Palace in Berlin.

"The mighty boycott movement against everything British began in China. Martial law lay over the foreign concessions, foreign marines landed at Shanghai, foreign businessmen organized and armed themselves into volunteer corps, and White Russian regiments in the foreign concessions were turned loose on our people. While the workers of America, Britain, and the Continent supported the Chinese revolutionary struggle, their ruling classes called for the suppression of 'the forces of anarchy and discord in China.' "

The American Senate, however, rocked with debate when Senator William Borah announced that the American people would like to see the rights and interests of China respected and extraterritoriality abolished; and when American business interests in China violently objected to such sentiments, Senator Borah threatened to expose them if they continued their pernicious conduct.

The anti-British boycott was complete in south China, and Chinese workers in British Hongkong began leaving the colony for the mainland by the thousands.

Then came June 23rd, when British and French troops on the island of Shameen at Canton fired point-blank into a parade of men, women, and children, who were marching along an avenue across from the island. Fifty-two people were killed outright and a hundred and seventeen wounded.

Immediately all workers of Hongkong went into action. Chinese seamen left all British ships, factory workers walked out, servants left all foreign homes, and for the next sixteen months the great port bastion of British imperialism lay in its own dust. Tens of thousands of Chinese workers poured into Canton where thousands entered the new revolutionary army while other thousands either became the armed guards of the Canton government or patrolled the entire Kwangtung coastline to prevent British goods from being smuggled into the country.

Up and down the coast, up and down the Yangtze River valley, the British began killing Chinese, a few here, a few there, and each killing hardened the Chinese and tightened the anti-British boycott. Class lines vanished and even the Peking warlord government which had again changed hands gave tacit support to the boycott in that ancient capital.

In Germany, General Chu and his comrades, together with the German working class, organized ten gigantic meetings within two months. Similar demonstrations were held in France, England, Holland, and the United States. The French government replied by deporting twenty Chinese leaders, and the British government demanded in vain that the German government do likewise. The German government, however, compromised by officially forbidding Chinese to participate in public affairs in the country. They might sit in a meeting, but any Chinese who arose to speak faced arrest and deportation. Three men who defied the orders were forthwith seized and ordered to leave the country within twenty-four hours.

General Chu now decided to return home. His comrades protested, urging him to remain a while longer in Germany and devote himself to a systematic study of economic problems and international affairs before reentering political life at home. Up to that time, he said, his studies had been of a more general and theoretical nature. He agreed with his friends that he needed systematic training.

From the autumn of 1925, therefore, we see Chu Teh sitting with German Marxist instructors, reviewing documents, reports, statistics, newspaper reports, magazine articles, and other material concerned with Chinese and international affairs.

"The statistical studies were very difficult but of the greatest value to me, because they taught me that ideas which are not based on fact are useless abstractions. Since that time I have been able to judge the seriousness of people, or the honesty of books and newspaper reports, by their use of facts instead of vague ideological fantasies."

Study was sometimes difficult for him also because of the news that reached him from China. No sooner had Dr. Sun Yat-sen's body been laid to rest than the reactionaries within the Kuomintang began organizing cliques to destroy the Three Policies on which the Canton revolutionary government was founded. Dr. Sun's only son, Sun Fo, became a member of the reactionary Western Hills clique which declared war on the Three Policies and established centers of action in imperialist strongholds such as Hongkong and Shanghai—actions for which their leaders were expelled from the Kuomintang during the second national congress of that party in January 1926. It did not prevent them, however, from continuing their work underground.

In the autumn of 1925, also, Mr. Liao Chung-kai, Sun Yat-sen's closest disciple and friend and author of his worker-peasant policy, was assassinated in Canton by men who were reported to have stated that they had been paid for the job by members of the right-wing Hu Han-min clique of the Kuomintang.

Storm clouds were again gathering over the Chinese revolution and General Chu began preparing to return home. But again he went back to his studies with a more peaceful mind after the second national congress of the Kuomintang. It was held in Canton in January 1926, and reaffirmed Dr. Sun's basic Three Principles and Three Policies. In a manifesto to the nation it warned that past revolutionary struggles had failed because the intellectuals had not allied themselves with the workers and peasants. The present revolution, the manifesto stated, "must reach its significance on the farm and in the factory," and the greatest service any Chinese could render to foreign imperialism would be to break the national united front.

One month after this manifesto was released to the Chinese nation, General Chu again was ripped from his studies by another menacing development. Chiang Kai-shek, president of the Whampoa Military Academy at Canton, had staged a *coup d'état*, apparently aimed at establishing his supreme power. Left-wing Kuomintang and Communist Party leaders and Soviet advisers fled from the city or went into hiding. Chiang's blow was also aimed at Dr. Sun Yat-sen's Three Principles. His coup was short-lived because, General Chu declared, Shanghai, and not revolutionary Canton, was Chiang's base of power.

Following protracted negotiations with the Kuomintang, a truce was patched up. A number of Communist leaders, anxious to preserve the national united front, agreed to resign their positions provided Chiang would adhere to Dr. Sun's Three People's Principles and Three Policies. Playing for time, Chiang complied. He issued a public statement in which he admitted his mistakes and pledged his adherence to Dr. Sun's Three Policies. Among the Communists who resigned their positions was Chou En-lai, chairman of the Political Department of the new revolutionary army. General Teng Yen-da, the brilliant revolutionary intellectual who had been Chu Teh's old friend in Berlin in previous years, took Mr. Chou's place. Chu Teh's old friend, Sung Ping-wen, remained vice-chairman under Teng.

"Chiang Kai-shek hated Teng Yen-da also," General Chu remarked, "but could do nothing about the matter at the time. A few years later, however, his agents secretly kidnapped Teng in Shanghai and took him to Nanking, where Chiang killed him. Chiang's *coup d'état* at Canton failed for the moment but he merely bided his time until he could reach Shanghai with the revolutionary army. He was appointed commander in chief of the Northern Expedition which was preparing to leave for the north in June or July. We made many mistakes in the Chinese revolution, and our dealing with Chiang Kai-shek in Canton in 1926 was one of them. Yet our party was young, weak, and inexperienced. We were merely one of a number of parties and groups in the national united front. Chiang's abortive coup, combined with other counter-revolutionary acts and outbreaks, alerted Chinese revolutionaries throughout the world. Many left for home and I hurried with my studies that I might be home by the time the Northern Expeditionary Army against warlordism and foreign imperialism got under way in July. For the next three or four months I studied almost night and day."

One evening in mid-June General Chu left his books and documents and joined a group of nine other Chinese with whom he went to a mass meeting on China in the Sports Palace in Berlin. By a special decree of the German government, no Chinese could take part in such a meeting, but there was nothing to hinder them from sitting in an audience and listening to what was said.

After the meeting, when they were leaving the hall, Chu Teh's group was suddenly surrounded by police, arrested and driven off in a Black Maria to Alexanderplatz police jail, where they were locked up for ten days while the authorities tried to find some law under which to hold them.

"I had been arrested twice before, but each time released," General Chu said, smiling a little. "This new arrest did not worry me. I was merely curious to learn what imprisonment was really like. The jail was calm and peaceful, and since I had been working very hard for months I used the time to catch up on sleep. Each morning a guard entered my little cell and placed a tin cup of thin coffee and a chunk of black bread on the table. After eating it, I exercised, sang a few songs to pass the time, and went back to sleep. At noon and at night the guard again entered and placed a plate of black beans and a chunk of black bread on the table and withdrew.

"So it went for ten days, when we were all brought to court, asked to show our passports and answer a few simple questions. The police judge then informed us that we were troublemakers and that we were ordered to get out of Germany within twenty-four hours.

"The Chinese ambassador intervened and got the orders of expulsion lifted from eight of our group, but not against myself and another comrade. We two had been arrested before and were suspected of having had a hand in preparing the big mass meeting. Of course, all of us had had a hand in it! The Chinese ambassador, however, told us that the British government had secretly demanded that we be expelled from Germany, and the German government complied.

"I was already prepared to leave for China, and I had just enough money left to buy a third-class railway ticket to Shanghai by way of the Soviet Union. My comrade also ordered to leave Germany went home by way of France, while I took my three trunks of books, maps and documents and set sail from Stettin for Leningrad."

As his boat nosed its way through the Baltic, General Chu paced the deck and tried to summarize his experiences in the preceding four years. He was a very different man from the one who had left China in 1922. Though worried about the counter-revolutionary outbursts in China, he was now totally free of the pessimism and confused despair that had once held him a prisoner. He felt that he had learned a lot about Germany and, through his associates and studies, about other Western countries. Above all, his years of studies with Chinese Communists in Germany had given him an explanation of why past Chinese revolutions had been aborted and how the present revolution could be saved. The alliance of the revolutionary intellectuals with the masses of workers and peasants was the key to China's future victory.

Basic in his new knowledge, he said, was the great law of the movement of history as defined by Engels and according to which all political, religious, philosophic or other ideological struggles are expressions of the struggle of social classes. "This knowledge of the law of the movement of history, combined with my other studies and experiences, gave me the key of understanding to Chinese history, both past and present," he declared.

Not only General Chu Teh, but other Chinese from every part of the world, were winging their anxious way homeward to take part in the decisive struggle against warlordism and imperialist control of their country. Because of the danger signals in China, he was now glad that he had kept his membership in the Communist Party a secret from all but his party comrades, and that he was known generally only as a Kuomintang member. The Canton revolutionary government was trying to neutralize or win over some of the less obnoxious minor warlords, and he felt that he might be of some service with his former military colleagues. In 1922, he remembered, General Yang Sen of Szechwan, once a 1911 revolutionary, had urged him to join his staff. Who could say— perhaps he could now play a political as well as military role in the new revolutionary wave facing China? But this time he would be able to avoid the mistakes which had filled so many years of his earlier life. He was forty years of age but felt that he was just beginning his revolutionary career.

Book V

On the Great Revolution

Chapter 15

IN MID-JULY 1926, Chu Teh was cautiously making his way through the International Settlement of Shanghai toward the adjoining Chinese city of Chapei, where the All-China Labor Federation and the Communist and Kuomintang parties maintained their concealed headquarters. He had already conferred once with Chen Tu-hsiu, Secretary-General of the Communist Party, who had asked him to return for a conference with a group of Nationalist (Kuomintang) and Communist Party members in charge of military intelligence. The southern revolutionary army had already left Canton on the Northern Expedition and Chu Teh's long connections with the militarists would be of value.

As he passed through the streets, Chu speculated on the great changes that had come over China within the past four years. The foreigners, once contemptuous of the Nationalists, were now filled with fear and hatred. The army of the Canton revolutionary government was called "Bolshevik hordes," and "forces of anarchy and discord." Chiang Kai-shek, commander in chief of the Northern Expedition, was called a "Bolshevik" and the instrument of his Russian military advisers. The Chinese press in the International Settlement and French Concession of Shanghai was rigidly censored, mass meetings or even small gatherings were forbidden, and Chinese homes were being raided and men dragged off to jail.

Passing through the streets, Chu smiled a little when he saw British police officers cursing as they scratched Nationalist posters off telephone poles. Further on he saw other officers directing Chinese policemen who with brushes and paint buckets were whitewashing Nationalist slogans off walls. Each day the slogans were washed off or painted over, but each morning the walls of the city were decorated with them again. Slogans were chalked on sidewalks, on the windows of business houses, and even on foreign motor cars.

Four years before, when he left China, the Chinese people had accepted the supremacy of the white man, and poor men cringed when foreigners pushed them off the sidewalk. Now the Chinese walked proudly with squared shoulders and looked the foreigner in the face. Labor unions were still illegal, yet the factory workers were organized, and wages had increased. Each cent of increased wages had cost the lives of men, women, and children. Chinese had died at foreign hands in many cities of China since Chu Teh had left the country but a new nation had arisen over their dead bodies. And now the final struggle against warlordism and foreign domination seemed at hand.

Reaching his destination in Chapei, Chu Teh passed through the front door of one house, went out at the back, walked through another and another, and finally reached the room where a group of men awaited him. Leaving them later he returned to the International Settlement and began the work assigned him. Some of his old Yunnan friends were still in the city. Seeking them out, he began collecting information about the warlord armies. Some of them introduced him to staff officers of warlord Sun Chuan-fang in Nanking. He talked for hours with them. The officers had loose tongues when talking with a military man whom they took for one of themselves. The British were supporting General Sun with ammunition and with money to finance his army of mercenaries who fought for nothing but their rice.

The general military situation at the time, as explained by General Chu, was like this:

The old Peking government was now controlled by the Manchurian warlord, Chang Tso-lin, a onetime bandit who had become master of his native Manchuria with the help of Japanese imperialism.

Shantung Province in the north was ruled by General Chang Tsung-chang, "another Japanese running dog," noted for his size and savagery, his wealth and concubines, as well as for the czarist regiments in his army. Chang was a man who received foreign diplomatic officials while in bed with a concubine or with one perched on his knee. A "rebel-killer," Chang was proud of his fifty concubines of many nationalities. He had, in fact, once walked into the roof garden of a big foreign hotel in Peking, followed by a platoon of concubines walking single file behind him.

Shansi Province in the northwest was ruled as a small medieval kingdom by General Yen Hsi-shan, who always allied himself with any warlord strong enough to hold Peking. If he ever felt strong enough, Yen would also try to make himself master of the capital.

The Yangtze River valley, which British interests regarded as their bailiwick, was ruled by two warlords, both supported by Britain. The lower Yangtze, including Shanghai and Nanking, and the provinces adjoining the river to the south, were ruled by General Sun Chuan-fang, while both sides of the river to the west and up to Szechwan were the stamping ground of General Wu Pei-fu, deposed head of the Peking government who was nevertheless allied with the new rulers. Wu's subordinate, General Tang Sheng-chi, ruled Hunan Province to the south but was dickering with the Nationalists. Wu was the most powerful of all the warlords. His headquarters was in Wuhan—the triple cities of Hankow, Wuchang, and Hanyang. He therefore controlled the greatest arsenal in China, that in Hanyang.

Szechwan Province in the west was still held by the two warlords, Liu Hsiang and Yang Sen, but Yang had been squeezed out of Chungking by his ally and now, with an army of about a hundred thousand men, made his headquarters in Wanhsien and fed on all eastern Szechwan. Weakened by his onetime ally, he had allied himself for protection with warlord Wu Pei-fu in the Yangtze valley.

General Yang Sen was the same man who had once been Chu Teh's comrade in the old Yunnan revolutionary army, but had broken away and set up business for himself as a warlord. Before leaving for Europe, Chu Teh had been assured by Yang that upon his return he would always find a position waiting for him on Yang's staff. Chu and his comrades now discussed this old connection and decided that he was the one person who might prevent Yang from entering the war against the national revolutionary army.

By the end of July, Chu had finished his work in Shanghai and Nanking and was on a boat bound for Szechwan. On his way, he was to stop at Hankow and perform a certain mission, before proceeding farther.

Landing in Hankow in early August, Chu found the city under martial law with Wu Pei-fu's troops patrolling the streets night and day, searching restaurants and teahouses every hour, and shooting down anyone who ran or resisted search. Marines from British warships in the Yangtze were guarding the British Concession and frisking every Chinese who entered or left. Terror hung over the city and the hatred was so thick that it could be cut with a knife.

Walking with all the arrogant confidence of a rich man above the law, Chu passed through the streets without being searched, entered a Chinese bank and left a letter for the secretary of the local Communist Party who was the chief labor leader in Hupeh Province. Next day he met this labor leader, together with a number of Kuomintang and Communist Party members in charge of military affairs and the workers' movement in the Wuhan cities. He had brought these men a dangerous order: as the southern revolutionary army drew near, they were to lead a general strike, paralyze communications, and the Hanyang arsenal workers were to seize and hold the arsenal for the revolutionary army.

His mission in Hankow completed, General Chu resumed his journey and a few days later landed at Wanhsien in eastern Szechwan. At General Yang Sen's headquarters, he presented his credentials as the representative of the Kuomintang to Yang.

"Yang received me as if I were his closest and oldest friend," General Chu said with a grim expression. "I had no illusions. Like all militarists, he was willing to join the side that paid the most, and he thought I had come to offer him money. Almost at once he began talking about his need of money to pay his troops, which garrisoned all eastern Szechwan where they levied taxes on the people and imposed transit duties on all goods passing through his territory. This was the system of all warlords at the time and he had plenty of money. British and other foreign ships navigating the Yangtze claimed extraterritorial rights, and Chinese merchants had begun using such foreign ships to evade paying the transit duties. Yang's customs officials inspected all such vessels for Chinese goods."

General Yang assured and reassured Chu Teh that he was very anxious to join the Nationalist cause but that he must have money to pay his troops. How much would the Kuomintang give him? After all, he argued boldly, Moscow was financing the Nationalist movement.

When Chu declared that he had brought no money and that Moscow was not financing the Nationalist movement, Yang thought he was only bargaining.

"All I can offer you is the certainty that our side will win and that if you fight, instead of joining us, you will have no future whatever," Chu told him.

Yang remained unimpressed and continued waiting to see which side would win. Day by day Chu talked with him about the Nationalist movement and day by day news of revolutionary victories kept pouring in. The Northern Expedition was rolling along, its way paved by the peasants and workers who rose in their millions. After futile fighting, General Tang Sheng-chi, warlord Wu's subordinate in Hunan Province, went over to the Nationalists. In the north, General Feng Yu-hsiang, who had joined the Kuomintang two years before, was leading his Kuo Min Chun, or People's Army, against the northern warlords. General Feng had become a Christian and had been the pride of missionaries who had fondly christened him "the Christian General." However, after Feng joined the Nationalists, the missionaries and other foreigners began referring to him contemptuously as "the so-called Christian General."

News of the great mass movement in south China worried Yang Sen even more than the defection of local militarists who, he knew, had their own plans. Peasant Leagues were spreading like flames across the south and barefoot peasants with big dirty hands were chasing the landlords to the great cities where the workers struck and chased them up and down the Yangtze. Such things were enough to scare any warlord, for they also were great landowners.

Yet Yang Sen did not send troops to support his ally Wu Pei-fu. In early September came the news of the general strike in Wuhan. The workers arose and fought and died, but the revolutionary army crossed the Yangtze, occupied Hankow and Hanyang and laid siege to the great walled city of Wuchang, which soon fell. The Fourth Nationalist Army, known as the "Ironsides," had written its name on the walls of the Wuhan city and on the walls of every city in south China, and one of its commanders, the Communist Yeh Ting, was now garrison commander of Hankow and was arming the workers. Other names of commanders, both high and low, in the Ironsides, were becoming household words in the homes of workers and peasants—names like Ho Lung, Lin Piao, Chen Yi and Nieh Jung-chen—and the names of such political leaders as Mao Tse-tung and Chou En-lai.

Even after the Ironsides took Wuhan, Yang Sen still dickered and wavered, and Chu Teh soon learned the reason. Landlords and industrialists fleeing from Hunan and the Wuhan cities had reached his headquarters with rumors of widespread conflict within the ranks of the Northern Expeditionary Army. Many officers in that army, they told Yang, were themselves landowners or the sons of landowners, or members of industrialist families. They had not joined the Northern Expedition in order to have lazy peasants who had never worn shoes and could not read and write seize and confiscate their land or other property. Peasant Leagues had sprung up everywhere and had taken over the villages, and some of them had even confiscated and divided the land. The Kuomintang government was opposed to such methods, but the peasants paid no attention to it. Chiang Kai-shek, commander in chief of the Northern Expedition, was fighting Communists and radical Kuomintang members over the Peasant Leagues and the labor unions, and was also demanding the suppression of the Political Departments in the army.

These "political workers" in the army, Yang was told, were a Russian importation and the center of all the trouble. They lectured the troops about all sorts of things, stirring up their fanaticism, and they spread out into the villages to help the peasants form leagues. Their voices were heard everywhere, stirring up the people and disturbing the social order.

It had come to such a pass that soldiers and peasants and workers thought themselves the equals of their betters and imagined they had all kinds of "rights."

What was worse, many of these "political workers" were women and girls who had shingled their hair and put on military uniforms like men. Never in Chinese history had there been such scandalous sights as girl students from respectable families marching with common soldiers and giving them wild ideas.

But all this sort of thing would soon end. The Nationalist army was torn to pieces by conflict and Chiang Kai-shek himself was demanding the end of the alliance with the Soviet Union whose advisers were responsible for the whole debacle. Sun Yat-sen had adopted the Three Policies calling for cooperation with the Communist Party, alliance with the Soviet Union, and promotion of the worker and peasant movements. But, reported the landlords, most "respectable" leaders of the Kuomintang were opposed to these policies and it was only a matter of time until they were put aside. Then the whole revolutionary movement would fizzle, and law and order would be restored.

Just at this critical moment, General Chu said, a British steamer came up the Yangtze and anchored before Wanhsien and, as was the custom, General Yang Sen's customs officials went out to inspect. As the customs boat approached the steamer, it was met with a hail of fire from the ship. The boat was sunk and all the men in it killed.

Furious, Yang Sen ordered his troops to occupy the vessel, which they did after considerable fighting in which a number of men on both sides were killed. From the time this incident began, Chu Teh and Yang Sen stood shoulder to shoulder, Chu advising Yang and Yang listening.

Negotiations for a settlement began, but, while they were going on, two British gunboats came up the river and tried to take the steamer by force. When they met resistance they turned their guns on Wanhsien and bombarded the city for two hours without pause. Yang Sen's shore batteries replied but at the end of two hours five thousand Chinese had been killed and Wanhsien was a sheet of flames. The British then seized the cargo vessel, threw the Chinese troops into the river, and steamed away.

News of the "Wanhsien incident" flamed through all China. The Nationalist government issued a blistering proclamation against this new British outrage, people's organizations of every kind did the same, and the Communist Party put out a manifesto recounting British crimes.

From his files of historical documents which he had collected and preserved for many years, General Chu brought out the creased sheet of paper on which the Communist Party manifesto was printed, and a part of which read:

The British have tried many previous provocations. Apart from the Shanghai, Hankow, and Canton massacres, at the beginning of the Northern Expedition British troops landed at Wuchow in Kwangsi and arrested Chinese engaged in the anti-British boycott. . . . When the Northern Expedition reached Wuhan, British gunboats openly helped Wu Pei-fu by bombarding our army. . . . On September 4th British gunboats anchored before Canton, arrested Chinese pickets, detained private boats, and by violence moved British goods into the city. . . . The Wanhsien bombardment was the fourth act of intervention against China. . . .

British imperialism has not only utilized every method to disturb the rear of the Northern Expeditionary Army, but has adopted every means to support the defeated Wu Pei-fu. They are also supporting Sun Chuanfang by giving him $10,000,000 in cash and 20,000,000 rounds of ammunition to prolong the power of the northern warlords and create internal disturbances. While supporting General Sun they are also proposing international armed intervention in China. The British Mediterranean Fleet has already arrived in Canton.

The manifesto ended with a call to the Chinese people to "destroy the very roots of British economic structure in China," and to give united and unwavering support to the Northern Expedition.

The one "positive result" of the Wanhsien incident, General Chu said, was that it forced General Yang into the revolutionary camp. After the fires had been put out and the dead buried, Yang sent Chu Teh to Hankow to pledge allegiance to the Nationalist army.

Arriving in Hankow, Chu saw the great hulks of British warships in the Yangtze, their threatening guns trained on the Wuhan cities, while British bluejackets glowered from behind their barricades in the British Concession at Chinese pickets or marching columns of students and workers who threw their arms into the air as they shouted:

"Avenge Wanhsien! Boycott British goods! Take back foreign concessions robbed from China! Uproot British imperialism!"

Hankow was a seething cauldron of emotions. Hope and fierce determination mingled with hate, and the people had no fear. A thousand workers had been armed and trained to maintain order while other thousands, unarmed, enforced the anti-British boycott. There were frequent demonstrations in which workers and students marched in long columns, holding banners aloft, singing songs and shouting slogans.

Watching them, sensing the laden atmosphere, General Chu recalled the 1911 Revolution when the world seemed young, newly born, and Chinese youth felt that it could move mountains and change the course of rivers. This revolution was different, he speculated, for workers and peasants provided its base. Yet the ghosts of past betrayals from within haunted him as he moved about Wuhan, listening to whispers and rumors, hearing a report here, reading an article in the press there. The old warlords had always been a danger, he knew, but now new ones seemed to be arising from within the ranks of the revolution itself.

Himself from the peasantry, he kept his eyes on the peasant movement which had burst like a mighty flood over south China and, together with the infant labor movement, was frightening high officers in the national revolutionary army who themselves were landlords or from landlord or merchant and compradore families.

General Chu remembered reading a number of articles on the peasant movement written by Mao Tse-tung, the man who was soon to become his alter ego and with whom his life thereafter became so intertwined that for years the public often thought them one man by the name of Chu Mao.

This man, Mao Tse-tung, was an educated peasant who had fought as a soldier in the 1911 Revolution, had played a leading role in the May 4th Movement in his native Hunan Province, had founded the first Marxian study group and later the first Communist Party group in that province. Mao had been a delegate to the First Congress that founded the Chinese Communist Party on July 1, 1921. A strangely erudite man given to profound speculation, Mao had been a newspaper and magazine editor, an essayist, a poet, and in 1925 had laid the foundation for the first underground peasant movement in his province. He had joined Sun Yat-sen's Canton government where he had organized the first training school for peasant leaders and had been elected to the Central Executive Committee of the Kuomintang.

The peasant movement, founded in Kwangtung Province by Sun Yat-sen, had seeped over into neighboring Hunan Province where, inspired by its Kwangtung brothers, it had taken the form of Peasant Leagues and armed Peasant Self-Defense Corps. Both before and after the Northern Expedition, the landlords and local militarists had fought it with all the savagery known to feudalism. There had been pitched battles in which thousands of peasants had died, there had been secret kidnappings and beheadings of peasant organizers and leaders, and the landlords had made a practice of calling in bandits from the hills to burn villages and slaughter peasants in the dark of the night.

When the Northern Expedition emerged from Kwangtung onto the Hunan plains, the peasants arose as it approached, disarmed the landlord militia, or Min Tuan, took over their villages and put the landlords to flight. Despite the Kuomintang program of land reforms—reduction of rent and the abolition of usury—many Peasant Leagues had confiscated and divided the land as had peasants in every revolutionary upsurge in Chinese history. By the time General Chu reached Wuhan, two million peasants in Hunan Province alone belonged to Peasant Leagues. With their families they represented at least ten million peasants, or half the peasant population of the province.

Reading Mao Tse-tung's articles on this mighty upsurge, General Chu seemed to see the clear outlines of possible future calamity. The peasant movement, like the labor unions, was meeting with fierce resistance not only from the old social forces, but from many high officers within the revolutionary army, including its commander in chief, Chiang Kai-shek, and in many places rightist Kuomintang leaders had arrested and imprisoned peasant leaders.

The issue had come to a head when the Ironsides Fourth Army took the Wuhan cities where the workers had risen to pave the way for its advance. By now some 300,000 industrial workers, or about half those in the triple cities, had already been organized by Communists into labor unions. The Kuomintang was on the horns of a dilemma. Revolutionary victories had been made possible by the labor and peasant movement which, in turn, threatened the leadership of the Kuomintang.

The Nationalist government was being moved from Canton to Hankow. The Kuomintang Central Committee which guided that government had already arrived, and its leading members were in secret conference with Chiang Kai-shek who was demanding that the mass movement be held in check, if not disbanded outright.

Chiang Kai-shek had many other demands on the Kuomintang. The Political Department in the army, which was the arm of the Kuomintang civilian power over the military, was a thorn in the side of Chiang and many other generals. Political commissars in the army were something like vice-commanders who had the right to approve or disapprove of military orders. The system, introduced by Sun Yat-sen on the advice of his Russian advisers, was designed to prevent the development of militarism which, in the past, had enabled individual generals to use their armies as private property and to become warlords. The staffs of political workers in the ranks of the army had the duty of educating the troops not only in general subjects but about the program, policies and goal of the revolution. Political workers also mobilized the peasants and workers to support the Northern Expedition, thus calling up mighty forces that threatened the feudal social order. Most such political workers both inside and outside the army were Communist or left-wing Kuomintang members.

Chiang Kai-shek was therefore demanding that the mass movement be disbanded or "kept in its place," and that the Political Department in the army be completely abolished because, General Chu heard, Chiang held that it interfered with military orders. Chiang further maintained that the mass movement, plus the political commissar system, plus the Communist Party, was of Russian origin and was therefore alien to the Chinese national essence. He therefore singled out Michael Borodin, the chief Russian political adviser, as the source of all evil and as his chief enemy. Behind Borodin, he held, hovered the shadow of the Communist International—which he had once hailed as the hope of the oppressed of the world.

Neither at that time nor later did Chu Teh ever place much emphasis on the Russian advisers, of whom there were many in the revolutionary army attached to the various army headquarters. He had never seen any of them and even later saw only two, and those at a distance when they were with Chiang Kai-shek. It was a period of great internal strife and confusion in which new and old militarists marched and countermarched across the national scene, changing sides time and again or juggling for power. He heard vague reports of conflicts between the Communist International and its representatives in China, and he even heard that Borodin and the leaders of the Communist Party of China—chief of them Chen Tu-hsiu—opposed the policy of the Communist International. A demand had arisen in Wuhan—a demand supported by Chu Teh also —that the workers and peasants be armed to save the revolution from threatened betrayal from within. What the policy of the Communist International was at the time he did not know, but the Chinese Communist leaders, supported by Borodin, refused to allow the workers and peasants to be armed lest such an action split the united front with the Kuomintang. They feared that this split might again bring feudalism and imperialism to the top.

Regardless of anything the Russian advisers might or might not suggest, General Chu added his voice to the chorus demanding that the masses be armed. In all his talks about this confused period in Chinese history, he concentrated on the land problem and the peasant movement which he considered basic to the revolutionary struggle. Chu Teh was one of the millions of Chinese who felt that the problems of China could be solved by the Chinese alone. He knew that whatever the Russians might advise, the revolution was not a Russian machination. The 1911 Revolution had not been a Russian machination, nor were the 1913 and 1915 revolutionary upsurges—a statement which he sometimes repeated as he continued talking of his life. The Russians, he said, had helped China by giving it a method of struggle. Nor, he declared, did Chiang Kai-shek object to foreign advice or even to foreign interference in Chinese affairs, as his later actions so eloquently proved. His desire "was that foreigners intervene on behalf of himself and his class."

Arriving in Wuhan in that early winter of 1926, Chu, however, had a specific mission to perform. He had been sent to Szechwan to neutralize General Yang Sen's army or to draw it into the national struggle. He had fulfilled his mission and had now come to pledge the allegiance of that army to the national revolution. He therefore tried to see Chiang Kai-shek, but found that the commander in chief was "so busy with his own plots" that he had no interest in such matters. Chu went to meet his old friend, Teng Yen-da, who was chairman of the Political Directorate of the army, from whom he learned that Chiang was not only demanding the suppression of the mass movement, but was insisting on his own military strategy as against the strategy of the Central Committee of the Kuomintang.

The Central Committee of the Kuomintang, together with the chief leaders of the Nationalist government, were insisting that the Northern Expedition continue its northward march until it had conquered and taken over the Peking warlord government. After that Shanghai, the stronghold of foreign imperialism, would fall to it almost automatically. Chiang insisted that first Shanghai be occupied, after which the Northern Expedition could continue.

Chiang's strategy was a "plot," General Chu said. Shanghai was his old stamping ground, the imperialist stronghold where he had once been a stock exchange gambler and where he had joined the underworld Green Gang whose leaders were enormously wealthy men, traffickers in opium and white slaves and gamblers indulging in every form of racketeering. The Shanghai compradore class were the go-betweens, brokers between foreign and native capital. Often landlords and bureaucrats, such men were intricately linked with foreign imperialism. Through their connections they had become rich merchants, factory owners, bankers, and agents for foreign firms in recruiting indentured workers to man foreign factories. These compradores together with their foreign masters, plus the Green Gang which served the compradores and foreign imperialism as hatchet men, were the social forces upon which Chiang Kai-shek could depend.

Talking with Teng Yen-da about these treacherous undercurrents, Chu Teh felt overcome with his old pessimism. From such despairing fears he reached out and clung like a drowning man to the revolutionary social theories which he had studied in Europe. The Chinese people alone could save China, he told himself, the Communist Party was the party of the poor. Although guided by revolutionary theory, it was nevertheless young and inexperienced and was, at the time, intoxicated by easy victories. In the vast human sea of China it had no more than fifty thousand members. Still fewer were the members of the Young Communist League, and there had been no time in which to train them.

The Communist Party's leaders, he declared with bitterness, were trailing along under the leadership of the Kuomintang merely because the Kuomintang held power, instead of asserting its own leadership on basic revolutionary issues. This "right opportunist" policy, as he called it, was the work of the party's secretary, Chen Tu-hsiu, who was an intellectual and a brilliant cultural leader but a man with no understanding of the land problem and the agrarian revolution. Chu added that Chen repeatedly defeated Mao Tse-tung's demands for a "broadening and deepening of the agrarian revolution and the arming of the peasants and workers." In the Fifth Congress of the Communist Party held in Wuhan in May 1927, he even refused to allow Mao's agrarian program to come up for discussion.

Chu apparently ignored the influence of the Russian advisers on Chen. He resolutely held to his thesis that the Chinese revolution had to be fought by Chinese on pure Chinese issues.

Chu himself was a man of little importance at the time. He had a job to do. Even if he did not believe in the success of this job, he was a man who would never give up unless the ground was washed out from beneath his feet. Teng Yen-da not only accepted the allegiance of General Yang Sen's army to the Nationalist cause, but ordered Chu to recruit a staff of thirty or forty political workers and take them back with him to Szechwan to introduce the political commissar system into Yang's army.

General Chu left with his political staff just as Chiang Kai-shek, again triumphant over the Kuomintang Central Committee, went down river to carry out his own plan for occupying Nanking and Shanghai. Arriving in Wanhsien, Chu Teh went at once to General Yang's headquarters and presented the official documents that brought the warlord's army into the Nationalist fold and that appointed Chu the official Kuomintang delegate, or political commissar. In amazement Yang looked on Chu's staff of forty political workers. He was still more amazed to learn that these men were henceforth to educate his commanders and troops in Kuomintang principles.

"Where's the money?" he asked Chu when they were alone. He smiled a little when told that there was no money, that the Nationalist government was fighting a revolutionary war, and that Yang received enough revenues to care for his own armed forces.

Again the long arguments about money began and again Chu explained the great financial problems of the revolution, adding that he and his staff, like all other members of the Nationalist army, received nothing but a minimum maintenance allowance. The arguments lasted the entire night following the receipt by Yang of an order from the Nationalist government to move his troops against warlord Wu Pei-fu and help the Ironsides drive him from Hupeh Province.

As for those political workers, Yang Sen declared, he could see no earthly use for them in his army. His soldiers needed no political education, for the simple reason that a soldier's duty was to obey orders and to die on the field of battle. What purpose would it serve for such men to begin acting like scholars, talking about things that were none of their concern? All this talk about democracy and improvement in the people's livelihood would lead to nothing but insubordination or open subversion. Nor did he intend to permit Peasant Leagues and labor unions to stir up trouble as they had in south China.

"Because of the military order from Hankow," General Chu said, "I had to compromise about the political workers, and even about the military order I was uncertain. Yang Sen finally agreed to allow my political staff to teach in his Military Training School where lower commanders were under training, but forbade them to teach anything but nationalism. They could say nothing about the other principles of Sun Yat-sen and nothing about his policies.

"When I had compromised to this extent, he began to find excuses why he should not move troops and help the Ironsides drive Wu Pei-fu's mercenaries from Hupeh. He finally moved a division of troops near Ichang, where they stopped, though Wu had a garrison so weak that we could have washed it into the Yangtze by merely spitting. Yang would not even spit. Instead, he began confiding in me that Wu Pei-fu was his old friend who had helped him build up his position in Szechwan, and that one couldn't fight a good friend."

Knowing the ways of warlords, Chu sought out a staff officer with whom he had established friendship and held a number of lengthy conversations with him. During Chu's absence in Wuhan, Yang had been holding secret conferences with representatives of Wu Pei-fu. A few days later this staff officer stealthily entered Chu's room at night, asked him to show no light, but to listen carefully. Yang Sen, he said, had agreed to throw in his lot with Wu Pei-fu once more and, with Wu, to march on the Wuhan cities. As a prelude to this step, he had also decided to murder Chu and his entire political staff.

Before the night was out, Chu had assembled and led his political staff out of Wanhsien and down over the mountain fastnesses toward Wuhan. Arriving in the Nationalist capital ten days later, Chu Teh wired back to Yang Sen:

"I warn you that if you try to fight us we will completely destroy you."

But Yang Sen didn't really wish to fight anyone, least of all an army that had already carved its name on the walls of all the cities of south China. The Ironsides attacked warlord Wu at once, drove him out of Hupeh and, in a confused battle in Hunan Province in which it also had heavy losses, broke his back forever. During this struggle, Yang Sen did not move a soldier to help his "old friend," but merely turned tail and fled back to his old feeding ground in Szechwan.

During the tragically confused months that followed, the Ironsides returned to the Wuhan cities, Chiang Kai-shek betrayed the revolution at Shanghai, the Hankow Nationalist government collapsed, and many of its leading Kuomintang members crept down the river to Chiang's camp. Yang Sen, too, allied himself with Chiang and, watching the disintegrating Wuhan government, swooped down on the villages and towns of Hupeh Province. Prowling from village to village like a lean and mangy leopard, he began killing every peasant who belonged to a Peasant League, every worker who had joined a labor union, and every girl who had bobbed her hair. Peasant heads were mounted on poles before recalcitrant villages, men and women were buried alive in mass graves, homes were completely stripped, and the night was made hideous with the running feet of the poor who had dared dream of liberty. The carnage cost Yang nothing because the people had not been armed and by then the Ironsides were far away, fighting in Kiangsi Province for the revolution.

Chapter 16

THE Ironsides was Chu Teh's love and he never spoke of it without emotion. When the Northern Expedition left Canton in mid-1926, it had 60,000 men, and by the time it reached Wuhan it had 200,000. The Ironsides, then known as the Fourth Army, left Canton with two divisions and one independent regiment, but when reorganized in Hankow at the end of the year into three armies it numbered 400,000 men.

Thousands of the new adherents to the Northern Expeditionary force were defeated troops from the old militarist armies that went over. This explained such later incidents as the looting and killing of a number of foreigners by Chiang Kai-shek's troops when they took Nanking. The new recruits to the Ironsides, however, were peasants or workers whom General Chu referred to as "uprising peasants and workers," or insurrectionists. Upon reaching Wuhan, thousands of printers, miners, Hanyang arsenal and other skilled workers had joined it.

The Ironsides was the most class-conscious, best trained and disciplined of all the Nationalist armies. Even its original forces, recruited in Canton, were Hongkong strikers and Canton industrial workers, while most of its officers, its young ones in particular, were Communists or Communist sympathizers who had been trained in the Whampoa Military Academy. Its Political Department was staffed almost exclusively with Communists. Clad with an armor of political conviction, the Ironsides had shattered all enemies in its way, called on the workers and peasants to rise, and cast confusion and terror among the feudal gentry and the warlords.

Its commander in chief, General Chang Fa-kwei, was a follower of the then leftist Kuomintang leader, Wang Ching-wei—chairman of the Nationalist government after Dr. Sun Yat-sen's death. General Chang regarded the Ironsides as his personal army to be placed at the disposal of Wang. His Communist subordinates regarded themselves as the instruments of nothing less than The Revolution itself.

When reorganized in Wuhan at the end of 1926, one of the armies in the Ironsides—the Fourth—was commanded by General Chang's follower, Hwang Chi-hsiang, while the other two, the Eleventh and Twentieth, were commanded by Communists, General Yeh Ting and General Ho Lung.

Yeh Ting was the thoughtful and reserved son of a well-to-do Hongkong family which sent him abroad, at his request, to study physics and chemistry. Giving up his scientific career to join the revolution, Yeh returned to China to join Dr. Sun Yat-sen. In 1922 he had rescued Dr. Sun's wife, Soong Ching-ling, from death at the hands of the local warlord who, at British instigation, overthrew the Canton republican government. Yeh Ting joined the Whampoa Military Academy after its establishment in 1923, became a Communist and a commander in the Ironsides during the Northern Expedition.

The other Communist commander, Ho Lung, was even then one of

China's most colorful personalities. The very mention of his name always brought a grin to the lips of his friends and comrades. During the war-lord years, Ho, a poor and illiterate peasant, seemed to have gained the idea that since almost everyone had become a warlord he might as well become one himself. His kind of warlordism, however, differed in that he raised an army of poor peasants like himself and chased out the land-lords of western Hunan, thereby winning the title of "bandit."

Most of his family seems to have been born as perpetual motion ma-chines. Even his elder sister, a big-footed woman almost as tall as himself who had been a laborer on the estate of a landlord, commanded a unit of his troops. In the '30s, at the age of forty-eight, she died with a gun in her hands while leading her troops in battle.

Ho Lung was a member of the ancient peasant secret society, the Ko Lao Hui, and was said to have held its highest title of Double-headed Dragon. In his youth he looked like a cross between a Taiping rebel and some central Asian chieftain of ancient times, and every inch of him, even in his forties, was Double-headed Dragon. Tall and powerful, he had no fear of man, ghost, or beast, so that landlords packed up and fled if his name was so much as mentioned. Before capturing a place, Ho had the uncomfortable habit of spreading rumors that he was miles away, then knocking on a landlord's door and saying with a grin:

"Well, here I am!"

The legends about him were legion, many of them perfectly true. His troops and friends could sit for hours listening to his humorous and dramatic tales of adventure. As a conqueror of women he was said to have had few peers, and to watch him striding across a field of wheat stubble was like watching the lithe movements of a panther. He paid no attention to military form and when once asked why he said he had only a regiment of men when he had thirty thousand, he threw back his head and, roaring with laughter, said:

"I can't count!"

When Dr. Sun Yat-sen founded the Canton revolutionary government in 1924, Ho Lung placed himself and his army at Sun's command, and immediately applied for membership in the Communist Party, which just as quickly rejected him. A brigade commander in the Ironsides during the Northern Expedition, he was made commander of the Twentieth Army at the end of 1926. Periodically he applied for membership in the Communist Party and periodically he was refused until, after his tenth application, the party grew weary and decided that the best way to dis-cipline if not to tame him was to take him in. A few hundred Wuhan workers were incorporated in his army to train his peasant troops politically. While he was in Hankow, he also received a few hundred peasants from the "East River Region" of Kwangtung Province who, under the leadership of the famous peasant leader, an intellectual and a landlord's son by the name of Peng Pei, had marched across the continent to join the Ironsides.

Peng Pei himself had a name to conjure with. As the first peasant organizer in the East River Region, Peng had begun the agrarian revolution by confiscating his own family's estate and dividing it among the peasants, an action which led them to believe him insane. They locked him up in their home, but the young man, inspired by Communist ideas, escaped to continue his organizing campaign. It was not until the early '30s that he was finally captured and killed in Shanghai by Chiang Kai-shek.

General Chu and his political staff of forty men fleeing from Yang Sen's army had reached Wuhan just after the Ironsides had been reorganized and was preparing to chase warlord Wu Pei-fu's mercenaries out of Hupeh Province. At the time, he said, about thirty percent of the soldiers in this army were Communists, and an all-permeating system of political education was drawing others in. That he had hoped to become a commander in the Ironsides there can be little doubt, but the Nationalist government appointed him, instead, as director of a new Military Training School which his old Yunnan Army had just established in Nanchang, capital of Kiangsi Province in the middle Yangtze River valley. The old Yunnan Army, renamed the Third Army, later again renamed the Fifth Route Army by Chiang Kai-shek, was now commanded by General Chu Pei-teh who still obeyed the Hankow Nationalist government but was leaning heavily toward the policies of Chiang Kai-shek. Since this army garrisoned all Kiangsi Province and had established its Training School at Nanchang, General Chu was ordered by the Hankow government to intensify the political training of the cadets who would be under his command.

The 1300 cadets in the new Military School were squad, platoon and company commanders who, during their eight-month course of study, were to serve as the Nanchang garrison and protect the mass movement against the sabotage of the right-wing Kuomintang. Chu Teh thus automatically became garrison commander of Nanchang. In addition, to unify all security organs, the government also appointed Chu Teh Nanchang's police commissioner. In addition Chu was also instructed to establish and direct a training school for the four hundred men of the Nanchang police force and train them to protect the mass movement. By virtue of his positions, Chu also became a member of the Nanchang Central Committee of the Kuomintang.

Since educated cadres, or trained personnel, in the revolutionary movement were too few to meet the national needs, each young Whampoa military cadet assigned to teach in the Nanchang Military Training School had to do the work of three men. While teaching in the school, they also had to lecture in both the Police Training School and in the Training School for the Peasant Movement which the Kuomintang established wherever it took over a region. Of these cadres, Chu Teh said, a number were Communists while others were left Kuomintang members. Their duties were to hold the ideological fort of the revolution.

The reactionaries in Nanchang were numerically weak but politically powerful because they were high army officers, officials, rich merchants or industrialists—and of these many were simultaneously landlords. As the internal conflicts over the mass movement grew, such men looked to Chiang Kai-shek rather than to the Hankow Nationalist government for leadership. As a member of the Central Committee of the Nanchang Kuomintang, Chu Teh was able to listen to their developing plans and to oppose their ceaseless campaign that the Peasant Leagues and labor unions be either suppressed or confined to supporting the military campaign. They were particularly opposed to the Peasant Training School in which some six hundred peasant men and a few women, drawn from the whole province, were under training as peasant leaders.

All the institutions under Chu Teh's direction taught the standard political subjects introduced by Sun Yat-sen before his death: methods of mass organization, the Three People's Principles and the Three Policies, the history of the revolution and something of the history and geography of China and of the world. The Military Training School devoted the major part of its time to military subjects, while the others devoted most of their time to political subjects, giving in addition some military training. The peasants were trained particularly in methods of mass organization.

Chu Teh said that he had no time even to think of personal matters while in Nanchang. From dawn to midnight he was engaged in administrative work of the Military and Police Training Schools and checking up on the work of his staff that taught in the Peasant School. He had to address these schools on special occasions and each Monday morning he conducted the memorial service to Sun Yat-sen in the Military Training School. There were meetings not only of the Kuomintang which he felt he had to attend but also Communist Party meetings where such problems as the organization and administration of special study groups of workers and students had to be solved.

Many of these Communist Party meetings were held in a room in the Peasant Training School, whose director was Fang Chih-ming. He was one of the ablest organizers and peasant leaders China had ever produced, an educated man and a mechanical engineer by profession. In the course of the May 4th Movement of 1919 in which he had been a leader, Fang had become a Communist. Chu described him as a tall, strong man about thirty years of age, a poor speaker in public and a man who was best at the conference table.

Of the 50,000 Communist Party members in the country and the 35,000 Communist Youth members, about a thousand were located in Nanchang and its environs. A few of these were students. Others were railway, dock, river, and pottery workers. The central theoretical organ of the party remained the old *Hsiang Tao*, or *Guide*, which Chu had first seen in Germany, but now did not always find time to read. Local party branches put out their own small newspapers, pamphlets and booklets, and established their own study clubs and schools.

Right-wing Kuomintang elements established secret organizations; in Nanchang they established the Sun Yat-sen Club. Once Dr. Sun was dead, men who had denounced his policies during his lifetime found his name a convenient cover. The rightist Kuomintang Sun Yat-sen Club in Nanchang soon became the secret general staff of the counter-revolution. Its members dared not come out in the open until the early months of 1927 when Chiang Kai-shek, in his march on Nanking and Shanghai, began suppressing Peasant Leagues and labor unions. The Yunnan Army in Kiangsi soon began doing the same, killing many labor and peasant leaders.

In mid-February 1927, the Nanchang reactionaries exposed their hand for the first time by paying gangsters, armed with clubs and iron bars, to attack a conference of labor delegates. A pitched battle was fought in the conference hall and in the street before it. Chu Teh arrested a number of gangsters. They excused their actions by declaring that they had acted on instructions from the members of the Sun Yat-sen Club.

One month after this incident, news came that General Liu Hsiang, warlord of Szechwan, had suppressed a revolutionary uprising in south Szechwan in which thousands of progressives had been put to death by the most barbarous methods. Two nephews of Chu Teh were among the slain. The uprising had been led by Liu Po-cheng, later known as the "One-eyed General," a onetime Szechwan militarist who had joined the revolution and become a Communist. Chu Teh had met Liu while in

Wanhsien and had even sent him into south Szechwan to organize the people in support of the revolution. He remembered the meeting well because Liu had walked into his office, plunked his Communist Party mandate on his table, walked over and given him a slap on the back that nearly felled him to the floor.

"Remember me?" Liu bellowed. "We met in south Szechwan years ago when I came from the Chengtu warlord to propose a dirty deal to the Protection Army against Yunnan and Kweichow!"

"Liu Po-cheng was a man who couldn't stand or sit still," General Chu said. "He told me how he had given up warlordism to join Sun Yat-sen, and how he had become a Communist. We talked the whole night through, each telling how he had searched for and finally found the Communist road. He had come to me for work in Yang Sen's army, but I sent him instead to south Szechwan, with letters to my wife and friends, to organize the revolutionary forces against Liu Hsiang. He had a native genius for organization and leadership. Within a few months he organized the progressive forces in all south Szechwan and led them in a great uprising against the warlord. Liu Hsiang threw in powerful forces which defeated him and slaughtered thousands, two of them my nephews who walked from Ta Wan to join him. Liu himself escaped and made his way to Hankow and later to Nanchang."

During this same dark period of revolutionary disintegration and mounting terror a special British expeditionary force, together with American, French and Japanese marines, landed at Shanghai, on which Chiang Kai-shek's armies were converging. On February 19th, three days after their landing, the Shanghai workers walked out in the first of three general strikes, all of them organized by Chou En-lai. General Sun Chuan-fang, warlord ruler in the lower Yangtze, struck with everything he had at the first and second general strikes, crushing them and beheading hundreds of workers as a bloody warning to others.

Undismayed, workers called their third general strike, which paralyzed the city in late March, as Chiang's forces drew near Shanghai. Spearheaded by three hundred men armed with pistols, the workers stormed police stations, garrison headquarters and, finally, the arsenal. With captured arms they fought and drove warlord Sun's troops from the entire Shanghai area, then sent out a delegation to welcome Chiang's troops to the city.

This writer was a friend of one of the members of this delegation. He was a railway engineer and had been a member of one of the workers' detachments that fought against a White Russian regiment in warlord Sun's army which was entrenched in the North Railway Station and along the railway. He had fought for one night and one day without rest, till the mercenaries were routed and driven out. As a member of the welcoming delegation to Chiang Kai-shek's armies, he had been jubilant. Upon reaching the headquarters of the advance Nationalist army, which happened to be from Kwangsi Province, he and his companions were thrown into confusion and consternation by the cold reception they received.

"The officers who received us listened to our speech of welcome. They just stared without replying one word," he said. "We had heard many rumors about the suppression of the workers' movement in territory occupied by Chiang's army, but we thought individual generals had been responsible for such acts. We thought reactionaries were spreading such rumors to split the united front. We had fought and thousands of our comrades had died, but Chiang's officers treated us like enemies. When we reported back to our Labor Federation headquarters, everyone was afraid but still we had guns in our hands and didn't think they would do anything against us."

Two days later, on March 24th, another branch of Chiang Kai-shek's force broke into Nanking and chased thousands of enemy troops through the city. As they fled, the enemy troops began looting, and soon Chiang's troops, many of whom had come over from the warlord armies, joined them. In the confusion that followed, the British and Japanese consulates and foreign homes were gutted. Six foreigners were killed and twelve wounded.

British and American gunboats immediately opened up on Nanking, bombarding until the disorders ceased, then sent marines ashore to escort foreign residents to the gunboats. Hundreds of Chinese were killed in the incident.

This "Nanking Incident," which threatened to unleash international armed intervention, was one of the numerous factors that induced Chiang Kai-shek finally to turn against the revolution. Chiang's course was already set, but now he could place blame for the Nanking Incident on the Communists whose political workers in his army, he declared, had been responsible for the outrages. The foreigners welcomed this interpretation, and both they and Chiang ignored the fact that the Ironsides, which was dominated almost completely by the Communists, was the most disciplined army in the country and had never engaged in looting or in physical attacks on foreigners.

General Chu Teh described the tragic aftermath of the Nanking Incident and the Shanghai general strike in these terms:

In the very midst of the Nanking Incident, Chiang Kai-shek landed

from a boat at Nanking but, instead of going into the city to restore
order, immediately changed to another boat and left for Shanghai where
he ordered the workers to surrender their arms, dissolve their pickets,
call off the general strike, and return to the factories. The workers, by
now thoroughly alarmed by menacing developments, refused. The Hankow Nationalist government had just published a decree proclaiming
that henceforth the military was subordinate to civilian authority. A
temporary civilian revolutionary government had already been established in Shanghai, and the workers declared that they would obey only
the orders of this government which in turn would receive its orders from
Hankow.

The workers had learned that Chiang Kai-shek, upon entering Shanghai, had at once entered into secret conferences with Chinese bankers,
factory owners, and the underworld Ching Pang (Green Gang), whose
members were rushing about between the headquarters of the French
Concession and International Settlement authorities. Chiang had entered
into no conversations with the revolutionary forces that had liberated
Shanghai. To them he gave nothing but peremptory orders to return to
their old servitude. The Green Gang, which consisted of tens of thousands
of thugs, opium traffickers, thieves, pimps and professional racketeers
linked with both the foreigners and Chinese reactionaries, was hated by
the workers and other revolutionary forces.

By this time, General Chu said, the web of international conspiracy
against the revolution stretched from every imperialist capital in the
world to Shanghai, and foreigners were already declaring that Chiang
Kai-shek was not a Bolshevik after all, but quite a good fellow. "The
foreigners enticed Chiang with one hand, while threatening international
armed intervention with the other."

Chiang's course had long since been charted, however. It was only
later that the full truth came out. Chinese bankers, backed by foreigners,
offered Chiang a loan, and foreign recognition, if he would break with
the revolution and establish his own military dictatorship. The extent
of this loan has been variously estimated from twenty-five to thirty
million dollars, but only in 1949 did this writer learn from the most
reliable foreign sources that the sum was, in reality, sixty million
Chinese dollars.

Conditions for this loan were that Chiang not only break with the
Hankow Nationalist government, but that he disarm the Shanghai
workers and drive them back to the factories, crush the Communists,
and break the Kuomintang alliance with the Soviet Union. It was not
until after World War II that some of the threads of this conspiracy

became definitely known. Chu Teh was convinced that foreign fingers were in the pie, but had no proof when he talked to me about it in 1937. However, after World War II, Mr. John B. Powell, owner and editor of the *China Weekly Review* of Shanghai, an enemy of the Communists and an all-out defender of Chiang Kai-shek, published his autobiography, *My Twenty-five Years in China,* in which such foreign participation was approvingly exposed.

Chiang Kai-shek knew that he could not depend upon the common soldiers in his own army to put down the Shanghai workers. He therefore had to depend on the underworld Green Gang, which had insufficient arms and ammunition for the job. Mr. Powell stated that Green Gang leaders, together with the French authorities of the French Concession, secured the active help of Mr. Stirling Fessenden, American chairman of the International Settlement. The Green Gang received five thousand additional rifles, with ammunition, and the right to pass through the International Settlement for an attack on the workers of the native city of Chapei, headquarters of the anti-militarist and anti-imperialist movement.

The Green Gang was to begin the carnage, after which Chiang's reluctant troops were to be told that the workers were rioting and murdering and that they were to go into action and restore law and order.

At midnight on April 12th, therefore, thousands of armed gangsters were allowed to pass unmolested through the International Settlement into Chapei. The foreign troops guarding the great gates that had been thrown up between the International Settlement and Chapei silently swung their doors open and the carnage began. The first attack was on the headquarters of the Shanghai Federation of Labor, where the chief labor leaders slept. All were murdered. After that the slaughter extended to every part of Chapei, while foreign police and detectives went on man hunts in the foreign concessions and turned their victims over to the gangsters.

Under cover of darkness, Chiang's troops were ordered into action to "put down the workers' uprising, the rioting and murder, and restore law and order." At the end of three days, some five thousand workers, left-wing Kuomintang and Communist Party members and non-party intellectuals had been slaughtered. Chu Teh's old friend, Sung Ping-wen, was among the slain. Chou En-lai, the organizer of the general strikes, was captured and delivered to a unit of the Kwangsi army, which allowed him to escape.

When the carnage was over, Chiang Kai-shek appointed the secretary of the chief Green Gang leader as secretary of the new, reorganized Federation of Labor. This same man was thereafter made Political Director of Chiang's army. Green Gang members, organized into battalions, were then sent out into the countryside and to towns and cities in the lower Yangtze River valley to repeat their acts of carnage.

The Central Committee of the Kuomintang at Hankow expelled Chiang from the party and stripped him of his command, but he merely organized his own Kuomintang, with himself as chairman, and his own military regime at Nanking. He received his loan, but it was two years before the imperialist powers granted him further loans, recognition, and sent him advisers to supervise the many departments of his government. The foreigners made him work for his money, and work hard, and would recognize him as China's ruler only after he had proved his "sincerity" —which meant the complete destruction of the anti-militarist and anti-imperialist revolution.

Chiang now became very popular with both the old and new warlords, who began joining his Kuomintang and entering his government. Many left Kuomintang members at Hankow began crawling toward Nanking, some of them pausing in Shanghai to search their souls before taking the final plunge. General Yen Hsi-shan, medieval warlord of Shansi Province, was appointed commander in chief of the "Northern Revolutionary Army" and, later, Minister of War in Chiang's regime. Before 1927 was out, Chiang had united with warlord Yen Hsi-shan of Shansi and warlord Chang Tso-lin of Peking and called for the extermination of "Communism," by which they meant the great social forces of the people unleashed by the Great Revolution. Chang Tso-lin of Peking celebrated the new alliance by arresting and killing hundreds of progressives in Peking, including girl students who were accused of indecency because they wore sleeves to their elbows instead of to the wrist.

Chu Teh was so staggered by the news of the Shanghai massacre that he could not even think. He had not been surprised when Liu Hsiang massacred in Szechwan, he said, but Shanghai was the very heart of the anti-militarist and anti-imperialist movement. Shanghai, however, was also the heart of Chinese compradore capitalism, a capitalism bound body and soul to foreign banking capital.

"Throughout the next ten years," General Chu declared, "the Chinese bourgeoisie, itself oppressed by imperialism, nevertheless formed a reactionary alliance with foreign imperialism and the Chinese feudal landlord class. Utilizing Chiang Kai-shek as a figurehead, the bourgeoisie betrayed the revolution and thus became the enemy of the people."

Shortly after the Shanghai massacre, the Communist Party held its Fifth Congress in Hankow. Chu Teh did not attend. Leading Kuomintang members attended and addressed the congress, among them Wang

Ching-wei, chairman of the Hankow government, who had recently returned from Europe. However, before proceeding to Hankow, Wang had held secret conferences with Chiang Kai-shek in Shanghai and, upon reaching Hankow, called secret meetings of his own left-wing Kuomintang followers at which his agreement with Chiang was approved.

Chen Tu-hsiu, Communist Party secretary, spoke to the congress, admitting his past mistakes in regard to the mass movement, but he still prevented the discussion of Mao Tse-tung's thesis on the agrarian revolution and the arming of the workers and peasants. Yet even after this congress, General Chu declared, the Communist Party did not arm the workers and peasants, but continued to trail after the leftist Kuomintang leaders in the belief that the final split could be prevented.

Throughout May, June, and July of 1927, reaction unleashed rivers of blood across the face of the country. Thousands of protesting peasants in Hunan Province, and hundreds of workers in Canton in the south, were slaughtered like pigs. The Yunnan Army in Kiangsi, whose Military School Chu Teh still headed, killed labor and peasant leaders and expelled and killed Communists who had fought in its ranks.

While the counter-revolution moved like a turgid flood across the nation, the Hankow government under Wang Ching-wei's leadership began shadowboxing with Chiang Kai-shek's threatening armies. The "Christian General," Feng Yu-hsiang, holding the balance of power between the two forces, emerged from secret conferences with Chiang to advise Hankow to suppress the Communists and send the Russian advisers home. Left-wing Kuomintang leaders who wished to do so, he said, should go abroad "for a rest." Wang Ching-wei was anxious to accept such advice but regarded himself, not the upstart Chiang Kai-shek, as Sun Yat-sen's successor.

Wang and his followers began maneuvering against Chiang for power and position. The Ironsides, which he considered his personal military instrument, was ordered down the river to north Kiangsi. Part of the army of the Hunan ex-militarist, Tang Sheng-chi, was also moved down the river while the remainder stayed in the Wuhan cities where they occupied the headquarters of the labor, peasant and student organizations.

At the memory of that far-off developing tragedy, General Chu Teh's eyes stared into the shadows of my room and his voice became low and harsh.

"Instead of turning to the workers and peasants for support against the counter-revolution unleashed by the Shanghai massacre, left-wing politicians and militarists began suppressing the mass movement. The

bone and blood of the Hankow government had been the people's movement, yet by mid-July it had been militarized. Deprived of mass support,
Wang Ching-wei and his leftist clique began rattling around in Hankow
like a few peas in an empty gourd. While they made threatening gestures
with the Ironsides against Chiang, some of the most loud-mouthed
budding politicians among them began crawling toward Nanking and
Shanghai. Dr. T. V. Soong, Minister of Finance, left. Dr. H. H. Kung
and Sun Fo were already in Shanghai. Both right and left Kuomintang
leaders wrapped themselves in the mantle of the dead Sun Yat-sen whose
only true spokesman was his widow, Soong Ching-ling, who condemned
both cliques. In a proclamation, Madame Sun denounced all who were
condemning the labor and peasant movement as a 'recent and alien
product.' Dr. Sun, she said, had called for a peasant revolution while
Russia was still under the heel of the czar. She declared that in 1927 the
peasants were more wretched than when Dr. Sun started the revolution
and that the suppression of the mass movement was a betrayal of the
nation. She was convinced, she said, that the millions of people who had
come under the influence of the revolution would continue the struggle
until they were victorious.

"Madame Sun, followed by a number of Kuomintang leaders who remained true to the principles of her dead husband, went into exile in
Europe. Among them was the Foreign Minister, Eugene Chen, who
nevertheless belonged to Wang Ching-wei's clique. A few months later
Wang himself went abroad, but he and Chen, with others of his special
entourage, later returned to China to fight for their own power. Wang
eventually joined Chiang, yet continued to struggle with him for power.
By then there was no difference between the two, politically. Because he
had more military power, Chiang had the upper hand.

"By mid-July 1927, the Great Revolution was finished. Leftist revolutionaries, followed by the Russian advisers, were in flight, rivers of blood
were flowing, generals were changing sides, and there was chaos and
confusion everywhere. Chiang Kai-shek was rising to power, drawing old
and new warlords to him and playing them off one against the other to
keep himself on top. As after the 1911 Revolution when Yuan Shih-kai
came to power, Chiang was being propped up by the combined forces
of foreign imperialism, the Chinese bourgeoisie, and the feudal landed
gentry. As with Yuan Shih-kai, Chiang was proclaimed by foreigners as
a patriot, a statesman, a great administrator, and the one strong man
capable of holding China together."

Chiang had learned at least one lesson from Yuan Shih-kai. Instead
of merely appealing to the Christian world to pray for him as Yuan had

done, he soon joined the Christian church. He also put aside his wife
and concubines and married Soong Mei-ling, sister of Madame Sun
Yat-sen and Madame H. H. Kung. General Chu Teh remarked that these
moves of Chiang were "clever strategy." By becoming a Christian he got
the "propaganda machinery of Christian missionaries behind him,"
while his marriage to one of the Soong sisters landed him in the lap of
the two greatest fortunes of China—the Soong and Kung fortunes.

This "clever strategy" was also designed to make him the legal heir
to the mantle of Sun Yat-sen, whose widow was now his sister-in-law.
The one link in this chain of maneuvers refused to fall into place—
Madame Sun had removed herself from the China scene to prevent the
name of her sainted husband from being used as a cloak by the counter-
revolution. Presuming on his relationship with her, Chiang cabled her
to return home from Europe and "behave herself," a message which
she ignored.

Book VI

The Agrarian Revolution Begins

Chapter 17

IN HER historic proclamation to the Kuomintang, Madame Sun Yat-sen had placed her finger on the very heart of China:

"We must not betray the people. We have built up in them a great hope. They have placed in us a great faith. To that faith we owe our final allegiance."

But the Kuomintang had already betrayed the people. The earth of every major city and of countless towns and villages in the interior had been watered with the blood of workers, peasants, and intellectuals. With wild cries of "Communism," reaction was killing poor men in whose hearts a great hope had been lighted. And true it was indeed that the Chinese Communist Party inspired, organized and led such men, for it was the party of the poor.

With the ruins of great hopes about it, this party now had either to fight or to surrender to its enemies. Long before, in the mid-nineteenth century, the great Taiping leader, Shih Ta-kai, had faced a similar dilemma and had said:

"If we fight we die and if we do not fight we die. So we will fight."

Knowing that history never repeats itself exactly, the Communists decided to fight—and live.

On July 18, 1927, General Chu Teh received a call to leave at once for a secret conference of the Communist Party in a small village not far from Nanchang in north Kiangsi. That same evening he entered a large hall where the chief Communist leaders had gathered. About him he saw many men known to him, but many of whose names he had only heard. Chou En-lai, who had escaped death at Shanghai, was there, and men called him simply "the man of iron." Liu Po-cheng, who had escaped death in Szechwan, was there. There was Su Chao-jen, secretary of the All-China Federation of Labor and Minister of Labor in the Hankow government, together with Tan Ping-shan, Minister of Agriculture. Also there were commanders and chiefs of staff of the Eleventh and Twentieth Armies of the Ironsides, together with their political leaders—names that have since made history: Yeh Ting, Ho Lung, Yeh Chien-ying, Li

Li-san, and Lin Tsu-han. The last had been one of Sun Yat-sen's earliest followers.

There were men whom Chu Teh saw but whose names he did not know. One of them was a tall, thin man named Mao Tse-tung, the peasant leader who was a member of the Political Bureau of the Communist Party and of the Central Committee of the Kuomintang.

General Chu confined himself to the barest outline of decisions taken at this conference:

"We reversed our former policy toward the Kuomintang. While continuing the anti-militarist and anti-imperialist struggle, we voted to arm the peasants and workers and begin the agrarian revolution. I spoke and supported this resolution. Yet even at such a decisive moment the agrarian policy which we adopted was extremely curtailed and we made no plans to use the Ironsides to confiscate the landed estates or even to support the peasant uprisings. Such actions were left to cadres of the people's organizations and of our party. Our party was young and inexperienced. It had grown so rapidly that we had been unable to consolidate it and educate our cadres in theory. We were first intoxicated by easy victories and then cast into despair by the counter-revolution.

"Our first action in carrying out the new policy was to be a military uprising of the Ironsides at Nanchang after which this army was to march to Canton and establish a new national revolutionary government. The uprising was to be the signal for harvest uprisings of the peasants during which they were to arm themselves with weapons seized from the Min Tuan, the landlord militia. As it turned out later, Mao Tse-tung was the only leader who used armed force to help the peasant uprisings. Mao led the Hankow garrison troops down into Hunan and used them to help the peasants, after which he enlarged his forces from the most active peasant volunteers.

"The policy which we adopted at this secret conference was summed up in these slogans: 'Continue the anti-imperialist, anti-militarist struggle. Fight Nanking, fight Chiang Kai-shek. Begin the agrarian revolution. Arm the people.'

"I cast my vote for all these measures. We were standing in the midst of chaos and terror, yet at last I felt a great burden fall from my shoulders. Up to that time I had had no voice in party policies, but had performed such tasks as were given me to the best of my ability.

"After the conference our comrades went to their designated posts. Mao Tse-tung left for Hankow to wait for the Nanchang uprising when he and a number of Whampoa Military Academy cadets in the Hankow garrison were to lead their troops southward into Hunan. Su Chao-jen left to prepare the labor organizations along the Yangtze for the uprising.

A number of men, elected to the Front Committee which was to prepare and lead the Nanchang uprising, left for Nanchang. I was elected a member of that committee. Among the other members were General Yeh Ting of the Eleventh Army and General Ho Lung of the Twentieth, with their chiefs of staff and political commissars. Liu Po-cheng was chairman of the Front Committee and Chou En-lai the vice-chairman. Other members were Yeh Chien-ying, Li Li-san, and Chang Kuo-tao, party leaders; and Tan Ping-shan, and Lin Tsu-han.

"Since I knew most about Nanchang, I was given the job of reporting to the Front Committee on all the forces which would be involved in the uprising, both for and against it. The time was short, but everything was clear to me. Our enemies would be a number of regiments of the Sixth Kuomintang Army which had been edging close to Nanchang; also a number of regiments of the Yunnan Army—the Fifth Route Army—in and around Nanchang; and we might have to contend with a division of the Yunnan Army which had moved up to within two days' marching distance of Nanchang. As the counter-revolution spread, all these troops were preparing to take over Nanchang and crush the mass movement.

"On our side we had all the people's organizations of Nanchang, such as the labor, peasant and student unions, and the Peasant Training School whose director, Fang Chih-ming, had also attended the secret conference.

"Most troops of the Ironsides could be depended on, but not its commander in chief, Chang Fa-kwei, or the commander of the Fourth Army, Hwang Chi-hsiang, both of whom were followers of Wang Ching-wei. They were trying to use the Ironsides in a horse trade with Chiang Kai-shek for power. Most troops of the Fourth Army were at Kiukiang on the Yangtze, where General Chang Fa-kwei had his headquarters. The branch headquarters of the Ironsides was at Nanchang, under control of General Yeh Ting, commander of the Eleventh Army. All of the Eleventh and Twentieth Armies were in and around Nanchang, and there was one regiment of the Fourth Army along the Kiukiang-Nanchang railway which was prepared to take part in the uprising.

"We could also depend on the entire police force of Nanchang which, like the Military Training School, was under my direction. However, even before I left for the secret conference, I had received orders from the Yunnan Army to graduate all the 1300 cadets of my military school and deliver them to headquarters for distribution among the troops. These cadets had not yet finished their training course, but the commander of the Yunnan Army was preparing to go over to Chiang Kai-shek and was preparing to seize Nanchang. When that time came, he wanted none of these young cadets in the city. Distributed among the troops, they would be helpless.

"I had been forced to obey this order, and all but three hundred cadets had been graduated and distributed. The three hundred remaining were ready to take part in the uprising. I tried to reach as many of the others as possible, but failed because the time was too short."

On the night of the uprising, Chu Teh, acting on orders of the Front Committee, gave a big dinner to all officers of the Fifth Route and Sixth Armies in the city. He invited only officers of and above the rank of regimental commander. Still regarding him as a Yunnan Army officer and a Kuomintang leader, they all came.

By nine that evening the dinner was finished and the guests were just settling down to play mah jong, with which General Chu planned to keep them occupied until midnight, when the uprising was to begin. At that moment the door opened and a battalion commander from Ho Lung's Twentieth Army entered in great excitement. This young commander was a native of Yunnan Province, and most of the men in the restaurant were his fellow provincials.

Chu Teh's heart sank into his shoes when this young commander announced in a confused voice that he had just received orders to disarm troops of the Yunnan Army in his section of the city. As a Yunnan native he did not know if he should disarm his fellow provincials or not. What should he do?

A dead silence settled over the room. Turning to his guests with a laugh, Chu Teh remarked that all kinds of rumors were set afloat in such troubled times, and that this meant nothing at all.

"Let us continue our mah jong game and not give ear to every whisper carried on the breeze."

Scraping back his chair, a general arose and said:

"It may be a rumor, yet I have already heard that there will be trouble this night. Let every man return to his post."

Everyone was now on his feet and preparing to leave. Not daring to invite too much suspicion by insisting that they remain, General Chu bowed them out with jokes and laughter. The moment they were gone he rushed to the Front Committee, where orders were issued that the uprising should begin at once.

It took time to get the new order to all the Ironsides units, but the sound of firing soon began and continued in a wave through the city as first one unit and then another received the order. Chu Teh and his comrades worked throughout the night, and by daybreak the city was in the hands of the Ironsides. It was hours before more distant villages were taken. Fuchow, a strategic town some forty miles to the southeast, was seized from an enemy regiment two days later.

Nanchang now became a sea of revolutionary banners, and tens of thousands of people and soldiers poured out to a vast meeting where a dozen platforms for speakers were erected. On the morning following the uprising, an emergency conference of the Communist Party was called. Chen Tu-hsiu was expelled as party secretary and Chu Chiu-pai elected. The new secretary was a famous writer who had been one of the chief leaders of the cultural renaissance.

The conference elected a Revolutionary Committee made up of Communist Party members and a number of Kuomintang leaders who had remained loyal to the revolution. Among them were Madame Sun Yat-sen and Eugene Chen, Foreign Minister in the Hankow government. On the morning of August 5th, the Ironsides, together with such members of the Revolutionary Committee as were then in Nanchang, were to march southward to Kwangtung Province and establish a new revolutionary government. To finance the expedition, an elected committee of the Ironsides and the Communist Party made the rounds of the city, confiscating money from bankers and other rich families.

At the same time, Chu Teh had been ordered to organize a new division, the 9th, which he was to command in person. His three hundred military cadets, the entire Nanchang police force of four hundred men, and a few score workers and students were drawn into this division, but nearly all the rifles captured in the uprising had already been taken by workers and peasants. The six hundred men and women of the Peasant Training School had loaded boats with rifles and ammunition and, covering them with straw, had pushed off downstream to their native districts in the province to begin the organization and arming of peasants. Fang Chih-ming, with a number of peasants, left for Iyang, his native district in northeastern Kiangsi where, in following years, they built up the Tenth Red Army Corps.

Chu Teh was therefore able to mobilize only about a thousand armed men for his new division.

The agrarian revolution was beginning.

Chapter 18

AT DAYBREAK on August 5th, two columns of Ironside troops, in parallel routes ten to twenty miles apart, began marching southward toward Canton. Chu Teh's troops, named the Vanguards, went two days in advance of the eastern column to prepare the people, buy food and arrange billets for the troops following them. The two columns converged at Ihwang for one night, held a conference, then continued marching and periodically converging in the following weeks.

Somewhere along the road beyond Ihwang, General Tsai Ting-kai, commander of the 10th Ironsides Division, got cold feet and led his troops due east into Fukien Province. In later months, he rejoined the former commander in chief of the Ironsides, Chang Fa-kwei. In the meantime Chang had taken two regiments of the army which had been with him at Kiukiang and marched southward by another route, reaching Canton and joining up with the local militarist in the hopes of holding the southern city as a stronghold for his leader, Wang Ching-wei.

When news of the desertion of the 10th Division spread through the ranks of the Ironsides, soldiers began deserting. The country was in chaos and they decided to go home. Wandering off in many small streams, they took their guns and returned to help their families in the harvest uprisings. Many excused themselves to their comrades by saying they did not wish to go so far away from their homes as Canton, others that their families needed their help against the terror.

Such men, General Chu said, were not lost to the revolution. They fought in the harvest uprisings and most of them later rejoined the revolutionary forces. Such events, he added, were typical of both the American Revolution and the American Civil War.

The Nanchang uprising had so disorganized their enemies that the Ironsides met no resistance until they reached the extreme southern part of Kiangsi. The landlords, who knew nothing of it, even came out and drove hard bargains with Chu Teh's Vanguards for grain.

"I also had time to study peasant conditions," General Chu said. "Kiangsi peasants were as heavily oppressed as those of my native province, but even more destitute, hopeless and fatalistic.

"Most of Kiangsi is mountainous, and the crops are poor. The landlords took as much as seventy percent of the crop as rent, and most peasants had to borrow from them at high rates of interest each year, so that they and their sons and sons' sons were bound by debt in perpetual servitude to the landlords. The peasants were so poor that they sopped up every drop of fat in cooking pans and could afford to buy only a handful of salt at a time. They would dissolve a pinch of salt in a bowl of water and dip their bits of vegetables in it when they ate. They were gaunt, half-naked, and illiterate, and lived in dark, insanitary hovels in villages surrounded by high mud walls which had only one gate.

"Shihching district was typical of many others. Most of this district was owned by the Lei family, two of whose men were Kuomintang army officers. One was a general with his own local army. The family had a big town house and also a big country home inside an ancient mountain fortress in which they stored their grain, money, and other wealth. Serf tenants cultivated their land, and they also had hundreds of land laborers who were virtual slaves working for nothing but poor food and shelter and such old clothing as the Lei family discarded."

Approaching the town of Juikin in south Kiangsi in late August, Chu Teh's Vanguards finally ran into patrols of two Kuomintang divisions based on Hweichang some thirty miles farther south. From the point of contact to Hweichang the Ironsides fought for four days and nights. It was their first battle of the agrarian revolution and a fierce one ending in victory, but when a reckoning was made it had cost hundreds of dead and around a thousand wounded. Chu Teh lost three hundred of his Vanguards.

Unable to carry so many wounded over the high mountain ranges through which they had planned to march, the Ironsides turned due east toward the walled city of Tingchow in the mountains of western Fukien Province. The revolutionaries of Tingchow, who had distinguished themselves during the Great Revolution, could be depended on to care for and shelter the wounded. Among them was a Christian family, some of whose members were trained medical workers and one of whose sons, Dr. Nelson Fu, was on the staff of the British Baptist Hospital in Tingchow.

General Chu's voice, which constantly changed according to the nature of the story he was telling, now became tender and was even touched with wonder.

"Dr. Nelson Fu and the British doctors in that foreign hospital took charge of our wounded men! The seriously wounded were taken into the hospital, the less serious in the homes of the people, while the lightly wounded went on with us."

The Ironsides were now in a territory every inch of which was known to Peng Pei, the peasant leader from the East River Regions of Kwangtung Province a few miles to the south. Peng Pei was the same man who, at the end of 1926, had led hundreds of militant peasants across the continent to join the Ironsides at Hankow. After the battle in south Kiangsi, Chu Teh had taken command of a regiment of troops, while Peng Pei and his peasants had become the Vanguards. These peasants fanned out in every direction to collect information about enemy troops and movements and to buy food and arrange for sleeping quarters for the troops.

The army was now in dangerous territory and within easy reach of enemy troops along the coast. Swiftness in movement now meant everything. Leaving Tingchow at one o'clock in the morning, Peng Pei led the Ironsides by forced marches due southward toward his native East River Region in Kwangtung which had been the birthplace of the first Peasant Leagues and Peasant Self-Defense Corps under the protection of Dr. Sun Yat-sen. By now the peasant movement in the region had been driven underground and the "tiger landlords" and their Min Tuan had emerged bloody but triumphant on top.

Moving with the speed of greyhounds, advance scouts of Peng Pei's Vanguards crossed the Fukien-Kwangtung border and spread the word among the villages that the Ironsides were coming. Behind them came the swift-moving troops. Swooping down, they overwhelmed and smashed the landlord Min Tuan along the route of march, crossed the border and entered the famous East River Region.

From this moment on down to the Han River, which opens into the sea at the port city of Swatow, their march became an almost continuous celebration. First small groups and then larger and larger groups of peasant men and women, armed with every conceivable weapon, came out to meet and join them, pouring out their bitter sorrows as they marched. Entire villages awaited them with food and drink and at the Han River boatmen by the hundreds had gathered to ferry them across the river where they halted to plan the battle for Swatow. A division of Kuomintang troops had already concentrated against them while another division was marching up from the south.

Long lines of peasants carrying big baskets of rice and vegetables slung from shoulder poles came into their encampments and with gleaming eyes exclaimed:

"You have come at last! You have come at last!"

Boatmen and boatmen came up the river from Swatow with news of enemy preparations, warning that British gunboats were in the harbor and that Kuomintang army officers were going and coming from them. There were rumors in Swatow that other Kuomintang troops were coming by sea, while peasants coming down from the north warned that still another enemy division was moving down from Fukien Province.

The first thing that Chu Teh noticed upon entering the East River Region was the large number of women. Fully two thirds of the peasant population were women and girls who, like the men, carried rice to them, ferried them across the river, or, with arms in hand, marched with them.

To explain this phenomenon, General Chu recounted the history of the southern Chinese provinces which, he said, "had been the first to feel the impact of imperialist aggression." Local militarists, bureaucrats, and the "tiger landlords," however, had also done their full share in bleeding the people white. As a consequence vast numbers of men for decades had been forced to seek a living by emigrating to Nanyang (the South Seas), while their womenfolk remained behind to maintain the native home. Most poor families depended on the two or three dollars a month sent to them by their menfolk overseas.

About two thirds of the population of the East River Region were therefore women who tilled the fields or worked as boatmen along the waterways or as stevedores at Swatow and other port cities. Women had been among the founders of the Peasant Leagues and had fought shoulder to shoulder with the men in the Peasant Self-Defense Corps. Like the men they had died in battle and their heads had been mounted on poles before their villages when the tiger gentry emerged triumphant.

"This was the first time I had ever seen physically strong and emancipated women in China," General Chu said. "The women had natural feet, they were barefoot like the men, and were strong and capable. Forced to shoulder every kind of responsibility, they had become emancipated from the ancient tyranny of fathers, husbands, and their in-laws. They nevertheless longed for their absent menfolk, and had many songs of longing for them.

"Some of us wept when we first heard these women sing a sad, militant ballad. It was a song in ten stanzas, each of which began with the words 'My beloved.' It was called 'The Ten Entreaties.' I will sing it for you."

Arising, General Chu went to the small harmonium in my room and sang this ballad, which began:

> My beloved, you are not so far away!
> Take your quilt and return to your native home.
> Do everything to join the revolution.
> Help the fight against rent and taxes.

The last stanza ran:

> My beloved, these are my ten entreaties.
> Have no fear of the White devils.
> Workers and peasants hand in hand,
> You take the rifle, I take the sword.

The word "White" was already used to describe the counter-revolutionary forces, while "Red" covered all revolutionaries. From the most ancient times the color red had symbolized happiness, hope and new life, while white had been the color of death. Even the faces or masks of the villains in the old operas or dramas were white or streaked with white while the hero's face was red or marked with red. The ballad of the East River peasant women which had moved Chu Teh and his companions to tears had therefore referred to all reactionaries as "White devils."

It was these women who became the eyes and ears of the Ironsides, its messengers and its supply and transport aides. Since speed was everything if the Ironsides were to reach Canton and establish the new revolutionary government, its general staff decided to smash the enemy division at Swatow before reinforcements could come up. Leaving Chu Teh in command of three thousand troops at the strategic river town of Sanhopa to guard against attacks from the rear, the main body of the Ironsides at once attacked Swatow. This battle, which lasted four days, was fought in early September, but after the first two days of fighting General Chu received nothing but rumors from the front. The entire forces of the Ironsides, with thousands of peasants, were engaged, he heard; the British gunboats in the harbor had shelled them; the enemy division from the south was near at hand, and other enemy troops were landing by sea. Then all was silent.

Since the Ironsides, in case of defeat, were to retreat to Sanhopa, General Chu took it that the fighting was still raging. On the fourth day, the enemy division from the north came down and, unable to find any boats to ferry them across, began bombarding them from across the river. Then, to Chu's consternation, instead of the Ironsides, enemy regiments began moving up against him from Swatow. Deploying his forces and the thousand armed peasant men and women who came to his support along the mountain slopes, overlooking the route from the east, Chu Teh directed a battle which lasted for one week.

The peasants who came to Chu Teh's support had come organized in battalions. Five hundred women organized by themselves into stretcher-bearing units cleared the battlefield. They worked without fear in the midst of battle, transporting the wounded to villages in the rear, where other stretcher-bearers carried them to villages farther inland. Still other organized units of old people and children carried food and water to the fighters, while barefoot women peasants served as runners for his headquarters, carrying orders to the various fighting units and swiftly running back with reports to his headquarters. Women scouts came into his headquarters day and night with reports on enemy movements and he was amazed at their detailed accuracy.

Still no word came from the main forces at Swatow. At the end of one week of fighting, Chu Teh had suffered fifteen hundred casualties, or half of his regulars, while hundreds of peasants had been killed and wounded. Unable to hold out, he gave the order to retreat. All the survivors, both regulars and peasants, concentrated upstream at midnight. Boatwomen ferried them across and the peasant fighters led the small column swiftly into the mountains to the north. At the town of Jaoping near the Fukien border they came upon three hundred men from Ho Lung's Student Training Detachment from whom the column learned of the disastrous defeat of the Ironsides at Swatow.

Heavy enemy reinforcements had come up and in four days of fighting the Ironsides had been cut into segments and shattered. The general staff had become separated from the troops. As Chu Teh learned later, they had taken refuge in a fishermen's village and from there they had been smuggled into Hongkong. Ho Lung and Liu Po-cheng had made their way to Shanghai. Liu went on to Moscow to study in the Red Army Military Academy while Ho Lung went up the Yangtze to his native regions of west Hunan to raise another army and continue the revolution. General Yeh Ting and Yeh Chien-ying stayed in Hongkong to care for Chou En-lai, who lay unconscious with malarial fever. After recovering, Chou also left for Moscow, while Yeh Ting and Yeh Chien-ying remained in the south and led troops in the Canton Commune in December, which also met with bloody defeat.

After the Ironsides were cut to pieces at Swatow, Peng Pei, the peasant leader, collected the scattered fighters and sent them inland to the Hailufeng district. There were altogether some two thousand of these men whom Peng Pei organized into a partisan or guerrilla detachment. Together with the peasants, these partisans confiscated and divided the land. On November 7, 1927, they called the first conference of workers, peasants and the urban poor and founded the small Hailufeng Soviet Republic. This first Soviet in China held out until March 1928, when the East River Region was overrun and devastated by "militarist troops"— a term which General Chu used to cover all Kuomintang or other reactionary armies. Villages were reduced to dust and the peasants hunted and killed by the tens of thousands. In 1929 this writer read a pamphlet, illustrated with photographs, which the Canton militarists put out in celebration. Some photographs showed the ruins of villages in and around which the bodies of the slain lay like autumn leaves. The pictures of well-fed, handsomely uniformed Kuomintang generals decorated the pamphlet side by side with the lean and keen faces of peasant leaders who had been captured and then beheaded.

Peng Pei remained in the region, keeping the underground Peasant Leagues alive until the early '30s. Then he went to Shanghai for a Com-

munist Party conference. He was captured and, refusing to betray his
comrades, was beheaded by Chiang Kai-shek's men.

After the defeat of the Ironsides, Chu Teh and his small column were
hunted men, pursued on every side by enemy troops and the landlords.
Halting for a short conference on the Fukien border, all but one hundred
of the peasant fighters turned back to join Peng Pei, while three of the
seven women nurses, who were too weak to keep up with the swift-
moving column, were released and told to go to Tingchow.

At this conference, General Chu proposed that the column march
through the mountains to the west until they reached south Hunan, where
the peasant movement was strong and militant. Chu's chief of staff, Chow
Shih-ti, supported by a number of other cadres, was so discouraged that
he proposed the army be disbanded. They were voted down because, as
General Chu argued, each man carried more than one rifle, others had
light machine guns and a few had mortars. There was little ammunition
or money left, but they could confiscate food from the landlords and
capture ammunition from the enemy. His proposals were supported, yet
confusion and despair hovered over the column as it began marching to
the west.

Chapter 19

ALL the tenacity and determination in Chu Teh came to the fore as the
small revolutionary column made its way through the mountains along
the borders of Fukien, Kiangsi, and Kwangtung provinces. Through the
pouring autumn rains they marched at night and slept in the forests
during the day. Moving or resting, a debate raged between those who
wanted the column to disband and those who insisted that it continue
the revolutionary struggle.

"The defeatists argued that the bourgeoisie had again betrayed the
revolution and, allied with the feudal gentry and imperialism, was too
powerful to resist," General Chu recalled. "The mercenary character of
the counter-revolutionary armies, and the landlord-militarist origin of
their officers, further strengthened the counter-revolution until the situation in the country was worse than when the Great Revolution began.
Thousands of party members had been killed, others had given up the
struggle, and some had even joined the enemy. Tens of thousands of

workers and peasants had been killed. They held Chen Tu-hsiu, our former party secretary, and all who had supported his policy, responsible for the disaster. These men had now formed a small Trotskyist faction and were attacking the Communists with propaganda that differed little from the Kuomintang. All these factors, they argued, were so overpowering that any continuation of the revolutionary struggle was sheer adventurism.

"I replied," said General Chu, "that their analysis of the counter-revolution was correct, but that their conclusions were so wrong that to accept them would be nothing but treason to the revolution. A few intellectuals with influential connections in counter-revolutionary circles might indeed save their lives and get jobs, and some might retire or go abroad, but the workers and peasants could do none of these things. The people had no place to which to retreat and they either had to fight until the agrarian and anti-imperialist revolution was complete, or allow themselves to be driven back into the swamp of feudalism and imperialist subjection.

"I argued that we were fighting a rear-guard action, and that all such actions were demoralizing unless men girded their spirits and continued the struggle. The workers and peasants were so poor that they had to fight or die, and to die fighting was more honorable than to die like a slave. The fires of hope had been lit in the hearts of millions of our people, and they needed only leadership such as we could give. Harvest uprisings had taken place in many points in the south. They had been crushed or driven underground in most places but the peasants had captured arms. We also had arms to reinforce them. To betray them would be treason. As for myself, I would continue to fight if only one man remained with me; and if he deserted I said I would raise up others. I refused to return to warlordism. I had chosen the road of the people's revolution and I would follow it to the end."

General Chu failed to convince the defeatists, who continued their demoralizing campaign, but he was supported by many young officers who, in the two decades that followed, made history in China: men like Lin Piao, Chen Yi, Chou Tze-kwen, and Wang Ehr-jo, all of them lower commanders in the column.

The money Chu Teh had was soon used up and the troops began to starve and some to desert. In the Chumeng mountains in Kiangsi, Chu therefore surrounded a landlord's home and asked for a "contribution." The landlord gave him $2000 which lasted until the column reached a village near the town of Hsinfeng in western Kiangsi. Here he called a conference to settle once and for all with the defeatists who, he charged, were responsible for the demoralization and despair of the troops, for desertions, and for the acts of robbery in which some of the troops had engaged.

Speaking fiercely, General Chu proposed that every man who wanted to leave the army should do so at once. His proposal was accepted and acted on at once. His chief of staff was the first to go, leaving for Shanghai. Even in 1937, ten years later, General Chu spoke of this "desertion" with hatred. Then others began to follow until over three hundred commanders and fighters had left. Fear and despair ate at Chu Teh's heart as he watched man after man step out of the ranks, stack his rifles, and leave.

"I feared the entire army would collapse," he said, as if reliving that distant scene. "At last the exodus dribbled away and ended. We had less than nine hundred men left. They were dirty and bedraggled, gaunt with hunger, but they stood upright and firm, and now many of them carried three or four rifles.

"We called a conference of squad commanders and made a hasty reorganization. We appointed a Confiscation Committee and I issued an order that this committee alone had the right to confiscate from the landlords. With the defeatists gone, a new spirit of hope took the place of despair and demoralization. Next morning we swooped down on Hsinfeng, smashed the landlord militia and confiscated rice and money from the rich. Two days later we took the large tungsten town of Tayu in southwestern Kiangsi, where we remained for a week to rest, reorganize, and call for volunteers among the peasants and the workers in the tungsten processing plant. A transport station of the Fourth Army of the old Ironsides, which had been left here by the army during the Northern Expedition, was stocked with a few hundred uniforms, blankets, and other supplies. The men in charge delivered them to us and joined our ranks. A few hundred workers and peasants also volunteered. Our Confiscation Committee did the rounds and confiscated rice and money from the rich, and gave such surplus as we did not need to the city poor.

"In Tayu we reorganized our troops into five detachments, each with a political director with the duty of educating the troops politically and drawing as many as possible into the party. The old military command system was replaced by a system of direct command. The army was renamed the Workers and Peasants Revolutionary Army, but we still kept the old Kuomintang banner. In a general meeting of fighters and commanders I was elected commander in chief, and Chen Yi my political commissar. Lin Piao commanded one of the five detachments. We held many mass meetings while in Tayu, informing the people of our program and intentions, and urged them to remain loyal to the revolution until we were strong enough to establish the people's power."

Near the end of the week in Tayu, General Chu received a staff officer —who turned out to be a Communist Party member—from Fang Shih-tseng, a general of the old Yunnan or Fifth Route Army whose troops now garrisoned southern Hunan and the bordering regions of Kwang-tung. General Fang wrote Chu Teh that, since they were old comrades and friends, he would not fight against the revolutionary troops but would help them. There was still a branch of the Communist Party in his army, he wrote, but its members had proved themselves good revolu-tionaries and he would not oppose their activities. He also wrote that he had learned that strong forces of the old Yunnan Army were marching against Tayu.

For the next twenty days the small revolutionary army remained in a market town in the mountains northwest of Tayu where it trained and educated its troops, revived the suppressed mass organization, and laid the foundation for the agrarian revolution. Messengers were sent to party branches throughout southern Hunan and Kwangtung provinces. They instructed the branches to send delegates to Kweiyang, in south Hunan, for a conference on November 26th to draw up plans for peasant upris-ings which would be spearheaded by the revolutionary army. At the same time General Chu sent a liaison officer to General Fang Shih-tseng's head-quarters to ask for clothing, blankets and ammunition.

Two hundred men who had formerly left the army returned during this stage and, as General Chu expressed it, "were accepted without prejudice." In the last week in the town the army was suddenly ordered to take up fighting positions against an unknown number of enemy troops bearing down on them from the mountains to the north.

The strange body of troops approached with shouts of joy. They turned out to be five hundred well-armed men, part of the Hankow garrison which Mao Tse-tung had led into Hunan Province to support the harvest uprisings after the Nanchang uprising. They were commanded by Chang Tse-chin and Wu Chung-hao, both Whampoa military cadets.

From these men General Chu learned that Mao Tse-tung was now on the strategic mountain range known as Chingkanshan in western Kiangsi to the north and near the Hunan border. Like similar mountain fast-nesses elsewhere in past eras of oppression, for decades under the pres-sure of extreme poverty and ignorance, it had become a bandits' refuge. The peasant movement during the Great Revolution had inspired social goals, and their leaders, Wang Tso and Yuan Wen-tsai, led them into fierce struggles for land redistribution. Beaten back by the counter-revolution which followed, they had returned to their old bandit habits until Mao Tse-tung led his troops and peasant followers into the area. He entered into an alliance with Wang Tso and Yuan Wen-tsai, and transformed Chingkanshan into a revolutionary training base for the agrarian revolution.

After dispatching representatives to Mao, Chu Teh led his small Workers and Peasants Revolutionary Army, now numbering about two thousand men, down through the mountains to the west to keep his rendezvous with Communist Party delegates who were to gather in conference at Kweiyang to make plans for peasant uprisings.

The story which General Chu told of this march sounded like something lifted from the immortal tales of the *Shui Hu Chuan,* or *All Men Are Brothers.* After the revolution was crushed and the old and oppressive ruling classes regained their sway, the country again swarmed with bandits. They drew desperate peasants into their ranks, established their rule over whole regions and went on bloody raids against more prosperous areas. In one night battle with a small bandit army, Chu barely escaped death in a village in which he and a company of troops were sleeping. In a swift maneuver to regain the main body of his army, one of his squads followed the bandits in retreat. Twenty of the bandits followed them through the dark, thinking they were with their own men. Reaching the assembly point, a roll call was taken and the twenty bandits found themselves surrounded by revolutionaries.

"After talking with them, we released those who were old-time bandits but invited the poor peasants with them to join us, which they did," explained General Chu. "Here and there we met or heard of small bodies of Kuomintang troops who were just wandering around the country without any goal. They would flee when we approached so that we were unable to talk with them. After reaching Kweiyang, we heard of the approach of a whole regiment of strongly armed troops of the Kwangsi Army and, not able to fight such a force, evacuated the city and took up positions in the hills. These troops turned out to be scattered remnants of a regiment who were on their way back to their native province. From what we could make out, all of them were deserters."

The Kweiyang conference of party delegates from south Hunan and northern Kwangtung lasted for three days, after which the delegates left for their homes to prepare for the uprisings which were to begin in mid-December. On the last day of the conference, a long column of peasant carriers arrived from General Fang Shih-tseng's headquarters with a few hundred uniforms and a considerable amount of ammunition. General Chu had just sent the five hundred Hankow garrison troops back to the mountain town of Chaling in eastern Hunan and was preparing to dispatch other troops to other regions when he received a call from the Communist Party in Canton. It asked him to march at once to help in an uprising also scheduled for mid-December.

He began marching southward at once, in early December. No sooner did they begin moving, however, than the peasants, thinking the revolutionary bell had tolled, began risings. Soon the small revolutionary army was completely engulfed in a fierce peasant revolution that stretched throughout south Hunan and northern Kwangtung. Peasants arose, attacked landlords and their Min Tuan, and sent desperate calls to Chu Teh for men to help them. Chu sent small units in every direction ordering them to rendezvous at certain points to the south and continue the march to Canton.

With a few companies of troops, Chu and his staff moved southward. Landlords, seeing their old Kuomintang banners and mistaking them for troops come to suppress the peasants, rushed out in wild joy.

On such occasions General Chu adopted tactics which caused the Kuomintang press for the next two decades to call him a "cunning and treacherous bandit chieftain." He had a lifelong habit of standing with his legs apart and his hands braced on his hips as he listened intently to matters of importance. In such posture he listened to the landlords' urgent plea that he use his troops to crush the despised peasant rebels. General Chu asked questions: Apart from the automatics which the men of the landlord families slung from their hips, just how many rifles or other weapons did their Min Tuan have? Just what had they already done to suppress the peasants, how many had been killed and how many imprisoned? What steps had they taken to get military help from Kuomintang Army units?

After all his questions had been answered, General Chu had the landlord Min Tuan draw up for inspection, and as these men and their masters stood at attention he disarmed them, delivered their arms to the peasants and turned them over to peasant justice.

Chapter 20

IT WAS mid-December before all the scattered units of the revolutionary army had assembled and reached the Shaokwan area in northern Kwangtung Province, some two to three days' march from Canton. By that time, the territory before them was swarming with Min Tuan and with "militarist troops."

While probing for a way through the mountains, the army met a company of armed cadets from the Officers Training Regiment at Canton who rushed towards them with hoarse cries of joy. These cadets told them that the Canton uprising had taken place on December 11th and that they and their regiment had participated in it. The Canton Commune, established during the uprising, had been crushed three days later by the combined might of Kuomintang troops and British gunboats. There had been a grisly massacre of thousands of workers, peasants, students, and revolutionary soldiers. Small groups of men who had escaped were trying to make their way to Chu Teh's army, as the company of cadets had done, to join it and continue the revolution.

General Chu Teh's summary of the national situation at this moment in history was something like this:

The Canton Commune unleashed a new wave of counter-revolutionary terror against the mass movement throughout the country. Everywhere were small islands of revolutionary resistance. With the two hundred cadets who now joined it, the Workers and Peasants Revolutionary Army under Chu's direct command totaled some seventeen hundred men. At Chaling to the northeast were the five hundred Hankow garrison troops and not far away from them at Chingkanshan were another thousand men commanded by Mao Tse-tung.

General Ho Lung was somewhere in northwest Hunan, again gathering a peasant army about him. Fang Chih-ming, the peasant leader, was leading the peasants in northeastern Kiangsi, while a small group of Whampoa Military Academy graduates were building a revolutionary base in the Tungku mountain area in central Kiangsi. Peng Pei was still leading the remnants of the Ironsides and the peasant partisans in the East River Region of Kwangtung.

The peasant revolt was already shaking Hunan, known as the domain of some of the most savage "tiger landlords" of China, landlords whom the peasants lumped together as "nobles." In the darkness of each night desperate peasants were picking off Min Tuan sentries, arming themselves, and storming the manor houses of the "nobles" who in turn led their Min Tuan against sleeping villages where they seized and killed peasant leaders and mounted their heads on poles as a brutal warning. It was a merciless, savage struggle with no quarter given on either side, ragged peasants attacking and fighting and dying with curses on their lips.

The tragic dramas being enacted in hundreds of villages in south

THE AGRARIAN REVOLUTION BEGINS

Hunan were no different from what this writer personally witnessed in later years when the landlords and their minions cast in their lot with the Japanese Imperial Army and fought the Communist guerrillas, most of them peasants, who operated against them.

Without food and shelter and carrying their wounded, the peasant rebels would enter a sleeping village at night, knock on a barred door, and say in a low voice:

"Brothers, open! We are a Peasant Self-Defense Corps. Give us shelter!"

Silence hung over the village, every hovel was listening yet not a sound came, not a ray of light glimmered. Inside the huts men and women, dressed in the rags they wore both night and day, had silently crept from their straw beds and were listening at the doors, the women whispering to their men:

"Don't open! Maybe it's landlord Wu and the Min Tuan!"

Again the peasant guerrillas knocked and an urgent voice said:

"Brothers! We have been fighting the Min Tuan. We have wounded."

After an endless silence one door would open and an old man would peer out through the crack and whisper with the peasants armed with spears, bird-guns and perhaps a few captured pistols and rifles. Swinging wide the door he would go out into the night and say to the listening houses:

"They speak the truth!"

As if in a dream, all the village doors swung open and men poured out, took straw from the stacks beyond and carried it indoors to make pallets on the earthen floors. Then the doors closed silently once more and the guerrillas and their hosts sat on the pallets and talked in whispers while the women lit flames beneath the cooking vat on the mud stove and brought rice from a jar for cooking.

Scenes such as this, repeated over all south China in succeeding years, caused General Chu to remark time and again that "the peasants of China are the most revolutionary people on earth" and that all they needed was good leadership, a sound program—and arms. And it was back into this small world in south Hunan Province that General Chu, in that black winter of 1927, led his troops and established the pattern of agrarian revolution that characterized the army which he and Mao Tse-tung led for the next twenty-two years.

Entering Ichang county, not far from the small walled city of the same name, he soon met a Peasant Self-Defense Corps. It was a few hundred strong, led by a youth of eighteen named Chen Kwang. He said that all members of his family except himself had been killed by the landlord for whom they had worked. Many other men of the corps told the same or a similar story, and Chen Kwang—who in 1937 became a divisional commander of the Eighth Route Army—had organized and led them in raids on the fortress homes of the "nobles." And now the corps had come to join Chu Teh's army.

The next addition was an intellectual named Hu Shao-hai. He identified himself as one of two Communist Party members from the city of Ichang. Because their families were landlords they had been able to live openly and legally, as legality went in such a reactionary stronghold. Hu reported that there were only three hundred Min Tuan guarding Ichang and that the city was ruled by a small clique of landlords who were simultaneously merchants and Kuomintang officials. This clique had sent him on a mission into north Kwangtung to ask for military reinforcements against the revolting peasants.

Such being the situation, Hu had a plan: would General Chu give him command of two hundred troops to lead into the city to disarm the Min Tuan and arrest the city's rulers?

General Chu selected two companies of his veterans. He told them to spruce themselves up and try to act like Kuomintang soldiers. On the morning of December 29, 1927, these two companies, led by Hu Shao-hai, marched into Ichang where the city's rulers received them with joy and invited their commanders to a banquet that same evening.

Evening came and the chief commanders of the two companies sat down with Ichang's rulers to the banquet. As they dined and exchanged toasts in the best rice wine, the two companies surrounded the astounded Min Tuan. This done, the two companies surrounded the banquet hall and the company commanders arose and said to their hosts:

"Gentlemen, you are arrested! Go quietly, for our troops now hold Ichang."

Followed by his troops, General Chu entered the city and next morning the red banner of the Canton Commune floated over its walls.

"From that time onward we used this banner," General Chu said. "It was red with a white star and a hammer and sickle in the center—the symbol of workers' and peasants' rule. During a big mass meeting next morning a Revolutionary Committee of representatives from the suppressed people's organizations was established, and on January 1, 1928, this committee organized the first Workers and Peasants Council, or Soviet, in Hunan.

"The Soviet established departments to deal with the armed forces, with finance, education, justice, and with labor, peasant, and women's affairs. The eight-hour day was proclaimed, wages were raised, and plans made for relief of the unemployed. The property of landlords, militarists and officials was confiscated and the landed estates proclaimed confiscated without compensation. Debts were annulled and usury declared a criminal offense. The Justice Department brought the arrested reactionaries to a mass trial and those found guilty of serious crimes against the people were shot. Lesser offenders were fined and released.

"I reorganized our army into one division of two regiments. The first regiment was made up of Ironsides veterans. The second was made up of the Peasant Self-Defense Corps that had joined us, and the new Ichang Workers Self-Defense Corps—about a thousand men in all. New volunteers kept coming in to join us and soon the second regiment had doubled in size, but it was not our policy at that time to enlarge our regular army to any great extent. Our policy was to organize and arm the peasants. Many cadres of the later Chinese Red Army—our present Eighth Route Army—came from this first great peasant struggle in Hunan. Wang Chen, who is now [1937] a brigadier general, and Hsiao Keh, who is now a divisional general, came from that struggle. Hsiao Keh was one of six sons of a peasant family, three of whom had already been killed by the Kuomintang. Another of his brothers joined our army at the time, but was later killed in action. Thousands of men in our army can tell similar stories."

After the occupation of Ichang by Chu Teh's forces, all southern and eastern Hunan burst into flames and peasants began dividing the land. They streamed to General Chu's headquarters for help against their landlords, and he selected cadres to return with them or sent small armed forces to aid them. Within a short time most of his troops were again scattered far and wide, and landlords were running for their lives to the great cities held by the Kuomintang or local militarist armies. When enemy troops threatened from the south, Chu Teh dispatched a couple of battalions of his veterans to mobilize and arm the peasants. When warlord Tang Sheng-chi moved troops into the district of Chenhsien to the north, Chu Teh sent still others. Finally Ichang was guarded by little more than a handful of the Workers Self-Defense Corps.

Three weeks after the occupation, two divisions of Chiang Kai-shek's troops began marching on Ichang. They were commanded by General Hsu Ko-hsiang, known as the "Peasant Butcher" because he had slaughtered thousands of peasants in Hunan in May 1927. The entire city took fright and evacuated to the villages. Chu Teh called back his troops and, together with the Ichang Soviet and the leaders of the people's organizations, withdrew into the mountains on the Hunan-Kwangtung border. In the first day in this region, the revolutionary army disarmed two thousand Min Tuan. Their weapons were turned over to the peasants.

With cries of "bandits!" the Peasant Butcherer sent two regiments to exterminate them. None of his men returned to tell the tale. Then he led five regiments in person against them. The pattern of military struggle adopted by the Revolutionary Army, which General Chu described, characterized his army in all the years that followed:

"We based ourselves on the people," he said. "Choosing our own battle-field and keeping the mountains to our back, we drew the enemy where we wanted him, then cut off his transport columns, attacked his flanks, then surrounded and destroyed him.

"When it became known that the Peasant Butcherer was in personal command, peasants armed themselves with everything from club to bird-gun and hurried by the thousand from every direction to help us. They wanted to catch the Peasant Butcherer alive. In a week-long battle, while our main forces attacked his main forces, the peasants destroyed his transport troops and hunted scattered groups as if they were leopards. When one enemy battalion was trying to escape over a wooden bridge, the bridge collapsed and hurled them into the river. The peasants hunted them up and down the river, shooting them in the water and beating to death any who crawled ashore. In the confusion of battle, the Peasant Butcherer hid himself in the bottom of a small boat that swirled down the river. That was a terrible disappointment to the peasants and many of them wept and cursed their bad luck. But two thousand of them armed themselves with good rifles during this battle.

"When we occupied Shihping, which the Peasant Butcherer had used as his headquarters, we found military supplies, food, and money for a whole division. The main street was so clogged that we had to climb over the supplies to pass. We captured enough guns to arm our entire 2nd Regiment with good rifles and light machine guns.

"I sent troops to pursue an enemy unit fleeing toward Ichang, which the Peasant Butcherer had occupied. This enemy unit ran right through the city, picking up the garrison as it ran, and ran into the mountains to the west, with our troops following. The peasants in the mountains and our troops in pursuit finished the lot of them off and the peasants got another five hundred guns."

The victorious revolutionary forces now returned to Ichang and re-established the Soviet, while Chu Teh led a few hundred of his veterans northward against the district city of Chenhsien where warlord Tang Sheng-chi had eleven companies of troops. On the way he met a group of peasants who had been inside Chenhsien to smell out the situation. To Chu Teh they reported:

"Six of the eleven companies of warlord Tang's troops in Chenhsien are not old mercenaries. They're students from primary and middle schools who have been conscripted and put in the Training Detachment to become officers. Most of them are under twenty, a few are kids of sixteen or seventeen. They're treated well and some are proud that they will be officers. These six companies have now left Chenhsien to march on Ichang to fight you. It's their first fight. They think you're bandits and if they're scared they'll fight. Why don't you pinch them off and if they fight rub them out?"

Chu's eyes gleamed as he stood listening, his hands braced on his hips. To Chen Yi and other staff officers with him he said:

"Six companies of educated youth—already with some military training! We need such men. We can send them to Ichang for retraining and then ask them to join us."

At a signal his troops gathered about him and sat down in the field, their rifles between their knees, while he and Chen Yi explained the importance of the six companies to the revolution. The companies were to be ambushed, disarmed and captured without one man being killed or wounded. They were to be treated like misguided brothers. When the attack began, slogans shouted should begin with "Brothers! Welcome to the revolution!" and such things, which would confuse and disconcert the students at first and perhaps prevent them from fighting.

This plan was carried out to the letter and every man of the six companies was captured and disarmed. They were escorted to a depression in the hills where Chu Teh and Chen Yi explained the nature and program of the Workers and Peasants Revolutionary Army. Chen Yi's speech, which was more like a conversation among friends, made the greatest impression on the captives because Chen Yi was himself from an old family of scholars. He explained that he had graduated from both Chengtu University in Szechwan and from a university in France, as well as from the famous Whampoa Military Academy founded by Sun Yat-sen in Canton. After explaining why he, a man from the same class as themselves, had chosen to continue the struggle against militarism and imperialism, Chen urged them to go peacefully with guards to Ichang to talk with other men like himself and Chu Teh. If they then wished to return to their homes, they could do so. They would even be given traveling money and military passes. Those who wished to fight for the revolution would be welcome, but they should realize that the revolutionary road would be long and bitter.

"Can we, the youth of China, fear suffering more than slavery?" asked Chen Yi, and many voices among the captives answered "No!"

A young commander in the revolutionary army stood up and explained that he also was a student whose entire family had taken part in the Great Revolution. When the counter-revolution began, one of his sisters and two of his brothers had been killed. Next a peasant soldier told of the tragic fate of his entire family who had struggled against the feudal landlords. As he talked the tears ran down his cheeks so that he had to cease speaking. Chu Teh looked at the captives and saw that some of them were also weeping.

Such meetings, which came to be known as the "Speak Bitterness Meetings," were typical of the Chinese revolution in the more than two decades that followed before it was victorious.

The six companies of educated youth were sent back to Ichang, where all but fifteen men joined the revolutionary army. When General Chu talked with me in 1937, many of them were military or political cadres in his army.

When the remaining five enemy companies in Chenhsien got wind of the approach of Chu Teh's column, they fled and Chu occupied the city without firing a shot. The Chenhsien Soviet was the second to be established in Hunan, after which all the villages established branches. After that other districts or county seats in southern Hunan fell to the revolution. By then Mao Tse-tung had swept down from Chingkanshan in Kiangsi and the Hankow garrison battalion at Chaling fanned out until, as General Chu expressed it, "the people's power was established in all south and eastern Hunan."

To the north of Chenhsien lay the large district of Leiyang with its district city of Leiyang where "the peasants and intellectuals were famous for their militance and heroism, and the landlords notorious for their ferocity." Chu Teh himself took command of troops to capture it. A few li before its southern gate he met about a thousand armed peasants who reported that the great landlords were in personal command of nearly a thousand well-armed Min Tuan and had built defense works on the southern approaches. They had omitted to erect any elsewhere, however, and the northern gate was always open and guarded by no more than half a dozen men.

Chu Teh again followed a plan proposed by the peasants. That night they marched through the hills to the east of Leiyang. As they passed through sleeping villages men got out of their beds, picked up such weapons as they had, and marched with them. The next morning, when the landlord commanders and the Min Tuan went out to their southern defenses to take over from those who had been on night duty, the revolutionary troops marched in and through the city and took them from the rear. Like hungry men, the peasants rushed on the Min Tuan and seized their weapons. Some of the landlords who fell into peasant hands were beaten to death on the spot.

The liberation of Leiyang and the establishment of the Leiyang Soviet were celebrated by the peasants for two weeks. Thousands of people poured into the city in orderly columns. After seeing the sights and attending mass meetings, they marched back to their villages. Each of the columns carried its great banners of the Peasant Self-Defense Corps—a big red field with a white plow in the center. The same banner was used by the Peasant Leagues and their Self-Defense Corps when Sun Yat-sen began the peasant movement in Kwangtung earlier.

Chu Teh was kept busy from morning to night with new volunteers who poured into his army and with the organization of peasant detachments who were sent back into the countryside to extend the revolution. He found time to speak at the daily mass meetings. There he first heard, and then met, a woman speaker who was known widely among the peasants as an intrepid peasant organizer. She was twenty-five years of age, and a powerful and intelligent speaker. She had natural feet, was physically strong, her hair was bobbed and her dark skin was pockmarked. She was not beautiful, but she had magnificent eyes that gleamed with intelligence and fiery determination.

She was introduced to Chu Teh as Wu Yu-lan, a writer and a member of an intellectual family that had played a leading role in the Great Revolution. Her two brothers immediately joined the revolutionary army and she joined its Political Department.

"Wu Yu-lan and I were married in Leiyang," General Chu remarked, and when I glanced up quickly he seemed somewhat embarrassed and hastened to explain. "It was not a conventional marriage. I had a wife in Szechwan whom I had not seen since 1922. We had sometimes corresponded but she had long since known that my life belonged to the revolution and that I would never return home. Both Wu Yu-lan and her family knew all this, but they were not bound by conventional forms. Of course Wu Yu-lan, like other women, kept her own name, had her own work in the Political Department, and spent the major part of her time out in the villages."

I interrupted General Chu to ask:

"Why are you so depressed when you speak of Wu Yu-lan? Didn't you love her?"

Staring grimly at some imaginary scene in the dim room about us, he replied in a hoarse voice:

"She was later captured by the Kuomintang. They tortured and beheaded her, then stuck her head on a pole and mounted it in one of the main streets of Changsha in Hunan, where she had been born."

After a long silence he shook off the memory and returned to Leiyang and related a hundred tales of peasant courage. The peasants were so emboldened by victories that they hurled themselves against regular Kuomintang troops and time and again were slaughtered. In April of 1928, for instance, two divisions of the Kwangsi Army, whose generals were planning to conquer Hunan and fight Chiang Kai-shek for the mastery of all China, occupied the big strategic and industrial town of Hengyang. Two peasant brothers known as Big Liu and Little Liu decided to drive them out and capture the city.

Without waiting for regular revolutionary troops, they assembled peasants and began marching, collecting others as they marched until there were some ten thousand hopeful fighters. They flung themselves on the two Kwangsi divisions before Hengyang. When the smoke cleared, the battlefield was littered with thousands of their dead, among them Big Liu and Little Liu.

During this same period, eight hundred miners from antimony mines at Shuikuoshan joined General Chu. Sung Chao-seng, a former blacksmith turned miner, had been one of the earliest Communists and labor organizers. A man of forty, Sung had led the antimony miners in many bloody struggles for their union and their study club, and had kept the union intact after the counter-revolution drove it underground. With iron bars and clubs, they had battled the mining company's armed guards, seized thirty rifles, and marched across country to join Chu Teh's army.

Called from his headquarters in Leiyang, General Chu stepped into the street to meet the miners. A number of them were little boys of eleven or twelve who, fearful that they would not be admitted to the army, were trying to look very tall. These children had been miners for three or four years, working the same number of hours as their men companions. Like many other poor children who joined the army, they were transferred to the Political Department to receive regular education whenever possible and to serve as orderlies or messengers about headquarters. These "little devils," as such children were affectionately called, grew up in the army and became cadres whose lives were devoted completely to the revolution.

In 1937, when General Chu talked of the miners, many were still in his army and had worked themselves up to become military commanders or political leaders. Sung Chao-seng, their leader, however, had been killed in action.

By April 1928, when five divisions of the Kwangsi Army opened their campaign against the revolutionary forces in Hunan, Chu Teh's forces consisted of about ten thousand men. Only a few hundred of them wore uniforms and most of them were barefoot until the women and girls of Leiyang started their big "sandal making campaign" which provided them with rope-and-straw sandals.

Many engagements with the powerfully equipped Kwangsi Army and with the troops of warlord Tang of Hunan proved to Chu Teh and his comrades that they would be destroyed by further fighting. In one battle with the Kwangsi Army, in which they had been supported by troops of Chu Teh's old friend, General Fang Shih-tseng, they had suffered heavy losses. General Fang had been forced back into Kwangtung Province.

Representatives of the Military Department of the Communist Party in both Chu Teh's and Mao Tse-tung's forces therefore met in conference. They decided that Chu's main forces should concentrate in the Linghsien district near the Hunan-Kiangsi border and withdraw to the strategic mountain base, Chingkanshan. From this base they were to turn all western Kiangsi and eastern Hunan into a base of the agrarian revolution. Many of Chu Teh's cadres, with plainclothes troops, were to remain in Hunan to keep the peasant movement alive.

Once the order of concentration was issued by General Chu, it was swiftly acted upon. One of the best departments developed by his army during this period, he said, was communications. The communication system spread in a network over all southern Hunan and eastern Kiangsi and spread further underground into "White" territory. It was manned entirely by peasants, some of whom could cover a hundred li, or over thirty miles, a day without much effort. The usual system was for a peasant to run for ten to twenty li, or three to six miles, and deliver letters, reports, or orders to another who sped on to the next station. Boatmen could travel more quickly, and, after horses were captured from the enemy, some messengers operated a pony express.

Chapter 21

FIGHTING and retreating and fighting and retreating again, Chu Teh's forces withdrew eastward. By the first week of May they were encamped in the Linghsien area preparatory to moving on to Chingkanshan. Kuo-

mintang armies in Kiangsi, who had been fighting Mao Tse-tung, by
then had occupied the main county seats in Linghsien. They had broken
the line of communications to Hunan, whereupon Mao Tse-tung had
stormed down from Chingkanshan to reopen the route. With two battalions he had come in person to meet Chu Teh at Linghsien.

This obscure meeting, where the two main streams of the agrarian
revolution mingled, proved to be one of the most portentous events in
Chinese history. Chu Teh had seen Mao Tse-tung once, but only across
a dim hall during a secret meeting, and they had never really met. From
the moment of their first meeting in Linghsien the lives of these two men
became so interwoven that they were like the two arms of one body. For
years thereafter the Kuomintang and foreign press often referred to
them as "the Red bandit chieftain, Chu Mao," and to the Red Army as
the "Chu Mao Army."

There were many striking similarities, as well as deep differences between the two men. Mao was ten years younger than Chu, who was now
forty-two. Both were educated peasants and both had taken part in every
revolutionary struggle since the 1911 Revolution. Mao had played a
leading role in the great May 4th Movement while Chu had existed on
its periphery and was stumbling in confusion in the morass of warlordism in Szechwan. Mao had organized the first Marxian study group
in Hunan and had been a delegate to the First Congress that founded the
Communist Party. After that he had been one of the chief party leaders
and a member of the Central Committee of the Kuomintang. He was a
writer of great power and insight—a political pamphleteer, a military
theorist, who sometimes wrote poetry.

In both appearance and temperament, Chu Teh was more of a peasant
than Mao. Both men were as direct, forthright and as practical as the
peasants from whom they sprang, but Mao was basically an intellectual
whose strange, brooding mind perpetually wrestled with the theoretical
problems of the Chinese revolution. Sensitive and intuitive almost to the
point of femininity, Mao nevertheless possessed all the self-confidence
and decisiveness of a pronouncedly masculine man. Both men were tough
and tenacious, characteristics more pronounced in Chu who, though
politically intelligent, was more a man of action and a military organizer.

Yet there was a strange contradiction in Chu Teh's nature. Beneath
his tough exterior hovered a deep sense of humility which in later years
often irritated Mao. This sense of humility was due not only to his poor
peasant origin and his peasant's respect for men of culture and learning,
but perhaps also due to an unconscious sense of guilt rooted in the years
he had spent as a militarist.

With his deep sense of character and integrity, Chu Teh seems to have discerned right away that he had met his alter ego, a man on whose judgment he could depend for the rest of his life.

Chu Teh's army continued its march through the mountains, guided by Mao Tse-tung's two battalions. They smashed the enemy troops that tried to impede their march and one week later they wound their way up one of the five or six narrow trails which were the only means of penetrating the famous strategic mountain region.

Chingkanshan was the general name for a mountainous area some 150 miles in circuit. Great forests of pine and spruce and bamboo rose on every hand, great flowering creepers wrapped trees in their embrace, and spring flowers cast their fragrance on the breeze. It was a region of great loveliness, yet shrouded in fogs for most of the year. When the fogs lifted, Chu Teh stared at towering volcanic peaks.

In the midst of this wild and relatively unproductive mountain region was a broad, circular valley surrounded by wooded slopes. In past ages, "bandit peasants" whose descendants now numbered fifteen hundred souls had founded five villages, each of them grouped around a well so that the valley was locally known as the "Five Big and Little Wells." It was in and around this valley that Chu Teh's troops constructed barracks, a training school, a hospital, an arsenal, and other institutions to serve as a training base and headquarters for the agrarian revolution which Mao Tse-tung had already begun among the peasants in the valleys and mountains beyond. Mao had also organized and begun the training of the peasants in the five villages, with the consent and help of their leaders, Wang Tso and Yuan Wen-tsai.

The peasants on the mountain depended for existence on their vegetable patches and on the sale of bamboo shoots, tea, and medicinal herbs. This had always been insufficient, so to make ends meet they had gone on marauding expeditions against distant towns. They had always left the local landlords unmolested.

"Banditry and landlordism have always gone hand in hand in China," said Chu Teh. "Landlordism breeds poverty and ignorance so that peasants often become bandits for at least part of each year. When, as in the Chingkanshan region, these banditized peasants are organized under leaders, the landlords make agreements with their leaders. Before we arrived on the mountain, Wang Tso and Yuan Wen-tsai received a little tribute from landlords and in return left them in peace. The landlords said, 'Don't raid us—raid others.' All this changed after we began the agrarian revolution, with the confiscation of the land and goods of the landlords and their distribution among the peasants. Then the landlords called in Kuomintang troops against us.

"Kuomintang troops garrisoned all the main cities and towns in six

districts surrounding Chingkanshan which we decided, after reaching
the region, to sovietize as a base from which to extend the revolution to
ever-expanding territory."

This decision was taken at a Communist Party conference immediately after Chu Teh's forces reached the mountain base. General Chu
called it "the most important party conference after the counter-revolution began." The conference reviewed the history of the revolution,
formulated far-reaching plans, and established the tactics and strategy of
revolutionary warfare. Mao Tse-tung advanced five basic characteristics
of Chinese revolutionary war which in turn determined the military and
political strategy adopted.

First, Mao said, China was a semi-colonial country of uneven political
development in which a few million industrial workers in a few modernized coastal and river cities coexisted with hundreds of millions of
peasants living under backward, semi-feudal conditions.

Secondly, China was a large country with abundant resources. It had
passed through the Great Revolution which had sowed the seeds of revolution which had sprouted into the Workers and Peasants Revolutionary
Army.

Thirdly, the Kuomintang, representing the counter-revolutionary bourgeoisie and the feudal landlord classes, had seized control of the country.
It had won the financial and military support, and would soon have the
official recognition, of the imperialist powers. Due to its control of the
country the Kuomintang could command great manpower and secure
the weapons with which to wage ruthless warfare on the people and their
armed forces.

A fourth characteristic of the Chinese revolution, Mao said, was the
weakness of the revolutionary army and its present location in mountainous regions where conditions were backward and unstable and where
it had no consolidated bases. Precarious food, clothing, arms, and other
material supplies would determine the tactics and strategy of the revolutionary army.

A fifth characteristic was the agrarian revolution and its leadership
by the Communist Party which enabled the revolutionary army, supported by the peasants, to exist, expand, and resist enemy offensives.

Mao stressed at the time and later wrote that the revolutionary army
had been able to exist and expand because its rank and file emerged
from the agrarian revolution and because the commanders and the rank
and file were politically one. The Kuomintang and local warlord armies,
on the other hand, opposed the agrarian revolution, received no help
from the peasants, and their ranks were rent with perpetual political

dissension, and their officers could not arouse the soldiers and lower officers to fight and die.

Accepting such analyses, the Communist conference formulated basic principles of struggle which, though often modified to conform with existing conditions, remained fundamentally the same for years. Chu Teh stripped the military tactics down to a few skeleton ideas:

(1) When the enemy advances, we retreat.
(2) When the enemy halts and encamps, we harass them.
(3) When the enemy seeks to avoid battle, we attack.
(4) When the enemy retreats, we pursue.

The Chingkanshan conference decided to reorganize Chu's and Mao's troops into one united force, called the Fourth Red Army because so many of the men sprang from the old Fourth Army of the Great Revolution era. Its banner was a white star with a hammer and sickle in the center of a red field. It adopted three main disciplines: (1) Obedience to orders. (2) Take not even a needle or thread from the people. (3) Turn in all confiscated goods.

Its eight additional rules were: replace all doors[1] and return all straw on which you sleep before leaving a house; speak courteously to the people and help them whenever possible; return all borrowed articles; pay for everything damaged; be honest in business transactions; be sanitary—dig latrines a safe distance from homes and fill them up with earth before leaving; never molest women; do not mistreat prisoners.

The conference further decided that, after transforming the six districts, or counties, surrounding Chingkanshan into a base of the agrarian revolution, these should be progressively expanded until they merged with still other similar areas in Kiangsi and adjoining provinces. In such regions the land was to be confiscated without compensation and distributed among the peasants; the peasants and other common people were to be organized, armed and trained, and, in so far as was possible, educated.

At that time, General Chu remarked, "We needed everything and had nothing. We put in vegetable crops on the mountain and we confiscated rice from the landlords in surrounding territory and laid in stores on the mountain for future use."

A peasant ballad composed at that time mentioned "the barefoot Chu Teh carrying rice up the mountainside." This must have been poetic

[1] [Wooden doors of peasant houses are hung on iron pins. Easily detached, they are often laid across Chinese flat stools and used as improvised beds.]

license because Chu declared that he had straw sandals and was not
barefoot.

In the military reorganization, he said, he was elected commander in
chief and Mao Tse-tung the political commissar. Mao directed all party
work in the army and among the masses, and all political-educational
work among the troops. The Political Department was "the lifeline of
the army," preventing it from degenerating into militarism. Its purpose,
Chu added, was "to create an educated, conscious, iron revolutionary
army dedicated to the liberation of the country and the emancipation of
our people." Compared with later developments, the political work was
primitive, yet even under the most harassing conditions the troops were
taught the history of the revolution, the history of foreign aggression
against China, and methods of mass leadership and organization. They
were also taught how to carry on propaganda with enemy troops; singing; and public speaking.

Of all the revolutionary troops, the old Ironsides veterans and the
Shuikuoshan miners were the swiftest, most disciplined, vigilant and
politically advanced, while the peasant troops took things easy and
"even in the midst of a campaign would stop by the wayside to cook and
eat." To raise their efficiency, Chu distributed Shuikuoshan miners
among them as military and political leaders, and also transferred five
to six hundred of peasant "uprising leaders" to a special Training
Detachment.

While on Chingkanshan, General Chu began collecting and binding
together the songs used by the army, adding to them, until by 1937 he
had a small booklet of about two hundred pages just large enough to slip
easily into his tunic pocket. This booklet was so dog-eared and thumbed
that some of its pages were illegible. It contained songs, short poems,
army rules, essays on the history and principles of the Communist Party,
and a list of the various national and international memorial days com-
memorated by the army.

These memorial days were both doctrinaire and symbolic: March 8th,
International Woman's Day; March 12th, anniversary of Sun Yat-sen's
death; March 18th, anniversary of the Paris Commune; April 12th,
anniversary of the Shanghai massacre; May 1st, international labor day;
May 4th, birth of the student movement; May 5th, birthday of Karl
Marx; May 21st, anniversary of the massacre of Hunan peasants by Hsu
Ko-hsiang; May 30th, anniversary of the Shanghai massacre by the British in 1925; June 23rd, anniversary of the Canton massacre by British
and French troops; August 1st, the Nanchang uprising; October 10th,
the 1911 Revolution; November 7th, the Russian October Revolution;

December 11th, anniversary of the Canton Commune; December 25th, anniversary of the Yunnan uprising by Tsai Ao in 1915; and January 21st, in memory of Lenin's death.

Some of the first songs in General Chu's songbook read like the outpourings of men just lifting themselves from slavery. Others were old folk melodies set to new words. One was "The International" and another "The International Youth Song." There were simple drill and shooting songs, and even the army rules were set to music. One was a propaganda song for use on enemy troops, and one recalled the Canton Commune. There was a nostalgic song about Chingkanshan which, curiously enough, was set to the music of the American song "Dixie."

Of the many folk melodies set to new words, one, entitled "Three Great Tasks," was a catechism to music:

> Our Red Army has three great tasks:
> To destroy imperialism and the feudal forces,
> To carry out the agrarian revolution,
> To establish the people's sovereignty.
> To each according to his needs,
> From each according to his ability.
>
> Our speech to the people must be friendly.
> Spread Red Army principles among the masses.
> Enlarge its political influence.
> To be a model Red Army man,
> Take not one needle or strand of thread
> From a worker or peasant.

Of the Chinese love songs, one had a Biblical ring:

> My beloved! I say farewell before our bed
> And tell you not to love me.
> We must travel the revolutionary road.
>
> My beloved! I say farewell before our door.
> We must walk the revolutionary way,
> Enduring all hardships for its sake.
>
> My beloved! I say farewell in our courtyard.
> Burden not your heart with thoughts of me.
> We must march the revolutionary road.

My beloved! I say farewell before our gate.
The dark days of hell are past,
The bright road stretches before us.

My beloved! I say farewell on the main road.
Write me, but send news of joy.
Send news of revolutionary victory.

My beloved! I say farewell by the riverside.
If you are captured and turn reactionary,
You can never find the right road again.

My beloved! Go quickly, quickly to the Red Army.
Return to me only in victory,
And we will open our hearts again.

Thumbing tenderly through this booklet of songs wrapped in a faded, ink-stained red cloth and crudely stapled together, General Chu recalled the wild crags and lush green valleys of Chingkanshan, the bamboo and fir forests, the shrubs and fragrant flowers and the clouds that shrouded it almost the year round. The roofs of houses were made from the bark of trees, and grass grew on them so that from above they looked like green flannel.

Chu tramped over the entire region, studying the terrain and defenses and talking with the bandit-peasant leaders Wang and Yuan. They told him of Old Deaf Chu, a bandit, who had said: "You don't have to know how to fight; all you have to know is how to encircle the enemy."

They had followed the advice of Old Deaf Chu and Chingkanshan had never been breached in their lifetime. Yet their followers were armed with weapons as primitive as bows and arrows. Their cannon were made from tree trunks. They would cut down a big tree, then hew the trunk in lengths of five or six feet each. Leaving one end solid, they hollowed out the rest and bored an ignition hole near the solid end. They packed the barrel with black powder, bits of iron, lead, and sharp pebbles.

These wooden cannon were placed in concealed emplacements along the five or six narrow trails leading up Chingkanshan, and when the enemy drew near they lit the fuse and ran for their lives. The gun went with the explosion, blown to pieces, but "they stripped enemy soldiers down to their skeletons."

The bows and arrows used on Chingkanshan had a span of five, six or more feet, the arrows were three to six inches in diameter and the tips poisoned. One end of the bow would be placed on the ground and the arrow released by a trigger operated by the foot.

"I learned a lot from the tactics of Old Deaf Chu," General Chu laughed. "Kuomintang armies all fought by the usual Japanese military tactics, always advancing in one column, with front and flank guards. Beyond this they knew nothing. But we split up into small, swift combat units which got in their rear and on their flanks, and attacked, cutting them into segments. There's nothing secret about such tactics. Anyone can learn them, and the militarists later tried to use them against us. They failed because such guerrilla warfare requires not only a thorough knowledge of the terrain of the battle area but also the support of the common people. The people hated and spied on the Kuomintang militarists, waylaid and destroyed small units and stragglers, and captured their transport columns. There came a time when enemy armies were afraid to advance after they sighted even one barefoot peasant watching them from a distance."

The Fourth Red Army took the offensive against the landlords and militarists in the six surrounding districts in the first week of June 1928. Within one week the Red Army cleaned three counties of all enemy forces, seized all their supplies, and took twelve hundred captives. Councils of People's Delegates were established in the county seats, and smaller councils in the villages. The land was divided among the peasants, the peasants were organized, armed and trained, and Women, Youth, and Labor Associations founded. The first break in the ancient subjection of women to men was made.

Enemy troops sent against the revolution from central Kiangsi were hurled back, shattered and bleeding. Not only did able-bodied peasants fight, but even children and the aged did their bit.

Tales of "Red bandit atrocities" filled the foreign and Chinese press in the great cities. General Chiang Kai-shek concluded temporary truces with rival militarists who had been fighting him, and then issued orders to 40,000 troops from three provinces to surround the Chingkanshan area and starve the "Red bandits" to death.

In the Hunan divisions ordered to blockade the mountain area from the north were two young officers who later played a tremendous role in Chinese revolutionary history. One was a battalion commander, Hwang Kung-lei. The other was Peng Teh-huai, a regimental commander in temporary command of a brigade. After the Second World War, Peng became deputy commander of the People's Liberation Army of which

General Chu Teh was commander in chief. In addition, there was a young company commander, Kung Ho-chan, who, when the revolution got too hot in the '30s, joined Chiang Kai-shek.

These three Kuomintang officers were secret members of the Communist Party. Their troops held the Pinghsiang-Liling mining region to the north of Chingkanshan. In July, when ordered to tighten the blockade, Peng Teh-huai led his brigade in insurrection. In the confusion, nearly half of his men changed sides half a dozen times. Eventually, with two thousand troops and hundreds of miners, he moved into the countryside, joined up with the peasants, and established a guerrilla area which later became the Northeastern Kiangsi Soviet District.

During this same period General Chu Teh led three regiments of the Red Army on a diversionary maneuver down into south Hunan to cut off blockading troops advancing from Kwangtung Province. His campaign embodied elements of both revenge and comedy. His old Yunnan Army friend, General Fang Shih-tseng, had by now forgotten such trivialities as friendship and had "turned over" to the counter-revolution. Chu Teh decided to teach him a lesson.

General Fang's troops occupied a south Hunan city, well stocked with ammunition. Swooping down upon this city, General Chu's troops surprised a few companies of Fang's troops drilling in a field. General Chu calmly walked into their midst while his troops disarmed the last man of them without firing a shot. Next Chu nonchalantly entered a big hall in the city where a few hundred men were listening to a lecture. At his order, his troops took all rifles and cartridge belts hung from the walls of the hall while the hundreds of men sat at their desks and stared in amazement. In the meantime the rest of his troops, equipped with shoulder poles and ropes, were carrying out boxes of ammunition.

The whole raid lasted no more than an hour, and by the time General Fang's troops caught their breath Chu Teh was leading his troops back toward Chingkanshan.

Heavily burdened with their trophies, General Chu's troops moved back to the mountains. They met Mao Tse-tung who had come with two regiments to help them. Mao reported that by now the blockade of Chingkanshan was almost complete. Alternately marching and laying down their burdens to fight off attacking enemy troops, Chu and Mao at last reached one of the small, tortuous trails and moved up into the wildness of Chingkanshan.

"From our base on Chingkanshan we could look down on the enemy troops," General Chu said. "We knew all their movements and even watched them cook their meals. On the last night of the autumn harvest festival, when the moon was full, we sent troops down the mountain to capture six enemy companies encamped at the base of one of the trails. A couple of hours later they marched up the trail with them and their supplies. The six companies, being peasants, joined us. A week later a battalion of the blockading troops deserted to us because they were Szechwan troops who had heard that I was also a Szechwan man."

More and more enemy troops came up to tighten the blockade. The Red troops swooped down the mountain on night raids for weeks, but these soon cost more ammunition than they were worth and resulted in heavy casualties. The mass movement in the countryside beyond had been crushed or driven underground. Rice was rationed on Chingkanshan where the troops had put in fields of squash. Week after week squash was their only vegetable.

From the end of September onward the fighting front was frozen and by December the Red troops began to starve. Five thousand men filled the hospitals and barracks. Some were wounded, but most of them were suffering from hunger and some had pneumonia and tuberculosis. It was wet and cold and they had little warm clothing.

In mid-December, Peng Teh-huai marched into the mountain area from the north with a thousand men, half of them peasants. Peng had built up a force of four thousand, but half had been lost in fighting. Leaving a thousand behind under Hwang Kung-lei's command, he had led the rest to Chingkanshan.

Following Peng's arrival, a conference was called and plans were made to break the enemy blockade. Peng was to remain on the mountain with fifteen hundred men and with the sick and wounded, while Mao and Chu were to lead four thousand others, including a number of women from the Political Department—among them Chu Teh's wife Wu Yu-lan— through the blockade and start guerrilla warfare to draw off the enemy. Each man and woman going on this expedition was to take just one pound of cooked rice in the pouch which each carried. Except for a few advance squads, who were to be issued a few rounds of ammunition each, all the rest of the ammunition was to be left on Chingkanshan.

Chapter 22

GENERAL CHU drew a rough sketch of the wild mountain range along which he and Mao Tse-tung led their four thousand through the enemy blockade. No one but the bandit-peasants of Chingkanshan knew

of this way of leaving the mountain stronghold, and few indeed had been
the men who had dared risk it. There was no path, not even the trace of
a trail, only a chaos of huge boulders and jagged volcanic peaks towering above yawning chasms.

At dawn on January 4, 1929, the column of gaunt and ragged men
and women began creeping single file along the jagged crest of this
mountain spur that connected Chingkanshan with the mountain range
that runs southward along the Kiangsi-Hunan border. The stones and
peaks were worn to slippery smoothness by no one knows how many eons
of fierce winds, rains and snow. Snow lay in pockets and an icy wind
lashed the bodies of the column that inched forward, crawling over huge
boulders and hanging on to one another to avoid slipping into the black
chasms below.

By nightfall they reached a small, sloping plateau of solid volcanic
rock where they ate half of the cold cooked rice which each had brought
along. Huddling together and linking arms they sat down on the slope
and spent the night, shivering and coughing. At daybreak they were again
creeping southward, and by late afternoon reached an overgrown trail
that led down a wooded mountain slope toward the village of Tafen,
where a battalion of enemy troops was stationed. Here they halted to eat
the last half of their cold rice. When darkness fell they began moving
stealthily down the trail, under strict orders not to make a sound, forbidden even to cough.

Reaching the foot of the trail, they surrounded Tafen village while
the squads with ammunition moved in and overpowered the enemy
garrison.

"We ate that night!" General Chu remarked with grim satisfaction.
"After talking with them, we released the captives. We had no plans to
train such men and, anyway, we wanted them to spread the alarm. We
hoped the blockading troops would come after us. We learned later that
they didn't. Troops from other places were alerted, instead."

Marching swiftly southward, the Red troops, as ragged as scarecrows,
struck like lightning at landlords and their Min Tuan, feeding and supplying themselves from their enemies and wrapping themselves in such
clothing as fell to them from landlord homes, and everywhere calling to
the peasants to destroy their ancient enemies.

Shattering the local garrison, they occupied the tungsten city of Tayu
in southwest Kiangsi where the people, knowing them from the past,
poured out to mass meetings. Here they remained for three days to revive
the suppressed mass movement, thus giving an enemy regiment time to
come up and, in a confusing and desperate battle, kill hundreds of them.

Chu and Mao gave the order to retreat, and for the next ten days the small army fought a desperate running battle through the icy mountains along the Kiangsi-Kwangtung border with enemy troops swarming against them from every direction, following them by the bloody tracks they left on the snow-covered paths behind them. Often without any food, and never with enough, burdened with their sick and wounded, they moved up and down the wintry mountains, covering fifty or sixty miles before resting in the open or in some town or village that opened its doors to them. After a few hours' rest, they began marching shortly after midnight to outstrip the enemy troops who operated only by day.

Approaching a village, they would send a man or two in advance, and the peasants would come out, collect rice for them and take and hide their wounded, their sick and exhausted. Each man left behind under the care of peasants was given his rifle and a few rounds of ammunition so that he might, upon recovery, begin organizing and training the peasants.

"We aimed so to train our men that even if only one escaped alive he would be able to rise up and lead the people," General Chu said. "We fought many battles during that terrible time and in one we lost two hundred men. In another, twenty of our men and one Whampoa cadet were captured. They joined an enemy regiment that garrisoned a south Kiangsi hsien (county or district). A few months later they led that entire regiment in insurrection and turned the hsien into a guerrilla base. It later became one of our strongest Soviet districts."

In still another battle, Chu Teh's wife, Wu Yu-lan, was among the missing. The girl was tortured and beheaded, after which the severed head was sent to her native city, Changsha, where the city fathers mounted it on a pole in one of the main streets as a warning to all who thought as she had. . . .

The Chinese lunar New Year season came, red New Year greetings gleamed on every door, and the sound of music came from restaurants and the homes of the wealthy. Down in the small district city of Juikin in south Kiangsi, a regiment of provincial troops returned to tell how they had destroyed most of the "Chu Mao bandits" and chased the remnants over the border into Fukien Province. In thanks for such good work the leading citizens of the town presented the regiment with a fine New Year dinner. Laughter mingled with the gurgle of wine and the odors of cooking food. Red candles gleamed on the long tables set up in the barracks. So secure did the regiment feel that not even a sentry was left on duty.

The fine food was on the tables and the soldiers had just seated themselves and reached for their chopsticks, when something like the scream of a bullet in flight brought a silence as deep as infinity. In openmouthed amazement they looked up at the "Chu Mao bandits," as gaunt as timber wolves, who seemed to have arisen from the earth and who stood in long lines about the hall, their guns at the ready. At a hoarse command, the regiment arose as one man, hands over their heads, out into the night where other ragged specters locked them inside a great stone ancestral temple and stationed guards to hold them there.

"We finished the New Year feast for them," General Chu laughed. "Next morning we moved northeast into the Tapoti mountains, with a division of enemy troops moving against us from two directions. But we had run enough, and in a conference we decided to get rid of our pursuers once and for all. We selected our own battlefield. Our troops discussed the plan of battle until everything was clear, then met in a mass meeting and with raised fists swore to destroy the enemy or die in the attempt."

As was his custom, General Chu described in detail the battle which was fiercely fought but which, he said, was "really very simple." Lin Piao led one regiment ten miles through the night to get in the rear of one enemy column before dawn, when the battle began. The enemy had everything while the Red troops had no more than twenty rounds of ammunition each. This was soon exhausted as they struck from every direction and with everything they had. They used their rifles or even branches torn from the trees as clubs. By the time the sun was overhead, they had completely destroyed the enemy division.

There were only about a thousand captives, and of these General Chu selected one hundred poor peasants. He asked them to join the Red Army, eat bitterness with it, and fight until it was victorious. The rest of the captives were released because "they were old mercenaries and opium smokers . . . we didn't want such men."

The Tapoti battle was a turning point in the agrarian revolution and in enemy morale. Thereafter enemy troops followed the Red Army only from a respectful distance while the Fukien troops withdrew to their own province, saying the whole thing was none of their business.

With their small bands of intrepid agitators going in advance "to prepare the peasants," the Red Army took the walled city of Ningtu in central Kiangsi a few days later. The local garrison and the landlords fled as it approached while the Chamber of Commerce, acting as had such organizations from time immemorial, pulled down the Kuomintang banner, ran up the red flag, and offered the army five thousand dollars and the keys to the city.

Chu and Mao accepted the five thousand dollars but refused an invitation from the Chamber of Commerce to a banquet. The army took over all the food and other possessions of the landlords, distributed the surplus to the city poor, and called a mass meeting of the entire civilian population. As in every town and city which it occupied, it also opened the prison doors, releasing all prisoners regardless of the charges against them because, General Chu declared, "crime is a class question." Many were political prisoners who had been kept in shackles and tortured until they were crippled for life. Others were poor men who had been imprisoned for petty offenses against private property, such as the theft of food or clothing.

After three days in Ningtu, the Red Army gathered up its wounded, its sick and exhausted, and the confiscated rice supplies from the landlords, and marched to the west toward the Tungku mountain base, which had already prepared to welcome it.

The march toward Tungku became a triumphal procession, with peasants pouring out from all the villages to help carry the wounded and the supplies. The town of Lungkang at the base of Tungku, a strong center of the peasant movement, turned out to welcome the Red troops and offer them the hospitality of its homes. Here Chu and Mao met Li Wen-ling, a former Whampoa military cadet who, with a company of guerrillas, had come to guide them up the mountain.

With his deep feeling for the beauty of nature, General Chu described Tungku much as he had previously spoken of Chingkanshan. This mountain was part of a forested range that stretches north and south through Kiangsi. It was in a high mountainous area, but not as impregnable as Chingkanshan, he said. Narrow trails led up over its four levels, and on every hand were forests of spruce and fir, flowering bamboo, shrubs and, in the spring and summer, wild flowers in great profusion. Near the summit was a broad and fertile plateau dotted with small villages and with the market town of Tungku near its center. In the fertile valleys that poured onto the plateau were other small villages.

Some twenty-five miles south of Tungku stood the large walled town of Hsingkuo which, a few weeks later, fell to the Red Army and was united with Tungku in the "Tungku-Hsingkuo Regional Soviet District."

The small hospital which had already been established in Tungku was too small to accommodate all the Red Army sick, wounded and exhausted, and many were invited into the peasant homes.

Here on this high plateau the Red troops rested and bathed. They repaired and boiled their ragged clothing to rid them of the lice that had tormented them. They doctored their torn feet, and made themselves sandals with strong rope soles and uppers of many colors. Their education did not cease even for a day. Each morning companies of troops could be seen at drill or maneuvers and after the first of their two daily meals they gathered to hear lectures by their military or political leaders or to take part in discussions.

Common educational subjects, such as reading and writing, were not taught methodically as they were later, but even in this dawn of the agrarian revolution commanders tried to find time to teach the illiterate. Paper and pencils were the sheerest of luxuries, but men would sit in a circle on the ground and trace Chinese characters and figures in the dirt with small sticks.

But the most powerful educational method evolved by the Red Army, and one which it practiced throughout its existence, consisted of the conferences in which past battles or campaigns were analyzed. In these conferences, every commander and fighter participated, including General Chu and Mao Tse-tung. All rank disappeared and men had full rights of free speech. Not only was the plan of battle or campaign discussed and, if men felt the necessity, criticized, but the individual conduct of any commander or fighter could be criticized. Of course men could defend themselves against criticism which they felt to be unjust, but if the charges were proved against them they would thereafter be disciplined by army headquarters.

General Chu placed the greatest importance on such conferences. They developed the men in every possible way, he said, and also kept the army democratic. By such methods, he said, men who failed to do their duty in battle, or who violated the democratic regulations of the army, would be demoted and reeducated, while men who distinguished themselves by intelligence or special courage were promoted from the ranks. At the same time the inarticulate peasant fighter learned to think and express himself on military, political and human problems. He learned the nature of a democratic army, as opposed to the old feudal militarist armies, he learned vigilance and responsibility, and he learned to value his own worth as a man and as a responsible member of a revolutionary army.

In similar conferences, plans for new battles or campaigns were placed before the army for discussion, and Chu Teh never failed to be impressed by the questions asked or ideas advanced by the rank and file in such gatherings.

"While our men had to obey orders in the midst of battle, we did not want them merely to accept and obey without understanding, as was the case with soldiers in the Kuomintang armies. We were a people's revolutionary army, building for the future."

He remembered one general mass meeting in Tungku where Mao Tse-tung and he were among the main speakers. "We are weak and small," Mao Tse-tung told them, "but a spark can kindle a flame and we have a boundless future." As so often, Mao explained the general strategy and tactics of the revolution which, he said, must begin with the seizure of small areas in the countryside and the construction of secure mountain strongholds such as Tungku and Chingkanshan which would eventually be united. "With time, and under certain conditions," he continued, "the people's power will be extended to areas that include large towns. From the liberation of a small part of the country we will thus advance to larger and still larger areas; and eventually we will liberate all China."

It was a strategy so simple and practical that any man could understand it, yet when viewed against a continent and through the haze of an unknown future it was complicated and beset by a thousand uncertainties.

General Chu had his own special repertoire. He never failed to emphasize two main lines of thought in all his speeches. First, he gave the troops and the people an historical background of the Chinese revolution, from the Taiping Rebellion onward, thus inspiring them with the conviction that they were the heirs of a great revolutionary tradition. Secondly, he repeated over and over again that "in a semi-feudal and semi-colonial country such as China, there can be no place for peasants and workers, no place for the Communist Party, for agrarian or other reforms, and no victory for the revolution, without armed struggle." This struggle of the peasants in the countryside, he declared, could succeed only if it had the support of the industrial workers and the petty bourgeoisie—including the intellectuals—in the towns and cities.

In that early spring of 1929, he frankly analyzed the national and international situation, in so far as he knew it, for the troops and the people. Chiang Kai-shek, he said, had ordered eleven regiments of Kuomintang troops to blockade the Tungku mountain stronghold. Chiang was also beginning a war with the Kwangsi generals for mastery of the country. He could not spare his best troops as he had been able to do for the blockade of Chingkanshan. In fact, Chu added, the Fukien provincial troops who, as everyone knew, were primarily professional bandits incorporated into the Kuomintang armies, had been ordered to take part in the Tungku blockade, but had failed to show up. Such troops, he said, wanted only to be "left in peace to collect taxes and sell opium in their own domain."

While thieves and robbers quarreled or fought among themselves, he said, the people should use the occasion to organize and arm themselves and build up their power.

In the northeast, or Manchuria, he further explained, there were conflicts and contradictions involving both the Chinese ruling classes and
the imperialists. The "Young Marshal," Chang Hsueh-liang, who ruled
Manchuria, had defied Japanese imperialism by raising the Kuomintang
flag and, to protect himself, had transferred all foreign affairs in his
region to Chiang Kai-shek's regime at Nanking. As Chiang had done in
his territory, the Young Marshal claimed the exclusive right to appoint
all members of the Kuomintang in the northeast, so that the Kuomintang
was nothing but an organization of officials and militarists. But the Japanese had not finished with the Young Marshal, nor with Manchuria.
Nor, for that matter, had the other imperialist powers, all of whom had
designs on that great region.

Thinking back on those far-off days, General Chu Teh admitted that
while there were conflicts and contradictions among the counter-revolutionary and imperialist forces, the revolutionaries also had problems not
easily solved. For example, he said, upon arriving on Tungku, he and his
comrades found a most curious situation among the Communist leaders
who controlled this stronghold. These men were the sons of landlords,
or even landlords themselves, yet they were by and large young, educated men who had played a serious role in the Great Revolution during
which period they had become Communists. Some of them were graduates of the Whampoa Military Academy and one had been an instructor
in that famous institution. All of them had taken part in the Nanchang
uprising, after which they had returned to their native homes in the
Tungku region to begin the agrarian revolution.

These "intellectuals," as General Chu called them, had done everything
for the revolution—except divide their own land among their tenants. As
benevolent landlords and as natives of the region, they had the support
of the peasants and of their own tenants.

Here, in the midst of the Communist Party and the agrarian revolution
which it had begun, were clear remnants of feudalism both in thought
and in action. The problem was further complicated for Mao Tse-tung,
Chu Teh, and their staffs because, at a moment when strong enemy forces
were concentrating against the Red Army, they dared not insist that the
native Tungku party leaders live up to the program and policies of the
cause to which they had pledged their lives. To have insisted on this at
such a moment might have precipitated a serious internal struggle. The
Red Army, therefore, could only wait for the revolutionary ferment to
work among the Tungku masses.

This ferment worked about a year later, when the agrarian revolution
swept Kiangsi like a flame. The Twentieth Red Army Corps of Tungku

natives, whose commanders and political leaders were members or followers of the Tungku leaders, arose in insurrection against the Red Army. Fearful of their own peasant troops, the commanders of this army dared not denounce the Communist Party and the Red Army as such. Instead, they denounced Mao Tse-tung and Chu Teh as false Communists, and set up their own small Communist Party.

Of all such local leaders, only one remained loyal to the Red Army. This man, later chief of staff of the Fifteenth Red Army Corps, was still with the Red Army in 1937 when General Chu talked with me, and was an instructor in Kangta, the Resistance University at Yenan. The others, however, failed to stem the tide of the agrarian revolution which by then had ceased to be the work of individuals.

Book VII

"Now Listen Closely to My Song"

Chapter 23

THE small "poor man's army," as the peasants called the Red Army, which gathered on the Tungku plateau in the early south China spring of 1929, hardly looked like an army at all. Yet it was the embryo of the great People's Liberation Army which swept over China twenty years later and shook the world.

After the Tungku guerrillas had been reorganized into its ranks, the army numbered around four thousand men. Of these, three thousand left on a campaign just eight days after reaching the mountain refuge for rest. The others remained behind to till the fields and guard the Tungku stronghold, and of these nearly three hundred were Chu-Mao veterans still in hospital or not yet strong enough to fight.

Of the three thousand leaving on the campaign, no more than half carried some kind of modern weapon while the others were armed with spears. A few were clad in remnants of what were once uniforms, the rest in the patched loose trousers and short jackets, rope sandals and odd assortment of headgear that the poor of China wear.

They were lean and hungry men, many of them in their middle or late teens, with big hard hands and thickly calloused feet, to whom life had been nothing but a round of toil and privation, insecurity and oppression. Most were illiterate. Each man wore a long, sausage-like rice pouch long enough to encircle one shoulder and tie at the opposite hip, a pouch now filled with enough rice to last for two or three days after which it would have to be replenished from the bins of landlords, or with rice captured from the supply columns of the enemy.

Their second article of equipment consisted of a cloth cartridge belt long enough to wrap around each shoulder, cross in front and back, and go around the waist. The belts of men with rifles now held a few rounds of ammunition each, but those worn by men with spears were empty. When Chu Teh made his final inspection he had said to the spear bearers:

"Each of you will soon carry a gun, and your cartridge belts will be filled."

There was nothing to distinguish Chu or Mao, or any other commander, from the rank and file. There is a faded old photograph taken
of Chu Teh in the summer of 1929. It shows a company of troops sitting
in a circle on the ground, their rifles between their knees and their faces
uplifted as they listen to him speak. Chu Teh is standing in the center
of the ring, his head uncovered and close-shaven and his clothing nothing but a pair of shorts and an open peasant jacket exposing the bare
skin beneath. His legs are bare and his feet encased in a pair of rope
sandals. He stands in his customary pose, his legs apart, his hands on his
hips, a humorous expression on his face.

So he must have appeared as he spoke to the big farewell mass meeting
of troops and peasants on the Tungku plateau in that early spring of
1929. He talked of the eleven enemy regiments that were concentrating to
the north, west, and south of the mountain stronghold. He may have said,
as he did a thousand times in later years, that "we must take advantage
of the contradictions among the enemy, win over the majority, oppose the
minority, and smash them one by one."

And the signs of conflict and contradictions among the enemy were
many indeed, as every man knew, because the eastern approaches to
Tungku were still free of enemy concentrations. Chiang Kai-shek, busy
fighting his rivals, the Kwangsi generals, had ordered troops from Fukien
Province to move up and complete the blockade around the mountain
from the east, but his orders were not obeyed because, as General Chu
expressed it, "these Fukien troops wanted to be left in peace to collect
taxes and sell opium." Nor, General Chu said, could Chiang spare his
best troops to fight the Red Army, but had ordered up second-rate local
forces. And now the Red Army was going forth to draw them off from
the mountain and to destroy them one by one.

Eight days is no time at all for weary men to rest, yet on the eighth
night after reaching Tungku, when the moon was high, Chu and Mao led
their three thousand down the eastern slopes and began the campaign.
In fighting a numerically superior force, the Reds not only used tactics
of their own invention to fit the situation on the spot, but they most certainly drew upon the tactics of Chinese and Mongol armies of ancient
times, of the Taipings in the nineteenth century, and on experiences won
in the Great Revolutionary period of 1925-1927, tactics which bewildered
Kuomintang commanders taught in Japanese military academies.

Reaching the foot of the mountain, small groups of the swiftest
marchers made off in the direction opposite to the main forces and made
feints at large towns to draw the enemy after them, then faded away in

the villages and appeared suddenly before other towns. All the while Chu and Mao were after the landlord Min Tuan in villages far away, arousing and arming the people and leaving cadres behind to continue what had been begun.

After a time the enemy was baying across all south Kiangsi, hunting for the elusive Reds who, guided by the peasants, made surprise attacks on them at night, pinched off their supply columns in swift, fierce raids, and disappeared only to appear again miles away shortly afterwards.

Then came the windfall of Tingchow, a turning point in revolutionary development. The Reds had not planned to take it. Following a twenty-hour march to evade numerically superior forces gathered against them, the army bivouacked on the mountain range that runs north-south along the Kiangsi-Fukien border but a short distance north of the walled city of Tingchow in south Fukien Province.

Tingchow was held by the ex-bandit chieftain, Kuo Fang-ming, who by successful banditry had become a great landlord and Kuomintang general. Kuo's troops, most of them professional bandits and opium smokers who had been incorporated into the Kuomintang armies, could be defeated if enticed out from behind the walls of Tingchow, but this would be impossible unless they believed their enemy was small and poorly armed.

They could come by one route only, and this was along a footpath that led from Tingchow northward through a narrow valley through which a swift and deep river ran. The Red Army was bivouacked on the mountain range overlooking this valley.

The Red troops sent their peasant guides into Tingchow to spread the news that the "Red bandits" were encamped just a stone's throw from the city, that their weapons were few and their ammunition none; then they pillowed their heads on their guns and waited for the morning to come.

Before noon next day two regiments of enemy troops came marching single file along the footpath through the valley. When runners reported that the enemy commander was riding in a sedan chair borne by four carriers, General Chu smiled, saying: "It may be General Kuo himself seeking merit." When the enemy was where Chu and Mao wanted them, Red outposts fired a few random shots and then ran noisily up the mountainside as if in fear. "Our outposts have fired and will draw them into the mountains," guessed General Chu. The enemy troops immediately took up the chase, climbing higher and higher, panting and sweating, and growing bolder as they met no resistance. The Red troops finally erupted from their concealed positions and the enemy turned and tumbled in terror down the mountainside with the Reds on top of them. There was some fighting on the footpath but the enemy remnants were soon pinned against the river and totally disarmed.

In the midst of this final action, a guard ran into General Chu's command post and shouted: "A big fat fellow in a fine uniform and hung with luxuries has been killed while trying to escape in a boat on the river!"

The big fat fellow proved none other than General Kuo Fang-ming, and the "luxuries" consisted of a huge gold watch and chain and a number of rings which he had worn on his fat fingers.

By nightfall the Red Army had taken Tingchow, disarmed the enemy troops within its walls, and by daybreak next morning had established its power over the walled towns and surrounding territory within a radius of fifty miles. And, as was the practice, Mao Tse-tung set to work without rest to revive the people's organizations and organize Councils of People's Delegates, or Soviets, exactly as had been done since the agrarian revolution began. Tingchow was the center for the entire region. Some landlords were captured, others fled to the great walled city of Shanghang to the south. Soon the land was being divided by village and town committees.

Chu Teh, who could work ceaselessly on no more than three or four hours of sleep, had his own work. Examining and then rejecting the captive enemy troops, most of whom were opium smokers as well as old professional bandits, he called for and got a thousand young peasant volunteers. Two thousand other peasants were soon organized by him and his staff into peasant partisans, the younger men into Red Guards. Everywhere in the liberated regions, squads of these young peasants could be seen drilling and learning the difficult art of marching in rhythm.

The Red Guards, a people's militia, were attached to agricultural production and armed chiefly with spears. These spears were often more effective than rifles in hand-to-hand contests in forested mountains. The regular peasant partisans were able-bodied young men, all of them better armed than the Red Guards. They formed a reservoir for the regular Red Army, but they fought only as auxiliaries, not as front-line fighters. Operating in the enemy rear, they waylaid enemy messengers and patrols, destroyed enemy camps and communications, sniped in the forests and carried on their own propaganda war by shouting to White soldiers:

"Brothers! Don't be dust for the landlords and generals! Shoot your officers who beat and curse you. Poor men should not fight poor men. Come over to us!"

Many small pictures from Tingchow were engraved on General Chu's memory and of these he mentioned three in particular. First, there was the body of General Kuo, which peasants came to see to convince themselves that their enemy was really dead. And, as they stared, Chu Teh heard them say: "There lies the greatest scoundrel in the world!"

He also recalled the two small Japanese-made arsenals which had provided General Kuo with most of his ammunition. Of the weapons captured in this operation, two thousand rifles and "tens of machine guns" were new and also of Japanese make.

But, above all, there was the factory, equipped with modern sewing machines—Japanese-made—which General Kuo had owned, as he had owned the arsenals, and which had made uniforms for his troops. The workers in such institutions had worked twelve hours a day, but now they organized their trade unions and established two work shifts of eight hours each to provide the Red Army with uniforms.

General Chu's voice even became tender when he spoke of those sewing machines. They were "a great thing for us," he said, "because until then all clothing which the men wore had had to be made by hand.

"But now we got our first standard Red Army uniforms," he said, smiling a little sadly at the memory. "They were grayish blue in color, each with a pair of leggings and a cap with a red star. They were not as fine as foreign uniforms, but to us they seemed very fine indeed. Some of our troops would go in small groups and stand in silence to watch the tailors operate the sewing machines. We had to evacuate Tingchow much later, but the arsenal and uniform factory workers went with us. They carried their machinery with them and set to work wherever we happened to be. The sewing machines went with us on the Long March in 1934-1935, and the tailors often set up shop in the open during that time. They are still with us, with their machines."

At General Chu's suggestion, I visited this uniform factory which had been established in Yenan in January 1937. The sewing machines with their Japanese marks were still there, and the tailors, now middle-aged, were thin, dark and solemn men who merely glanced up at visitors and fell to work again.

Tingchow proved to be a turning point in the history of the Chinese revolution. It was there, a few days after its occupation, that a messenger arrived from the Central Committee of the Communist Party in Shanghai, with reports on the national and international situation and with important documents of another nature. Among these were reports and decisions of the Sixth Congress of the Communist Party which, because of the terror in China, had been held in Moscow in the summer of 1928; and with these were decisions of the Communist International which followed shortly after it and reached the same conclusions. This was the first time in two years that the forces led by Chu Teh and Mao Tse-tung had had contact with their party's Central Committee. They had gone their own way, acting in accordance with necessity and conviction.

Only a few hours after this Shanghai messenger arrived, a peasant walked into Chu Teh's headquarters. He opened his jacket, and drew from the lining a piece of cloth with a few lines of small writing on it, signed with the name of Peng Teh-huai. Peng was the young commander whom Chu and Mao had left in command on Chingkanshan when they broke through the enemy blockade around that mountain stronghold in January 1929. What had happened since then they did not know, but Peng's letter announced that he was now in Juikin with his troops and wished to know if Chu and Mao could join him there or if he should come to Tingchow. Juikin is a small district town in south Kiangsi some two to three days' march to the west of Tingchow.

With a number of military and political representatives and a battalion of guards, Chu and Mao left at once for Juikin, taking the Shanghai messenger and the documents with them. In Juikin, Peng Teh-huai, a grim and austere man, told them the following story:

After Chu and Mao left Chingkanshan in early January, the enemy merely tightened its blockade of the stronghold. Finally the enemy made a surprise attack. One enemy soldier was sent up the face of a mountain cliff, with a rope tied around his waist. He reached the top, and drew others up after him. They killed the Red Army guards at a small, obscure mountain pass. Thousands of enemy troops then poured through the pass and fell upon the beleaguered revolutionaries, some six thousand of whom by then were slowly dying in their hospital and barracks from starvation.

Peng had tried to hold the enemy back long enough to allow as many as possible of his sick and wounded to escape into the forests. A few crawled away, but were hunted down and slain. Others were put to the sword in their beds. The barracks and hospital were burned to ashes. Every house, every building on Chingkanshan was burned to the ground and the defense works were blown up.

Snow was falling during the grisly slaughter and a wintry wind wailed a mournful dirge. Peng collected survivors until there were some seven hundred, whom he led up through the crags and over the boulders along the same route of escape used by Chu and Mao. His troops were in a much worse condition than those that had left at the turn of the year, but they began striking blows at the enemy the moment they escaped the blockade. Everywhere they searched for Chu and Mao, but could not find them. Here and there they heard of their passing from peasants, but then the trail was lost again. Peng had speculated with the idea that they had been killed, and had set to work to build up the Red Army and organize the mass revolution alone. Many peasants had joined him until now, at Juikin, they had fifteen hundred.

Peng had been in western Kiangsi when he heard rumors that Ting-chow had fallen to the Red Army. Turning about he had smashed his way eastward and, after destroying the enemy garrison, he had occupied Juikin and begun organizing and arming the peasants.

Such was the tale told by Peng Teh-huai, at the Juikin conference which lasted for three days and the most of three nights after Chu and Mao arrived with their comrades. The reports and decisions brought by the messenger from Shanghai were studied and discussed, but Chu dismissed this aspect of the conference with the terse and grim remark: "We accepted the decisions and began carrying them out."

With a thread of communication established with the outside world, Chu and his comrades felt that they were no longer operating in darkness. The reports from Shanghai, written in microscopic script on the thinnest of rice paper, told them of the conflicts and contradictions among the imperialist powers abroad, and in China of their control over Chiang Kai-shek's Nanking dictatorship in which foreigners now sat as advisers in all strategic positions. A British official from India was "adviser" to the Ministry of Foreign Affairs, Americans sat in high position in finance and communications, and British, American, Belgian and French financiers were planning the purchase or part-purchase of industries or of such mines as the famous tungsten mines at Tayu in southwestern Kiangsi. The foreigners were also having a holiday in China selling arms and ammunition to Chiang Kai-shek and the old and new warlords allied with or against him. The reports also detailed the conflicts between the old and new Chinese militarists.

While China was being looted, and Chiang Kai-shek and the Kwangsi generals, with their different foreign backers, were fighting for the mastery of China, many regions of the country had begun to erupt in revolutionary struggle. Peasants had risen and been slaughtered in many places in the Yangtze River valley and northward. Islands of resistance had established themselves as far north as Shantung. Fang Chih-ming, the educated peasant, was building up a peasant army in northeastern Kiangsi; the peasant leader, Peng Pei, was still leading partisans in the

East River Region of Kwangtung Province to the south; and Ho Lung, the "Pancho Villa of China," was building up a peasant army in the mountains of western Hunan.

In the western and southern reaches of Kwangsi Province to the south, a still greater revolutionary uprising was taking place. Kwangsi garrison troops had arisen in insurrection and established a great partisan area inside of which the people ruled themselves in village and town councils. One year later, however, the Kwangsi generals returned to the province, after suffering defeat at the hands of Chiang Kai-shek. Their troops, supplied by the French in Indo-China, uprooted the partisan area with fire and sword. Six thousand of these Kwangsi revolutionaries fought their way through the mountains to south Kiangsi where Chu Teh organized them into the Sixth Red Army Corps.

Delving into his memories of those early days, General Chu recalled one of the Shanghai reports about the activities of "Trotskyist and right-opportunist cliques." These ex-Communists, he said, were accusing the Communist Party, or Chu and Mao more specifically, of having "retreated to isolated mountains in the interior to engage in military adventurism and banditry instead of returning to the industrial cities to lead the struggle of the proletariat and urban petty bourgeoisie for the completion of the democratic revolution."

"Behind these empty phrases about democracy and human rights hovered treason to the revolution!" General Chu snorted. "In a semi-feudal and semi-colonial country like China, the simplest democratic rights for the people had to be fought for with guns in hand. In Shanghai, Hankow, Canton, and other cities, workers and intellectuals were being beheaded in the streets for demanding free speech, press, assembly and the right of organization, and for demanding the right to defend themselves in court when arrested. Anyone who used the word 'imperialism' was automatically branded as a Communist, to be killed if captured. The eight-hour day, increased wages, and the abolition of child labor were all branded as Communist banditry, as was the idea of free trade unions.

"From the very beginning, Mao Tse-tung and many others of us had understood that the Chinese people could win democratic rights only by the armed defeat of the counter-revolutionary henchmen of foreign imperialism. Many people neither understood nor wanted to understand this, but the simplest peasant existing under a landlord owner, or the simplest worker laboring under the whip of domestic and foreign reaction, knew it. As for Mao and myself and the troops which we commanded—

we had no intention of laying down our guns and offering our necks to the Kuomintang butchers."

Under the chairmanship of Mao, therefore, the Juikin conference mapped two separate military-political campaigns. The first of these was to be led by Chu and Mao, who were to smash the power of the counter-revolution in south and central Kiangsi and transform these areas, together with western Fukien, into a central revolutionary base. This base in turn was to be progressively enlarged until it united with other islands of the people's resistance in south China.

The second campaign was to be led by Peng Teh-huai, who was to return to the Chingkanshan area to revive the people's movement if possible. After that he was to proceed to his old base in the Pinghsiang mining region of northwestern Kiangsi which in turn was to be consolidated and expanded until it embraced adjoining territory in Hunan and Hupeh provinces and eventually linked up with the Central Soviet Region established by Chu and Mao in the south.

After two weeks of rest during which time they received new uniforms from Tingchow, Peng Teh-huai and his troops marched off to fulfill their mission, while Mao and Chu returned to Tingchow. One week later Mao took a thousand men and marched off to central Kiangsi to drive enemy troops from Hsingkuo, a walled city lying in the mountain range some twenty-five or thirty miles south of the guerrilla base at Tungku. Hsingkuo and Tungku were to be united in a powerful revolutionary base where Red Army schools, hospitals, arsenals, and other institutions would be secure.

After Mao left on this mission, Chu Teh selected and deployed troops further to organize and train partisans in the Tingchow and Juikin areas, and then, a week afterward, also left Tingchow on a campaign through south Kiangsi. The walled city of Ningtu, which lies a few miles to the east of Tungku and which the Red Army had already once occupied, was his final objective.

As a rule General Chu described such campaigns in military detail, giving full reports on the battles fought, the number and types of weapons captured, and the nature and amount of enemy supplies seized, building up a picture of the long and painful growth of the revolution. As the "father of the Red Army," as he was often called, he was the living embodiment of its exhausting struggles and patient educational development.

Yet for all his emphasis on military affairs, he was an unpredictable man, and his simple manner and commonplace appearance most deceptive. There were times when he described campaigns without more than the barest mention of battles, though these were never-ending. Instead, he would recall and graphically describe the dreadful lot of the common people, much as a sociologist might do, or speak of the magnificent beauty of forested mountains with their somber cliffs shrouded in clouds, and compare them and their wild flowers with those of his native Szechwan. A steady stream of deep interest in and love of folk music also ran through his recollections at all times, until one was constrained to speculate about his development had he been born in other times and circumstances.

Now, in describing his whirlwind campaign through south Kiangsi during which he fought the landlord Min Tuan and provincial armies, the sociologist in him came to the fore. In these regions, he said, the peasants lived in small villages surrounded by crumbling walls in which there was only one gate. Inside these walls were two rows of squalid thatch-roofed mud hovels bordering a street which became a quagmire in the rainy season. In dry weather the open gutters on either side of the street were filled with decaying refuse.

The dark hovels had one door and no windows. Inside, the beds consisted either of pallets of rice straw on the earthen floor, or of boards stretched across trestles and heaped with rice straw which served both as mattress and covering. Too poor to afford the luxury of covers, the people slept in the only clothing they owned—loose trousers and jackets of many generations of patches. There might be a crude wooden table with benches, for family meals. The stove, made of mud, was fed through a vent beneath the iron vat above, which was the only cooking vessel, and fuel was dried grass and twigs gathered from the hillsides by children. Rice bowls were of clay with broken pieces riveted in place. Chopsticks were whittled out of bamboo.

No ray of culture ever penetrated these villages, which were breeding places of sickness and disease, and often of terrible crimes. Rents, as high as seventy percent or more of the crops, usury, crop failures, requisitions by provincial and local armies kept the death rate high and the peasant families small. General Chu held that at least seventy percent of the population consisted of poor peasants—tenants—and land laborers, and almost all were illiterate. Schools existed in market towns and cities, but only those able to pay tuition and provide decent school clothing for their children could afford such luxuries.

The "hundred-headed" landlords, as the peasants called them, lived in the large towns and cities, safely enthroned behind strong walls. Here they acted as officials, judges, juries and executioners. Commanders of the Min Tuan, they used local garrison troops to supervise the reaping of the harvests lest the peasants bury some of the grain which the landlords claimed as their due.

The dark peasant pessimism, or rather indifference, to the torment called life, began to break like ice under the spring breezes when rumors fled "from east and west" that a peasant named "Chu Mao" was leading a "poor man's army" against the nobles. This man, it was said, possessed magical powers by which he was able to command a whirlwind or summon the clouds to shield his army against its enemies.

The lean brown men dressed like peasants who went in advance of the army to tell the peasants of its coming spoke in concrete rather than magical terms. At their words the peasants lifted their heads and, often without waiting for the army's approach, fought with their primitive weapons until they were crushed by the Min Tuan from the cities. The heads of peasant leaders were mounted on poles before offending villages, and at night women crouched at the base of the poles in desolation. In the words of Tu Fu, the great Tang dynasty poet, whom General Chu called the greatest of China's classical poets, "the darkness choked with tears."

Many were the peasants who escaped death and, exhausted and with bloodshot eyes, made their way to Chu Teh. Some wept in bitter desolation at the death of son or brother, some said with hate-filled voice: "Let me fight!" Chu Teh, his eyes narrowed to small, hard points, listened to their stories and said to young commanders about him: "Give them guns and train them on the march!"

Thus the muttering of the coming peasant storm, which twenty years later was to destroy an ancient oppression, eddied around Chu Teh in south Kiangsi, around Mao Tse-tung marching with his thousand men on Hsingkuo, and around Peng Teh-huai farther away to the northwest. And around other men in a dozen places in China.

"We never had to lay siege to any village," General Chu said. "Whole villages poured out and often walked for miles to wait for us, but the strongholds of the landlords had to be taken by storm. Our miners, whom we had organized into an embryonic engineering corps, would excavate holes in the walls of such towns or cities and fill them with the black powder that the peasants manufacture and sell to make firecrackers. If the explosion failed to blow a hole through which our troops could enter, the peasants would bring bamboo ladders which we used to scale the walls. Often women and children marched along, carrying baskets and shoulder poles, to clean out the rice bins of the landlords. Our troops would fill their pouches with three days' rations of rice, and the peasants would take the rest. Everywhere we left trained men behind to organize and lead the peasants."

Smashing east and west, north and south for weeks, Chu Teh finally swept northward against the powerful walled city of Ningtu. He had once taken it without firing a shot, but now it was garrisoned by a whole regiment under a Kuomintang officer, Colonel Lei Shih-ning. Colonel Lei was a member of the great landlord-militarist family of the nearby Shihcheng district, and the head of this family was a general in Chiang Kai-shek's army. Colonel Lei, so the peasants said, had a harem of thirty women, and he had boasted that he would mount the head of the "Red bandit chieftain" Chu Mao on the walls of Ningtu.

Unable to blow up the strong walls of Ningtu, the Red Army laid siege to it. Then the troops took it by assault, going up the long bamboo ladders which the peasants brought and mounted against the walls. Hundreds of Red soldiers and many peasants died in that struggle but the city, with its entire garrison, was finally taken.

In those days there was no sharply drawn line between military and political work, so that everybody did everything, and Chu Teh's name appeared as a member of the Ningtu Soviet while peasants in distant villages announced him as chairman of their Peasant Leagues. Chu Teh was not an individual, a person, but a symbol, a name confused with the Red Army; and Red Army men also often ceased to have individual names but were addressed by peasants simply as "Mr. So-wei-ai," or "Mr. Soviet"!

"Wherever we went," General Chu said, "we always opened the prison doors and released prisoners regardless of the charges against them. Crime is a class question, and real criminals were never among those prisoners. Instead, they were always poor men unable to pay their debts or taxes, or those who had been jailed for petty crimes against private property. We always found at least some prisoners who were suspected of belonging to peasant or workers' organizations, or to the Communist Party, though most such men had already died or been killed. Those left alive were shackled, and the chains had worn sores in their legs so that they often could not walk at all. All were covered with lice, their hair was long and matted, and many had tuberculosis, heart ailments, or were dying of dysentery or typhoid. The prison-keepers furnished no food, which had to be supplied by the families of the victims. The prison authorities kept most of this food themselves, so that the prisoners were like skeletons."

General Chu always found time to talk with the captive enemy soldiers. Those in Ningtu were very poor, illiterate and simple-minded peasants who, General Chu said, "had been taught nothing except how to shoot a gun." After a general explanatory meeting with the regiment, General Chu invited all who wished to do so to join, but said that those who did not wish to would be given traveling expenses to return to their homes.

Some joined and were sent to the Tungku mountain base for education and training, while the others were set at liberty as promised and, as General Chu said, "to work like yeast among the peasants and Kuomintang soldiers."

Colonel Lei Shih-ning, commander of the enemy regiment, had changed into civilian clothing and hidden when Ningtu was occupied. He was found, dragged out of his hiding place, and led before Chu Teh, whose head he had promised to mount on the walls of the city.

Considering the man's reputation for sexual prowess, Chu expected to see a big beefy Lothario, for a harem of thirty women surely called for physical endurance of a high order. Therefore when Colonel Lei was escorted into his headquarters between two grinning guards, Chu was struck speechless. Before him stood a little shrimp of a fellow, the smallest man he had ever seen, and now in captivity one of the most craven.

"So you're the fellow with thirty concubines, who swore to mount my head on the walls of Ningtu!" Chu exclaimed in amazement. A roar of laughter from his staff workers and guards destroyed the last shred of the little man's composure.

"Now listen!" Chu said to the little man, "we ought to shoot you, but we won't if you obey our orders. In your home in Shihcheng are many rifles, machine guns, cases of ammunition, silver, and tons of rice looted from the peasants. You haven't paid your soldiers for five months either —you've salted that away also. Now all of these guns, ammunition, money and rice, shall be delivered to us here and in addition we will give you a list of medicine which will have to be bought in Shanghai or some other big city. Until all of these things are in our hands, you will remain our prisoner. After that we will set you at liberty."

The "little turtle," as the Red soldiers called him, wrote a letter which one of his soldiers took to his family in Shihcheng. A few days later his chief wife came riding into Ningtu in a sedan chair, followed by columns of bearers with everything demanded except the medicine. She spent that night with her husband, but some of Chu's staff workers laid idle bets that instead of sleeping with him she gave him a good licking for costing the family so much by allowing himself to be captured. The thing that stumped them, they said, was why she wanted to ransom the fellow at all.

Three months later, when the Red Army was campaigning in Fukien Province, the Lei family finally delivered the demanded medical supplies. Chu had taken Colonel Lei along as a prisoner but now, in fulfillment of his promise, he gave him a safe-conduct pass and released him with the cool remark: "If we catch you a second time things won't go so easy with you!"

A few days after the occupation of Ningtu, Mao Tse-tung came down the mountains from the west where he had fulfilled his mission and took charge of political work in the Ningtu district. General Chu recalled the slogans that called down from the walls of the city: "Confiscate and divide the land! . . . The eight-hour day! . . . Raise wages! . . . Equality of men and women! . . . Equal pay for equal work! . . . Arm the people! . . . Eradicate illiteracy! . . . Destroy opium! . . . Strike down the Kuomintang, running dog of foreign imperialism!"

The Ningtu victory was short-lived and two weeks after occupying the city the Red Army was again on the march. Three enemy divisions were bearing down from the north with blood in their eyes. The army first helped the Ningtu Soviet and the people's organizations to evacuate to mountain villages, then set out, followed by two enemy divisions, for its base in Tingchow. This was also menaced by other enemy divisions moving up from the coast and from Kwangtung Province in the south.

Selecting the weakest link in the enemy chain, which in this instance was the Fukien troops coming up from the coast, Chu and Mao led the Red Army past Tingchow and in a lightning blow captured the walled city of Lungyen, the supply base of the Fukien Army, where they seized military supplies of all kinds and ten thousand pounds of opium.

Here Chu and Mao both spoke at a big memorial meeting for the Red Army dead. It was attended by throngs of civilians from the entire region who had never before heard of dead soldiers being honored. The captured opium was burned in a bonfire during the meeting, with Chu Teh ceremoniously lighting the fire. In the future, Mao told the throngs, free China would honor every soldier or civilian killed in the course of the revolution, would give his family pensions and educate his children at state expense.

It was in this memorial meeting that General Chu developed a theme which he repeated a thousand times in the years that followed. Reviewing the history of the Chinese revolutionary struggle from the time of the Taipings onward through the 1911, 1915 and 1925-1927 revolutions, he urged the people never to forget that they were the heirs of a great and sacred revolutionary tradition which in turn was a part of the liberation struggle of colonial peoples and of the world's oppressed.

Years later this writer often heard General Chu address similar meetings, and his method was always the same. He was not a particularly good speaker, his voice was weak for outdoor audiences, and there was nothing dramatic or oratorical about him. He was more like a teacher, and like a teacher would often pause to ask: *"Tung pu tung?* (Do you understand?)*"* and if voices replied that they did not he would repeat and elaborate in other, or simpler, terms.

In western and southern Fukien, and in south Kiangsi, where the people continued to struggle, there now came hard days. Powerful enemy forces occupied all the main towns and cities and the people fled to the villages, buried their few precious documents, and fought as best they could from a thousand ambushes. Then the Red Army split in two. One section under Mao Tse-tung remained in western Fukien to harass the enemy while Chu Teh led the other in a great diversionary maneuver down into Kuomintang territory as far as the coast in an effort to cut the enemy supply centers and draw at least the Fukien armies away from the Soviet base.

Marching by night, turning back in his tracks to waylay enemy forces following him, and slashing them in a thousand small battles, Chu Teh made swiftly for the great coastal port of Changchow.

"The Red bandit chieftain Chu Teh is rampaging through Fukien, murdering peasants, burning and raping," screamed the Kuomintang press in the great cities, while Chu Teh's forces were being guided by peasants through the night and sheltered in their villages during the day. Heads rolled in the cities, and the Japanese, who regarded Fukien Province as their sphere of influence, asked Chiang Kai-shek if he was able to crush the Red bandits or if they would have to do it for him. Chiang pleaded for time and more arms and ammunition from the foreign powers; and he got them.

Chu remembered August 1, 1929, anniversary of the Nanchang uprising. After a fierce battle with a force twice his own, his troops crossed a swift river on ropes slung from trees on either bank. On these ropes he and his troops crossed the river, hand over hand. They paused to rest in a sunny meadow where grazing cattle stared at them with melancholy eyes, and where regimental commander Liu An-kung, killed before the year was out, spoke to the resting troops about the rise of fascism in Europe from which he had but recently returned. Italian fascism had come to power under Mussolini, he said, and international bankers were propping up German capitalism in an effort to destroy the German Republic. A second world war was being planned, he declared, and nothing could stop it unless the working class of the world organized and united, and unless the Chinese people could overthrow Chiang Kai-shek's dictatorship and turn China into a base of peace and progress.

By September 1st of that year Chu Teh was back in the Soviet regions of western Fukien from which the provincial enemy armies had fled while those from Kwangtung had withdrawn in disgust at Mao Tse-tung's ceaseless harassment. But Mao now lay dangerously sick with malaria and there was no quinine to cure him. This was the time of year when malaria took a greater toll than warfare, and the expensive quinine tablets sold by merchants in the interior consisted of bicarbonate of soda with just enough quinine to give them a slightly bitter taste.

The Red Army Medical Corps, a primitive organization at best, sent one of its members through the enemy lines to buy quinine in Shanghai. When he returned in triumph from his mission they sent him again. But this time he never returned, but was captured and beheaded en route, and no further life could be spared.

But Mao Tse-tung's life was saved, though with difficulty, and Dr. Nelson Fu, the Christian convert from the British Baptist Mission in Tingchow who had joined the Red Army and headed its Medical Corps, made periodical visits to the mountain village where Mao hovered between life and death.

Chu Teh still led the Red Army, penning up enemy troops inside the walls of Tingchow while striking at and taking many other towns that had been lost in previous weeks. Not even malaria ever seemed to have a chance with him, though why this was he never knew. Forty-three summers had passed over his head, he had crossed in and out of the doors of death a thousand times, and still he did not know the meaning of sickness.

"Why was it that even the malarial mosquito failed to make an impression on General Chu?" I once asked Dr. Nelson Fu, who shook his head in wonderment.

"Who knows?" he answered. "The man is just naturally tough. I remember that he had a single strip of cotton cloth with which he covered himself at night, but no mosquito net. I sometimes saw him, but when we had time for a little talk he was merely curious to know why I was a Christian and what Christianity was. He was curious about everything. He was a little rough for my taste and he had a sense of humor that the peasants and soldiers liked. And he was always optimistic. But, of course, none of this explains why he never caught malaria!"

Chapter 24

WHEN General Chu came again to resume the story of his life, he spoke of song and battle; for he was a man to whom singing was a part of life and whose own life and thinking had been moulded by battle.

"Until we came," he began, "the people seldom sang. Of course there were a few old mountain songs, sung chiefly by individual men singers; but it was the revolution that released the energies of the people and gave birth to all kinds of songs—some very simple, even primitive, such as men sing when emerging from serfdom or slavery, but some more developed. They would be laughed at by rich people who like poems or songs above love, wine and moonlight or about the beauty of a concubine's eyebrows. They were songs in which the peasants expressed their hopes, or even the new things they had learned to lead them to freedom. It was the Red Army that taught the people mass singing. The peasants in the mountains of Fukien and Kiangsi also made up new words to old melodies and sometimes created completely new ballads."

Such a new ballad was the "Ballad of Shanghang," which was almost a running narrative of what the peasants had learned from the Red Army. It was punctuated with expressions of pity for the poor and of hatred of the landlords who used the walled city of Shanghang in south Fukien as medieval lords of Europe once used their castles:

> Now listen closely to my song:
> Workers and peasants are very poor,
> Eating bitterness while landlords eat meat,
> Working while the landlords play,
> Ah, so hard!
>
> First we must unite and raise the red banner.
> Second, sew a badge upon our sleeve,
> Third, destroy reactionaries in the village,
> Fourth, capture rifles from the landlords.
> Arm ourselves!

We the masses must be clear!
Destroy the militarist Lu Han-min
But not the captive soldiers,
Poor men like ourselves,
Ah, so poor!

Enter Shanghang, disturb no merchants
And always protect the poor.
Capture the landlords and tiger gentry,
No compromise with them!
Bandits, all!

Never forget the hundred-headed landlords:
Militarist; moneylender; magistrate;
Tax collector; police chief; Min Tuan leader;
Chamber of Commerce and Kuomintang masters,
Dog-men, all!

Red Guards and peasants be clear!
The date to attack Shanghang is decided.
We march during the mid-autumn festival.
The man-eating landlords must die!
The people live!

Exactly as the ballad related, in mid-September Chu Teh led two regiments of regulars and detachments of Red Guards against the walled city of Shanghang in south Fukien. As they marched peasants picked up saws, axes, and spears and marched with them. On a late afternoon General Chu and his staff stood on a wooded mountainside, with the setting sun in their eyes, and looked down at the old walls of the landlord stronghold lying in the valley at their feet. There was only one way to approach this city by land, and that was through the western gate. This gate was heavily fortified and open only a few hours each day. The other three gates were closed and sandbagged from within.

General Chu and his staff looked over the scene with a practiced eye. Chu Teh had no intention of attacking from the west as the enemy expected. He turned to regimental commander Lin Piao at his side and pointed to a row of hills before the western gate and said:

"A couple of mortars on those hills can create enough of a row to draw all the enemy troops to that sector of the city while we scale the walls and take them in the rear."

They knew the terrain already, for the Red Guards had described it in detail and had even drawn crude maps in the dust. Just to the north of the city, the Toku River swerved and made a complete horseshoe bend around the north, east, and southern walls of the city, but between that bend and the ancient walls was a broad strip of land which would come in handy this same night; and just before the northern gate was a wooded hill which General Chu marked out as his first command post.

General Chu had a keen sense of drama, and the whole scene below them reeked with drama and comedy. Here they stood, thousands of them, in a forested mountain, looking down on their enemies who knew nothing whatever of their presence. Enemy soldiers were placidly bathing and washing their clothes in the river below, or lolling on its banks, and did not even hear the peasants and Red troops sawing down giant bamboo to make ladders to scale the walls and attack them this very night.

When darkness fell, Shanghang became a fairyland. It had an electric light plant and the city's rulers and defenders had strung electric lights all around the top of the city walls in the belief that they enabled the armed patrols pacing them at night to discover any possible attackers on the earth below. In fact, the lights merely spotlighted the patrols so that Red Guards had made a practice of crossing the river at night, coming down into the horseshoe bend, and shooting out the lights above. This, General Chu said with a smile, had been "in the interest of target practice" and to disturb the enemy. The city's defenders no longer paid any attention to these nuisance raids, which could be also turned to advantage on this night.

After the moon was up the plan was put into effect. Lin Piao marched off with one regiment of troops to the south of the city. Peasants had assembled boats to enable them to cross the river, after which they were to march back and get inside the horseshoe bend around the city from the south. At the same time Chu Teh left with the other troops and the Red Guards for a northern ferry where the peasants had lashed boats side by side in the river, held in place by long poles driven into the river bed, with boards placed across them to form a bridge for rapid crossing.

Once they were across, a few men with mortars left for the low hills facing the western gate of the city "to create a row and draw the enemy in that direction."

By midnight Chu Teh had established his command post on the low hill before the northern gate inside the horseshoe bend, and his troops and Red Guards, with peasants carrying ladders, were all around the northern and eastern stretches of the city wall. Something went wrong so that Lin Piao didn't reach the southern wall until after the attack began.

Sharpshooters gave the signal to the mortars to the west by shooting out the electric lights on the walls above. The enemy guards merely took shelter, thinking this was another nuisance raid of the Red Guards. Then the mortars began shelling the western gate and the enemy brigade within rushed to that sector of the city. The peasants rushed up and hoisted their ladders. The Red troops and Red Guards, followed by Chu Teh and the peasants, went up in a steady stream and poured down into the city streets.

It wasn't such a pushover as Chu Teh had expected, for the enemy brigade and the armed landlords, with no avenue of escape, fought until noon next day. By then all had been disarmed, and the landlords were herded into the filthy centuries-old prisons after the prisoners in them had been released. The medieval despots watched in shivering terror as the Red troops carried out political prisoners who had been so savagely treated that they could not walk. Some even had lost the power of speech.

Mao Tse-tung, still sick from malaria, was carried into the city on a stretcher. From his sickbed he directed all political work, including the revival of the people's organizations and the organization of the Shang-hang Soviet. Peasants from far and near poured into the city to celebrate the victory, take part in the division of the land, and participate in the trials of the hated landlords. With twisted lips General Chu recalled those trials. Aged parents, widows, fathers and brothers walked up to the landlords and cried out:

"Where is my son? Where is my brother? Where is my father?" Receiving no reply, they attacked them with their bare hands. The Red Guards, set to maintain order, refused to obey orders of their commanders to protect the prisoners.

After only a few days in Shanghang, Chu Teh was on the march again, cleaning all south Fukien of enemy forces. Finally, in late October, he and his troops erupted into the adjoining East River Regions of Kwangtung Province where the famous Ironsides had been destroyed two years before. This time he was again defeated by the Nineteenth Route Army, which hurled against him its three full divisions, armed to the teeth. He lost hundreds of men, but one of the greatest losses to him was regimental commander Liu An-kung, one of the most brilliant and highly educated Red Army commanders. General Chu's heart seemed to be a scroll on which were engraved all the battles of the revolution and the names of all the men who had died under his command.

After leaving two companies of volunteers to reinforce the East River

Regions guerrillas, late November saw him again retreating northward through the mountains into Kiangsi Province. He grieved as he marched.

"The Kuomintang could afford to lose thousands of men," he remarked sadly, "but our men were not pawns in the ambitious games of militarists. We educated each Red Army fighter so that, in case of defeat in battle, he could raise up a new army and continue the revolution. Each of our men was a precious revolutionary asset."

He knew that there would be many defeats or partial defeats and many thousands would die before his hopes for China could be realized. Yet he reacted passionately at each defeat and at every death under his command. He tried but failed to draw comfort from the fact that his troops were carrying hundreds of new captured weapons, or ammunition and other supplies. It was only when he met a peasant partisan detachment in the mountains along the Kwangtung-Kiangsi border that some of his gloom lifted.

There were over six hundred of these partisans, and of these near to two hundred were Red Army veterans who had followed him and Mao Tse-tung through the enemy blockade around Chingkanshan nearly a year before. Sick or wounded, they had been left with the peasants to recover during that bitter winter when the Red Army fought a desperate running battle through these same mountains. Each such man had been given his rifle and a few rounds of ammunition and told, upon recovery, to organize and lead the peasants in partisan warfare.

Those who survived had done so. Contacting one another, they had organized a small regiment which was modeled on the parent body, even to the political workers in each squad. Rejoining the Red Army, they now led Chu Teh into a secure partisan area where his troops could rest while he sent messengers to Mao Tse-tung in Fukien.

The messengers returned with reports: During Chu's absence, powerful enemy forces had captured all the walled cities, including Shanghang, but the countryside still remained in the hands of the people. Mao had withdrawn to a secure Soviet district, Kutien, in the Fukien mountains, where the Ninth Conference of Red Army Delegates, long planned, was to convene on January 1, 1930—just two weeks away. Each company under Chu Teh's command was to elect delegates to the congress.

Fighting his way toward Kutien, Chu tried to recapture Shanghang. He failed, but drove the enemy from Tingchow for a few days. Enemy reinforcements arrived and he gave it up. Chu Teh arrived in Kutien early in the morning of the New Year. The villagers received him and his troops as if they were returning from a great victory.

"The crops were good that year," General Chu said, interrupting his narrative, "and after the landlords were driven out and the land divided, the people had enough to eat and a surplus for the army. They poured into Kutien district by the thousands, each with his own bedding and a week's food, and each group with gifts for us. They brought great quantities of rice, with chickens and ducks, and even drove pigs and cattle before them that we might have meat for the New Year.

"Our troops and the people cooked and ate together and at night the streets resounded with drum and gong, bursting firecrackers, and singing. Paper dragons danced to the light of thousands of colored lanterns and I wrote down a new song which the partisans sang as they marched in. It began:

> "You are poor, I am poor,
> Of ten men, nine are poor.
> If the nine poor men unite,
> Where, then, are the tiger landlords?"

Observing a Red Army practice followed since the days of its inception, General Chu delivered his annual military report to the Kutien Conference of Red Army Delegates. Mao Tse-tung reported on political problems, not only of the army and the Soviet regions, but on the state of the nation and of such international developments as were within his knowledge.

These were portentous times, Mao reported, for the great economic depression of the capitalist world had begun and the Kuomintang regime, linked to foreign imperialism, was dragging China down deeper into colonial subjection. Within less than three years of the Kuomintang dictatorship, Mao reported—and Chu mentioned the same facts in his report—the major shares in Chinese mines, steel, iron and textile industries had passed into foreign hands. British and Belgian capitalists were trying to buy the famous tungsten mines in Tayu, in Kiangsi, which accounted in part for the insistence of these foreign capitalists that Chiang Kai-shek destroy the Red Army and restore "peace and order."

China was in a perennial economic depression, yet this was growing deeper as the world depression deepened. Factories in the great Chinese cities were closing down, throwing new thousands of workers into the ranks of the unemployed. Cheap child and woman labor was replacing men in such factories as still operated, yet even children and women had staged strikes of desperation which had been broken up by club and gun. Falling prices and Chiang Kai-shek's new war with Marshal Feng Yu-hsiang in north China had driven new millions of peasants into bankruptcy. These peasants were turning to banditry, vagabondage, or to the warlord armies for the sake of their daily bowl of rice.

As the armed force of the masses, the Red Army alone offered a revolutionary solution for the deepening poverty and subjection of the Chinese people, Mao declared. But to achieve this goal, certain reforms had to be introduced into the army. The resolution which he presented to the conference on future policy had been formulated after long consultation with Chu Teh and other leaders.

First, he said, the higher organs of the army and party must first reach decisions, after which they were to be discussed until understood and agreed to by the rank and file, thus reversing a practice in use up to that time—a practice that had led to many military defeats.

Secondly, the "absolute equalitarianism" of the army would have to be brought to an end because it had also led to disunity and sometimes to defeat. Up to that time the troops had objected to any discrimination whatever in the distribution of food, clothing, the carrying of burdens, the distribution of billets and orders, and the use of horses. They had even objected to special food for the sick and wounded, and insisted that every person carry the same load, regardless of age, sex or physical capacity, and they had criticized any commander who rode a horse as undemocratic.

Food and clothing, Mao declared, could and should be shared and shared alike by fighters and commanders—the sick and wounded required special consideration. Nor could every person carry the same burden as everyone else; such things had to be determined by capacity. Certain army organizations required larger billets and more orderlies to carry out their work, while officers who rode a horse worked far into the night and long after the fighters had gone to a just night's rest.

Mao gave many intellectuals in the army a working over because of their "idealist" tendencies. Such men, he said, concocted abstract theories out of their heads instead of studying concrete social, military and political problems and reaching decisions based on fact.

Mao's resolution was accepted by the conference, after which the delegates returned to their units and called general meetings where it was discussed and debated until accepted. General Chu held that the reforms led to a great strengthening of the army and enabled it to liberate all central and south Kiangsi, and even recapture the walled cities in western Fukien which it had formerly lost. This territory, known as the Central Soviet Districts, was then expanded until it embraced most of Kiangsi and Fukien provinces.

From January to April 1930, Chu Teh was in personal command of the main forces of the Red Army, waging a swift and hard-hitting campaign against the old Yunnan Army in which he had once been a brigadier and which Chiang had ordered back into Kiangsi to tear the "Red bandits" out by the roots. By June, these Yunnan troops were so shattered and disaffected that Chiang had to replace them with fresh troops.

The manner in which the Yunnan Army disintegrated amused General Chu. Not only did those troops sabotage the orders of their officers, he said, but they made a regular practice of sending reports to him by peasant messengers. Large numbers also would pay a peasant a dollar or two to guide them to the nearest Red Army unit.

As early as January, when the campaign began, a Yunnan Army "Bandit Suppression Officer," Colonel Lo Ping-hui, led his regiment over to the Red Army, and fought in its ranks until death claimed him thirteen years later.

Mao Tse-tung, who also commanded troops during this particular campaign, immediately took over the reorganization and reconstruction of the newly liberated territory. General Chu allowed no grass to grow under his feet before calling up and organizing as many young peasants as possible.

Following the usual establishment of the Councils of People's Delegates (the Soviets) in the various cities, towns and villages, all old taxes were abolished, General Chu recalled. A single progressive tax on the grain crop was introduced instead. Since the army supplied itself by capture from the enemy, the tax revenue was devoted entirely to reconstruction. Usury and opium were forbidden, mortgages and papers of debt returned, primary schools and cooperatives of various kinds formed, and the first small Peasant Bank established.

Before redistributing the land, Mao Tse-tung sent teams of political workers to survey land conditions. It was the first survey ever made in the region. It revealed that seventy percent of the land—including big estates, temple and ancestral lands—was owned or controlled by landlords who constituted one to two percent of the population. Of the remaining thirty percent of the land, about half was owned by rich peasants and the remainder by middle and poor peasants.

The survey classified seventy percent of the peasants as poor, twenty percent as middle peasants, and ten percent as rich. A rich peasant was one who owned his land and worked it but also hired laborers and, like the landlords but on a smaller scale, engaged in usury. A middle peasant was one who owned his land and cultivated it, employed no hired labor, and did not engage in usury. A poor peasant was a tenant who might own, at best, a small piece of land.

With this survey as a guide, the land was redistributed among the landless peasants and the agricultural laborers. Middle peasants whose holdings were too small to support their families also shared in the distribution.

The Cultural Department of the Soviets turned temples into free primary schools for poor children. At night, when the children moved out, adult illiterates came in. Temples were also used for the training of mass organizers, or as headquarters for mass organizations of the army. There were few teachers, no textbooks, little paper, and not even blackboards. The Red Army captured Changsha in Hunan in July of that year, and the city of Kian in Kiangsi in October; Kuomintang printing presses were confiscated and moved to the countryside. Only then could primers, small newspapers, and booklets for mass education be published. The first mass booklets consisted of a simple series entitled *Talks with Peasants, Talks with Workers, Talks with Soldiers,* and *Talks with Women.*

Thus began what General Chu called "the greatest study movement in Chinese history," a movement reflected in slogans painted on walls, cliffs, and even the trunks of trees: "Learn, learn, and learn again! . . . Study until the light fails! . . . Study as you plow! . . . Study by the reflected light of snow!"

Memories of that first hungry search of the "oppressed and injured" for knowledge filled General Chu with both pride and melancholy. In those days, he recalled, the army had to do almost everything. Every man in its ranks able to impart knowledge spent any leisure moment he might have in teaching the peasants what he knew of common and political knowledge. Teachers were few and far between, and the occasional primary school teachers who announced the opening of a school for children in some temple would appear at the stipulated time to find almost the entire village, from old grandfathers to mothers with babies at their breast, sitting side by side with their children on the school benches and spilling out into the temple courtyards. They did the best they could, and after a time selected the most advanced children to become "little teachers" to the others.

Women's work, poor until then, made rapid progress under the guidance of the special Department for Women and Youth Affairs which each local Soviet established. Women became the most militant advocates of the equality of the sexes and adopted their own methods of dealing with such of their menfolk as proved recalcitrant.

The greatest problem was economic. Kiangsi was a poor province and trade with the Soviet and Kuomintang areas was weak and sporadic. Salt in particular, as well as many other products, was scarce and expensive.

During this period of reconstruction General Chu was primarily occupied with military matters. He had to deal with islands of enemy troops or with an occasional regiment that sought renown and a bonus from Chiang Kai-shek for "Red extermination" activities. Just what reports such troops sent to Nanking General Chu never knew, but he felt certain they hardly conformed to the facts. One such regiment advanced bravely up from a Kwangtung city in the south. Chu waylaid them in the mountains and his troops fell upon them like a landslide. They chased the remnants straight through their city base and on the way back picked up all the supplies at their stations. By then his reputation for uncanny maneuvers was such that a whole enemy brigade in Juikin—the future Soviet capital—mutinied and fled as he approached and the speed of their departure was such that even his runners failed to catch up with them.

Those were months so filled with work, he said, that he never even saw his wife, who was off somewhere organizing women in the new Women's Associations. This casual reference introduced his fourth wife, Kang Keh-chin, the peasant girl whom he married in late 1929, some nine or ten months after the woman writer, Wu Yu-lan, his third wife, had been captured and beheaded by the Kuomintang.

Kang Keh-chin was a peasant girl in her late teens at the time, a strongly built young woman who had been an agricultural laborer on a landlord's estate until she fought with the peasants as Chu's army swept over the country. She was illiterate when he first met her, but by 1937 she was a cadet in Kangta, the Anti-Japanese Resistance University in Yenan that trained military and political leaders for the army. Like other women cadets she had been in military uniform for years, and now lived in the women's dormitories of Kangta except for the one day of rest a week when she was at liberty to visit her husband and friends.

General Chu was both fond and proud of Kang Keh-chin to whom he referred as a "girl who grew up and was educated in the army—a typical Red Army product." From the time she joined the army she had studied and done such work as had been given her by the Communist Party of which she had become a member. She had made the Long March over the great plains, rivers, and snow mountains of China and by 1937, when this writer met her, she was a grave, disciplined and hard-working veteran. About Chu Teh she spoke as she might have spoken of someone distant from her. This was her analysis: perhaps his greatest qualities were his tenacious loyalty and personal integrity and his lack of personal political ambitions—qualities that enabled him to subordinate himself to the civilian authority of the party which guided the army. In addition he was a kind and, on the whole, an even-tempered man who loved the troops and was loved by them in turn.

Yes, she replied to a question, he was a disciplined student of military and political books, when he could get them, and he read and underscored newspapers and reports, allowing nothing to escape his attention. The lectures which he delivered in Kangta were always carefully prepared, and he was an exacting teacher, as she, who was one of his students, well knew. In mass meetings attended by troops and civilians, he used simple language and often repeated it if they did not understand. His sense of humor was not as bitingly satirical as that of Mao Tse-tung.

Neither General Chu nor Kang Keh-chin seemed to place any emphasis on the great discrepancy in their ages. At that, it was not at all apparent, for even at the age of fifty-one he remained strong and vital and at the height of his powers. They appeared remarkably well matched. Both were peasants, as strong and elemental as the soil that had given them birth, and though simple and commonplace in appearance their shrewd intelligence belied their apparent unsophistication. She had clearly learned a great amount from him and had depended upon his guidance, yet there was about her the tremendous independence of the new revolutionary women of China. At the age of forty-three he had found a life companion, a woman able to accompany him and share every aspect of his life for better or for worse. What they meant to each other, neither said—they took each other for granted, as well-adjusted married people do. And marriage, in China, is taken for granted.

Chapter 25

WHEN June 1930 dawned, Chu Teh was in the walled mountain city of Tingchow in western Fukien Province, waiting for Mao Tse-tung and other party leaders to come over from Kiangsi for an important conference. In the previous five months there had been a few days of rest for his troops, but not for him. For those five months he had marched on his own legs with his troops. At the age of forty-four his lean body was as tough as steel and he could do with as little as four hours of sleep or less. From now on it would be less.

A messenger had just arrived in Tingchow from the Central Committee of the Communist Party in Shanghai where, as in other Kuomintang cities, there was a perpetual open season on all Communists and other revolutionaries. This messenger had brought two resolution-orders to the Red Army, both of them signed by Li Li-san, chairman of the Organization Bureau of the Communist Party and then the most powerful member of its Politburo.

One of these orders was a complete plan for army reorganization, not only of the forces of Chu and Mao, but of all Red Armies in other parts of the country which were to be brought under a single, centralized command, with Chu Teh as the commander in chief and Mao Tse-tung the political commissar, or supreme party representative. The other document was an order for the Chu-Mao forces, and others elsewhere, to leave the rural areas and capture the great industrial cities. As during the Great Revolutionary period, the industrial workers in the great cities were to arise in general strikes.

This new strategic plan, which embraced the whole country, called for the shifting of the center of revolutionary gravity from the rural to the industrial areas on the theory that the dispossessed proletariat alone could lead the agrarian and national revolution to a swift and victorious conclusion.

Looking back at those plans and orders, General Chu declared that Li Li-san and his supporters had little faith in, or understanding of, the Chinese agrarian revolution or of the Councils, or Soviets, through which the masses exercised power. Nor did they trust the policy directed by Mao Tse-tung which was founded on the facts of the military and political situation of China. Li Li-san was quoted as having said that "by such tactics our hair will be white before the revolution is victorious."

In accordance with the new orders, the four main Red Armies were reorganized in army corps: the First Red Army Corps of which Chu Teh was to remain commander in chief and Mao Tse-tung the political commissar, or party representative. Ho Lung's forces in western Hunan and Hupeh provinces were to become the Second Red Army Corps. Peng Teh-huai's forces in northwestern Kiangsi were to be the Third Red Army Corps. The guerrilla forces in the mountainous regions north of the Yangtze in central China were to be the Fourth Red Army Corps. Hsu Hsiang-chien was the military commander and Chang Kuo-tao the political commissar of this latter corps.

While Chu and Mao were skeptical about the theory upon which the whole new strategy of the revolution was based, they were irrevocably opposed to one particular aspect of the plan of reorganization of their forces. All weapons, so ran the order, were to be concentrated in the hands of the Red Army. This meant that the peasant partisans were to become a regular part of the army and were to leave the Soviet areas with the army in the campaign against the industrial cities. Both Chu and Mao rejected this plan because, General Chu explained, it would have denuded the Soviet regions of armed defenders, left them wide open to enemy occupation, and deprived the Red Army of a revolutionary base. However, he said, "we accepted it in theory," which meant that they organized the peasant partisans into three small armies, under the First Red Army Corps, but ordered them to remain where they were as defenders of their native soil.

General Chu's attitude toward the new strategy was expressed in these words:

"Mao and I were very skeptical about the whole plan, but we had been isolated in the interior for years and such information as we had about the national and international situation was incomplete. We therefore had to accept the analysis of such conditions sent us by our Central Committee. We knew of the great capitalist depression and we knew generally that the situation in China was far worse than when the Manchu dynasty was blown over in 1911. We had to accept the Central Committee's analysis which stated that the country was on the eve of a nationwide upheaval.

"Despite this, our army and, insofar as we knew of them, the other Red Armies, were still weak and poorly armed. Even if we succeeded in capturing a few industrial cities, we doubted our ability to hold them even with the help of the industrial workers. The counter-revolutionary forces were numerically superior and infinitely better armed than we; and we were more convinced than in the past that the imperialist powers which supported the Kuomintang dictatorship would actively intervene against us to protect that dictatorship. Though Chiang Kai-shek was at war with Marshal Feng Yu-hsiang, we were also convinced that he was planning a big campaign against us and that it would begin very soon.

"Apart from Mao and myself, there was very little opposition to the Li Li-san line. We had no choice but to accept it. By June 19th, therefore, the reorganization of our army was complete—we had twenty thousand men—and we took the first oath of allegiance to the revolution. After that, every branch of the Red Army took the oath of allegiance on August 1st, the anniversary of the Nanchang uprising in 1927."

The nucleus of the Revolutionary Military Council, the sovereign military-political body and the forerunner of the Chinese Soviet government, was also organized at this time, General Chu said. The council comprised all commanders and political commissars of the various Red Army corps in every part of the country. General Chu added that this body was "little more than a theory at the time because our communications, which were by messenger only, were so poor that we could not reach the other Red Armies."

Swallowing their doubts, on June 22nd Chu Teh and Mao Tse-tung jointly signed an order of the day which, after summarizing the national situation as described to them by the Central Committee, described the tasks, routes of march, and assembly points of each army taking part in the campaign against the great cities. These troops under their command were to concentrate in a city in central Kiangsi and then fight their way through enemy territory to the provincial capital of Nanchang in the extreme north of the province. After occupying this city they were to take Kiukiang, which lies on the Yangtze just to the north of Nanchang, then sweep westward along the Yangtze toward the great Wuhan cities of Hankow, Hanyang, and Wuchang, the birthplace of the 1911 Revolution.

Simultaneously, Peng Teh-huai's Third Red Army Corps was to leave its base in northwestern Kiangsi, march westward and occupy Changsha, the capital of Hunan Province, after which it was to wheel northward against the Wuhan cities. The Second Red Army Corps under Ho Lung from the west and the Fourth Red Army Corps under Hsu Hsiang-chien and Chang Kuo-tao from the north would meanwhile be converging on Wuhan where the industrial workers were to arise in a general strike as they had done during the Northern Expedition in 1925-1927. This triple city, "the Chicago of China," which commanded the Yangtze to the east and the west and the Peking-Canton railway to the north and the south, would fall to the combined forces of the Chinese people; and after Wuhan —all China.

"From the literary viewpoint," I remarked, carried away by Chu's narrative, "the strategy was stupendous, dramatic: a vast army marching to liberate the oppressed city population . . . the masses arising to smash the chains of a century of subjection . . . a nation reaching for the stars!" General Chu Teh's eyes narrowed and the expression on his face grew increasingly quizzical.

"Oh, there was plenty of drama in it!" he replied with a short little laugh, "but this was not an exercise in literature. Our army was not vast—it was small and armed only with light weapons. The militarist armies were large, with artillery, and the country's resources to draw on, and the naval vessels of the imperialist powers patrolled our inland and coastal waters and lay at anchor before the great cities. The strategy was pure adventurism—an effort to leap over great difficulties and problems that had to be faced and solved before China could be emancipated.

"Mao and I sensed this but lacked sufficient information to reject the plan; and we were practically alone in our misgivings."

Swarms of their political workers went in advance of the troops, calling on the peasants to arise. Enemy troops hid or scattered or fell back on Nanchang as the Red Army slashed its way across the length of Kiangsi Province.

"We gathered tens of thousands of peasants to us as we marched," were the exact words of General Chu. "We armed them on the spot and distributed them among our combat units to be trained on the march. Martial law lay over all the great cities, new enemy divisions poured into them, and the heads of workers and intellectuals rolled in the streets. General strikes had been prepared but the workers' leaders were dead. Unless we liberated them, the workers could do nothing."

On July 29, 1930, in the sweltering heat of summer, Chu and Mao approached Nanchang in the far north of Kiangsi and looked into the distance at its powerful defense works. On that date the news flashed through China that Peng Teh-huai's Third Red Army Corps, supported by clouds of peasants and by workers and intellectuals inside the city, had occupied the Hunan provincial capital of Changsha and proclaimed the Soviet government of three provinces—Hunan, Kiangsi, and Hupeh—with Li Li-san as its absentee chairman.

The threat to Nanchang by Chu and Mao and the occupation of Changsha brought the foreign powers directly onto the battlefield in support of the Kuomintang.

American, British, Italian, and Japanese gunboats had already evacuated all foreigners from Changsha, but on July 30th, one day after the occupation, they returned. Lying in the Hsiang River they began a four-day bombardment that set great fires and killed thousands of troops and civilians in the city. The bombardment was led by the United States gunboat *Palos*. Under cover of the foreign bombardment, the local warlord, Ho Chien, who had fled the city as the Red Army advanced, moved up.

On the evening of August 3rd, the Red troops and all the civilian organizations that had supported them began the evacuation of Changsha, taking with them the printing press, newsprint, rice, money and other material confiscated from counter-revolutionary forces. Railway workers on the branch line that runs eastward from Changsha into the mining

areas of northwestern Kiangsi spent that night shuffling back and forth
with their one railway engine and three cars as they evacuated first the
wounded and then the confiscated supplies.

On August 4th, warlord Ho Chien returned to Changsha. Within a
week he slaughtered so many thousand civilians that merchants and
industrialists issued a manifesto condemning him as a "butcher who
knows only how to kill innocent people."

During this same period, on August 1st, Chu and Mao threw their
lean, sweating soldiers against the defense works around Nanchang,
neither sleeping nor resting as their troops fell like autumn leaves under
the fire of enemy artillery. Chu Teh's face became the color of clay and
even seemed to have a faintly greenish tinge, as this writer saw later
under similar circumstances during the national Anti-Japanese War. Men
were dying at his command and no man knew what the outcome might be.

Twenty-four hours later he and Mao ordered their army to withdraw.
They moved westward toward Wuhan in three columns, with an interval
of a few miles between each column. They encountered a representative
of Peng Teh-huai on the way and gathered in the forested mountains of
northwestern Kiangsi where they united with Peng's army and held a
conference to debate Li Li-san's orders. These called for the reoccupation
of Changsha and taking the Wuhan cities against which the Second and
Fourth Red Army Corps were already converging.

Mao Tse-tung questioned this policy and was supported by Chu and
Peng in particular. General Chu said that in his opinion—and he was
supported by Mao and Peng and many other men—the Red Army was
neither equipped nor trained to fight positional warfare, which would
be necessary from this time on. Enemy reinforcements pouring into
Changsha alone had thrown up three lines of defense works, reinforced
by electrified wire entanglements. The defenses of Wuhan were still more
powerful and many foreign men-of-war were anchored in the Yangtze
waiting to turn their guns on the Red Army. To attack such overwhelming
enemy forces and powerful equipment might result in the annihilation of
the Red Army and in the crushing of the revolution for decades to come.

All such arguments were voted down, however, and the second attack
on Changsha began in the first week of September and lasted until the
evening of September 13th. Peasants and workers by the thousands
helped the army throw up trenches, transported rice and ammunition,
and cleaned the battlefield of the dead and wounded. But human flesh,
even when inspired, cannot endure against steel. At 8 P.M. on September
13th, Chu and Mao took one of the most serious steps of their careers,
a step which precipitated a grave crisis in China's revolutionary movement. They repudiated the Li Li-san line, which was the policy adopted

by the Central Committee of the party of which they were leading members, and ordered their troops to withdraw from Changsha. They dispersed in eight different columns and returned to Kiangsi Province to concentrate on the 30th of that month, near Kian, the citadel of absentee landlordism and second to Nanchang as military headquarters of Kuomintang armies.

Their orders, which were supported by Peng Teh-huai and most but not all commanders, forced the withdrawal of the two other Red Armies converging on Wuhan. It compelled the Communist Party to call off all its plans for a nationwide armed uprising against the Kuomintang dictatorship. Yet, General Chu declared, any other decision would have resulted in the destruction of "the living heart of the revolution." The Li Li-san policy was pure "adventurism," he added—a romantic gamble with little to support it.

General Chu had the ability completely to forget his immediate surroundings and to relive those tragic days when his troops defied death and dropped in hundreds before enemy artillery. Under the cover of darkness groups of men adopted every contrivance to break the electrified wire entanglements around enemy defenses, and their bodies lay in small mounds where they had met their death.

The army even bought fifty water buffalo from the peasants and tried to use them as "living tanks" to break the wires and enable the troops to get at the enemy beyond. This was a trick lifted from the ancient *Tales of the Three Kingdoms*. The animals were lined up facing the electrified wire entanglements while peasants tied strings of firecrackers to their tails. The firecrackers were lit but instead of dashing forward and breaking the wires the great terrified beasts lunged in every direction, scattering everyone in sight. General Chu's smile was slightly twisted at the memory of a stunt that had worked shortly after the time of Christ but not in 1930.

When he finally issued the orders to retreat there were many party members who protested, some of whom even denounced him and Mao, yet the troops obeyed without question and hotly replied to all arguments against their leaders whom they regarded as bone of their bone and blood of their blood. Neither Chu nor Mao needed to defend themselves, nor could they for that matter, because they had moved with their headquarters to Peng Teh-huai's base in northwestern Kiangsi. After picking up a thousand new miner volunteers they and Peng left for the rendezvous near Kian where they found all their troops loyally awaiting them.

Mao addressed the assembled troops, regiment by regiment, explaining the reasons for the retreat from Changsha, and followed this with an explanation of the plan of battle to take Kian. And when Chu went

among them, the troops gathered about him as always, touched him with
their big rough hands, and he rested his arms about their shoulders as
they talked together as soldiers talk.

Kian fell at midnight on October 4, 1930, and while Mao took over
the civilian administrative work and directed the organization of the
Kian Soviet, Chu moved beyond the city walls to deal with the ten thousand new worker and peasant volunteers who poured into the army. The
city itself had become a teeming throng of peasants who slept knee-deep
in the streets at night and, as General Chu expressed it, "after seeing the
sights and attending mass meetings, marched back to their villages,
taking their landlords with them for trial." Fully a million peasants
entered and left Kian in the two weeks the city was held by the Red Army.

General Chu remembered Kian especially because there he unearthed
important documents in enemy military headquarters. Some of these
documents dealt with plans for the first big "Red Extermination Campaign." Chiang Kai-shek's war in north China had ended and he was
transferring a hundred thousand Kuomintang troops to Kiangsi against
the Red Army. The war was to start in late October.

The other captured documents dealt with the so-called Anti-Bolshevik,
or A. B., Corps, a cloak-and-dagger outfit of the Kuomintang secret
police which had a network of sabotage and terrorism throughout the
Soviet areas. The documents filled General Chu with foreboding because
the names of A. B. members in the Soviet areas were given in code which
the Communists were unable to break for many months. There had been
enough carelessness, however, to provide important clues, such as a
receipt for money openly signed by a landlord in the Tungku-Hsingkuo
Soviet District. One of the chief Communist leaders in this district, Li
Wen-ling by name, was the son of this same landlord. General Chu could
not believe that Li Wen-ling was connected with the A. B. Corps, yet
here was a document signed by his father.

Until that time the Red Army had a committee to deal with secret
enemy machinations, but it was only after Kian that it organized its
special Committee to Combat the Counter-Revolution and began serious
work. Even after the A. B. Corps codes were broken, General Chu said,
the Red Army made no arrests. Instead, members of the new special
committee made friends with A. B. members, joined their secret groups,
and worked until the entire enemy network was in its hands.

By then, General Chu declared as if recalling a horrible nightmare,
"many of our best comrades had been secretly murdered; one of our
armies of Tungku troops had mutinied under the leadership of the sons
of Tungku landlords, and such confusion and suspicion had been created

that no man knew if he could trust his brother. A. B. members had organized secret superstitious religious groups to predict the destruction of the Red Army, and to isolate the masses from us they even founded 'Free Love' societies where the landlords used the women of their own families in an effort to seduce Red Army fighters."

The Red Army had a rigid code of morality without which the peasants would have fought them, and it was this reputation for morality that the landlords tried to destroy. They failed. Chu Teh's method of dealing with the problem was to go directly to the troops, explain all the tactics employed by the A. B. Corps, and urge vigilance. Specially trained bodyguards protected him, Mao, and other leaders, but three of these bodyguards were secretly murdered before the back of the A. B. Corps was broken forever.

In early 1937, when General Chu told me of this long struggle against the tortuous Machiavellism of a predatory ruling class fighting for its ancient privileges, I once watched him and the chief of the Committee to Combat the Counter-Revolution, at a big dinner. At the time, the chief of this committee was a man who had been a miner from the age of eleven and who had become one of the earliest labor organizers of China.

To observe Chu Teh and this miner together was to understand the difference between the Chinese peasant and the Chinese industrial worker. In social gatherings General Chu was as calm and relaxed as a cat. At all times he was a man who could lose himself in any market place where peasants gathered to sell cabbages and gossip to their hearts' content. Every inch of him, from his commonplace appearance to his movements, was peasant.

The chief of the Committee to Combat the Counter-Revolution, however, could not have disappeared in any peasant gathering. There was no rest or relaxation, no elasticity in him. Dynamic and alert, in both expression and movement he was the embodiment of controlled energy which frequently characterizes the industrial workers in Western countries during great struggles.

It was undoubtedly due to this man, and to many others like him, that Chu Teh, Mao Tse-tung, and other Red Army and Communist leaders had not been murdered by their secret enemies. I thought again of this man when the People's Revolutionary Army marched into Peking in January 1949, and published notices ordering all members of the Kuomintang secret police, the Blue Shirts, to surrender their weapons and register with the Peking police or be wiped out.

In obedience to this order, a suave professor in Tsinghwa University near Peking presented himself at police headquarters to register as a "captain" in the Blue Shirts which had spread terror among students, professors and intellectuals in particular. He was duly registered and told to resume his teaching in Tsinghwa as before, but the new chief of police quietly informed him:

"You have made a slight mistake in your registration. You were not a captain in the Blue Shirts—you were a lieutenant colonel!"

Book VIII

Red Phalanx

Chapter 26

LOUD hosannas sounded over Shanghai and other great Chinese cities in that late October 1930, when the curtain went up on the first big Red Extermination Campaign. Chiang Kai-shek was the hero of the hour, fresh from victory over his northern rivals. Now he was transferring 100,000 of his troops against the "Red vermin" in Kiangsi.

Communism was the one irreconcilable anti-imperialist and anti-feudal force in China, the only organized force whose members had proved that they were willing to die for a principle. Such men were dangerous but, being weak, could be destroyed if attacked in time. Now was the time and the outcome seemed certain. For who were the Reds in Kiangsi but peasants and workers, the most despicable of human creatures? Did not the whole world know that the Chinese peasant cared not at all who ruled him but wished only to be left in peace to till his few feet of earth?

The Kuomintang press and its foreign fellow travelers made a great noise. The former proudly published the most complete details of the armies marching against the Reds, and even of their routes of march. But no word came from the Red armies, above all nothing from Chu and Mao whose army, it was said, had been driven from Kian by victorious Kuomintang troops. The Red Army consisted of nothing but "remnant bandits" who would soon be completely surrounded and exterminated.

Down in Kiangsi, Chu and Mao and their comrades studied the Kuomintang press most carefully, and General Chu made a point of marking and underscoring each military report of which the Kuomintang was so proud. The Red Army still had no radios, yet its communications and intelligence service had improved greatly, and the Kuomintang military press reports tallied with its own. It still had no news from Shanghai, but Chu and Mao had sent delegates to Shanghai to oppose the Li Li-san line of the Central Committee of the Communist Party. Whatever the outcome, they knew they were right.

In mid-October, Chu and Mao and their comrades held a military conference in Peng Teh-huai's headquarters to the north of Kian. Here they decided to evacuate Kian, because to hold that city against forces twice as numerous as theirs would entail sacrifices they were not prepared to make. They would withdraw 40,000 of their main forces into consolidated Soviet territory where they would have the complete support of the people. In this region lying between the Tungku mountain base and the walled city of Kwangchang they would, as General Chu put it, "select our own battlefields and, by swift concentrations, surprise attacks, and dispersals, encircle and attack first one and then another of the enemy divisions sent to exterminate us."

Of the whole campaign that followed and which lasted four months, General Chu selected one specific battle as an example of how the Red Army fought. This same battle must have been in the mind of Mao Tse-tung when he later wrote in his military textbook, *Strategic Problems of China's Revolutionary War*:

In military history there are instances of defeat in one battle which nullify all the achievements of previous successive victories, and of victory in one battle following many defeats which develops a new situation.

This specific battle, which caused the entire Kuomintang campaign to collapse, was fought in the last days of December 1930, against the 18th Division commanded by General Chang Hwei-chang. General Chang's other two divisions were the 28th and 50th, and the three of them were the backbone of the Kuomintang armies. They were full, regular divisions, excellently equipped with foreign weapons and excellently supplied.

Before describing this decisive battle, General Chu digressed to tell of treachery in the ranks of the Red Army itself, a treachery which threatened to turn the tide in favor of the enemy. In the midst of weeks of fighting, he said, Liu Ti-tsao, son of a landlord, led his Twentieth Red Army of Tungku peasants in mutiny. Liu was supposed to defend the Fukien region near Kian, despite A. B. Corps documents captured in Kian in October which had proved that at least one of the landlord families of Tungku was connected with the secret Kuomintang cloak-and-dagger organization.

Liu Ti-tsao and Li Wen-ling, the chief political leader in the Tungku-Hsingkuo area, whose family was proved to be in connection with the A. B. Corps, had been among the most determined followers of Li Li-sanism which Chu Teh and Mao Tse-tung were fighting. Just when and where the connection between Li Li-sanism and the A. B. Corps took place, or just how and when these leaders passed over from Li Li-sanism into the A. B. Corps, Chu and his comrades learned only much later.

Despite all the complications and confusion General Chu was convinced that landlordism in Tungku, which the Communists had not yet cleared out, was the real cause of the mutiny of the Twentieth Red Army.

Of course Liu and Li did not dare to expose their real motives to their peasant troops. They therefore accused Chu Teh of being "just another Chiang Kai-shek" and Mao Tse-tung a "Party Emperor" who had betrayed the Communist Party. Their oratory produced the desired mutiny and they killed many Communist leaders in the Fukien region. They fled subsequently into Kuomintang territory west of Kian where they established their own small Communist Party and began turning out one confusing manifesto after another. In one such document Chu Teh was suddenly praised as a noble soul while Mao was branded as a traitor, while in another Mao was praised and Chu denounced.

Despite all their camouflage, General Chu declared, the Red Army judged by facts, and these facts were clear: the Kuomintang armies took no action whatever against the mutineers. In the end the Tungku peasants began to realize it too, escaped and made their way back to the parent body, where they were accepted, reorganized and reeducated.

Yet the mutiny had enabled the Kuomintang Nineteenth Route Army to occupy Hsingkuo, and General Chang Hwei-chang's 28th Division to occupy Tungku. The partisans and the people on Tungku had fought the enemy but their villages had been destroyed and hundreds of people were killed. Finally they fled eastward to the main body of the Red Army.

Such was the situation when Chu and Mao and their staff decided to fight a decisive battle and break the back of the 18th Headquarters Division of General Chang Hwei-chang.

General Chu drew a rough sketch of the battlefield where this struggle took place. He marked enemy headquarters and positions and the location of his own headquarters, combat units, reserves, field hospitals, and reception stations for enemy captives. He also indicated the positions of the people's forces which, as Red Army auxiliaries, were to attack small enemy units and transport columns as well as to transport Red Army supplies and clear the battlefield of the wounded.

The headquarters of Chu and Mao was in a small mountain village just four miles from Lungkang where General Chang Hwei-chang's headquarters was located. General Chang's 28th Division was on Tungku mountain directly above them to the east, while his 50th Division was at Nientow to the northwest. Peng Teh-huai's Third Red Army Corps was deployed, for holding operations, between Lungkang and the 28th and 50th enemy divisions. One day's swift march to the south and southwest were the troops of the Kuomintang Nineteenth Route Army.

Red Army communications were good, General Chu said, and his headquarters messengers, all young peasants, were very swift. At 8 P.M. on December 29th he and Mao issued meticulous orders for the coming battle, which was to begin at dawn next morning. These orders to all their main combat and reserve units included instructions to hold the customary "political mobilization" meetings during which the military commanders were to inform the troops of the plan of battle and everything that was known about enemy strength, positions, equipment, and morale. The political leaders were to explain the significance of the battle to the campaign and the revolutionary movement as a whole.

One point in General Chu's orders instructed all Red Army units to maintain close contact and exchange intelligence, and to pay special attention to the collection of medical supplies and to "preserve any captured radio sets."

The battle began at dawn on December 30th when the troops of Lin Piao and Hwang Kung-lei drew the 18th Division out of Lungkang by attacking and retreating until the enemy could be split into segments and destroyed. Hwang Kung-lei's troops were peasants and miners from northwestern Kiangsi where General Chang Hwei-chang's three divisions had previously destroyed hundreds of villages and exterminated entire families that had sons in the Red Army. Hwang's troops therefore fought with bitter hatred in their hearts. These troops, General Chu said, "fought right before our headquarters, and enemy machine-gun bullets splattered against our walls."

At the height of the battle General Chang Hwei-chang ordered his 50th Division to reinforce his 18th but "we captured his wireless station immediately afterwards." The 50th Division started marching. Somehow it received no further communications and when it met Peng Teh-huai's troops outside Nientow, it withdrew and waited. The 28th Division on Tungku made no move at all, nor did the Nineteenth Route Army to the south.

By noon a thousand men of the 18th Division had been killed and the other nine thousand captured and disarmed. General Chang and his staff, with all his officers, were among the captives. War trophies included eight thousand rifles, light and heavy machine guns, trench mortars and other small fieldpieces, the precious radio set of the 18th Division—with its operators—as well as field telephones, medical supplies, horses and large quantities of provisions. Money for the entire three enemy divisions was also captured.

"We immediately held a mass meeting of the captive soldiers," General Chu said, "where we told them why we were fighting and invited those who wished to do so to join us. Three thousand joined us and we gave three dollars to each of the others and told them to go home."

The enemy had had superior fire power and supplies yet "our troops were superior in conviction, morale, and swift maneuvering." This explained this quick and decisive victory, as well as the collapse of the entire enemy campaign that rapidly followed, General Chu explained. Surprise played no role because fighting had been going on for over two months and the 18th Division had expected some kind of attack.

Furthermore, General Chu said, the "Whites"—as he, in common with the Red Army and the people, called Kuomintang forces—were in Soviet territory where the entire population regarded them as mortal enemies. Still another reason for the victory was psychological: "The enemy believed their own propaganda that we are bandits—and bandits can be easily crushed."

The conversation which General Chu Teh had with General Chang Hwei-chang immediately after the latter's capture was the kind that dramas are made of. The captive general, clad in a smart khaki uniform decorated with his insignia of rank, with polished black knee boots, was hustled into Chu's headquarters. There he saw a few men as lean and poorly clad as coolies. It was clear, General Chu remarked in a voice that had grown cold and hard, that "he believed we were ignorant bandits who would soon be defeated by his other two divisions, when he would be released.

"Though his defeat and capture had stunned him, he was still arrogant and tried to outwit me. He was a big fat fellow whose headquarters was stocked with all kinds of delicacies, and though he had a riding horse he had chosen to travel in a sedan chair on the backs of carriers."

General Chang's first haughty question was "How much will you demand to release me?" Chu replied with dignity: "I am not a merchant! You will be tried before your own troops, and before the troops of one of our armies whose families you have exterminated in northwestern Kiangsi." Some of the captive general's insolence seemed to crack.

"I asked him," General Chu told, "if he would be willing to teach in the new Red Army academy which we were planning to establish. He said he would but I knew he was only playing for time—he expected his other divisions to rescue him. I asked him which White armies he would advise us to attack next. I needed no advice from him because our troops were already moving against his 50th Division, but I wanted to see what kind of man he was. He advised us to attack the Nineteenth Route Army

and he even gave us military information about that army which conformed with our own intelligence reports. He was betraying his own
side and he thought he was outwitting us."

"Just to show General Chang how we could destroy his other divisions," General Chu took him and his captive officers along when the
Red Army smashed the 50th Division within the next twenty-four hours.
The Reds then wheeled against the 28th Division on Tungku. It fled. By
then the Nineteenth Route Army had begun retreating from Hsingkuo,
and did not stop until it reached its native Kwangtung Province in the
far south.

Within less than three weeks after the victory over the 18th Division,
the enemy armies collapsed under the swift blows of the Red Army, and
the first Red Extermination Campaign came to an inglorious end. With
his staff, General Chang was then put on trial before three thousand of
his own troops, the civilian population of Tungku, and the troops of
Hwang Kung-lei's army whose homes and families had been destroyed by
him. By then, General Chu said, Chang Hwei-chang's insolence had
turned to fear. He was condemned to death and, with his staff, beheaded
by troops whose families had been slaughtered by them.

A number of weeks later a messenger from the Central Committee of
the Communist Party reached General Chu's headquarters from Shanghai. He carried a letter asking for General Chang's release in return for
which Chiang Kai-shek offered to release many political prisoners and
to pay a sum of $200,000.

"We were sorry we had executed him," General Chu remarked, "not
because of the money but because Chiang Kai-shek killed many of our
imprisoned comrades in reprisal."

The victory of the Red Army really frightened the Kuomintang and
its foreign supporters and financiers and unleashed a new wave of terror
throughout Kuomintang China. By the end of 1930 Generalissimo Chiang
Kai-shek had appointed himself Minister of Education of his Nanking
regime and issued a manifesto stating that his "heart was pained" by
students who had "fallen prey to Communism" and had called meetings,
distributed handbills, and even "opposed their university Presidents—
which is tantamount to opposing the government." The Generalissimo
declared that he was "not afraid to shoot students," and set about
proving it.

Five universities were closed down and scores of students secretly
arrested in Shanghai, never to be heard of again. The Shanghai press
laconically reported that sixty students in Peking National University,
another dozen or so in Tientsin, and scores in Canton, Changsha, and
Hankow, had been arrested. On February 7, 1931, twenty-four young

writers, artists and actors were arrested by the British police in Shanghai and delivered to the Kuomintang garrison commander who, that same night, shot them in a mass grave which they had been forced to dig.

In February 1931, the monthly issue of the Kuomintang's *Anti-Red Suppression Monthly* at Nanchang published an interview with a high Kuomintang officer who said:

If the Government cannot find a better method of solving the Red bandit problem than it is using today, it will be obliged to isolate all those regions and kill the last person with poison gas. Every man, woman and child from ten to sixty is either a spy for the Reds or is a member of the Red Army.

Chapter 27

WHEN General Chu next came to resume the story of his life, I proposed that he select a typical day out of the year 1931 and tell me what he did from morning to night.

After some reflection he said it would be impossible because he could not remember everything he did in any particular day, but that he would try. This was the story he told:

"I had a lifelong habit of arising very early. I slept only after my work was finished, which was very late—nearly always after midnight. My life has been built around disciplined work and study, yet my work and studies were never regular because in such warfare as ours there was much work that had to be supervised directly by headquarters.

"Generally, but not regularly, I lectured to the troops on military subjects and I frequently inspected nearby troops to see their organization and work. I attended regular staff conferences and there were also party meetings once or twice a week as well as headquarters cell meetings. There were frequent conferences with heads of various army departments, and still others to deal with special problems that arose. Before each battle there were one or two mobilization meetings of the combat units, where military commanders reported on our plans and enemy conditions and our political leaders explained the significance of the battle or campaign and the political tactics to demoralize or win over the enemy during fighting.

"Following each battle, if there was time, but always after each campaign, we held two conferences: the first of commanders and the second of commanders and men together where the battle or campaign was analyzed. I tried to attend such conferences, which were of the greatest technical and educational value for our army. Each fighter and each commander had complete freedom of speech in these joint conferences. They could criticize one another or any aspect of the general plan or the way it had been carried out. In this way we were able to correct mistakes, weed out weak commanders, and promote men on merit. Through them we aimed to eliminate all feudal practices, keep our army democratic, and develop voluntary discipline among the fighters. Any man who had shown cowardice or bad judgment, or who had violated orders in the midst of battle, had to explain his conduct and learn to correct his mistakes. Any commander who cursed or struck a fighter or otherwise violated army rules had to answer before this court of public opinion; if guilty he was dealt with by headquarters. The results of such conferences were published in pamphlets and used as study material throughout the army."

There was much other work, he continued, and he told of the spring plowing and sowing, and the harvests, when every army man not occupied with military duties helped the peasants. Whenever possible General Chu did his share of field work and "found it an excellent way to maintain my health." Red Army recreational and cultural activities were relatively weak in those days, but a few dramatic troupes toured the Soviet districts to play to the troops and the people, and if they played anywhere within reach of headquarters General Chu was sitting on the ground or on one of the benches in the front rows. The army had some songs, he said, but singing was not as highly developed as in Yenan at the time he talked.

"There were also daily intelligence and other reports which had to be read and dealt with," he proffered next. "I read every newspaper or book I could find but it was not easy to get books and magazines in those days. An occasional package of books came in from Shanghai, but they were in such demand that others often seized them before I had a chance at them. At that time I was trying to improve my knowledge of Marxism-Leninism and I read and reread any book on such subjects that reached us. During the first enemy Extermination Campaign we captured many books and pamphlets on military strategy and tactics which I read and which were useful to our army."

During the occupation of both Changsha and Kian, the army had confiscated Kuomintang printing presses and removed them to the country.

It now published a *Military Fortnightly* which contained reports about other Red armies, partisan areas, and general conditions of the whole country. At that time there was a movement among teachers and professors in Shanghai, Peking, and other Kuomintang cities, to prepare textbooks for the Red Army and the primary schools in the Soviet areas. These manuscripts were smuggled through the enemy lines and either printed or lithographed, and General Chu found time to go through those intended for the troops.

"After the defeat of the first enemy campaign," General Chu continued, "our troops were scattered over a large area. Peng Teh-huai commanded on the northern front where we had occupied two new districts. Peng cleaned out the walled city of Nanfeng, which had been held by General Hsu Ko-hsiang the 'Peasant Butcherer' who had been hanging on until Chiang Kai-shek could prepare the second Kuomintang Extermination Campaign against us.

"Because of these preparations we enlarged our army, established supply depots at various strategic points, and trained our troops. Enemy airplanes were now bombing us periodically, while the A. B. Corps intensified its activities everywhere. A. B. activities sometimes kept us in conference the whole night through.

"Because of the bombings, as well as our food supply, our headquarters moved four or five times within four months. Food was a serious problem because it was spring sowing time, our territory was small and our resources limited, and we had to conserve rice to meet the coming enemy campaign. Our troops confiscated rice from landlords, but there was a limit to this and we not only helped the peasants plow and sow but our troops reclaimed wasteland, which was poor in any case.

"Our army had a system of Soldier Committees in each division which managed supplies, maintained discipline, and directed educational and entertainment activities. Throughout the spring of 1931 these committees led the campaign to conserve food. They reduced our rations so that we ate meagerly twice a day, at ten and four. The food was poor and we were hungry all the time. Only the sick and wounded had enough.

"We also developed an air-raid warning system throughout Soviet territory, and our Engineering Corps, made up of miners, constructed good air-raid shelters for the troops and the people. These miners were highly skilled workers who could do many things, including the manufacture and use of explosives. Many of them were deaf from explosions in the mines where they had previously worked. Even before joining our army their political level was very high because most were old party members who had been labor organizers and leaders from the earliest days of the labor movement. I often took part in conferences called by them to initiate new defense methods.

"My days were crowded with still other work. Since we were the armed forces of the people, our army until then had been tied up with all mass activities. We helped rearrange the old Soviet districts and consolidate the people's sovereignty in new ones. We confiscated the food and land from the landlords, helped divide the land, established mass organizations and the Soviets, and led the plowing and sowing campaigns to increase production.

"In early March 1931, we received resolutions passed by the Fourth Delegates' Congress of our party which had met secretly in Shanghai. We had sent delegates to this congress, which finally repudiated the Li Li-san line and affirmed ours. The resolutions which we now received instructed us to introduce the systematic education of our troops and to make a clear division of labor between our army, the Soviets, and the mass organizations. The congress also called on us to arrange for an All-China Soviet Congress, to meet in south Kiangsi on August 1, 1931, the fourth anniversary of the Nanchang uprising.

"We began work on the resolutions by calling a conference of party delegates from all the Soviet districts and we moved our headquarters once more, this time to a small mountain village, Shantang, which had a big family temple large enough to house our headquarters and the conference delegates.

"The conference lasted for nearly a month. Among other things we arranged for committees to prepare for the All-China Soviet Congress on August 1st. However, the new enemy campaign began soon and the congress had to be postponed, first to November 7th and then to December 11th. December 11th was the anniversary of the Canton Commune.

"After the Shantang Conference, which I attended as one of the presidium and sometimes the chairman, our work became much better. The Soviets and mass organizations henceforth became independent of our army. Personal relationships in the Soviets, which had played a considerable role in some places, were eliminated, and these Councils or Soviets became efficient administrative organs dealing with such problems as finance, land, communications, the local armed forces, health, education, production, and the problems of women and children. The Soviets were organized in pyramidal form from the village up to the Region, then to the Province. After December 11, 1931, the highest organ was the Central Soviet Government at Juikin, of which Mao Tse-tung was chairman.

"We also established regular lecture hours on military and political subjects for our troops and intensified the campaign against illiteracy. Many intellectuals arrived from the outside to help us, but they were still too few and our Medical Corps was still weak. Shanghai printers and other industrial workers from different cities began coming through the enemy lines to join us.

"I also kept my eye on the new radio school which we had established after capturing the wireless set from the 18th Division. Its chief, Wang Chen, joined us and at once organized the radio school. Wang is still director of our radio school here in Yenan and is called 'the father of radio.'

"After joining us, Wang began intercepting enemy messages from which we learned that General Kung Ping-fang's 28th Division had a new wireless outfit. Our radio students began clamoring for it and I told them they should have it. From intercepted enemy messages we also learned of enemy supply dumps which were being established behind the fortified defense positions which were being constructed in preparation for the Second Extermination Campaign. We learned all about these fortifications because the Kuomintang conscripted peasants to build them.

"By April our food and ammunition problems were very serious, and to avoid using up our supplies for the second campaign we began borrowing rice from the peasants, promising to return it by a set date. When peasants asked me how we could set a date, I asked them if we had ever failed to keep a promise to them. They said we had not and we all laughed," and General Chu added proudly "for the peasants knew what that meant."

By the time General Chu finished talking it was past midnight. His fine white teeth gleamed in the candlelight as he yawned and remarked quizzically:

"Such was a typical day of my life in the spring of 1931!"

Chapter 28

IN EARLY May, 150,000 Kuomintang troops under the supreme command of General Ho Ying-chin, Minister of War in the Nanking regime, took up positions behind their defense works which by then ran zigzag across Kiangsi from Kian on the west to Chienning in Fukien Province

294

on the east, a distance of some 700 li, or about 250 miles. The Second
Extermination Campaign began.

General Chu remarked dryly that the Red Army knew everything
about these enemy defenses because the peasants forced to build them
had told their location and even explained just how deep the trenches
were, just how many loopholes each fort had, how many bricks or stones
had been used in them, and had drawn rough sketches in the dust to show
each path leading up to them.

"We planned to use the same tactics as in the first campaign. That
meant to draw the enemy out from behind their defenses, entice them
into Soviet territory where they would be at the mercy of our troops and
the people, and in big sweeping flank movements attack their rear and
destroy them. We first decided to destroy the 28th and two other divisions
between Tungku and Kian. We needed the food and munition dumps
behind the enemy defense lines—and our radio school kept clamoring
for that 28th Division's new wireless set."

After issuing battle orders to Red Army regulars and partisan auxiliaries, on the night of May 16, 1931, Chu Teh and Mao Tse-tung moved
their headquarters to the Tungku mountain stronghold where the Medical Corps had established two rear base hospitals. The masses were so
confident of victory that thousands of them gathered at various points
with stretchers of every description to transport Red Army wounded and
with baskets and carrying poles to carry away captured enemy supplies.

Instead of shunning all mention of ancient feudal concepts which still
lingered on in the minds of the peasants, General Chu spoke frankly of
them. The peasants, he said, refused to obey his orders to transport the
enemy wounded to Red Army hospitals and to treat them the same as
they treated their own wounded. Mass meetings were called to explain the
order, but Chu found that it was useless to talk about modern rules
of warfare. The peasants could not understand why they should act
humanely to enemy soldiers, even when wounded. After all, they had
been sent to wipe them off the face of the earth. The only argument that
impressed them was that such men could be won over to the revolutionary
cause, yet even then they remained reluctant and some of them resentful.

Three nights before the enemy offensive was scheduled to begin—
and Chu Teh knew the exact date—the main Red Army forces made
forced marches into the enemy rear in the Kian area. Because of enemy
bombers they marched only at night and fought on moonlit nights. On
dark nights they attacked in the earliest dawn.

Fighting was supposed to begin on the night of the 17th, but no sound
of gunfire reached Chu and Mao. Two more days passed and still they

had received no report and heard no sound of fighting. Hwang Kung-lei's Third Red Army had been ordered to hold the front between Tungku and Kian while Peng Teh-huai and Lin Piao's troops in particular were to attack the enemy rear, yet no news came even from Hwang and no sound echoed in the valleys beyond.

The silence was so ominous that Chu Teh took his chief of staff and two companies of guards and started down the mountain to the west to investigate. He had nearly reached the foot of the mountain and was in a narrow valley abutted by two mountains when he suddenly came face to face with the advance guards of the 28th Division which was marching directly up the mountain.

"We could only scatter along the forested mountainsides and fight and retreat," General Chu said, "but I could see by the cautious movements of the enemy that they did not know how strong we were. Three hours later, when we were approaching the Tungku plateau and when Mao had readied our headquarters, hospitals and the people to retreat, I saw that the enemy had begun to draw back. The distant sound of gun-fire reached me—our Third Red Army was attacking the rear of the 28th Division. By nightfall most of that division had been disarmed. General Kung Ping-fang was among the captives but he had learned something from the first campaign: he wore an ordinary soldier's uniform without any insignia of rank and mingled with the soldiers. When we gave each captive soldier three dollars and told them to go home, General Kung lined up and took his three dollars—the only time in his life that he had accepted so little money. He outwitted us, but we got his guns and supplies, and our radio students crooned over his new wireless set with its generator, both intact."

A messenger arrived with a report from Peng Teh-huai that same night. This was a second messenger. Peng's first messenger had been captured and killed. For two days and nights Peng's Third Red Army Corps had fiercely assaulted both the front and rear of the enemy 43rd Division—a division of northern troops—capturing their mountain fortifications and chasing them into the valleys where half were disarmed and the rest fled to their brother 47th Division at Shuinan.

The whole western front was now in the hands of the Red Army, yet Chu Teh's voice became disconsolate at the memory of the two battles because they netted "only" 7000 rifles, machine guns, mortars and other weapons together with medical supplies and great quantities of food, ammunition and considerable money. This poor haul, he said, was because the 28th and 43rd Divisions were only half the size of the 18th Division which had been destroyed in the first campaign.

Deploying partisans and a few companies of regulars to hold the liberated area, Chu and Mao took their headquarters with the radio school, and joined their main forces which began rolling in one of the most dramatic offensives in the history of their army.

Thousands of peasants, including women and children with baskets and carrying poles, eddied around the army as it drove against the walled town of Shuinan where remnants of the 43rd Division had joined the 47th. After one regiment of these northerners was disarmed, the others fled eastward, leaving the great supply dumps behind them. The Red troops laughed as they spoke of "our White supply troops."

Chu Teh made a quick inspection of the supply dumps which the peasant thousands were already cleaning out, and the peasants laughed as he said to them:

"Didn't I tell you that we'd return all borrowed rice on a set date?"

Something like awe was in General Chu's voice as he remembered the swift thoroughness with which the peasants worked. Swarming like ants, they filled their baskets and lumbering carts drawn by water buffalo, while the thrifty women and children swept up the last grains of rice with their hands. The older men, women, and children moved in disciplined columns back into Soviet territory, while younger men, organized into battalions, moved eastward with the Red Army with rice and ammunition for the troops and, like the troops, seemed completely oblivious of the pouring spring rains.

As he talked of that campaign General Chu appeared to be living through it once more.

"Our offensive rolled forward and for the next fifteen days our troops fought and slept alternately. Combat units fell to the earth and slept while others arose from sleep and took up where they had left off, attacking in great sweeping movements into the enemy rear. Two days after Shuinan, at Peisha, we disarmed the 47th and remnants of the 43rd Division. These big northerners shook their heads and complained that they were not used to fighting in the mountains or in the rain. They were hustled back to our enemy reception stations by peasant partisans, and our own and the enemy wounded were transported back to our hospitals.

"I have never needed much sleep, but I hardly remember sleeping at all in the next two weeks. We were determined to teach the enemy a lesson they would never forget. Our troops swept forward like a flood, shouting slogans as they fought, singing, and fighting with wild fury for each inch of ground, and the enemy went down before them. The rains poured, enemy bombers could not operate, and we chased the enemy troops into flooded rice fields where we dragged them out, covered with mud. They wore full regulation Kuomintang uniforms, with leggings and shoes or sandals, while our troops wore thin shorts and jackets and were barefoot. I think I wore sandals, but I don't remember. Yes, Mao and I wore the same clothing as the fighters. I remember the heavy packs of enemy troops, which were filled with loot from our villages.

"Deep in Soviet territory where the enemy had driven a wedge we found villages burned to ashes and the corpses of civilians lying where they had been shot, cut down, or beheaded. Even children and the aged. Women lay sprawled on the ground where they had been raped before or after they had been killed. After that only the seriously wounded could be induced to leave the battlefield, and a fierce song crashed over our lines day and night:

> Fear not the rain of bullets
> Or the forest of enemy rifles!
> Advance! Kill!
> Take the cripple Ho Yin-ching alive!

"Along every road and path I saw peasants transporting our wounded and enemy wounded to the rear. Some had stretchers made of doors of houses, or boards, slung on ropes, and many carried the wounded on their backs. Despite our orders to care for the enemy wounded as our own, the peasants had their own method of obeying the order and expressing their hatred of the Whites. When tired, they would lower the White wounded man to the ground and curse or kick him or even tear a branch from a tree and beat him, all the time cursing him:

" 'White bandit! Raper and murderer! Paid dog of the landlords!'

"They would then pick up the wounded man and carry him until weary and then would lower him and ask him: 'Why should I carry a dog like you on my back?' and beat him. Though some people tried to stop them, I had no time, for we were rolling forward and fighting without rest.

"In the Ningkang area, to the north, we met more divisions of northern troops of the Twenty-sixth Route Army which Chiang Kai-shek had transferred to Kiangsi. Chiang did not trust this army, which had once belonged to Marshal Feng Yu-hsiang. We had a number of party comrades in this army and discontent among its troops was widespread. When we first contacted them, three regiments surrendered to us without firing a shot, and the others retreated. We left them in peace to think things over, while we rolled forward."

The final battle in this great campaign took place on May 29th in the Chienning district in Fukien Province, the end of the enemy defense works. Here the Red Army met the Sixth Route Kuomintang Army under Liu Ho-ting who for years had been one of the most notorious bandits of Fukien Province. Liu had been made a Kuomintang general and his ten thousand bandit followers organized into the Sixth Route Army.

"On the moment we attacked his troops," General Chu said with bitter hatred, "Liu fled from his headquarters inside Chienning city, and his troops followed him. We chased them right through the city and onto the bridge over the Min River. Some of our troops had already crossed and were waiting on the banks beyond.

"That bridge soon became so packed with bandit troops, horses and luggage that no one could move. Our machine gunners on the west bank poured a hail of fire into their ranks and they began throwing away their guns and hurling themselves into the river where our troops picked them off, while our troops on the bank beyond seized and disarmed everyone who succeeded in crossing."

With the capture of Chienning the Red Army, after leaving combat units behind, wheeled and went back along the enemy fortified lines, smashing them along the entire length. They seized whole new districts on either side which political workers began "consolidating" into Soviet districts.

When the enemy fortifications were thoroughly destroyed, the Red Army again wheeled, southward into the Soviet territory against the Nineteenth Route Army from Kwangtung Province in the far south. This army was also expert in retreating and did not stop until it had reached its home province. This retreat, General Chu said, was due to a new conflict between the generals of Kwangtung and Kwangsi provinces on the one hand, and Chiang Kai-shek on the other. Now that the Red Army had brought two Extermination Campaigns to ridicule, foreigners and the Chinese ruling class had become violently critical of Chiang Kai-shek, and the southern generals were trying to convince the representatives of the foreign powers in China that they could succeed where Chiang had failed, and thus be worthy of foreign recognition and support.

General Chu Teh summarized the Second Extermination Campaign in these words:

"This campaign lasted twenty days and twenty nights. During that time our army marched over three hundred miles, fighting day and night, pillowing their heads on their rifles on the earth while the rains poured.

In that time we defeated thirteen White divisions, killed at least ten thousand enemy troops, and disarmed over twenty thousand. Our trophies were too great to remember: they included some 20,000 rifles, with other weapons; money, blankets, medicine, clothing, wireless sets with generators, field glasses, mine throwers, automatic pistols, hand grenades, and great stores of rice, flour, and ammunition. Among the captives were many army doctors whom we ordered to work in our hospitals and some of whom later joined our party and remain with us still. A few, however, got entangled in the network of the A. B. Corps and murdered some of our wounded commanders. We shot them."

This campaign, General Chu said, "brought sorrow to thousands of peasant homes." Apart from the peasants slaughtered, the Red Army alone had four thousand casualties while the Red Guards and other partisan units lost heavily. Yet neither death nor suffering could crush the revolutionary ardor of the people and there were moving scenes in the great memorial meetings that followed the victory.

Because of the espionage of the counter-revolutionary A. B. Corps, the Red Army no longer accepted White captive soldiers en masse, but carefully screened each man before admitting him as a volunteer.

"We spoke frankly to such volunteers," General Chu said, "and never offered anything but bitterness and long struggle before victory would be ours. But we were certain of final victory. We could now attract only men willing to give up their families and perhaps their lives, or men whose families were already bankrupt or destroyed so that they had no hope except in the revolution. Such men we took into our army. We kept the others for two or three weeks of education in the history of the Chinese revolution and the principles and policies of our party and army. After that we gave them traveling expenses and allowed them to go where they wished.

"The second enemy Extermination Campaign proved to us that Kuomintang officers tried and partially succeeded in brutalizing their soldiers by ordering them to rape, burn, plunder and murder so that they would not dare surrender to us. In this way they tried to make their troops immune to our propaganda and make them fight hard to prevent capture."

Despite these brutalizing tactics—which incidentally the Imperial Japanese Army also used in China during the Second World War for the same reasons—there was nearly always someone in almost every Kuomintang regiment or division who managed to send reports to the Red Army by peasant messengers or who left messages behind. These messages and reports, whose authors he never knew, moved General Chu to deep emotion. Some reports, he said, were awkwardly written in unlettered script, but others were clearly the work of educated men because they were systematically composed and well written and gave the plans, location, and number of arms of the White troops with whom they served.

"By comparing them with our own intelligence reports, we found them to be exact," General Chu declared. "After occupying a place we often found some chalked message on tables or doors telling us just where the enemy unit was going."

General Chu also said that the Red Army espionage network was now well organized and stretched throughout Soviet territory and into Kuomintang regions. The army had special schools to train intelligence workers, many of whom were women and boys, while still others were peddlers and itinerant handicraft workers whose work took them far and wide in Kuomintang territory, working for or selling goods in the homes of the rich and poor alike, or into military camps of the enemy.

One section of the intelligence service made a study of enemy codes, documents, publications, and of talks with captives. Another section gathered information in newly occupied regions. Still another was historical—it made complete studies of each enemy army, with its commanders and soldiers: just what province the army came from, what changes had been made in it, its past history and organization, its fighting ability and so on. From such studies, General Chu explained, "we finally decided the best methods of working with each particular enemy army."

From the historical files of the Red Army which he had collected and preserved for many years, General Chu placed reports from his field commanders of that period at my disposal. Many were more exciting than anything a fiction writer could conjure up from his imagination. General Peng Teh-huai's reports, for example, were marvels of concentrated military and social fact in which not one superfluous word appeared. There was one from him dated May 17, 1931, just as the Second Extermination Campaign began. It was written in microscopic handwriting on both sides of a yellow postcard. Following a description of the battle that began that night, Peng wrote:

Enemy left much rice and flour here. Masses hate White bandits and helped us greatly in fighting. Wounded soldiers transferred to Yangmeiling Soviet area. Enemy soldiers are northerners; have not been influenced by us. Feudal relations between them very strong. Did not surrender until wounded. We marched too far—eighty li [twenty-seven miles] before fighting. Our troops very tired.

Reporting on one of his divisions which captured the enemy mountain defense works, Peng wrote:

Our side: dead and wounded, commanders and fighters, about one third of this division. In some units about one half of our cadres dead and wounded.

The reports always began: "Commander in chief Chu: Political Commissar Mao" and ended simply: "Peng Teh-huai."

All reports from Peng and other commanders gave concise details about their own and enemy troops, losses on both sides, captives, trophies, transfer of the wounded, problems and worries, and many ended: "Please instruct us about our work."

One report from Hwang Kung-lei, commander of the Third Red Army, was written across a military cap captured in battle. A number of reports from a divisional commander and his political commissar, who sounded very young, always ended: "Hail to complete victory in this second period of the war!"

General Chu also gave me a copy of a peasant ballad in nine stanzas which was born of the second campaign. The first stanza ran:

> Warlord Chiang Kai-shek
> Sits trembling in Nanking!
> Mobilized a great army to suppress the revolution,
> Ai-yoh! Ai-yoh!
> Sent paid hounds to suppress the revolution!
> Ai-ya! Ai-ya!

"We held memorial meetings, we sang, we worked and we planned after the Second Extermination Campaign," General Chu concluded. "We were victorious but we had had heavy losses and our troops were very tired."

> Bombers in the air above,
> Wire entanglements on the earth below.
> Powerful White armies for open attack,
> Concealed agents for secret destruction.

Then came the agent Hwang Mei-chuan
To bribe his nephew Kung-lei
And split the great Red Army.

Imperialist hunting dog Chiang Kai-shek
Reached Nanchang in summer's heat.
In parallel columns his armies marched
Over long distances to south Kiangsi.
Left-wing Commander Chen Ming-shu
Unleashed his hordes on Kwangchang.
Right-wing Commander Chu Hsiao-liang
Raped and killed at Nanfeng.
Central-route Commander Sun Lien-chung
Fed his horses on the crops at Kian.

The iron Red Army with discipline firm
Enlarged its ranks. Summoned partisans
And armed the masses to win the war.
In Lichuan, Chienning, and Taining
It fulfilled two missions:
Seized and divided the land,
And provisioned itself for battle.
Peasants rid themselves of twin evils—
Landlords and the feudal gentry.

Five new districts were Sovietized
And combined with Fukien-Kiangsi.
With horses fattened and fighters fed,
We met the advancing enemy.
Our men fell like autumn leaves,
Crying: "White brothers, come over to us!
Poor men should not fight poor men!"

The Whites fled, their arms shattered,
Burning villages and forests
And slaying the people.
On the ashes of our burnt homes
We rebuilt the Soviets
And tightened the people's sovereignty.
The Red Army is tempered in a thousand battles!
            —Red Army Ballad,
                "Victory in the Third Campaign"

Book IX

The Long March

Chapter 29

SONG OF THE LONG MARCH

In the wild autumn wind of October
The Central Red Army began the Long March,
And under the starry heavens passed through Yutu
And fought victoriously at Kupu and Hsintien.
In November, occupying Ichang, Lingwu, Lanshan, and Taochow,
The second enemy blockade line was broken
And the dog Ho Chien's liver turned cold.
In December we crossed the Hsiang River.
The Kwangsi warlords trembled.
Three blockade lines were broken irresistibly
Like the splitting of bamboo.
In December, in the fragrance of plum blossoms,
We entered Kweichow and crossed the Wu River
And in quick succession occupied ten hsien.
The Red Army's name spread to the four seas.
In February, at Tungtze and Tsunyi
The army reformed and reorganized.
We developed guerrilla armies in south Szechwan
And new volunteers joined us.
In March we fought back to Kweichow again
And reoccupied Tsunyi,
Crushing eight regiments of warlord Wang,
Wiping out two divisions of Hsieh and Chou.
In April we turned southward,
Fought from Kweiyang to Kunming,
Crossed the Golden Sands River in triumph,
And marched through western Szechwan.
In May at Lutingchiao
We sent Liu Wen-hwei reeling backward

And crossed the Ta Tu River at leisure.
The names of the Seventeen Heroes were written on our banners.
In June's hot weather the snow still mantled Chiachinshan.
Two armies, the First and Fourth, united at Fankung.
In July we entered northwestern Szechwan
Where the Black Water River flows
And green wheat ripples in the wind at Lihwa.
In August we advanced, fearless of hunger and cold,
Through the dread Grass Lands
Which few men have ever crossed.
The Red Army conquered all, struggled in bitterness
To fight the Japanese and save China.
In September we left Panchuchen, marched to the northeast
And crossed the Latzekiu and Weiho.
Fighting infantry and cavalry,
We reach north Shensi.
The Red Armies of the north and south united,
Shattering the enemy's new extermination campaign
And uniting the people to save China.

NEITHER facts nor figures, nor the names of a hundred rivers and mountains, can ever explain the historical significance of the Long March of the Red Army. Nor can they describe the tenacity and determination nor the suffering of the hundred thousand men who took part in it.

From Kiangsi and Fukien, from which the march began, and across the great plains, the wild rivers, and mountains of eternal snow to northwest China, was an estimated distance of 25,000 li, or about 8000 miles. Chu Teh marched farther. While Mao Tse-tung led the main column of the army directly on to the northwest, General Chu remained with troops for an additional year in the Chinese-Tibetan borderland of Sikang, reaching the northwest only two years after leaving Kiangsi.

"In early September 1934, after long preparation," General Chu began, "we called many chief political and military cadres to Juikin and informed them of our plans for evacuation. Hsiang Ying, vice-chairman of the Soviet government and a member of the Central Committee, came from the eastern front. We informed him that he was to remain in the Central Soviet District as the party leader and political commissar of all the armed forces and political cadres left behind to continue the struggle. Chen Yi, who had been commanding troops on the Hsingkuo front, was to remain as supreme military commander. Nieh Jung-chen, Chen's political commissar—who was sick with malaria—was to go with us.

"The armed forces left behind were: 5000 men of the 24th Division commanded by Chow Chien-ping; 3600 men of the Fukien Red Army; 2400 men of the Kiangsi Provincial Red Army; 2400 men of the Kiangnan Red Army; and 15,000 of the Anti-Japanese Vanguards, in northeastern Kiangsi.

"We left many of our ablest military, political and mass leaders behind. One was the chairman of the All-China Federation of Labor, who was captured and beheaded by the Kuomintang seven months later. Ho Shu-kang, Commissar of Justice, and Chu Chiu-pai, former Secretary of the party and now Commissar of Education, were also left behind because Ho was in his middle sixties, while Chu was slowly dying of tuberculosis. Chu Chiu-pai had been one of the leaders of the cultural renaissance and a member of the Central Committee of the Kuomintang under Sun Yat-sen's leadership. Ho and Chu were to be smuggled to Shanghai. Eight months later they were captured by the Kuomintang and beheaded at Lungyen, together with a number of women leaders.

"We also left behind about 20,000 of our wounded, scattered in mountain hospitals. After recovering, these men left the hospital and reported for duty. Maimed men were given money, sent to their homes, and allotted a pension of $50 a year. These pensions were paid out so long as our comrades in Kiangsi had money.

"The enemy used twenty full divisions to occupy the main Soviet cities and towns. They never succeeded in completely conquering the countryside where the people had arms, but they did succeed in slaughtering hundreds of thousands of people. Large numbers of women and girls were captured and sold at five dollars a head to Kuomintang soldiers, officers, landlords, and brothel keepers.

"All the landlords and loafers who had fled in previous years returned with the White armies and became officials, but they never dared go into the villages where the peasants shot on sight. The White occupation of Soviet districts was very slow and bloody, but the armed forces which we left behind were never exterminated."

One hundred thousand men and thirty-five women were selected to go on the Long March. Eighty percent of these were seasoned, disciplined veterans, the others were party and government cadres, and people who had played a leading role in the revolutionary movement.

The chief engineer of the Central Red Army Arsenal told me the way the evacuation was organized. In late September, he said, he received orders to destroy certain heavy arsenal equipment and guns. This done, the arsenal was divided into six units, one to be taken on the Long March, the rest to be distributed to five different regions in Kiangsi and Fukien. One hundred arsenal workers were to make the Long March, the others were sent with the arsenal machinery to the various Soviet regions. The arsenal workers and staff, together with five hundred Red Guards, all organized into companies, carried the arsenal machinery and supplies throughout the Long March.

"On October 13th," this engineer continued, "the Manchurian engineer who was director of the Central Arsenal stood with me on a big meadow and watched our six hundred men march past. Each man carried five pounds of ration rice and each had a shoulder pole from which hung either two small boxes of ammunition or hand grenades, or big kerosene cans filled with our most essential machinery and tools. Each pack contained a blanket or quilt, one quilted winter uniform, and three pairs of strong cloth shoes with thick rope soles tipped and heeled with metal. The people also gave us presents of dried vegetables, peppers, or such things. Each man had a drinking cup, a pair of chopsticks thrust into his puttees, and a needle and thread caught on the underside of the peak of his cap. All men wore big sun-rain hats made of two thin layers of bamboo with oiled paper between, and many had paper umbrellas stuck in their packs. Each man carried a rifle.

"Everyone going on the Long March was dressed and equipped the same. Everyone was armed.

"Though we were in Soviet territory and the people turned out to bid us farewell, we marched at night to get accustomed to night marching before entering enemy territory. On October 14th we reached our concentration point, Kwangtien. The First Red Army Corps under Lin Piao, which had been fighting on the Hsingkuo front, and the Third Corps under Peng Teh-huai, which had come from the eastern front, had already left to clear the way for the rest of us. Liu Po-cheng, chief of staff directing field operations, had gone with them.

"Some of our rear organizations had already reached Kwangtien, and others poured in throughout that and the following day. I saw General Chu Teh and Chou En-lai ride in with General Headquarters, followed by Mao Tse-tung and the Central Committee. Mao was thin and emaciated.

"At sunset on the 15th we began moving out through the mountains to the southwest. The order of march was issued by General Chu Teh. The first column consisted of a regiment of the Red Army University under the general command of Yeh Chien-ying, chief of staff to Chu Teh's headquarters. Next came General Headquarters, the Revolutionary

Military Council, and the party's Central Committee. Then came the Soviet government, party and Young Communist League members, and a part of the Anti-imperialist League. There followed the Supply Department; our arsenal unit; printers with their printing presses and supplies; the Government Mint; the Sanitary Department with doctors and nurses and 120 sets of stretcher-bearers—four to each stretcher; the Red Army uniform factory—with many tailors carrying sewing machines; and long columns of men carrying supplies for each department.

"The Seventh Red Army Corps protected our left flank, and the Ninth Corps protected our right. The Fifth Red Army Corps, whose commander was Tung Ching-tan, was our rear guard.

"I remembered Hsiang Ying, one of the first labor leaders of China, who came to Kwangtien with Chu and Mao. Hsiang Ying stood on a knoll and watched us leave, then returned to the 24th Division. A few weeks later he wired Chu Teh that the division had just destroyed one enemy brigade at Hweichang, south of Juikin, but the enemy was so powerful that the division was splitting up into battalions for widespread guerrilla warfare.

"On October 21st our First and Third Red Army Corps passed through the first enemy defense line in the Hsinfeng region. The rest of us followed. On November 3rd, we passed through the second defense line, and ten days later broke the third along the Canton-Hankow railway. The enemy knew nothing about our movements until we had broken through the second defense line and were in their rear.

"Once in enemy territory we often marched at night to avoid air raids. Night marching is wonderful if there is a moon and a gentle wind blowing. When no enemy troops were near, whole companies would sing and others would answer. If it was a black night and the enemy far away, we made torches from pine branches or frayed bamboo, and then it was truly beautiful. When at the foot of a mountain we could look up and see a long column of lights coiling like a fiery dragon up the mountain side. From the summit we could look in both directions and see miles of torches moving forward like a wave of fire. A rosy glow hung over the whole route of march.

"We marched through Kiangsi and along the mountain ranges of the Kwangtung, Hunan, and Kwangsi borders. For weeks at a time we fought our way across the plains, capturing cities and supplying ourselves from landlord warehouses and enemy ammunition dumps. We marched in three parallel columns—the First Corps on our right, the Third on our left, we in the center, and the Fifth Corps in the rear.

"Ninety thousand enemy troops swarmed into south Hunan alone, and the warlord, Ho Chien, was so scared that he scorched the earth of eight districts to prevent us from linking up with Ho Lung's Second Red Army. While burning and destroying, Ho Chien told the country that we were devastating south Hunan. The Kwangsi warlords also drove peasants from our route of march, then burned villages and told the people that we did it. We often saw villages burning far to the south where we had never been, and we sometimes captured Kwangsi agents in the act of setting fire to villages. We shot them down.

"Our First and Third Corps often made forced marches to occupy towns and cities and protect villages. In such places we always confiscated the property of the landlords and militarist-officials, kept enough food for ourselves, and distributed the rest to poor peasants and the urban poor. When we captured great warehouses of salt, every man in our ranks filled his pockets and ate it, like sugar. Our medical workers searched everywhere for quinine and other drugs, but never found sufficient.

"We also held great mass meetings. Our Dramatic Corps played and sang for the people, and our political workers wrote slogans and distributed copies of the Soviet Constitution and the Fundamental Laws of the Soviet Government. If we stayed in a place for even one night we taught the peasants to write at least six characters: 'Destroy the Tuhao (feudal gentry and landlords)' and 'Divide the land.'

"When hard pressed by superior enemy forces, we marched in the daytime, and at such times the bombers pounded us. We would scatter and lie down; get up and march, then scatter and lie down again, hour after hour. Our dead and wounded were many and our medical workers had a very hard time. The peasants always helped us and offered to take our sick, our wounded and exhausted. Each man left behind was given some money, ammunition and his rifle and told to organize and lead the peasants in partisan warfare as soon as he recovered. Sometimes one or two companies would become separated from our main forces during battle, but they merely retreated into the mountains and developed partisan areas.

"General Chu often made inspection trips of all units, encouraging everyone, but the morale of our forces was high in any case. General Chu was very thin and tough, although a tender-hearted man. He was old and his face deeply lined. He was never sick and never pessimistic."

As a matter of fact, Chu Teh was forty-eight in the year the Long March began.

The Long March was not only a great epic in the history of revolutionary warfare, but the seedbed for great folk literature. In the two-volume history of the Long March, written in the form of stories, poems, sketches, and diary notes by hundreds of Red Army men of every rank, I found this story:

Our most bitter trials came when we had to pass along narrow and dangerous mountain paths, through narrow passes, across narrow bridges, or swim icy streams. At such times our advance troops slowed down and the rear ones would take one step forward and stand for ten. We could not move forward and we could not sit down to rest. Some men fell asleep as they stood.

At other times we marched through storms with a fierce wind and rain whipping our bodies. Under such circumstances we would not use our torches and the paths were slippery and dangerous. Sometimes we covered only a few li a night, and, soaked through, had to bivouac in the open.

There was Laoshan (Old Mountain) on the Kwangsi border where we went up a mountain so steep that I could see the soles of the man ahead of me. Steps had been carved out of the stone face of the mountain, they were as high as a man's waist. Political workers went up and down the columns encouraging our struggling men and helping the sick and wounded. . . . News came down the line that our advance columns were facing a sheer cliff and that there was no way of getting the horses up. After a time came the order to sleep where we were and continue climbing at daybreak.

The path was no more than two feet wide at any point and even if one succeeded in lying down he could not turn over without rolling down the mountainside. There were great jutting boulders everywhere and even the path was covered with sharp stones.

Since there was nothing else to do, I folded my blanket, placed it beneath me, and tried to curl up on the path. I was so weary that I fell asleep. Sometime during the night the cold awoke me. I wrapped the blanket about me and tried to roll myself up in a little round ball, but I still could not sleep. I lay and watched the twinkling stars in the sky. They looked like jade stones on a black curtain. The black peaks towering around me were like menacing giants. We seemed to be at the bottom of a well.

Up and down the path I saw many small fires lit by men also awakened by the cold. They were sitting around and talking in low voices. Apart from their faint voices the silence was so great that I could hear it. It was sometimes near, sometimes far away, sometimes loud and sometimes faint, and at other times like spring silkworms eating mulberry leaves. I listened intently and it sounded like a complaining mountain spring, then like the distant murmur of the ocean. . . .

Next morning my group finally reached the sheer cliff that had stopped us the night before. It was Leikungyai (Thunder God Rock), a solid cliff of stone jutting into the sky at about a ninety degree angle. Stone steps no more than a foot wide had been carved up its face, and up this we had to go without anything to hold onto. Horses with broken legs lay about the foot of the cliff.

Our medical units suffered the most because the sick and wounded had to get off the stretchers and either crawl or be pushed, dragged, or carried up. The women comrades of the Medical Corps ceaselessly comforted and helped the men in their care without once showing any sign of weariness. . . .

Old Mountain was the most difficult mountain we had climbed so far. . . . But after crossing the River of Golden Sands, the Ta Tu River, the Great Snow Mountains, and the Grass Lands, it seemed very small indeed.

In January 1935, after suffering heavy losses, the Red Army broke into Kweichow Province, smashed enemy fortifications, crossed the Wu River, and seized Tsunyi, a city on the road from the capital, Kweiyang, to Chungking in the north. By that time, Chiang Kai-shek had drawn armies from all the Yangtze provinces, built roadblocks, and fortified all Yangtze crossings to prevent the Red Army from crossing into the north. Simultaneously, the Szechwan warlords began a reign of terror, trying to arrest and destroy every person suspected of even the mildest liberal leanings.

In a Kuomintang newspaper at the time, General Chu found a news item about his second wife, Yu-chen, and son. Kuomintang militarists had fallen upon his wife's home in Nanchi and destroyed everything. Chu Teh's son, a student of nineteen, the report laconically remarked, had escaped but was being "hunted down." General Chu waited in the hope that his son would make his way to the Red Army. He never heard of his wife or son again. There was no doubt in his mind but that they were killed by the Kuomintang.

Though outnumbered a hundred to one, the Red Army now turned on the enemy and began four months of distracting maneuvering warfare of which both Chu and Mao were masters. The opium-sodden troops of the provincial warlord were no problem, and were soon shattered and immobilized, General Chu said, but Kweichow was swarming with

200,000 of Chiang Kai-shek's best troops, and Chiang himself arrived at the provincial capital, Kweiyang, to take command.

The Red Army completely destroyed five enemy divisions, recruited nearly 20,000 new volunteers, and its intrepid political workers penetrated every town and village in the province to hold mass meetings and organize the people. The army encircled Kweiyang, but found itself too heavily outnumbered. Chiang Kai-shek, however, fled Kweiyang.

Among the records of this period which General Chu preserved, I found many roughly penciled notes among his papers, many of which had apparently been jotted down while he was resting at small villages, or late at night before he slept. One mentioned a mass meeting in Tsunyi on January 15th at which he spoke in memory of Karl Liebknecht and Rosa Luxemburg, and during which enemy bombers plastered a nearby town. This same note mentions that trade unions had been organized but "members are afraid they will be killed if the Whites return"—as indeed two hundred of them were.

Other notes reveal General Chu's ceaseless preoccupation with the living problems of the people. One read:

Corn, with bits of cabbage, chief food of people. Peasants too poor to eat rice; sell it to pay rent and interest. Rice seized by militarists as "war rice tax." . . . Peasants call landlords "rent gentry" and themselves "dry men"—men sucked dry of everything. Three kinds of salt: white for the rich; brown for middle classes; black salt residue for toiling masses. Even black salt so expensive peasants place small chunk in a bowl and rub cabbage on it when eating.

It was apparently while resting in a village that Chu Teh jotted down these lines:

Poor hovels with black rotten thatch roofs everywhere. Small doors of cornstalks and bamboo. . . . Have seen no quilt except in landlord houses in cities. One family of 10 persons here. Two board beds, one for husband, wife, baby; one a shelf for grandmother. Others sleep on earth floor around fire, without covering.

Another note read:

People digging rotten rice from ground under landlord's old granary. Monks call this "holy rice"—gifts from Heaven to the poor. Taoist and Buddhist temples everywhere, Christian churches in cities. Christian converts preach four slogans: "Boycott Japanese goods! Buy British and American goods! Fight the Reds! Believe in God!"

General Chu most certainly was in a hovel in a village when he jotted down these lines:

Young land laborer thinks himself too humble to join Red Army because Army is "book learning" army. Said he had worked for landlord for 5 years and was paid 3000 coppers for the 5 years (Ch. $27.99), with food. Landlord fled when we approached; laborer took rice, flour, corn and came home. Buried it from warlords. Went back and brought mother one quilt, one pair trousers.

While discussing the Kweichow campaign, I showed General Chu a number of old clippings from the Chinese and foreign press which I had preserved because they reported, and "confirmed," his death. These reports, which emanated from a Chinese, Thomas Chow, chief correspondent of Reuters news agency, were typical of both Chinese and Western reporting about the Red Army at the time. The first report, dated April 9, 1935, read:

It is now revealed that Chu Teh was killed during a battle at Chutaoshan (Pig Head Mountain) in the Tsatsu area. Chu was leading his column of troops in an effort to reach Kweiyang. . . . His body has not been encoffined. . . . It is wrapped in red silk and carried by his close followers. . . . Chu had been suffering from a serious wound before he met his death. . . . His close followers in the Red Army offer sacrifices before the red silk-wrapped body at close intervals when they have a chance to take a brief rest in their escape for life. . . . It is now confirmed that the Red Army consists of no more than 10,000 men.

A contemptuous smile formed about General Chu's lips as he read this report which, incidentally, was about the tenth time he had been reported killed. He pushed the clippings aside and said:

"I once read a report in the *Shun Pao* of Shanghai about an American YMCA speaker who said the Red Army gets recruits by surrounding a village and cutting off the ears of every man who refuses to join it!"

I asked General Chu if he had ever been wounded. "No," he said. "I have never even been sick for a day in my life. To tell the truth, though, I caught a cold while we were in the Snow Mountains . . . the Kuomintang often reported my death . . . that outfit can't tell the truth!

"Chiang Kai-shek offered $250,000 for my head, for Mao's, and others.

He even published price lists for heads, according to rank—from squad commander up. His planes dropped these over our lines. Men were insulted if their names were not on the lists or if only a few hundred dollars were offered for their heads."

General Chu continued speaking of the Kweichow campaign. By April, he said, enemy armies were concentrated in north, east, and south Kweichow. The Yunnan Army had also moved into the south, leaving the western route into Yunnan Province open. Unable to shake off such heavy enemy forces, on May 1st the Red Army suddenly drove westward through northern Yunnan over mountainous territory well known to General Chu from the past. In order to get the army across the River of Golden Sands—which crashes along the Yunnan-Szechwan border— before enemy bombers could discover it, Lin Piao was sent with one division to make a feint at the provincial capital, Yunnanfu, and draw enemy armies and bombers after him.

While Lin's division was making a loud noise on the road to Yunnanfu, Liu Po-cheng, chief of staff of field operations of the Red Army, led vanguard forces in a forced march directly across northern Yunnan. On the night of May 4th he reached the ferry crossing at Chou Ping Fort, disarmed the astounded Szechwan garrison, seized nine large boats, arms, ammunition, food stores, and the complete war plans and orders of Chiang Kai-shek. The rest of the army followed and crossed in safety.

On the way to Yunnanfu, Lin Piao's division captured an enemy caravan of military and medical supplies on its way to Kweichow. When his division came within sight of the gates of Yunnanfu, Chiang Kai-shek and his wife, who had flown there from Kweichow together with other Kuomintang figures, hurriedly left again. Lin's division now wheeled northward and three days later crossed the River of Golden Sands at Chou Ping Fort, destroyed the boats on the northern bank, and disappeared into the wilderness of mountains and forests of Lololand. The Red Army was not heard of again for three weeks.

The Red Army was moving northward through the mountains and forests of Lololand toward the torrential Ta Tu River, while Chiang Kai-shek flew to Chengtu in Szechwan and ordered the warlord armies in the west "to repeat history by destroying the Red Army at the Ta Tu River as the Taiping Army under Shih Ta-kai was destroyed."

General Chu spoke contemptuously of Chiang's order, saying:

"We repeated the observation of Karl Marx that world historically important events and persons occur, as it were, twice—'the first time as tragedy, the second as farce.' " Chiang Kai-shek waited in Chengtu for months, but history had still not repeated itself.

Chapter 30

CONSIDER the great historical drama being enacted in the vast mountains and primeval forests of distant Sikang Province.

The Chinese Red Army, now no more than sixty or seventy thousand men—for their losses had been heavy and they had left many partisans behind—was marching northward through Lololand. Chu Teh had known this route in 1922. And forty thousand men of the Taiping Army had, just seventy-two years before, trodden along the same paths up the terrible Fire Mountain where no tree or shrub or blade of grass grew and not a drop of water could be found. Tung Pi-wu, "Old Tung," consoled the "little devils," sons of soldiers who were to grow up in the army, by telling them the ancient story of Monkey who crossed this same Fire Mountain on his way to India to search for Buddhist manuscripts, but the mountain was so hot that all the hair on Monkey's behind was burned off—which is the reason monkeys have bare bottoms to the present day.

"If that is true," one Red Army little devil laughed, "why is not your long mustache burned off?"

"Ah, if Monkey could cross this desolate mountain and live happily ever after, sure *we* need have no fear," Old Tung replied, turning the subject.

The thirsty Red Army found water at last in scattered small villages surrounded by terraced fields of rice and sugar cane, and in a sparkling river washing the feet of other fields. And they bathed in the river at night, "treading the faint reflection of the moon," as one Red Army man put it, before spreading their blankets on the soft sand, "looking at the moon and talking of many things." Sometimes the Red Army built bonfires on both sides of a river, and cursed their "dead balls" engineers for failing to bridge the Lolos' broad deep river for them.

To cement friendships with the semi-savage Lolo tribesmen whose ancestors had waged war on the Taipings, Chief of Staff Liu Po-cheng was not above drinking an oath of blood brotherhood with the chieftain of a Black Lolo tribe. Until then the Lolos had greeted the Red Army with a long-drawn-out war cry that sounded: "Wu yu! . . . wu yu! . . .

wu yu! . . ." at which the Lolo warriors, naked to the waist, had seized
their spears and attacked like swarms of hornets from every mountainside.

A Red Army man who knew the Lolo language went out and arranged
for a meeting with the Black Lolo chieftain. At a pond called Hai Tze
Pien, the chieftain met and talked with Liu Po-cheng. It was there that
the chieftain killed a chicken and let some of the blood drop into two
bowls of water. He said as he did so:

"On this day, in this month, Commander Liu and Hsiao Yao-da, on
the banks of the Hai Tze Pien, become blood brothers. If at any time
either of them betrays the other, he will die like this chicken!"

Commander Liu took one bowl of the bloody water and spoke in a
loud voice for all assembled Lolos and Red Army men to hear:

"I, Commander Liu Po-cheng, and Hsiao Yao-da, today at Hai Tze
Pien, become blood brothers. If I ever violate this oath, Heaven will kill
me and the earth destroy me!"

After Liu had drunk, the Lolo chieftain lifted his bowl and also proclaimed in a loud voice:

"I, Hsiao Yao-da, and Commander Liu, today become blood brothers.
We are willing to live and die together. If I ever betray this oath, I will
die like this chicken!"

And he drained his bowl.

The Black Lolo chieftain, with many of his warriors, then escorted
the Red Army through their territory, and when they came to the tribal
border the chieftain ordered twenty of his slaves, who were White Lolos,
to guide the Red Army northward, and remain with it to learn its ways
of fighting, and then to return and teach his tribe how to fight the
Szechwan warlord Liu Wen-hui. The Red Army taught the White Lolos
indeed! These men became Communists before returning to Lololand,
but what happened to them thereafter General Chu Teh did not yet know.

In late May, Lin Piao's vanguard division reached the Ta Tu River
at the market town of Anshunchang—the very place where Shih Ta-kai
and the Taiping Army perished.

The savage river tumbled down from the towering, dead mountains—
outposts of the Tibetan ranges covered with everlasting snows. The river
roared like thunder and cast up rainbow mists as it crashed against the
cliffs. The river broadens out at Anshunchang, where there was a ferry
crossing with three ferry boats, each large enough to take eighty men at
one time. Only one ferry was tied up at Anshunchang, while the other
two were on the northern bank where a garrison of Szechwan troops had
built fortifications and was waiting to obey Chiang Kai-shek's order to
"destroy the Red Army as the Taipings were destroyed."

It is at this crossing, so runs the legend, that the spirits of the Taipings wail on dark nights, crying for vengeance, and it was here that General Chu, who had come up with Lin Piao's vanguard division in advance of the main forces, told a group of men the tales which the Old Weaver had told him in his childhood about Shih Ta-kai's revolutionary army.

In the midst of his stories a soldier came up and said: "We bought and slaughtered a hog. I snitched the liver and a few other pieces for you. Suppose we have a meal!"

"Good!" General Chu exclaimed with gusto. "I'm a good cook! Come, you cut up the meat and I'll do the cooking."

A dozen men followed him into the house where he had established headquarters, and stood about sniffing the odors of the cooking food while listening to his tales of the Taipings. When the food was ready and being eaten, General Chu turned to the soldier who had "snitched" it for him and said: "If you lay your hands on some tripe, bring it along and I'll cook it to make your mouth water!"

By the time they had eaten their meal, all preparations for Lin Piao's division to cross the river were completed. The ferry was pushed far upstream, where eighty men boarded it, set up machine guns and shoved off much as had the Taipings some seventy years before. They landed on the north bank with machine guns rattling and rifles crackling. They captured the ferries and sent the lot back to bring others. By next day, the entire division had crossed and the enemy redoubts on the north bank were in Red Army hands. Then the main forces came up. But enemy bombers had turned up also and began plastering the ferry and Anshunchang. The only other place where the river could be crossed was at Luting village one hundred and forty miles upstream where a famous suspension bridge had been built in past ages. There were also Szechwan garrison troops, and strong defenses, at Lutingchiao, as the suspension bridge was named, but Lin Piao's vanguard division could take them in the rear while the main forces crossed.

The decision was acted upon at once, and the two columns began marching, signaling each other across the river. At night they marched by the light of pine torches. Only after a cruel eighteen-hour march did the columns halt to sleep for four hours. Then they got up again and continued toiling along the narrow paths up and down the monstrous mountains.

A few hours before they reached Lutingchiao, Lin Piao's division fell behind. They signaled that they had encountered enemy troops. The main column pushed on fiercely and reached Lutingchiao at dawn on May 30th, the tenth anniversary of the Shanghai massacre. They decided to cross Lutingchiao by some means on this historic day, to prove that history never repeated itself save as a farce.

General Chu described the famous suspension bridge as made up of about twenty heavy iron chains embedded in huge piles of cemented stone on both banks of the river, each chain "as thick as the diameter of a rice bowl" and two or more feet apart, with iron bars to hold on to. The river at this point narrowed to about three hundred yards. Luting village, with the enemy redoubts, was on the north, and only a few houses stood on the south bank. The enemy had prepared a welcome for the revolutionary army by removing all plank flooring of the bridge up to about a hundred yards from the north bridgehead. So for about two hundred yards there was nothing but iron chains swaying over the roaring torrent five hundred feet below.

Lin Piao's division had still not come up, and no one knew how many enemy troops it had to cope with. There was no time to lose. The bridge had to be crossed, a new bridge floor laid. The troops began felling trees from the surrounding forests, and collecting planks, doors, and everything which could be used for a flooring. At the same time volunteers were called for to make the first crossing.

Whole units volunteered, but first honors went to a platoon commanded by Ma Ta-chiu. Then a second platoon was chosen. The men of both platoons strapped their guns, swords, and hand grenades on their backs, and Platoon Commander Ma Ta-chiu stepped out, grasped one of the chains, and began swinging, hand over hand, toward the north bank. The platoon political director followed, and after him the men. As they swung along, Red Army machine guns laid down a protecting screen of fire and the Engineering Corps began bringing up tree trunks and laying the bridge flooring.

The army watched breathlessly as the men swung along the bridge chains. Ma Ta-chiu was the first to be shot into the wild torrent below. Then another man and another. The others pushed along, but just before they reached the flooring at the north bridgehead they saw enemy soldiers dumping cans of kerosene on the planks and setting them on fire. Watching the sheet of flame spread, some men hesitated, but the platoon political leader at last sprang down on the flooring before the flames reached his feet, calling to the others to follow. They came and crouched on the planks releasing their hand grenades and unbuckling their swords.

They ran through the flames and threw their hand grenades in the midst of the enemy. More and more men followed, the flames lapping at their clothing. Behind them sounded the roar of their comrades, and, beneath the roar, the heavy THUD, THUD, THUD of the last tree trunks falling into place. The bridge became a mass of running men with rifles ready, tramping out the flames as they ran. The enemy retreated to their second line of defenses, but Lin Piao's division appeared suddenly in their rear and the battle ended.

The battle of Lutingchiao lasted just one hour. Seventeen men were killed, many scorched and wounded, and a few severely burned. A staff officer who was with Chu and Mao while the bridge was being crossed told me that Chu made no sound, no sign, but stood like a man turned to stone. He knew that the fate of the Red Army was being decided at that moment, that twentieth-century Chinese workers and peasants were succeeding where other Chinese warriors of past history had failed.

By late afternoon when the enemy began bombing the bridge and village, General Chu ordered a withdrawal. That night he spoke at a memorial mass meeting.

General Chu told his audience that seventeen heroes had sacrificed their lives to pave the way for the army's advance to Moukung where the Red Army was to meet the Fourth Front Red Army and proceed to north China to fight the Japanese.

May 30, 1935, he said, was a historic day. It was the tenth anniversary of the massacre of Chinese students and workers at Shanghai by British imperialism. And seventy-two years before, in May, Shih Ta-kai had attempted his crossing of the Ta Tu River.

After briefly reviewing seventy-two years of Chinese history, General Chu went on to a theme on which he often spoke in following years:

"Heroism is an ancient concept," he said. "In the past, individual heroes arose above the masses, often had contempt for the masses, and sometimes tried to enslave the masses. The Red Army embodies a new concept of heroism. We create mass heroes of the revolution who have no self-interest, who reject all temptation, and are willing to die for the revolution or live and fight until our people and country are liberated.

"The way before us is even more difficult than the one behind us. We must cross some of the highest mountains in the world, glacier-clad mountains wrapped in eternal snow, and often we will have to break our own paths. We must cross torrential rivers, construct our own bridges. In this vast region of the Tibetan-Chinese borderland are war-like tribes who fight all Chinese. Chinese oppressive regimes for centuries have tried to exterminate these tribesmen, and have succeeded with some. But we must try to make friends and work with these oppressed tribes as we have worked with Chinese workers and peasants.

"In the vast regions before us are also many enemy mountain forts and a hundred thousand enemy troops under orders to exterminate us. Kuomintang planes, which never molest the advancing Japanese, will bomb us even in the mountains of eternal snow. We will often have to march at night to avoid them. Our difficulties are great, our enemies are many, but there is no mountain and no river we cannot cross, no fort we cannot conquer."

Chapter 31

ON THE map, it is less than a hundred miles from the Ta Tu River to Moukung where the Central Red Army planned to meet the Fourth Front Red Army from Szechwan for the final march to north China. It was seven weeks before the unification took place.

Ten days were spent in preparing to cross the glacier and snow-clad mountains ahead, and another week in rest after this had been accomplished.

There was also some fighting before the march began. A regiment of Tibetan braves came down from Tachienliu to reinforce the Szechwan troops. The Tibetans were clad in sheepskin coats and their Chinese officers in fur-lined uniforms. The officers had brought their concubines along—baby-faced women hung with jade and swathed in beautiful white fur, and, like their masters, riding fine horses. Since the Red Army needed fur garments, it did not take them long to strip the Tibetan regiment, including the baby-faced concubines. They also took the horses, and the boxes of silver which the officers were carting with them.

In preparation for crossing the first snow ranges ahead, General Chu issued an order of the day which instructed each man to be as warmly clad as possible and to carry enough food and fuel to last ten days.

The order included a report on the some 100,000 enemy troops in the vast Chinese-Tibetan borderland between Luting and the Kansu provincial border in the far north. Of these General Chu said:

All such enemy forces have poor fighting power and have been defeated by Red Armies in the past. They are incapable of constructing new forts, standing guard in the fierce cold, or of prolonged fighting. Our army has better fighting power and, since our troops and political leaders are very active and courageous, we are confident of our ability to defeat them.

This was followed by orders about fighting tactics in the great snow mountains where "the paths are narrow and dangerous, the distribution of troops difficult and, under some circumstances, fighting is altogether impossible." Troops were to move no more than six or seven hours a day. They had to be prepared to build shelters, and to use white camouflage in certain regions. Enemy boats were to be seized, or leather and wooden boats prepared, to facilitate the crossing of rivers. All frontal attacks on the enemy were to be avoided, night attacks carefully planned, and all attacks "simultaneous and continuous until the enemy capacity for resistance is completely shattered."

This order of the day, like other orders, reports, letters and articles by General Chu in the next eighteen months, was written on paper which told an eloquent story of the backward, primitive life in the vast Chinese-Tibetan borderland. Some were written on the reverse side of old military maps roughly torn into squares; some on cheap, soft paper of many gaudy colors which Chinese use for New Year celebrations; others on coarse, thick Tibetan paper decorated with Tibetan designs or on pages torn from military account books. And some on great square sheets of coarse paper from which previous Tibetan printing had been roughly washed off with water or chemicals.

One of General Chu's articles, written about the time the above order of the day was issued, was entitled "How to Win Enemy Soldiers to the Anti-Japanese Anti-Chiang Front." It contained this significant quotation from a letter which a captive Szechwan soldier had written his family:

While I was in the Szechwan Army, our officers told us the Red Army cuts out the tongues of all captives before killing them. My whole company was captured but we were not even searched. A Communist talked with us. He asked us how many rich men were soldiers. We said no rich men are soldiers. He asked us what we and our families got from the warlords for whom we fought. We said our families just get more taxes and we soldiers were often not paid for months. He asked us why we fought for the warlords. We said because we were ordered. He said we fought poor men like ourselves and helped rich landlords and warlords who are running dogs of Chiang Kai-shek and the Japanese dwarfs. He asked us to join the Red Army but said if we didn't want to, his army would give us expense money to go home. We are now in the Red Army. It is very different from the Szechwan Army. Its officers and soldiers live and eat alike and no officer can curse or beat a soldier. We have lectures and meetings and we sing.

Since General Chu Teh was too busy to discuss this period of his life with me, he referred me to men who could give details of the march northward, and placed important documents written by himself at my disposal.

A political worker with whom I talked said he thought the worst mountain to cross was Kuchow, which was not so high as others but was completely covered with forests so dense that they shut out all light. The troops climbed this mountain in a pouring rain, wading in mud up to their hips and pulling themselves out by the branches of trees.

"After that," the man continued, "the Chiachinshan range was the worst—most of our comrades thought it the worst of all. When we came to it we had already crossed many mountains and many of our men were exhausted. Before crossing, General Chu Teh made an inspection of every unit, looking at our shoes, lifting packs to test the weight, inquiring about everyone's health, and instructing medical units to march in the rear to care for exhausted or older people who fell behind. He encouraged us to put forth every effort.

"Chiachinshan is blanketed in eternal snow. There are great glaciers in its chasms and everything is white and silent. We were heavily burdened because each man had to carry enough food and fuel to last ten days. Our food was anything we could buy—chiefly corn, though we had a little buckwheat and some peppers. We carried our food in long cloth pouches over our shoulders. General Chu carried his food like everyone else. He had a horse but he gave it to sick or wounded men to ride.

"We would not have suffered so much, or had such heavy losses in life, if we had been able to buy rice. The change from rice to a corn diet gave our men diarrhea and other stomach disorders. The corn passed straight through them—they couldn't digest it at all. Another torment was lice. Wherever we slept in the huts of the people, the lice seemed to come up out of the earthen floor to settle on us. Everybody had lice, everybody hunted lice."

Of all the men who talked of crossing Chiachinshan, however, Tung Pi-wu seemed the most graphic. A learned man of fifty, Mr. Tung was one of the earliest Communists. In describing the crossing of Chiachinshan, he said:

"We started out at early dawn. There was no path at all, but peasants said that tribesmen came over the mountains on raids, and we could cross if they could. So we started straight up the mountain, heading for a pass near the summit. Heavy fogs swirled about us, there was a high wind, and halfway up it began to rain. As we climbed higher and higher we were caught in a terrible hailstorm and the air became so thin that we could hardly breathe at all. Speech was completely impossible and the cold so dreadful that our breath froze and our hands and lips turned blue. Men and animals staggered and fell into chasms and disappeared forever. Those who sat down to rest or to relieve themselves froze to death on the spot. Exhausted political workers encouraged men by sign and touch to continue moving, indicating that the pass was just ahead.

"By nightfall we had crossed, at an altitude of 16,000 feet, and that night we bivouacked in a valley where there was no sign of human life. While most of us were stretched out exhausted, General Chu came around to make his usual inspection. He was very weary, for he had walked with the troops. Yet nothing ever prevented him from making his rounds. He gave me half of a little dried beef which he had in his pocket. He encouraged everyone and said we had crossed the worst peak and it was only a few more days to Moukung.

"To avoid enemy bombers, we arose at midnight and began climbing the next peak. It rained, then snowed, and the fierce wind whipped our bodies, and more men died of cold and exhaustion.

"The last peak in the range, which we estimated to be eighty li (twenty-seven miles) from base to summit, was terrible. Hundreds of our men died there. They would sit down to rest or relieve themselves, and never get up. All along the route we kept reaching down to pull men to their feet only to find that they were already dead.

"When we finally reached a valley and found a cluster of tribal houses, we gathered around and rejoiced at the mere sight of human habitation. The tribespeople had fled because we were Chinese, and centuries of cruel oppression had engendered in them fear and hatred of every Chinese. We had a number of Lolo tribesmen with us, but they also could not understand the tribal language in these areas.

"I lost track of time, but I think it was middle or late June when we finally reached a broad valley dotted with many tribal villages of huts or black yurts made of yak wool. Here were great fields of barley, two breeds of wheat, millet and peas, and herds of pigs, yak, sheep and goats. We established such friendly relations as we could with the tribespeople and bought food from them. We paid for our food with national currency.

"By that time we had so many sick and exhausted men that our main forces decided to rest for a week while Peng Teh-huai led eleven regiments ahead to establish contact with our Fourth Front Red Army in the Moukung, Lianghokow, Lifan and Maohsien districts. The Fourth Front Red Army had occupied these areas for a number of months, but there were still many mountains and rivers to cross before we reached it. The mountains were not so terrible as those behind us, but the whole territory ahead was peopled with fierce Fan tribes who fought every step of our advance."

One of the political workers who went with Peng's vanguards told this story:

"For four days we fought Fan tribesmen in the Black Water River region and finally reached a shabby little village called Weiku. The people had evacuated and destroyed the rope suspension bridge over the river. They took up positions on high, precipitous cliffs directly behind Weiku and rolled huge boulders down the mountainside against us. Peng had to send troops to drive them away.

"Everywhere from the cliffs and mountains we heard the tribal horns calling men to battle: WUNG-G-G-G! WUNG-G-G-G! WUNG-G-G-G-G-G-G!

"Our troops had begun building a pontoon bridge when we saw a column of armed men coming down from the hills on the far shore, running and shouting, but the roar of the river was so great that we could not hear them. One of them wrapped a message around a stone and hurled it across to us. It read:

" 'We're Fourth Front Red Army troops. Forty li up the river at Inien is a rope suspension bridge where you can cross.'

"On the way to Inien we passed through empty tribal villages where the Fan tribesmen again hurled boulders down from overhanging cliffs. The river at Inien was wider than at Weiku and the rope suspension bridge had been destroyed. Again we saw marching men, and when they reached the bank a Fan guide who was with them threw a message across the river to us. It was from Hsu Hsiang-chien.

"We all marched back to Weiku where our engineers constructed a pontoon bridge and we crossed the Black Water River and united with our comrades. We embraced, we sang and wept."

After a week of rest, the main body of the army followed along the same route taken by Peng Teh-huai. Before leaving, General Chu issued this order:

Though the environment is very difficult, our military-political educational work must continue without interruption. Six major disciplines must be observed: (1) Obey orders; (2) Act swiftly; (3) Keep time; (4) Love and protect your weapons; (5) Pay attention to sanitation; (6) Be kind and courteous to one another and to the tribespeople.

"Be kind and courteous to the tribespeople" must have been a discipline difficult to obey. The route of march was dotted with the corpses of

Peng's men who, weary from marching and fighting, had straggled behind. The tribesmen had murdered them.

When I asked General Chu what his attitude had been at such times, he replied:

"When attacked, we drove the tribal warriors away, but we tried not to kill. We left their homes as they were, taking nothing, hoping they would understand that we were not enemies. Peng Teh-huai's troops had tremendous success with the tribespeople afterwards. He even organized a Tribal People's Government over a large territory—exactly as we had done in Kiangsi."

When the main forces of the Central Red Army at last met advance troops of the Fourth Front Red Army, the battered, emaciated southerners broke ranks and ran toward their comrades, shouting, weeping, and singing. Many were so overcome with joy that they could not even speak.

On July 20th, in a pouring rain, they marched into the village of Erhokuo, in the Moukung area, to unite with the Fourth Front Red Army officially. Posters and slogans had been put up everywhere, field telephone wires were strung from village to village, and on a meadow stood ready a speakers' platform.

What happened at that meeting, and at the conference of the Politburo of the Communist Party immediately afterwards, was told me by different men.

Chu and Mao came out of the village in the pouring rain to await the arrival of Chang Kuo-tao, political commissar of the Fourth Front Army. They had already had long talks with the Fourth Army military commander, Hsu Hsiang-chien, with other officers and men, and what they learned had been disturbing.

A Red Army political worker explained the situation in these words:

"The Fourth Front Red Army had about 50,000 men. They were big, brave fellows from Szechwan, Honan, and Hupeh. They were poor peasants or former slaves, and anything could have been done with them. They had fought with great heroism and they had suffered. Chang Kuo-tao had taken good care of them physically—they were well fed and warmly clothed—but he had done almost nothing to educate them generally or politically. Chang had been appointed political commissar of this army by the Central Committee of our party. His duty was clear: to develop the troops politically to prevent the army from becoming an instrument of any ambitious military leader.

"Chang Kuo-tao had transformed the Fourth Front Red Army into his own personal instrument. He had—following a good old Kuomintang custom—built up a powerful clique of officers as his personal followers. He had organized the army on the Kuomintang pattern and even introduced the same officer rank. He had established special privileges for himself and his clique—the best clothing and food, for example—and kept thirty horses for himself and his bodyguard.

"Of course Mao and Chu and a few other commanders in the Central Red Army each had a horse. Mao had to ride because he was sick, and he had one bodyguard. Chu Teh also had one bodyguard. Except when he inspected army units, Chu Teh gave his horse to others to ride. We often protested because he had to direct the whole army during the Long March, but he said nature had given him a particularly strong body and that other men needed his horse.

"Chang Kuo-tao had contempt for the whole Central Red Army because we were so ragged and battered and were now numerically weaker than his army. Before leaving Kiangsi, we had fought a million enemy troops for months. Our men went on the Long March directly from the battlefield. In the nine months of fighting and marching across the plains, rivers, and mountains, we had suffered heavy losses. We had left most of our sick and wounded with the peasants; we had also left companies along the way to develop partisan warfare, so that we had only 45,000 men left when we reached Moukung.

"We had approached Moukung as men approach an oasis in a desert. Because of this we were appalled at the attitude of Chang Kuo-tao and his officer clique. They acted like rich men meeting poor relatives.

"Chang Kuo-tao's arrogant attitude was clear from the very beginning. When we held our unification meeting at Erhokuo, he came riding in with his mounted bodyguard of thirty men, like an actor coming onto the stage. Chu and Mao rushed forward to meet him, and he waited for them to approach him. He didn't even meet them halfway. General Chu's speech to the assembled troops praised Chang Kuo-tao's long revolutionary record, but when Chang spoke he introduced Chu Teh to his army merely as 'a man who has struggled with us for eight years.'

"Our party alone could determine the policies and program, strategy and tactics, of all the Red Armies. They had been decided on the Long March to north China. The guiding Politburo had called a conference at Erhokuo, following the unification meeting, where our continued march northward was to be mapped. Despite all this, in his speech to the assembled troops Chang Kuo-tao announced his own private program, stating that the vast borderland regions of Sikang and western Szechwan were an ideal place to establish a Soviet base and 'build a new world.'

"We had not made the Long March in order to stick in the high

Tibetan-Chinese borderland while the Japanese continued lopping off province after province, and Kuomintang traitors continued surrendering.

"Of course, in every great revolutionary upheaval, all kinds of problems arise and mistakes are made. Problems must be solved and mistakes corrected. The mistakes of the Fourth Front Red Army leadership were therefore discussed frankly at the conference of the Politburo. Chang Kuo-tao, however, was not a man to accept criticism or admit mistakes readily. He was even arrogant enough to point to the good condition of his 50,000 troops and to the losses and poor condition of ours, by which he implied that he was the only man capable of leading the Red Army. Instead of carrying out the northern policy, he insisted that we remain in the borderland and develop it into a revolutionary base.

"The conference was stormy, but before it ended Chang had promised to eradicate all personal militarist habits and all militarist practices in the Fourth Front Army. He continued opposing the northern policy, arguing that Chiang Kai-shek had thrown 100,000 troops across our route of march. The best strategy, he said, was to march back over the same route we had come, to Tienchuan, take the Tibetan city of Tachienliu, and establish our power in Sikang Province. He was voted down and the northern policy reaffirmed.

"Chu Teh reminded Chang Kuo-tao that while Chiang Kai-shek had sent 100,000 troops against us, we also had around 100,000 troops. Since the Fourth Front Army was rested and in good condition, General Chu proposed that it open the northern route by taking the Sungpan region, thus seizing positions of great strategic importance. Chang refused outright, saying the enemy defense works were too powerful.

"We finally compromised by dividing our troops into two columns to continue the northern march. The first, or eastern column, led by Mao Tse-tung, consisted of the main forces of the Central Red Army from the south. The second, or western column, under the general command of Chu Teh—Liu Po-cheng was Chu Teh's chief of staff—consisted of the Fourth Front Red Army which Chang Kuo-tao commanded and our southern Ninth and Fifth Red Army Corps.

"We began moving at once. Our eastern column reached Maoehrkai, seventy miles from Sungpan, where it remained for three weeks to rest and prepare for crossing the Grass Lands, and to wait for Peng Teh-huai's troops to come up. Peng's troops were collecting food supplies for the whole army. They were also organizing the tribespeople into a Tribal People's Government.

"The western column reached the banks of one of the raging rivers that pour down from the great Kunglai mountain ranges. It halted to reconnoiter for a place to cross. Chang Kuo-tao declared that the river could not be crossed and that the column had no alternative but to turn back into Sikang Province—which was what he intended doing all along! He insisted that Chu Teh and Liu Po-cheng should turn back with him. Both Chu and Liu were Szechwan men whose names were famous throughout west China, and Chang Kuo-tao wanted to use them for his purposes. Chu Teh also had the only radio generator in the army.

"General Chu and Chief of Staff Liu said a crossing of the river could be found and, if that failed, the western column could join the eastern at Maoehrkai and continue the Long March. That same night Chang Kuo-tao brought up special troops of the Fourth Front Red Army, surrounded General Headquarters, and took Chu Teh and his staff prisoner. Chang ordered Chu Teh to obey two commands:

"The first was that he denounce Mao Tse-tung and cut all relations with him.

"General Chu replied: 'You can no more cut me off from Mao than you can cut a man in half.'

"Chang's second command was that Chu denounce the party decision to move into north China and begin the anti-Japanese anti-Chiang war of liberation. General Chu replied:

" 'I helped make that decision. I cannot oppose it.'

"Chang Kuo-tao said he would give Chu Teh time to think things over, and if he still refused to obey these two orders, he would be shot. Chu replied: 'That is within your power. I cannot prevent you. I will not obey your orders!'

"A number of factors prevented Chang Kuo-tao from carrying out his threat. First, there were the Ninth and Fifth Red Army Corps who wanted to take Chu Teh and his staff back to the eastern column. Chang Kuo-tao warned them not to try! Faced with this situation, which would have led to bloody fighting on the high plateau of central Asia, Chu Teh and his staff finally turned back with Chang Kuo-tao.

"The western column, now commanded by Chang, marched back into Sikang Province, where it remained until Ho Lung's Second Front Red Army of 35,000 men came up one year later. Ho's army had made the Long March along the same route taken by the Central troops but, instead of crossing the terrible mountain ranges as we did, swung west, encircled Tachienliu, and joined the Fourth Front Red Army.

"When Ho Lung and his political commissar, Hsiao Keh, learned what had happened, that Chu Teh and his staff were working as best they could with Chang Kuo-tao, he seriously advised Chang to allow Chu to assume command and lead all the Red troops into north China. By then

Mao's column had reached northwest China and had developed a powerful revolutionary base directly across the route of a possible Japanese
advance. By then, also, political conditions throughout the country were
better for the revolution and the food situation in Sikang so bad that
Chang Kuo-tao agreed. General Chu therefore assumed command and
led the Red forces northward to rejoin Mao Tse-tung. Chang, however,
still retained control of the Fourth Front Red Army, whose troops had
still not been educated properly."

General Chu Teh never talked with me about the year he spent in
Sikang as the virtual prisoner of Chang Kuo-tao. By the time we reached
that part of his life, the Japanese had invaded China below the Great
Wall and he went to the front. I therefore had to depend on others, and
on his writings on military and political subjects during that period.
From these it seemed clear that not only had General Chu become a
writer of power during his year in Sikang, but that he had done everything possible to help Chang Kuo-tao in the struggle against the Szechwan
warlord armies.

One report written by him during this period was an analysis of the
warlord armies. Another, apparently written at Kangtze in western
Sikang, and undated, was on tactics to be adopted in fighting in mountains of eternal snows. Mixed in with these pages I found two sheets of
gaudy pink paper on which he had jotted down fragments of two old
Chinese poems which had apparently fitted his unhappy mood:

> Tears flooded the Yellow River,
> Regrets loaded the three peaks.
> Hwashan* sank beneath their weight.
>
> .   .   .   .   .   .
>
> A peach tree outside the beloved's gate,
> Beneath the tree an iron bridge.
> Crossing the bridge the lover grows weak,
> Crossing the bridge the beloved loses strength.
> Only when the iron bridge rusts away
> Will love vanish.

Chu Teh kept himself informed on world affairs via his radio. That
was revealed in his detailed analysis of the tactics employed by the

* Hwashan is a mountain peak in south Shensi Province.

Abyssinian armies, and of the support of Italian fascism by the imperialist powers.

Still another document, dated December 25, 1935, was a lengthy open letter to the officers of the Szechwan armies. Tersely and powerfully written, it began with an historical analysis of China's struggle for independence from the mid-nineteenth century down to that moment.

This letter analyzed not only the notorious Tangku agreement between Tokyo and Nanking, but also the terms of the secret Ho-Umetzu agreement signed in July 1935, by which the Nanking government agreed to suppress completely the anti-Japanese movement in China.

The document reveals both Chu Teh's deep historical knowledge and vision, as well as the consuming passion with which he pursued the struggle under the most disheartening circumstances. The following are verbatim extracts:

For two months now the Abyssinians have been fighting for the independence of their country. Though Abyssinia has a population of only ten million and a territory of only 300,000 square miles, its people are still fighting an imperialist power many times their numerical and military strength.

We Chinese have many tens of millions of square miles of territory, a population of 400,000,000, and a history that began four thousand years ago with our Hwang Ti ancestors. Yet the Kuomintang government has not lifted one rifle to resist the Japanese enemy but, instead, has progressively surrendered our territory to the Japanese.

The Abyssinian War and the Japanese invasion of China are part of the same imperialist war of invasion, partition, and colonialism. These are skirmishes which will spread into a second world holocaust in which no country can remain neutral. In this coming world war China will become a vast battlefield—it will be the meat and the imperialists will be the butchers. . . .

We, all of us, were born in this country. We exist here; it is our only home. How, then, can we be so slavish as not even to think of saving our country from ruin? You, Szechwan officers, have many million of soldiers, and you have good modern weapons. Why can't you even dream of following the example of little Abyssinia whose dark soldiers are fighting gloriously for their independence? Why should not brave and gallant men in our country also step out to fight for national survival? . . .

Traitor Chiang Kai-shek, who is willing to sweep the way for imperialism, destroys or bans all anti-Japanese organizations, thus demonstrating his loyalty to Japanese imperialism. Is there any living Chinese who wishes to be a man without a country?

The appeal continued with a proposal that the Szechwan armies form a national united front with the Red Army and fulfill three conditions: (1) end the civil war; (2) grant democratic rights to the Chinese people in all territory held by the Szechwan armies; and (3) guarantee the right of the people to organize and arm themselves into Anti-Japanese Volunteers. It ended:

If you accept these terms, please appoint representatives to consult with us. If you still continue to take orders from traitors and continue to attack and carry out the orders of Chiang Kai-shek to suppress the people and exterminate the Communists, then you are the vanguards of imperialism, sweepers of the path for imperialism. . . . The anti-Japanese mission now rests on the shoulders of the Chinese masses, and if you wish to fight Japan you must not fear the masses, but must share responsibility with them. If China sinks deeper into subjection, *you* will not escape. When the nest falls, the eggs are broken. Your goal is glory and wealth, yet if China is destroyed, what matter if you have wealth and own 100,000 mu of land? . . . If you reject our offer and continue selling China and acting as servitors of Japanese imperialism, the final result will be the ruin of our country and your families, and the destruction of your own reputation and bodies. You can then never escape the punishment of the people. Decide: which way do you choose?

That the Szechwan generals continued to "sweep the way for Japanese imperialism" is clear, not only from history, but from an article written by Chu Teh following two battles between the Red Army and the troops of General Yang Sen, at Tienhu and Mingyah in Sikang, during which many Szechwan soldiers went over to the Red Army.

Many pages of this article gave advice about the treatment and education of prisoners of war. After captives are disarmed, the article reads, they should be divided into two different groups: the officers in one, the soldiers in another, each group assigned different billets. The soldiers "should be treated very well, the officers kept under surveillance." The soldiers should be screened and the more politically conscious trained and asked to join the Red Army. Methods of dealing with the soldiers were these:

We must first comfort the soldiers, ask them where they come from and what work they did before they became soldiers. Ask each man what he gets for fighting for Chiang; if wounded what he gets; if killed what his family gets; if neither wounded nor killed, what he gets. The reply will always be the same—"Nothing"—but we must ask it again and again. We must also ask detailed questions about conditions in the homes of each soldier. This done, we must use these facts to prove to the soldier who are his friends and who his enemies. After he has thus become class-conscious, we must compare our policies and actions with those of the Kuomintang; compare the principles and actions of the Kuomintang with the Kungchantang (Communist Party). Which party, which army, represents the interests of the workers and peasants, and which the landlords and capitalists; which educates and develops the soldiers, which keeps the soldiers in darkness; which is for, which against, Japanese imperialism.

We must start with the realities of the soldier's existence: the oppression and insults, the cursing and beating to which he is subjected by landlords and capitalists for whom he worked, and by army officers after he became a soldier. We must never forget that while in the White armies the soldier has little or no care if sick or wounded, and is left to die without care. After leaving the White armies he is penniless and homeless, yet forced to pay high taxes, and high interest on any money he may borrow. We must discuss all these things and compare them with the way our army treats soldiers.

Some captives will want to join the Red Army, some will want to return to their old army and lead a revolt from within, and some will want to go home and join revolutionary activities of some sort. Those who wish to return home must first be taught guerrilla tactics and methods of dividing the landlord estates. Those who merely wish to return home to see their families should still be taught how to organize guerrilla detachments and divide the land. Those who wish to fight the Japanese can be trained in the Red Army. Even the old professional soldiers must be given constant training before being released because they can be very useful for propaganda in the old armies.

The division of the land has a great effect on the captive soldiers, because some of them come from Soviet regions and their families have already received land. The majority have been forcibly conscripted by the warlords and gentry, and some have fought the Red Army for years. Many do not want to fight. All of them repeatedly told us that they fought because their officers constantly told them that the Red Army splits open the stomachs of captives. They also fought because high officers hold petty officers responsible for desertions, and the petty officers kept a sharp eye on every man under their command.

In our work with the captives, we must expose the lying and deceptive propaganda of the Kuomintang, demolishing every idea voiced by the Kuomintang. We must convince the captives that they must fight the Japanese invaders.

The conditions in Sikang where General Chu Teh spent one year of his life under duress can be understood by at least one incident as related to me by one of his staff:

"Since Red Army troops were workers and peasants who know every kind of work, they spun and wove and made woolen uniforms from yak, sheep, or goat's wool; or made skin garments and boots. The altitude was so high and the air so rarefied that water boiled at a very low temperature. Under these conditions, cooking took so much time that the food was only half done. . . .

"Following one battle, I was with Chu Teh and a column of men moving along a mountain path. We came to a group of black yurts such as the tribesmen use for dwellings. They had fled, of course, as Han (Chinese) troops approached, taking all food with them. We went into one of the yurts and found fifteen of our men who had gone in advance. They were sitting cross-legged on the earth around a pile of cold ashes. We called out but they did not reply. They sat with heads bowed, like statues. We went up and touched them. They were frozen to death. The tribesmen had taken their guns and packs. In another yurt we found five others, sitting around a pile of cold ashes, each with a shot through the back."

Chapter 32

I ONCE listened to a number of Red Army men in Peng Teh-huai's headquarters talking about the Long March. One of them remarked:

"Speaking of the way comrades should act, I'd like to ask which of you stole my needle during the Long March! I haven't mentioned it until now, but I'm reminded of it because I still don't have any needle."

Everyone smiled, and one man answered:

"Perhaps you gave your needle to some village girl to prove you were rich! I've seen Chu Teh spin and weave, but I've never seen you even sew a button on your jacket."

"Chu Teh had a lot of time on his hands in Sikang," the man-who-had-lost-his-needle replied. "When we came out of the Grass Lands, I didn't have anything worth sewing a button on. That was when we began eating rats. We cleaned every village of rats. They tasted awful but we ate them. I pitied the dogs and cats."

Another man spoke up:

"I remember when we came out of the Grass Lands and broke through enemy lines into Kansu and saw Chinese peasants. They thought we were crazy. We touched their houses and the earth, we embraced them, and we danced and sang and cried."

The Grass Lands! The Grass Lands! Every man talked of the Grass Lands. The first Red Army column, led by Mao Tse-tung, crossed the Grass Lands in September 1935. One year later General Chu Teh led the rest of the Red Army through that same dread region of terror.

The Grass Lands is a vast and trackless swamp stretching for hundreds of miles over the high Chinese-Tibetan borderland. As far as the eye can reach, day after day, the Red Army saw nothing but an endless ocean of high wild grass growing in an icy swamp of black muck and water many feet deep. Huge clumps of grass grew on dead clumps beneath them, and so it had been for no man knows how many centuries. No tree or shrub grew here, no bird ventured near, no insect sounded. There was not even a stone. There was nothing, nothing but endless stretches of wild grass swept by torrential rains in summer and fierce winds and snows in winter. Heavy black and gray clouds drifted forever above, turning the earth into a dull, somber netherworld.

The Red Army marched along the eastern fringes where the swamp was less deep and where there were often narrow strips of land which tribal horsemen used on rare occasions. Each man carried enough food and firewood to last eight days, and Lin Piao's First Front Red Army, which spearheaded the march, also carried bamboo screens to build shelters for those coming after. The food carried by each man consisted of parched wheat and tea.

One Red Army man wrote of crossing the Grass Lands in the *History of the Long March:*

Friendly tribespeople around Maoehrkai, who had been influenced by Chinese culture and were therefore more friendly, told us that we would freeze to death if we did not have woolen socks and sheepskins. We prepared as best we could but we couldn't buy enough skins or woolen garments for so many men.

Just before entering the Grass Lands, we heard shots in our rear. A party of tribal horsemen had fallen upon some of our stragglers and seized their guns. We marched ten hours on the first day, then lay down and slept on the narrow freezing path, tying the high grass on either side into a kind of tent above us.

On the fourth day we came to a stretch where we sank into muck up to our knees and our horses had to be pushed and beaten out. The clouds rolled heavily above, and except for the rustling grass it was a land of the dead.

I asked a comrade how he would describe the Grass Lands if he were a writer. He said he would describe it as a desert except that everything was water-grass instead of sand, that one could die of thirst in a desert but there was plenty of water here, and that the sun shone in a desert but never here. He said: "I've heard that you can sometimes see a mirage in a desert, but we do not even have that comfort here." We finally agreed that the Grass Lands was a place where your feet were always soaked, where the hoofprints of the horses disappeared immediately, where men and horses fell into the muck between the grass clumps and shivered in the bitter cold after they were dragged out. We agreed that we could not really describe the dreary waste about us.

Another Red Army man, Moh Hsu, kept a diary in which he wrote:

Today I discovered a comrade struggling in the muddy water. His body was crunched together and he was covered with muck. He gripped his rifle fiercely, which looked like a muddy stick. Thinking he had merely fallen down and was trying to get up, I tried to help him stand. After I pulled him up he took two steps, but the entire weight of his body was on me, and he was so heavy that I could neither hold him up nor take a step. Urging him to try and walk alone, I released him. He fell on the path and shrunk together, but he still clung fiercely to his rifle and tried to rise. I tried again to lift him but he was so heavy and I so weak that it was impossible. Then I saw that he was dying. I still had some parched wheat with me and I gave him some but he could not chew, and it was clear that no food could save him. I carefully put the parched wheat back in my pocket, and when he died I arose and passed on and left him lying there. Later, when we reached a resting place I took the wheat from my pocket but I could not chew it. I kept thinking of our dying comrades. I had had no choice but to leave him where he fell, and had I not done this I would have fallen behind and lost contact with our army and died. Yet I could not eat that parched wheat.

As the days passed, more and more corpses lay along the route of the march, many in the shelters built by the vanguard troops. Exhausted men had lain down in the shelters to gather a little strength, and those who came after found them dead. Little piles of parched wheat lay near the head of each man—comrades had left food which they themselves needed. Fires had burnt into piles of cold ashes.

Sometimes the rain poured so fiercely that a man could not hear the voice of the one behind him. The rain would be followed by a fierce, freezing wind. The sun would come out for a few moments, then be swallowed up, and the rain again come down in sheets.

When men came to a shelter they would crowd inside and try to build a fire, only to find that their wood was soaked and would not light.

On the sixth day they saw the faint, distant outlines of low hills with smoke here and there; and their rejoicing knew no bounds. Next they saw a few stones in the path, and they picked them up and exclaimed at their beautiful meaning. On the eighth day they again saw smoke, and the next afternoon some distant trees and low houses. They pushed forward like famished men in a desert, but an order came down the line: "Turn left and make another dew encampment tonight."

They obeyed in silence, and when they came to firm earth they found bushes covered with red-gold berries hanging in grape clusters which they ate. After days of eating only a few grains of parched wheat in hot water, the sour berries tasted delicious.

The next evening they came to a deserted tribal village where all houses were made of yak manure, which was so inflammable that special fire patrols had to be organized. Some of the buildings were huge structures of thirty or forty rooms. By then all the provisions of the army had been used up and the men began eating anything they could find: unripened wheat from the fields, grass, wild greens, berries. Some of the rich tribesmen, who had fled before the Hans, had secret storehouses in their great homes. These were built into the walls and completely sealed up. The Red troops discovered them, tore down the walls and distributed the food. Some men boiled cowhides for twenty-four hours and then ate them; or they boiled big leather boots and drank the broth.

Every rich Fan tribal family had a special religious hall in which Buddhist manuscripts and bowls of sacrificial food—nuts, dates, rice and cheese—were kept; and on the altars were figurines of gods and animals painted green or red. One Red Army unit of twelve men was billeted in such a hall for a number of days while the army was cruising far and wide to find and buy wheat.

One of the men of the unit of twelve returned one evening and noticed that some of the altar figurines had disappeared. When he asked the reason, one of his comrades gave him a bowl of steaming hot wheat porridge with butter floating on top. The fragrance was so delicious that he almost fainted. His comrades had scraped the paint from the figurines and found them to be made of wheat and butter.

"We were so selfish that we kept the secret," this man said. "At each mealtime we would peel the paint off a few more images and cook them in water with the handful of wheat which was our only army ration. We were so demoralized by hunger that we secretly planned to raid the family altars of other homes. But one day, after treating two famished comrades, our secret came out, and after that our living conditions sank deplorably!"

Chiang Kai-shek had even shipped a division of the famous Nineteenth Route Army into the borderlands, but after two regiments were destroyed in battle with the Red Army its commander fled and eight hundred soldiers surrendered. These soldiers told the Red Army that almost all their old commanders had been replaced by Blue Shirt (fascist) officers who spread propaganda that the Red Army cut off the ears, gouged out the eyes, and ripped open the stomachs of all captives. One soldier hit himself on his head with his fist and exclaimed:

"What a stupid head I have to believe such lies!"

Another captive laughed and remarked: "If you beat your head for each lie our captain told us, you'll beat your brains out!"

"I don't have to hit myself at all because I never believed that ghost talk," another declared. "Our officers said we were being sent to the north to fight the Japanese devils. Only after we got into this wilderness did we know we were being sent to fight our own countrymen. I'm going to join the Red Army."

Another soldier spoke up:

"I'll go with the Red Army until we get out of this savage country, then I'll go home."

"You'll never reach home!" his comrades protested. "You'll be grabbed and stuck back into Chiang Kai-shek's army before you're halfway home. . . . How can you reach home without money!"

"I'll beg my way home, and even if they grab me and stick me into Chiang's army again, I won't fight!"

"When the time comes you can't be your own master! Your officer will shoot you in the back if you don't fight!"

"That kind of talk makes me sick!" the beleaguered soldier exclaimed. "If I'm ever sent to fight the Reds again, I'll surrender my rifle again."

Starving and fighting, the Red Army finally broke through the enemy fortifications on the Kansu border and poured down onto the Kansu plains. It was an army of ragged skeletons, with hundreds of men coughing their lungs out, yet it smashed one militarist division after another, seizing rice, uniforms, money and medicine. By then Mao's column had only twenty thousand men—perhaps the hardest, toughest, and most politically conscious veterans in the world.

On October 20, 1935, after many fierce battles with Hu Tsung-nan's fascist troops, with Moslem and Manchurian armies, Mao's column finally reached north Shensi Province and united with ten thousand Red Army partisans under Liu Tse-tang, who had been fighting in this region since 1927. Hsu Hai-tung's regiment, left in the northwest by the Fourth Front Red Army in 1934, had now grown to a division and was fighting in eastern Kansu.

On October 6, 1936—one year later—Chu Teh led the other Red troops along almost the same route of march, and made contact with Lin Piao's First Front Red Army in the district city of Huihsien in southern Kansu.

On almost the same date the Young Marshal, Chang Hsueh-liang, commander of the old Manchurian Army which was driven out of Manchuria by the Japanese in 1931, wired from Sian, Shensi, to Generalissimo Chiang Kai-shek, proposing a national united front with the Red Army against the Japanese. Chiang angrily rejected the proposal and ordered the Young Marshal to close down his new Military-Political Training School at Sian which, he charged, was filled with Communists. Marshal Chang replied that his school accepted any man who loved and was willing to fight for his country.

Generalissimo Chiang called an "Anti-Red Military Conference" in Loyang in the north where he informed the assembled northwestern generals that China's chief enemies were not the Japanese but the "traitorous Red-bandits." His crack commanders in Kansu, Generals Hu Tsung-nan and Wang Chun, agreed with him, but the Young Marshal, who had already lost a number of regiments to the Red Army, had his own thoughts.

During these events, the Japanese army was driving westward into Suiyuan Province to encircle and lop off five north China provinces whose mines, railways, and other strategic industries were essential for Japan's planned conquest of all China. General Fu Tso-yi, governor of Suiyuan, began fighting, but an enraged nation knew his troops could hold out for only a short time. Thousands of north China students were pouring into Suiyuan to fight, but the three divisions which Chiang Kai-shek felt constrained to dispatch to Suiyuan never went near the front nor did they fire one shot at the Japanese.

The Japanese drive, together with Chiang Kai-shek's new Extermination Campaign against the Red Army, had the appearance of a Japanese-

Kuomintang pincer movement not only against the Red Army, but also against the Manchurian troops under the Young Marshal, and the Shensi provincial "Pacification Army" under General Yang Hu-chen which was allied with the Manchurian Army. Chiang interpreted the reluctance of these northwestern armies to fight the Red Army as nothing but "poor discipline and leadership," a state which he decided to correct by calling a special Anti-Red Military Conference in Sian on December 11th. Sian was the headquarters of the Young Marshal and also of General Yang.

In preparation for the Anti-Red Extermination Campaign—which was to follow the Sian conference—Chiang shipped new divisions into Kansu Province in the northwest, together with enough rice, ammunition, money, and clothing for the entire campaign. Hundreds of armed secret police, with a radio transmission set, were also secretly dispatched to Sian to prepare for an armed uprising against the Young Marshal.

Many national and international events convinced the embittered Chinese Communists and other Chinese that an actual Kuomintang-Japanese conspiracy existed against all anti-Japanese forces of the nation. The Tangku and Ho-Umetzu agreements gave credence to this belief, as did a number of public statements by both Japanese and Nanking officials.

Shortly after Mao Tse-tung's column reached northwest China, for example, the Japanese Foreign Minister, Koki Hirota, proposed a Tokyo-Berlin-Nanking anti-Red pact "to prevent the Bolshevization of Asia." Shortly afterward Hirota made this statement before the Diet:

The suppression of Communist activities in our part of the globe and the liberation of China from the Red menace is, therefore, a matter of vital importance not only for China but for the stabilization of East Asia and of the world. . . . It is the desire of the Japanese Government to cooperate with China in various ways for the eradication of Communism.

Hirota added that, "much to Japan's regret," there was still student agitation in China "which contravenes the very spirit of our program," but that "it is expected that the present situation will soon be rectified by the Chinese authorities."

Though the Nanking regime never signed the Tokyo-Berlin Anti-Comintern Pact of November 1936, still Chiang Kai-shek's Foreign Minister, General Chang Chun, repeatedly assured Japan that "China" was determined "not to relinquish, even temporarily, her firm stand against the Communists."

In early 1935, General Chang Chun, known as one of the chief pro-Japanese leaders of China, had officially assured the Japanese government that his government appreciated its concern about Communism in China "because internal agitation in one country is bound to be felt by its neighbors," and that the Chinese government had waged a relentless struggle against the "Red menace" until "we are confident of the early liquidation of the whole trouble."

Chiang Kai-shek's new Anti-Red Extermination Campaign was therefore undertaken, if not with direct Japanese cooperation, at least under the watchful eyes of their military and diplomatic representatives in Nanking and other major cities of China. Sian, headquarters of the Young Marshal, was the only strategic city in the country without Japanese "observers." In Szechwan Province the people attacked such Japanese. Kuomintang troops and the secret police prevented similar actions elsewhere. Thousands of Chinese patriots, including lawyers, bankers, and newspapermen, were being arrested, imprisoned or killed by the Kuomintang as "Communists" because they called for the end of civil war and the establishment of a united front against the Japanese.

Such was the political and military situation into which General Chu Teh led the Red troops out of the Tibetan-Chinese borderland into northwest China. The Long March was being completed and the Red Army keeping its rendezvous with history.

The meeting between General Chu Teh's forces and the First Front Red Army under Lin Piao's command was described by a young American physician, Dr. George Hatem, who went to the Red Army in the summer of 1936. Dr. Hatem, a graduate of medical schools in Switzerland and in Beirut, Syria, joined the Red Army Medical Corps and remained with it through all the momentous years that followed.

In his letters and diaries, this American physician described how the First Front Red Army occupied six counties in central and south Kansu to receive the advance of General Chu Teh's forces coming down out of the borderlands. Every household in the district city of Huihsien, and all surrounding villages and towns, set aside rooms to accommodate Chu Teh's troops, while the First Front Red Army transported food supplies and 40,000 new winter uniforms—made in the Red Army uniform factory—to care for them.

A peasant walked swiftly for four days to deliver the first letter from General Chu Teh to the First Front Red Army, then walked back with an answer.

General Chu's vanguard division reached Huihsien on October 7, 1936, Dr. Hatem wrote, but passed on through to leave room for the troops behind them.

Troops of the Fourth Front Red Army with General Chu Teh and

Chang Kuo-tao arrived on the 8th. The rest of the Fourth Front Army arrived the next day, but the Second Front Red Army under Ho Lung and Hsiao Keh, which had served as rear guards, arrived only on October 19th and 20th.

These troops were in relatively good condition and excellently equipped, Dr. Hatem said. Since they had fought many battles on the way, each man was burdened with extra rifles, machine guns and ammunition. There were so many men, however, that the 40,000 new winter uniforms were too few and others had to be prepared. Ho Lung's ragged army received new uniforms only two months later.

Dr. Hatem described General Chu Teh as "thin as a ghost, but strong and tough, with a full growth of beard and clad in a lousy skin coat." Chu changed into a new winter uniform and coat, he added, but kept his beard until he reached Paoan in northwestern Shensi where Mao Tsetung had established the Soviet Government and general Red Army headquarters.

Dr. Hatem wrote in one letter:

The most striking thing about Chu Teh is that he does not look like a military commander at all. He looks like the father of the Red Army. He has the most piercing eyes, he is slow to speak, quiet, and with a wonderful smile. He carries an automatic, and is a sharpshooter and a heavy smoker. He is fifty, but looks much older, and his face is deeply lined; yet his movements are vigorous and his health excellent. His headquarters is a bustling beehive with messengers and commanders coming and going, the phone ringing all the time and radiograms being sent and received.

Chang Kuo-tao, the political commissar, is fat, tall and smooth. I wonder how he kept so fat while others lost every ounce of excess weight.

Chu Teh had just stepped into his headquarters in Huihsien when Chen Keng, divisional commander in the Fourth Front Red Army, telephoned him. Chu Teh became very excited. The reunion of the Red troops in the region was held in the late afternoon of the following day— to avoid bombings, which are daily. . . .

What a reunion! Men threw their arms around each other, laughing and weeping at the same time, or walking arm-in-arm and pouring out questions about other comrades. Chu Teh was completely swallowed up.

A number of buses along the Sian-Lanchow highway had been captured and sent to transport the sick and wounded. The Fourth Front Red Army were peasants who had never seen a bus before. They were afraid to ride in the thing. Though sick, they preferred to walk to the hospitals. . . .

At Siaohochen on October 26th there was a great mass meeting of all Red troops in the region. Lin Piao and other leaders gave a complete report on the northwest, on the war between the Red and White armies, and on the continued advance of Japanese armies into Suiyuan. Chiang Kai-shek had ten divisions under Generals Hu Tsung-nan and Wang Chun, fighting the Red Army in Kansu.

For months the Red troops had been appealing to these divisions to unite with them to fight the Japanese. Under orders of Chiang, the Young Marshal, Chang Hsueh-liang, continued to order Tungpei (Manchurian) troops to fight the Red Army, but many had joined the Red Army instead, which now had a cavalry division made up entirely of former Tungpei cavalrymen.

As early as October 20th, Mao Tse-tung had ordered the Red Army not to fight any Kuomintang troops unless in self-defense, but to intensify their united front propaganda. He also ordered that no more Tungpei troops be accepted into the Red Army. By October 27th the Red Army began drawing back before enemy forces while political workers posted united front appeals everywhere. General Hu Tsung-nan merely moved up more divisions against them. Dr. George Hatem's diary described the events that followed:

October 29. News that four divisions of Hu Tsung-nan are trying to surround us. We know their exact positions and plans. . . . One of General Hu's cavalry commanders arrived at headquarters today to say he had orders to attack us at a certain place at 11 A.M. tomorrow morning. Since General Hu uses an airplane to watch his troops, this commander said, he himself would have to make a show of fighting, but he advised us to pass through his region at 6 A.M., which gives us five hours leeway. This development forced us to change our plans and we began marching rapidly by day. Enemy planes found us and began bombing. They have destroyed many hamlets.

October 30. Heard Chu Teh speak for the first time at the Red Army Military Academy. He speaks clearly and distinctly. He's enthusiastic and confident about the future. He advised the students to study night and day to meet the great tasks before China in the coming anti-Japanese war. Ho Lung also spoke. What a pep talker he is! He has a voluminous and clear voice and speaks with many gestures, raising the fighting spirit of the lost, lethargic or weary person.

November 1. Went to Northwest Party Bureau. . . . In Bureau read a copy of October 3rd issue of *Ta Kung Pao* from Tientsin which says Red Army under Mao Tse-tung was disastrously defeated at Huihsien. At Huihsien, Chu Teh's forces concentrated without fighting. Mao Tse-tung was at Paoan, *1300* li away at the time.

November 3. Hid in cave during air raid with commanders of two Tungpei regiments who came over to Red Army with their troops. Talked with them for three hours during the air raid. They and their troops want national united front against the Japanese. Talked with their troops later, who are sad and depressed because the Red Army is sending them back to their own Army to spread united front principles. Heard Chu Teh speak to both regiments in a meeting on a hillside. Chu talked of urgent necessity for them to return and convert their comrades to anti-Japanese united front. Chu is a very serious, convincing speaker, not dramatic. Organizes his ideas carefully and presents them slowly and clearly like a teacher, often repeating. Soldiers with wistful, sad faces gathered around him later. Chu Teh is like a father. He loves all soldiers. . . .

November 9, 10, 11. First, Second, Fourth Red Army commanders in daily meetings with Chu Teh and staff. Chiang's armies still concentrating against us, but we refuse to give up more territory. Momentous days before battle with many meetings of Red Army warriors to explain why we evacuated great regions in effort to preserve all troops for the anti-Japanese war and to win over enemy to united front. General Wang Chun killed in airplane crash. We found his body. Chu Teh knew this fellow in Szechwan. . . .

November 23-24. The battle finished. The Red Army attacked at dusk when bombers could not come. A bitter cold wind from Ninghsia plains swept down. Fingers of Red fighters became so numb they could not pull triggers or even remove caps from hand grenades. So they launched bayonet charge. Many grabbed White soldiers and disarmed them, and others used their potato-masher hand grenades as clubs, beating Whites over the head with them. Red (Tungpei) cavalry chased one White regiment which fled in wild disorder. Dead enemy soldiers litter the paths for miles around. I saw 150 dead Whites piled up at one end of a valley, other hundreds in other places. Hundreds of Whites fell into ravines and empty wells. We have spent a day pulling them out with ropes.

Talked with captives who said they had been brought by rail from Hunan, and told they were being sent to Suiyuan to fight the Japanese.

When taken off trains to fight the Red Army they were promised double-pay—but never got it. They say Fascists permeate their ranks, driving them on, telling them lies about atrocities of Red Army. They are now being well treated and educated, attending daily lectures and dramas and mingling with our troops. General Hu Tsung-nan reforming his lines.

December 3. I'm back at Paoan, headquarters of Soviet Government and Red Army. Chu Teh and Mao Tse-tung and staffs met and held long conferences. Hear men talking of Chang Kuo-tao as "The Slick."

These are the conditions under which the epic Long March ended, just two years, one month, and nineteen days after leaving Kwangtien in Kiangsi Province. The reunited Red troops now numbered some 80,000 effectives, or about the combat strength of the Central Army when it left Kiangsi in October 1934. Gathered on the plains and mountains of the northwest, it was a force unique in history.

At Yenan, which became Red Army headquarters on January 1, 1937, Chang Kuo-tao was finally brought to trial before the Central Committee of the party which he had helped found but whose basic principles and policies he had violated. He and a few officers loyal to him defended themselves against the testimony of their own men, of Chu Teh and Liu Po-cheng, and other men of their staff whom he had taken prisoner.

In this trial, General Chu Teh made no mention of the treatment which he himself had received at the hands of Chang, but confined himself to Chang's violation of Red Army and party principles and policies. Suave and furtive, Chang apologized for his treatment to Chu Teh, and accepted the verdict of the trial—which was to study until he had rectified his mistakes.

In the summer of 1938, after the Anti-Japanese War began, a group of Kuomintang military men who visited Yenan to confer on military problems smuggled Chang Kuo-tao to Hankow, where he joined the staff of General Tai Li, head of the dread Blue Shirts, the secret police.

While talking with General Chu about this incident, I once remarked that thousands of Chinese were actively helping the Japanese conquer China, and that even one of the founders of the Communist Party had now joined the secret police to help hunt down Chinese progressives.

General Chu replied that China is a semi-feudal country that had been a semi-colony under the major imperialist powers for a hundred years. During that century, he said, Chinese governments had been the sordid instruments of Western imperialism. Peking, Nanking, and Shanghai had been nurseries of traitorous plots to sell national interests to the highest bidders.

China, he declared, certainly had more traitors than most countries in revolution, but this was because China was greater in extent and population.

"America also produced large numbers of traitors during your Revolutionary War," he reminded me. "Even if you were not taught about them in school, still large numbers of Americans actively served the British tyrants during your own war of liberation. Consider Franco and his henchmen who are selling Spain to Hitler and Mussolini! Consider the White Russians who sold out to the capitalist powers and fought their own people during the October Revolution. Look at India and Korea; look all over the world and you will find men who are always willing to betray their own people for power and money.

"Our party has also had traitors. The Chinese revolution is like a train that starts out on a long journey. Some men get off at side stations, others get on, but the vast majority will remain on until the train reaches its destination. Chang Kuo-tao followed a rightist opportunist policy which resulted in serious losses to our army. However, the correct leadership of our party and the political consciousness and loyalty of our troops led to the correction of his policies and to the strengthening of our army and party. Chang can cause the death of many more men, but he cannot turn the course of history. Our party and army will lead the revolution to a victory which will influence all oppressed colonial peoples as well as the people of the whole world."

Book X

Rendezvous With History

Chapter 33

Gloom shrouds the spring day,
Taiheng peaks tower fiercely.
Loyal hearts shed no tears on these great heights.
Strong wills demand a northern expedition.
A hundred million new army menaces the enemy,
Ancient Shansi has created many heroes.
Three years I've given to hard fighting.
We drink to the defeat of the dwarf devils.
                              —CHU TEH

WHEN Chiang Kai-shek and his staff arrived in Sian on December 7, 1936, for the Anti-Red Conference, Chiang established himself at the Lintung Sulphur Springs outside the city, while his staff put up at the Sian Guest House within the city walls. The situation was what Chu Teh would have called "politically favorable."

Before he could carry out another large-scale Red Extermination Campaign, Chiang would first have to control the Manchurian (Tungpei) Army, which was determined to fight nothing less than the Japanese. To change this "subversive" trend, the Generalissimo would first have to rid himself of the Young Marshal, Chang Hsueh-liang, his deputy commander in the northwest, who for years had surrounded himself with young men who harbored "dangerous thoughts" about democracy and the necessity of driving the Japanese from Chinese soil.

The Young Marshal and his staff were prepared for Chiang. Instead of resuming the civil war, they had drawn up a plan for an anti-Japanese united front of all Chinese armies. Their program included the granting of civil rights to the Chinese people, the abrogation of all laws and restrictions on the anti-Japanese movement, the release of political prisoners, the realization of the last will and testament of Sun Yat-sen, and the formation of a National Defense Government of all parties, groups, and organizations.

Instead of calling a general conference at which such plans could be presented and discussed, Generalissimo Chiang summoned first one and then another high Manchurian officer to whom he offered rank and money if they would unseat the Young Marshal and lead their army against the Communists.

He had success with only one—a general who was soon assassinated by a young Manchurian officer. The others reminded the Generalissimo that the Japanese had occupied their homeland and killed their families, and that the Manchurian Army wanted to fight the Japanese instead of their own countrymen. Chiang remained adamant.

At dawn on the morning of December 11th, therefore, Marshal Chang's troops went into action. The headquarters of Chiang's secret police and of the Kuomintang, and the home of Shao Li-tze, Chiang's governor of Shensi, were raided, and every man in them arrested. The Sian Guest House, in which Chiang's staff was housed, was invaded and the officers hustled out of bed, shoved into motor cars, and driven to the Young Marshal's headquarters.

While Sian resounded with machine guns and rifles, a young Manchurian officer led troops to Lintung where they shot down and killed Chiang Kai-shek's nephew—one of the most hated fascists of the country—as well as a number of his bodyguards. Chiang fled in his nightshirt, but was captured and taken into Sian to Marshal Chang and General Yang Hu-cheng. There the Generalissimo was assured that he was being forcibly detained that he might hear and discuss the demands of the anti-Japanese armies of the northwest.

Manchurian armies throughout the northwest were simultaneously taking over all the ammunition, rice, and clothing dumps which Chiang had built up for civil war. At the same time the main Red Armies marched to within a few miles of Sian and drew a cordon across the province while Chu Teh and Mao Tse-tung took over and established headquarters at the small town of Yenan in the north.

Three days after Chiang's "kidnapping," as the Kuomintang and foreigners called his detention, a new Military Affairs Council, to which all anti-Japanese armies, including the Red Army, were invited to send representatives, was established in Sian. The Young Marshal, who had seized twenty-five bombers and fighters assembled on the Sian airfield for the Anti-Red campaign, sent one to bring Red Army representatives to the Military Affairs Council. Chou En-lai, chief of the Red Army delegation, thereafter joined in the enforced conference with Chiang.

The full story of the "Sian incident" has never been told, nor did the book which later appeared under Chiang Kai-shek's name tell the facts.

Despite denials, Chiang agreed to end the civil war—which had already been brought to an end by the Sian incident—and to begin negotiations with the Communists for the formation of a national united front against the Japanese invaders.

Chiang's detention set reactionaries of the whole world in motion. Japanese generals from Manchuria and north China immediately gathered in a secret military conference in Tientsin, undoubtedly to decide if the moment had come for the all-out occupation of China. Mussolini's daughter, whose husband had formerly been minister to China, sent frantic cables to the Young Marshal to release Chiang, while American, British and French diplomatic officials kept the wires hot with messages to their governments. American and Kuomintang broadcasters in China declared that General Chu Teh was in Sian, that red flags were flying from its walls, and that Red Armies were looting, slaughtering, and raping helpless girls and women north of the city.

These developments, which threatened to bring China into the Axis fold, seem the only possible explanation for the editorials in the Moscow press which condemned the arrest of Chiang Kai-shek as a "Japanese-inspired plot"—charges which aroused great hostility among the Manchurian troops. These charges, however, made clear to the Communists that Moscow felt any action against Chiang would help the fascists.

It was Chiang's own promise to prepare to defend China against Japanese imperialism that led to his release. To prove his own "sincerity," on December 25th the Young Marshal released Chiang and flew with him to Nanking. There the Young Marshal was brought to trial, sentenced to prison, and immediately pardoned and released. Chiang, who regarded any affront to his person as a criminal offense, arrested the Young Marshal and imprisoned him in his own home in Chekiang Province. From that date on the Young Marshal remained Chiang Kai-shek's personal prisoner.

With Chiang's release, the long and tortuous struggle for the organization of a national united front began. The Young Marshal's imprisonment demoralized the Manchurian Army, which was soon split up by Chiang and scattered over the country—some of its divisions later joining the Communists. In mid-January the extreme rightist general, Hu Tsung-nan, took over Sian, and patriots fled in every direction, some to the Red Army and some to north China from which they had come, to continue the struggle.

Yenan now became the focal point of the anti-Japanese movement of the whole country. A living river of workers, students, professors, teachers and cultural leaders soon began pouring to north Shensi, making great detours to avoid hostile Kuomintang armies who still declared that "the Japanese are only a skin disease, while the Communists are a disease of the heart."

General Chu, Mao Tse-tung, and their staffs were in almost continuous conference in Yenan. In February 1937, when Chou En-lai headed a Communist delegation to Nanking, Chu and Mao, representing the Red Army and the Communist Party respectively, addressed a long telegram to the Central Committee of the Kuomintang, then in session in Nanking, in which they appealed for a national united front and offered to make important concessions provided the Kuomintang introduced democratic reforms throughout the country. If the united front were formed, they wired, the Red Army would change its name and place itself under the general command of the Central Military Council, provided it were given the same treatment as other armies. In order to draw every element of the country into the anti-Japanese struggle, they offered to stop the confiscation of landlord estates and to transform the northwestern Soviet regions into a Special Administrative District administered by the Communists but under the direction of the central government. They declared their intention to carry out fully the principles and policies of Sun Yat-sen in this region.

In return for these concessions, the Communist Party and the Red Army urged the Kuomintang to give the masses something worth fighting and dying for by restoring civil liberties to them. They should also release all political prisoners and grant the people the right to organize and arm themselves for the anti-Japanese struggle.

However, it was months before the united front began to take concrete form. Interpreting the Communist offers as surrender, the Kuomintang tried to use the situation to destroy the Red Army, insisting that four of its seven divisions be disbanded and the other three reorganized into a new army staffed by Kuomintang officers. The Communists argued against the disbandment of any of their troops, and suggested a brotherly exchange of officers between the Red and Kuomintang armies—a suggestion which caused the Kuomintang to drop the subject like a hot potato.

Talking with me about these Kuomintang maneuvers, General Chu declared:

"Our army would be destroyed and there would be no resistance to the Japanese at all if we accepted the Kuomintang proposals. Chiang and his clique do not really want to fight the Japanese, yet Chiang realizes that if he does not, he will be swept from the stage of history by our own and other anti-Japanese armies, and by the Chinese people. Our army may have to accept subsidies and ammunition for only three of our divisions, but we will not disband the other four because war with Japan will most certainly start soon and all manpower and national resources of the country must be mobilized for victory. The Kuomintang has refused us new guns of any caliber, and we will get no clothing, blankets, or medicine; at best we will get ammunition and money for three divisions.

"After the war begins, however, all our troops will go to the front. We will root ourselves in the people as we have always done, and mobilize, train, arm and educate them. We will survive and fight."

Shortly after this conversation, a Kuomintang military delegation arrived in the northwest to inspect the Red Army, then came on to Yenan where I also had gone when the army of Hu Tsung-nan took over Sian.

During the week's stay of the Kuomintang military delegation in Yenan, I saw General Chu in the role of host to generals and colonels who had fought him for ten years. Instead of the blunt, simple soldier I had learned to know, he now appeared with all the graces of the old social order, yet without any of its indirectness and obsequiousness. Through his graciousness ran a cold stream of dignity, gravity and self-confidence. At the first breakfast of welcome to the Kuomintang officers, which I also attended, he welcomed them in these unadorned words:

"This is a historic moment marking the end of a decade of bloody fratricide in which millions of the best sons and daughters of our country have died. Had this national united front been formed years ago, China's manpower and natural resources would have been preserved, none of our territory would have been lost, and we would today be strong enough to meet the Japanese on equal terms.

"China is now entering a new era, and the Red Army and the Communist Party will do everything within their power to consolidate and maintain the united front for the purpose of waging a war of national and racial survival.

"Some people still say China is too weak to fight Japan. It is not. We can mobilize, train, and arm our people in the midst of battle. The history of the Red Army proves this. *We* are not afraid of the Chinese people. Our people are good people and require only to be told about the causes and purposes of the war of resistance, and helped to solve the problems of their livelihood."

When I asked General Chu later what the Red Army troops thought of the united front, he spoke with the utmost frankness:

"Our troops are workers and peasants. They are not intellectual, cultured men. Their ideology is Red Army ideology. As peasants and workers they have hated landlords and militarists all their lives. They knew how to work before, but it is now very difficult for them to be called upon to work with every person willing to fight Japanese imperialism.

To retrain them, we have called hundreds of cadres to Yenan to pass through special training courses in Kangta (the Red Army College) on the principles and tactics of the united front. After completing their courses, they will return to the army and others will be trained. Our army must be a model in carrying out the united front.

"Until now our chief Red Army discipline has said: 'We are the sons of the workers and peasants, and the interests of the workers and peasants are ours.' We must now say: 'We are the sons of the Chinese nation and the interests of the nation are our interests.' We must teach our troops to realize that if China becomes a Japanese colony there will be neither a Kuomintang nor a Kungchantang (Communist Party), but only a nation of slaves. We must keep our eyes on the goal and not be diverted by intrigues or hostility from the right, or from the infantile left."

Yenan was soon bursting at the seams with the thousands of youth who kept pouring in from every part of the country. New schools had to be organized to accommodate them. The North Shensi University, the Lu Hsun Art Academy, and a special school at the Red Army front near Sian were founded. Mao Tse-tung and Chu Teh, like other leaders, somehow found time to lecture in the new schools, but General Chu still devoted most of his teaching time to Kangta.

Yenan was a small place unable to accommodate so many people. To solve the housing shortage the Reds began excavating caves in the loess cliffs up and down the valleys. Students who had never before done a stroke of physical labor now took up picks and shovels and, together with the troops, began transforming the whole region into a small city of cave dwellers. After the war began Yenan grew to a small city of 50,000 people.

The hard shell of reaction began to crack here and there, and in April a party of Shanghai printers, with a new printing press, arrived on Red Army trucks from Sian. *The New China Daily,* poorly printed until then, appeared in a new dress, and on April 20th the *Emancipation Daily,* central organ of the Communist Party, made its bow to the world.

The leading article in the new *Emancipation Daily* was on the Spanish Civil War. Written by Chu Teh it was, like many of his chief articles, historical. Following an account of Spain's long struggle for democracy, he wrote:

There are around 100,000 Italian and German fascists fighting in Spain today. . . . Spain is not only fighting for her own independence, but is fighting to prevent western Europe from falling into German and

Italian hands. . . . The Spanish people have the support of international
democratic forces—American, German, French, British, Italian, Polish,
Russian and other volunteers. . . . Many people believe that China will
also have a civil war like that in Spain, but there will be no such civil
war because we have a united front for war against Japan. Anyone who
wants to stir up civil war in China is merely helping the Japanese.

The Special Administrative, or Yenan, Border Region, into which
the old Soviet region had been transformed, was the only place in China
that voiced support for Republican Spain. Posters sent to China by the
Spanish Republican government soon plastered the walls of Shensi towns
and villages.

Chapter 34

WHEN Japanese imperialism began its attempted conquest of China by
striking at the Twenty-ninth Route Army near Peking on July 7, 1937,
the united front had still not been consolidated, and Chiang Kai-shek had
still not made up his mind to fight. Despite this, the Special Administrative Border Region was put on a war footing, and within twenty-four
hours the commanders who had been studying in Kangta began marching southward to rejoin their troops, while other hundreds left their units
and marched to Yenan.

Ten days after Japan began the invasion of China, Chiang Kai-shek
finally issued a proclamation calling for resistance and stating that there
could be no turning back. By then the Japanese had occupied Hopei
Province and were pouring into northwest China. By August 13th their
armies began the campaign which led to the fall of Shanghai and, by
December, of Nanking.

Only at Shanghai did Chiang Kai-shek's armies really begin to fight,
and only when Nanking was menaced did the Kuomintang agree to
active cooperation with the Red Army. On August 9th, General Chu Teh
and Chou En-lai, with a group of Red Army and Communist Party
representatives, flew to Nanking for a conference of the National Military
Defense Council.

On September 6th, three divisions of the Red Army were reorganized into the National Revolutionary Eighth Route Army, with General Chu Teh as commander in chief and Peng Teh-huai as vice-commander. Not one new gun was given the three divisions—the 115th, 120th, and the 129th—and the only medical supplies issued to them consisted of three pounds of iodine crystals and two pounds of aspirin tablets. They were, however, supplied with ammunition and money for three divisions.

These three divisions, forty-five thousand men strong, left at once for the front in Shansi Province. They still wore their old Red Army uniforms and caps. Not even one blanket had been issued them. One of Chiang Kai-shek's lieutenants later remarked cynically to me:

"The Reds boasted that they captured all their guns and supplies from us in the past. Let them do the same with the Japanese!"

One month after the Eighth Route Army left for the front, I joined General Chu Teh's headquarters in the Wutai mountains in northeastern Shansi, which by then was in the Japanese rear. On September 25th and 26th, the 115th Division under Lin Piao's command had fought and won the first Chinese victory over the Japanese at the Great Wall pass, Pinghsinkwan.

During all this time, Communist representatives in Nanking were urging Chiang Kai-shek to permit them to assemble all the old Red Army guerrillas which had been left in Kiangsi and Fukien provinces when the main Red Army went on the Long March. However, it was not until Nanking fell to the Japanese and 200,000 civilians and captive soldiers were slaughtered that the Minister of War issued an order to these guerrillas to concentrate along the lower reaches of the Yangtze to be reorganized into the New Fourth Army.

As these emaciated, ragged and battered peasants marched from the mountains of the old Soviet districts, landlords and their Min Tuan waylaid them, sniping and killing wherever possible. With gnawing bitterness, Hsiang Ying and Chen Yi, their commanders, ordered that not one shot be fired in return, and that the columns march at night through dangerous areas.

The New Fourth Army, numbering 11,000 men, assembled in south Anhwei in April 1938, and was placed under the command of General Yeh Ting, with Hsiang Ying as vice-commander. Chen Yi was commander of a division which left at once to penetrate the Nanking area. The whole army was assigned a fighting zone about fifty miles wide and one hundred and fifty miles long, directly along the banks of the Yangtze. The War Ministry had planned things beautifully. The New Fourth Army was ordered not to leave its zone even for maneuvering operations against the Japanese. In their rear, in the Nanking area, was stationed an army made up of the same terrorist bands of Shanghai and Nanking gangsters which had once been used to exterminate villages in Soviet territory. These gangsters, whose supreme commander was General Tai Li, chief of the Kuomintang secret police, were excellently equipped and provisioned, and assigned the task of hemming in the New Fourth Army and driving it directly against Japanese columns.

There was no doubt in the minds of informed Chinese and foreigners that the Kuomintang expected the Japanese to achieve what they themselves had been unable to do: exterminate the Eighth Route and New Fourth Armies.

When I arrived at General Chu Teh's headquarters in the Wutai mountains in late October 1937, the Japanese were already driving on Taiyuanfu, the provincial capital, from two directions: through the mountains from the north; and from the east along the branch railway which ran from Shihchiachuang up through deep gorges to the capital. Kuomintang and provincial armies were holding the Japanese on the northern front, Tungpei and other Kuomintang divisions, with the 129th Division of the Eighth Route Army, were holding them on the east. The other two divisions of the Eighth Route Army were using mobile and guerrilla tactics in the enemy rear.

Ho Lung's 120th Division was ranging far and wide in north Shansi while regiments of Lin Piao's 115th Division were campaigning through northeastern Shansi and eastern Hopei provinces, where they had already driven the enemy from a number of occupied district cities and even attacked the Peking-Hankow railway.

Like all the Kuomintang forces, the old warlord governor of Shansi, Yen Hsi-shan, would not permit the people to be organized and armed unless they were already in enemy-occupied territory. The Eighth Route Army, which operated in enemy-occupied territory, was therefore organizing, training, and arming the people on the same pattern that had proved so powerful in south China during the civil war years. Peasants, workers, merchants, women, youth, and children's organizations had been founded. The older men in villages and towns were being organized into Local Self-Defense Corps. Able-bodied young men, formed into Anti-Japanese Guerrilla Detachments, were fighting as auxiliaries of the Eighth Route Army. Armed with captured rifles, these detachments were the reservoir from which the Eighth Route replenished its losses.

General Chu Teh's headquarters in the Wutai mountains was in a large white building, formerly a landlord's home, where two Chinese newspapermen and I found him sitting on a stool while a barber shaved his head clean. He waved and shouted a greeting, and later led us into a room papered with great military maps that stretched from floor to rafters. After pointing out Japanese and Chinese positions, he explained Eighth Route strategy and tactics:

"Strategically, we aim at sustained warfare and at the attrition of the enemy's fighting power and supplies. Tactically we fight quick battles of annihilation. Because we are militarily weaker than the enemy, we always avoid positional battles, but engage in combined mobile and guerrilla warfare to destroy the vital forces of the enemy while at the same time we develop guerrilla warfare to confuse, distract, disperse, and exhaust the enemy. Our guerrilla warfare creates such difficulties for the enemy that our regulars can launch mobile attacks under favorable circumstances."

He explained future plans:

"Our plan is to establish many regional mountain strongholds in the enemy rear throughout north and northwest China—such as this one in the Wutai mountains where the enemy's mechanized forces cannot operate. Our regulars can return to such bases for rest, replenishment, and retraining, guerrilla forces and the masses can be trained in them, and small arsenals, schools, hospitals, cooperative and regional administrative organs, centered there. From these strongholds we can emerge to attack Japanese garrisons, forts, strategic points, ammunition dumps, communication lines, railways. After destroying such objectives, our troops can disappear and strike elsewhere. We will consolidate and use these strongholds to enlarge our fields of operation until our defensive strategy can be turned into a strategic offensive. Chiang Kai-shek has agreed to this plan and the Wutai Regional Base is being organized with his permission."

As we talked, General Peng Teh-huai entered. Generally a grim, dour man, he was now very gay as he told us of hourly reports of small victories over a vast territory in the enemy rear. General Chu listened with narrowed eyes, his shabby cap with its faded red star shoved back on his newly shaved head.

"You must investigate our methods of mass mobilization and training," General Peng exclaimed, with a happy wave of his hand. "The people are like the sea and we are like the fish swimming through it. This is a national revolutionary war. Victory will depend on the courage, self-confidence and fighting power of our troops and on brotherly relations between commanders and fighters; and on our close cooperation with other Chinese armies. We are carrying on intensive political work among our troops and the people. The people have rallied to us to the last man, woman, and child."

General Peng braced his hands on the table and continued:

"You'll find a lot of inspiring slogans and posters, of course, but of greater importance is the gradual process of educating our troops, the guerrillas, and the people. Our aim is to develop deep national consciousness, and to educate and inform our troops and the people about the condition and designs of the enemy. Everyone must realize that victory cannot be had for nothing. The war has only begun!"

General Chu's eyes remained narrow, tense points as he replied:

"True! But the Kuomintang armies must also make many changes! Kuomintang officers still curse and beat their soldiers—they enforce unreasonable obedience. These are feudal practices! They must be replaced by friendship, mutual respect, confidence and help. Sorrows and happiness must be shared by all. Living conditions of officers and soldiers should be approximately equal so everyone can take part in the war wholeheartedly!"

"Will all that be done?" I inquired skeptically, and the ever optimistic Chu Teh answered:

"It will take time. Our army must be the model. As the war continues, the Kuomintang armies will have to reform or be defeated. Why are so many Chinese puppets fighting in the Japanese army? Why do the Japanese boast that they will conquer China with Chinese? Why! Because the Kuomintang has done nothing to wipe out feudal conditions in the country and feudal practices in the armies. We must convince the Kuomintang, and we must win over the puppet troops."

Chu and Peng told us of the destruction by Lin Piao's division of one Japanese brigade at Pinghsinkwan, and of other battles in which the Japanese never surrendered unless wounded. Even the wounded pretended to be dead, they said, and when Eighth Route stretcher-bearers bent over them, they sprang up and killed on the spot. When Ho Lung's troops destroyed enemy transport columns, the Japanese clung to the trucks until cut off. Searching the pockets of the Japanese dead, Ho Lung's troops had found a number of anti-war handbills signed by the Japanese Communist Party and the Japanese Anti-fascist League.

General Chu became excited when he talked of these handbills.

"Perhaps we have been killing our own comrades!" he exclaimed. "But we can do nothing else! Our troops must now learn enough Japanese to shout to the Japanese soldiers that we do not kill captives. Enemy soldiers are taught by their officers that we torture and kill all captives!"

General Chu placed one of the handbills, already translated into Chinese, before us. A part of it read:

Pity those 200,000 brothers who died during and after the Manchurian Incident! For whom? For what? For the militarists—for the ambition and avarice of our own militarists! Shall we play into their hands once more? . . . Dear comrades-in-arms! Demand that the militarists give back the lives of our brothers. We must arise and turn our guns against our real enemies—the militarists and financial magnates. Only by beating them down can we achieve permanent and genuine peace in the Far East.

Even before these handbills were taken from the pockets of the Japanese dead, a branch of the Political Department of the Eighth Route Army had been engaged in propaganda work with the enemy. This "Enemy Work Department," directed by men who knew the Japanese language, was now ordered to develop their work swiftly and to start teaching the Japanese language to the troops—activities which eventually spread throughout the Eighth Route and New Fourth Armies.

While talking about Japanese soldiers General Chu exclaimed with cold hatred:

"The Japanese prefer death to capture, but their desperate fighting is not mere bravery. It is guilt and fear! They have killed so many of our people, and outraged so many women and girls, that they are afraid to be captured by us. They openly boast of their 'slaughter battles.' They believe we will torture and kill them as they torture and kill Chinese soldiers who fall into their hands. From now on we will make a special point of capturing Japanese."

On the evening following this conversation, General Chu received orders to move at once to the branch Chengtai railway to the south where the Japanese who had broken through were marching on Taiyuanfu.

The light burned in his headquarters throughout that night, and at dawn we were marching southward over the dry, forbidding ranges of eastern Shansi. Ho Lung's division remained in north Shansi, while General Nieh Jung-chen, one of the administrative geniuses of the Eighth Route Army, remained with two battalions of the 115th Division in the Wutai mountains which he eventually developed into the powerful Chin Cha Chi stronghold in the enemy rear. The rest of the army moved with Chu Teh's headquarters and crossed the Chengtai railway just as the Japanese 20th Division, preceded by planes, began pouring through the gorges from the east.

In the first three days of November, the 115th Division of the Eighth Route Army, joined by the 129th Division which had just inflicted losses on the Japanese column, began a running battle against the enemy division. The first two uninjured Japanese were captured in this battle, one a radio operator, one an infantry captain. A column of over four hundred pack horses laden with supplies of every kind, including food, medicine, ammunition, and winter overcoats, was lopped off. A group of thirty Manchurian peasants who had been conscripted to care for the pack animals were also captured.

These operations, however, did not prevent the Japanese from occupying Taiyuanfu on November 13th. After that General Chu left the 129th Division in the railway region to prevent the Japanese from consolidating their power, while General Headquarters and the 115th Division marched southward through Shansi, slogging through freezing rains and a soggy snowstorm, and halting in villages and towns to hold mass meetings. Everywhere organizers were left behind to transform the interior of the province into a base of Chinese resistance.

In one town, where the two Japanese captives were presented as speakers, pandemonium broke loose and hoarse voices shouted: "Kill the devils!" Eighth Route speakers were still trying to silence the crowd when cries of "Chu Teh! Chu Teh!" sounded, and General Chu strode to the platform where the magistrate, who was presiding, stepped forward and said:

"We have all heard of Chu Teh for many years. He is here in the flesh and he needs no introduction from me!"

General Chu first spoke on the role of the people in the war of resistance; this done, he asked the people to realize that the Japanese soldiers were workers and peasants who had been conscripted and sent to China by the Japanese warlords and financial magnates. The Japanese people had not made this war, he said, and large numbers of Japanese anti-fascists had already been imprisoned or killed for opposing it. The Eighth Route Army intended to capture, educate, and train Japanese soldiers to fight their own rapacious ruling classes, and to help China win the war.

This was the first time the people in these regions had ever heard such ideas. One of the Japanese captives, the radio operator, stepped to the front of the platform and said:

"I am a soldier, but I am also a worker. The Japanese militarists want this war, but the Japanese people do not. I was conscripted against my will and sent to your country, but until I was captured I did not know the Chinese people could be so kind. In the future I intend to stand side by side with the Chinese people."

General Chu Teh later told me of the insolent attitude of the Japanese captain after his capture. Lin Piao had gone into a village hut where the man was held, but the captain remained seated and ordered Lin to provide him with chicken, eggs, and rice to eat!

In a cold, level voice, Lin replied: "Do not misunderstand the kindness with which we treat you. It does not mean that we are your inferiors. We serve you rice while we ourselves eat millet. I hear that you struck a peasant who came to look at you. We won't kill you for this, but if you ever strike a Chinese again, we will whip you in public!"

General Chu's lips tightened and his eyes became hard points as he told this story.

"We made the fellow walk until today," he said. "Today I gave him my horse to ride; also a box of captured Japanese cigarettes. He was embarrassed, but took them. He will learn!"

General Chu also gave me a copy of an order to all Eighth Route Army troops which he and Peng Teh-huai had just issued. It read:

Japanese soldiers are the sons and brothers of the toiling Japanese masses. Under the deception and coercion of Japanese warlords and financial oligarchs, they have been forced to fight against us. Therefore:

(1) Any kind of injury or insult toward Japanese captives is strictly forbidden, and no confiscation or damage to their personal possessions is allowed. Commanders and rank-and-file fighters of our army who disobey this order will be punished.

(2) Special care and proper medical treatment shall be given to all sick or wounded Japanese captives.

(3) All possible conveniences shall be given to help Japanese captives who wish to return to their country or to their original troops.

(4) Those Japanese captives who wish to remain in China or to work for the Chinese army shall be given proper work, while those wishing to study shall be helped to enter a suitable school.

(5) Facilities shall be given to those who wish to correspond with their families or friends.

(6) Japanese soldiers killed in battle shall be buried and a proper headstone or board erected over their graves.

General Chu explained Point 3 of this order:

"If we allow Japanese captives to return to their troops we will destroy the propaganda lies of their officers that we torture and kill captives. We showed that order to the two Japanese captives. They told us of a Japanese military law which states that no Japanese taken captive in battle shall be allowed to return to his country, while one who returns to his army after capture shall be shot.

"Despite this, any Japanese captive who wants to return to his original troops will be allowed to do so. If his officers kill him it will merely arouse unrest among their troops. The time will come when Japanese soldiers will surrender to us without fighting, or desert and join us."

A few days later I heard General Chu talking to the Japanese captain whom he had just given some flaky biscuits bought in a village. The captain bowed his thanks, ate the biscuits thoughtfully, and began to talk:

"There ought to be an international movement to change the present method of settling affairs. Here we are, Chinese and Japanese, and one American, all quite friendly!"

"You are now marching with such a movement—that is why you are alive," General Chu replied. "There are men in your own army who are also a part of that movement. We have taken anti-war leaflets from their pockets on the battlefield."

"I have heard nothing of such leaflets!" the captain exclaimed.

"You were an officer! The time will come when Japanese soldiers will help us defeat Japanese warlords."

"It's not so easy to defeat the Japanese army!" the captain remarked dryly.

"Yet it will be done!" General Chu retorted.

Marching through slush, speaking at mass meetings, at small conferences of Communist Party branches, General Chu finally led his troops into the Hungtung region of south Shansi where some rested and studied while others moved to the west of Taiyuanfu where the Japanese had established positions. The dry wheat fields around General Chu's headquarters were soon dark from morning to night with a harvest of tall, strong peasant volunteers under training.

Sitting in General Chu Teh's headquarters one night, sipping American coffee, we talked of everything and nothing. I had been on a trip to General Wei Li-hwang's headquarters at Lintung and upon my return found that a New Zealand journalist, James Bertram, and a United States Marine intelligence officer, Evans F. Carlson, had arrived at headquarters. Carlson had brought the coffee. Bertram passed on to the front and Carlson now sat sipping coffee from an enamel cup and listening to our talk. I was telling of an air raid on Lintung while I was talking with the Kuomintang general.

"We ran across a drill field to a cave just as the planes came back the second time," I said.

"Who reached the cave first?" one of General Chu's staff inquired politely. "And who left it last? Was it General Wei?"

"I must say that General Wei's staff is more stylish than you fellows!" I remarked. "They wear fine woolen khaki uniforms, high leather boots polished like mirrors, officers' belts, and insignia of rank. They have fur caps and winter overcoats with fur collars."

"They may be more stylish than us, but we are more important!" General Chu remarked, grinning. "The Japanese pay more attention to *us!* They have just posted proclamations on the walls of Taiyuan and other places offering rewards for any information about us or for any document issued by us. They say they've come to China just to exterminate us!"

"Are you going to read that copy of the New Testament sent you by that foreign missionary in Hungtung?" I asked him. For an old missionary had indeed sent him a copy of the New Testament in Chinese, and in return General Chu had sent him a copy of *What Is Fascism?*

"I read everything!" General Chu speculated. "Who'd ever think I'd be exchanging gifts with a missionary? I hear his Bible School has sent out some converts to turn our troops into Christians."

"They did!" I replied. "They even tried to convert me and were angry when I wouldn't be converted."

"We'll see who converts whom!" General Chu remarked laconically.

Who converted whom was right! On January 14, 1938, Dr. Walter Judd—subsequently a leading United States Congressman but then medical missionary at Fengyang, Shansi—wrote a medical missionary friend of his in Hankow, who in turn passed the letter on to me. Judd wrote:

Most people believe that Yen Hsi-shan has made a deal with the Japanese. In fact, the vice-commander of the army told me in person while I was treating his venereal disease six days ago that there would be no more fighting here, that China's strength was too small now, too shattered, and there would have to be a "political settlement." I know the leaders of the Shansi troops feel that way. . . . The officers believe in a political peace but the soldiers don't. . . . And I know the 8th Route Army is not party to any deal with the Japanese. They are organizing the countryside, especially in the mountains, preparing to make their own clothes, etc., so as to be self-sufficient for as many years as necessary to wear the enemy out. Fully half of the students in our mission school have joined up with the 8th Route Army, several of our preachers and teachers have also joined. They have left $30 and $70 a month jobs to get

$10 jobs and they are bursting with enthusiasm and devotion about it. I wonder often why we can't succeed in capturing the imagination of Chinese for this work in the churches. It was precisely that sort of vision and devotion which the missionary challenge meant to me. But I have been singularly unable to arouse in my colleagues that which it meant to me. I suspect a large part of the reason for our failure is because we haven't asked our church converts to sacrifice enough. They've had too soft and easy a job—we haven't demanded their all, as the 8th Route Army does. . . .

Yen Hsi-shan invited the 8th Route into Shansi because he thought he could hold the Japanese off indefinitely and the 8th Route would be as lukewarm or worse toward Nanking as he was and, in the settlement after the Japanese were smashed, they would be satisfied with what he would give them as their share. Now he finds he's got the Japanese as his masters, and he must get the most out of them that he can. The 8th Route has become a decided embarrassment to him. Most people here think it will transpire that his present trip to Hankow is a go-between for the Japanese, the Japs promising generous treatment for the Central Government, etc., if they will break loose from the 8th Route and accept most of what the Japanese have seized in the North, the Shanghai customs, etc. . . . It is interesting that when the Japs occupied Taiku, they occupied and looted every house except the home of H. H. Kung which was promptly sealed by the "economic co-operation" gang and protected even from Japanese troops . . .

Dr. Judd made one mistake in his letter. His converts had not deserted him for "$10 a month." They had deserted him for fifty cents or less a month, and sometimes not even that! Chu Teh's salary at the time was three dollars a month, but he didn't get it, because all money received from the Chinese government was being spread over all seven divisions of the Eighth Route Army. Eighth Route Army officers had been allowed the same salaries as Kuomintang officers, and the troops likewise. All this money was pooled to provide food and clothing for everyone. A man with ten cents in his pocket was regarded as practically a rich man.

Evans F. Carlson, a captain in the United States Marine Corps at the time, looked on this passing scene with growing amazement and regarded General Chu Teh with something approaching awe. For years he had heard of Chu as a "bandit" but when he met him in the flesh, and after he had studied the practices and educational system of the army, he exclaimed to me:

"Up to this time, the only practicing Christian I ever knew was my own father, a Congregational minister. Chu Teh is the second practicing Christian."

"Chu Teh's no Christian!" I protested.

"I don't mean one of those hymn-singing, grace-saying Christians!" Carlson replied. "I mean one who devotes himself to freeing and protecting the poor and the oppressed—who practices brotherly love instead of grabbing as much as possible for himself."

Carlson's remarks led to many discussions which were never finished because the end of 1937 had come and the Japanese had begun a new offensive to occupy all Shansi and to wipe out the Eighth Route Army. Carlson left with Eighth Route troops for the Wutai mountains, I left for Hankow to collect medical supplies, clothing and money for the Eighth Route Army and the northwestern guerrillas, and General Chu Teh led two regiments, and detachments of new recruits, eastward into the Taiheng mountains to help Kuomintang troops stop advancing Japanese divisions.

Chapter 35

IN a savage offensive in the early months of 1938, the Japanese occupied the main cities of Shansi and drove Kuomintang armies either across the Yellow River or into pockets on the borders of the province. Six enemy columns, marching by different routes, converged simultaneously on the Eighth Route Army stronghold in the Wutai mountains. There they bogged down and gradually advanced into northwestern Shansi where Ho Lung's 120th Division had established another guerrilla base in the mountains on the Shansi-Suiyuan border.

In this same offensive a part of Lin Piao's 115th Division, reinforced by local partisans and with regulars from Yenan, fought fiercely in western Shansi to prevent the Japanese from reaching the Yellow River and crossing into the Yenan Border Region. Lin Piao himself was dangerously wounded in this campaign.

It was in this offensive that General Chu Teh, over the protests of many of his comrades, took personal command of the two regiments and of detachments of new recruits, helped them against the Japanese in the Taiheng mountains, and barely escaped death in a number of fierce battles.

Preceded by bombers and fighters which ranged the skies from dawn to dusk, the Japanese finally broke through, occupied all walled cities in south Shansi, and began patrolling all major highways and railways through the province. They held the main cities. The Eighth Route Army and peasant partisans held onto the countryside and devoted themselves to tearing up railways, destroying bridges and waylaying enemy trucks along the highways.

Eleven counties in southeastern Shansi which fell to the enemy during this offensive were recaptured by General Chu's forces by mid-1938. A new mountain stronghold in the enemy rear was established in the Taiheng mountains on the Shansi-Honan border, where the chief administrator was a professor from Peking National University.

An Australian nurse, who had made her way to General Chu's headquarters, returned to Hankow—the temporary national capital on the Yangtze—with grisly tales. General Chu's headquarters, she said, was in a town in a broad valley in eastern Shansi. To reach it she had passed through hundreds of villages which had been bombed and burned by the Japanese. She had seen thousands of new shallow graves, and countless unburied corpses. Survivors in the villages were crawling about in the debris of their homes, tending relatives or neighbors who were dying.

The Eighth Route troops were sharing such food as they had with the people, but they also had little, and the field hospital near General Chu's headquarters was jammed with sick and wounded army men and civilians.

General Chu Teh had given this nurse freedom to work where she wished. He had given her such medicine as his hospital could spare, and had sent a bodyguard to help her. She had worked in villages until her body also became bloated with beriberi. Then she left for Hankow to save her own life.

This same terrible period inspired General Chu Teh to jot down a few short poems in his notebook, which he later sent me. One of them read:

> I draw in my horse on Taihengshan.
> White winter snows are flying.
> Fighters shiver in thin coats,
> Night after night killing dwarf bandits.

In midsummer, 1938, General Chu passed through the Japanese lines to the west, crossed the rolling Yellow River with its cliffs shrouded in clouds, and rode on to Yenan to report on one year of war of the Eighth

Route Army against the Japanese. This report was delivered to the Sixth Plenary Session of the Central Committee of the Communist Party, of which he was a member, that autumn.

The report stated that in the first year of war the Eighth Route Army had suffered 25,000 casualties, about one third of them killed. Of these, seven thousand had been members of the Communist Party. By that time, Eighth Route troops were operating across all north China from the mountains of Shensi to the Yellow Sea, and from the Yellow River in the south up into Jehol Province of Inner Mongolia where they had founded another mountain stronghold and were coordinating their operations with the Manchurian Volunteers. They had even raided Tsinan, capital of Shantung, and had attacked the coal mines and power plant that serviced Peking. Students and some professors from the American missionary university at Yenching, six miles from Peking, were working with Eighth Route guerrillas, and many Yenching graduates had joined them straight from the university. (Before the war ended, seven hundred Yenching graduates had joined the Eighth Route Army.)

In his report General Chu stated that the activities of the Eighth Route Army and the civilian guerrillas in the north had prevented the Japanese from crossing the Yellow River and moving southward against Kuomintang armies. The Japanese had been forced to halt to divert troops to guard their lines of communication and convoys, to drive away attackers, repair roads, railways, and bridges. They had also begun building forts as the Kuomintang had done during the decade of civil war, and had begun "pacifying" the population by wholesale massacres.

As he had proposed in conferences in Nanking when the war began, General Chu again advocated a national strategy and the adoption of tactics based on "China's strong points and the enemy's weak points." China, he declared, could not defend itself "by remaining rooted in positions and waiting to be blown out by the enemy." Instead all Chinese armies should choose favorable terrain and timing and avoid any engagement on equal terms with the more powerfully equipped enemy.

Though the Eighth Route Army had suffered heavy casualties, enemy losses had been 34,000. Enemy captives, most of them Chinese puppets, totaled 2094 men, while 1366 Manchurian soldiers who had been conscripted and inducted into the Japanese army had gone over to the Eighth Route Army with all their Japanese equipment.

Considering the poor equipment with which the Eighth Route Army went into the war, its captured war trophies were impressive. These included 6387 rifles, 171 light machine guns, 84 heavy machine guns,

72 fieldpieces, 25 mortars, 190 motor cars, 847 trucks, four radio sets, six radio speakers, nineteen telephone sets and nine field glasses. There were also five cases of poison gas—the Japanese considered all means justified in fighting the Eighth Route Army.

The army had also destroyed twenty-four enemy planes on an airfield in north Shansi—for which Chiang Kai-shek had rewarded it with $20,000; also five enemy tanks, five armored cars, and 901 motor cars and trucks. By the end of 1937, while I was with General Chu's head-quarters, thousands of Eighth Route Army troops were already wearing captured Japanese overcoats.

As the Eighth Route Army increased its strength and spread its influence across all north China, alarm spread and grew among Kuomintang reactionaries. When the news reached Hankow that the Eighth Route Army had introduced changes in all regions liberated from the enemy, the old cry of the "Communist menace" began to sound. In every liberated area of the north and northwest, all men and women over eighteen were given full suffrage rights. They elected their own village and town administrative organs to take the place of the old Kuomintang officials who had either fled before the Japanese or had joined them and headed local puppet governments. Since most traitors were big landlords, the peasants had confiscated and divided their land in the Liberated Areas. The peasants were also cultivating the estates of landlords who had fled but had not turned traitor. Such land was not confiscated but the peasants had no intention of paying rent to men who had fled from the enemy.

With these developments in mind, General Chu said:

The Central Government should spare no effort to improve the people's livelihood so as to enlist the people's material support and mobilize manpower. The Government should also encourage and aid patriotic organizations and activities, and organize the masses to participate in the war directly or indirectly.

After one year of war, during which the Chinese government had released political prisoners and allowed some degree of liberty to the people in the territory it controlled, there were serious signs that the reactionaries were again coming to the top. Premier Wang Ching-wei, supported by large numbers of followers, had been ringing the alarm bell of "Communist banditry" and urging the government to accept Japanese peace terms. The reactionary "C. C. clique" within the Kuomintang also campaigned against, and prevented, the organizing and arming of the people. If the war continued, Wang Ching-wei warned, the Kuomintang would lose China to the Communists.

Knowing that he would be swept into limbo if he surrendered to the Japanese, Chiang Kai-shek rejected all enemy peace proposals. He was as fearful of his Red allies as Wang. During the summer of 1938, for instance, Chiang dispatched a special army, with appointed Kuomintang officials, into north China to take over areas liberated by the Eighth Route Army. At the same time, Kuomintang troops along the Yellow River began raiding the Liberated Areas. Other Kuomintang troops in western Suiyuan Province on the northern frontier of the Yenan Border Region began making truces and alliances with the Japanese for joint attacks on the Eighth Route Army.

In mid-October 1938, while the Japanese armies were converging on Hankow, General Chu Teh flew to the capital for a conference with the National Military Defense Council where he warned against all such activities and pleaded for the introduction of democratic reforms throughout the country. Only such reforms, he urged, could improve the livelihood of the people and give them something to fight for, and if necessary, to die for. In support of his arguments, he reported on the achievements of the Eighth Route Army which had turned the north into a bulwark against enemy exploitation. The elected village and town councils were fully democratic, he argued, and the Communists had restricted Communist participation in elected bodies to no more than one third.

General Chu had no success whatever, yet he still assured the government that the Eighth Route Army, as well as its younger brother, the New Fourth Army fighting along the lower Yangtze, would maintain the united front and do everything within their power to develop close and brotherly relations with Kuomintang armies.

Two months after the Japanese occupied Hankow on October 25th, Premier Wang Ching-wei and a number of his followers mysteriously left Chungking by plane for Indo-China. From there he made the jump to Shanghai and the Japanese. In March 1939, Wang headed the Japanese puppet government at Nanking which announced its purpose to be the "extermination of Communism."

In an article published in the Yenan press on July 18, 1939, General Chu Teh described the growing power of Kuomintang reaction and the twin dangers of civil war and surrender to the Japanese:

From the time Hankow fell to the Japanese in late 1938, we realized that powerful cliques within the Kuomintang were preparing the way for

surrender by splitting the national united front and resuming civil war.
We have documents proving that three Kuomintang armies in southeastern Shansi, south Hopei, and western Shantung, have formed what
they call an "inter-provincial joint defense" agreement against the Eighth
Route Army. One of these armies, commanded by General Lu Chung-lin,
was sent by Chiang Kai-shek to take over areas which we had liberated
from the enemy. It entered one of our Liberated Areas, where it disbanded all local administrative organs and installed old feudal officials
who had fled before the Japanese in 1937. It also surrounded, disarmed,
and disbanded the local people's forces, and replaced them with a "Peace
Preservation Corps" whose function was to suppress the anti-Japanese
and democratic activities of the people. Reforms which we had introduced, such as reduced rent and the abolition of usury, were declared
illegal, and old as well as new taxes imposed on the people. Villagers
were again conscripted by press gangs, and only those able to pay General Lu three thousand dollars can buy themselves off.

These activities went hand in hand with the progressive suppression
of the people's activities in all territory controlled by Chungking. All
publications and organizations not directly under Kuomintang control
were suppressed, concentration camps founded, and even the new industrial cooperatives were regarded as potentially subversive because they
were jointly owned by those who worked in them. One Kuomintang
politician told me that the Communists had a network of cooperatives in
the north, and that cooperatives must therefore be Communist institutions. Such institutions, he said, might be useful during the war, but
would be a danger afterwards because the workers would become so
independent that they would not return to the old factories.

Until March 1939, the Communists desperately tried to smooth over
all incidents threatening a renewal of civil war. In late March, however,
in the dead of night, Kuomintang troops fell upon a transport station
of the New Fourth Army in Hunan Province and buried every man in
it alive.

Abandoning their former reserve, Mao Tse-tung and Chu Teh wired
Chungking, and released their wire to the press, disclosing the full details
of the atrocity. They demanded the immediate punishment of the men
responsible for the crime, an official apology, and an assurance that no
such atrocity would be repeated.

In August, General Chu again wired Chiang Kai-shek, this time in
confidence, informing him that General Shih Yu-san, commander of the
Kuomintang Sixth Army on the Hopei-Honan-Shantung border where

the Liberated Areas began, was actively collaborating with the Japanese in joint attacks on the Eighth Route Army. Though General Shih Yu-san was an unscrupulous warlord with a long pro-Japanese record, Generalissimo Chiang immediately rejected Chu Teh's charges.

General Chu repeated his accusation. Chiang did not reply. On August 24th, Chu Teh and Peng Teh-huai sent Chiang a long documented wire, quoting one of Shih Yu-san's orders to his officers. This order read:

Under orders of Generalissimo Chiang, and for the sake of our country, people, existence, and development, our army must exterminate the Communist bandits who are an obstacle in the war of resistance. . . . In the present stage we are to clean out the Communist-bandits, and in the second stage we are to carry on the war with Japan.

(1) If the Sixth Army comes in conflict with the Japanese, you shall immediately withdraw and send representatives to the Japanese to explain. When Japanese planes come, spread a white cloth on housetops and give orders to your troops not to shoot.

This was followed by orders explaining methods of communication with the Japanese: flag signals during the day and colored flares at night. When on the march, the distance between the Sixth Army and the Japanese was to be at least ten li (about three miles). By an understanding with the Japanese, the Sixth Army was to carry out no actions after eight o'clock at night.

The order concluded:

When the Sixth Army is opposed by Communist-bandits and has other than garrison duties to perform, you must notify the Japanese. When necessary we will send troops to help the Japanese fight the Communist-bandits.

Generalissimo Chiang Kai-shek rejected this telegram as a fabrication, but General Shih Yu-san's treason became so open that Chiang was forced, a few months later, to arrest, try and shoot him. After this execution a Kuomintang politician remarked in my presence:

"Shih Yu-san wasn't a bad fellow! He said that only one who has been a traitor can really appreciate the beauty of patriotism."

By December 1939, the danger of civil war became so menacing that General Chu Teh left the front for Yenan where he could be in constant contact with Mao Tse-tung and the Central Committee. In a letter which he wrote me three years later, he said that "the first undisguised military operation by Chiang Kai-shek against the Eighth Route Army was the December Incident of 1939."

This "incident" developed almost simultaneously with two others. First, a Kuomintang army commanded by General Chu Hsui-ping in south Shansi openly joined with the Japanese in a mopping-up campaign against the Eighth Route Army. Almost at the same time Kuomintang and Japanese forces in Suiyuan began a simultaneous attack on it from the northern frontiers of the Yenan Border Region. General Hu Tsung-nan chimed in with an offensive on the southwest borders of the Yenan Border Region. General Hu operated with planes and artillery and his forces destroyed hundreds of villages, killed thousands of people, and occupied a number of districts of the Border Region.

For the first time since the Anti-Japanese War began, General Chu Teh withdrew troops from the fighting front to protect the Eighth Route Army rear and the Yenan Border Region.

The Kuomintang attacks were so undisguised that the international press reported on them. On January 6, 1940, for instance, the *New York Times* reported that General Chu Teh had "sent a strong message to Generalissimo Chiang Kai-shek demanding cessation of attacks by the Central Government troops," quoting General Chu's charge that "the Communists were being attacked in the rear while fighting the Japanese."

In his annual military report in 1940, as well as in a number of articles, General Chu Teh stated that 1940 was the year when danger signals were so many that it seemed civil war would begin on a wide scale. This was the period when Chungking began to disintegrate under the impact of many developments favorable to the Japanese: (1) the permanent closing of the French Indo-China railway into Yunnan Province, and the temporary closing of the Burma Road by the British—actions which cut Chungking off from sea-borne military supplies; (2) the beginning of the European war; and (3) the founding of Japan's puppet "Central Chinese Government" headed by Wang Ching-wei, which proclaimed its purpose to be the extermination of Communism.

Instead of introducing bold and courageous democratic reforms which would have aroused all the latent strength and enthusiasm of the people, as had similar reforms in north China, Chungking sank deeper into reaction and corruption. A few generals led their armies into the Japanese camp.

The Kuomintang not only suppressed every mention of the treachery of its armies, but threw up a protecting smoke screen by charging that the Eighth Route and New Fourth Armies were not fighting the Japanese. As early as January 1940, one of Chiang Kai-shek's chief generals, Chen

Cheng, publicly charged that the Communist armies were merely "roaming around the country, stirring up the people and disturbing the social order."

Chu Teh and fifteen of the chief Eighth Route Army commanders called General Chen's bluff. They officially asked Generalissimo Chiang Kai-shek to send General Chen Cheng on a tour of north China to inspect their armies in action, their hospitals filled with wounded men, the people's resistance forces, and personally to investigate Kuomintang armies which were not only trading with the Japanese but collaborating with them in campaigns against the Eighth Route Army. Generalissimo Chiang ignored their request. The charges against both the Eighth Route and New Fourth Armies continued.

In early August 1940, after long planning, Chu Teh and Peng Teh-huai issued final orders for a hundred-regiment offensive against the Japanese.

The hundred regiments of the Eighth Route Army which waged this amazing offensive, General Chu wrote me, were all volunteers chosen because of their willingness to disrupt and defeat the blockade of "imprisonment and extermination" strategy which the Japanese had introduced in the north. Every unit of the Eighth Route Army took part in the campaign, he said, but only the strongest volunteers were taken into the hundred regiments.

All north China, from the mountains of north Shensi to the shores of the eastern sea, and from the Yellow River in the south to Manchuria in the north, became a battlefield over which fighting raged night and day for five months. The fighting was fierce and ruthless as the hundred regiments struck at the enemy's entire economic, communication and blockade system. Enemy-held coal mines and power stations, railways, bridges, highways, trains and telecommunications were destroyed. The countryside was littered with telephone and telegraph wires and poles. Great stretches of northern railway were ripped out, the ties carried away, and the rails carried to small arsenals in the guerrilla mountain strongholds. Enemy trucks and motor cars were destroyed, ships in the harbors along the Shantung coast blown up, and enemy warehouses and administration buildings in Tsinan and Chefoo wrecked. Thousands of liberated railway workers and miners joined the Eighth Route Army.

By the time the offensive ended in late December, 2933 Japanese forts had been destroyed; 20,645 Japanese, including eighteen officers, killed or wounded; and 281 Japanese taken prisoner. Over 51,000 Chinese puppet troops had been killed or wounded and 18,407 taken prisoner, about half of them former Kuomintang soldiers. Vast quantities of arms and ammunition and other supplies had been captured and put to immediate use.

How the Japanese took these events—and guessed at the Kuomintang reaction—was best expressed in an editorial in the reactionary Tokyo daily, the *Kokumin Shimbun,* on December 27, 1940:

Chungking is surely worried over the increasing influence of the Chinese Communists. . . . The restless activities of the New Fourth Army along the lower Yangtze have also become a menace to peace. . . . The Tientsin-Pukow railway has been hard hit in its transportation. Activities of the Eighth Route Army have penetrated all North China and constitute a cancer to the maintenance of peace. . . . The Chiang faction now faces a dilemma. . . . It is not altogether unimaginable that Japan, too, may be seriously affected by Communist influence if Chungking fails to pacify the Communists.

Whether Chungking acted on Japanese promptings, or whether it had merely reached the same conclusions as the Japanese, at any rate, in December 1940, the Chungking High Command ordered the New Fourth Army to evacuate the fighting zone where it had operated for nearly two years. It was ordered to cross the Yangtze at specified points, and march to north China by designated routes. Chungking had already begun withholding money from the New Fourth Army, its food was meager, and its troops still had no winter uniforms.

General Yeh Ting argued with the High Command. He was convinced that the New Fourth was being forced out of the Yangtze River valley to facilitate surrender negotiations with the Japanese, and knew that it would be exterminated by the Japanese and puppet troops if it marched along the routes designated. The majority of his troops, General Yeh Ting said, which now numbered 40,000, were local volunteers—peasants whose homes were in the region, or workers and intellectuals who had left Shanghai, Nanking, and other Japanese-occupied cities. These men fought best over familiar terrain and especially for their native districts.

His pleas were rejected and the evacuation order repeated. The New Fourth Army now accepted the order, but asked for back pay, for the right to cross the Yangtze and march along routes chosen by itself, for ammunition, and for winter uniforms against the fierce northern winters.

Chungking gave the army $200,000 back pay, and issued ammunition, but no uniforms. By January 7, 1941, all but 9000 of the New Fourth Army had already crossed the Yangtze at points chosen by themselves. The remaining 9000 consisted of General Headquarters, the army's

Military-Political Training School, two rear base hospitals filled with patients, also headquarters guards and part of one division.

On January 7th, when these forces began moving toward the Yangtze, they were surrounded by 50,000 Kuomintang troops sent in from other areas. A bloody slaughter began. Vice-commander Hsiang Ying was killed in action, General Yeh Ting wounded and taken prisoner. The wounded and sick in the hospital column were simply put to the sword. As men fell dying or dead, women political workers and nurses took up their guns and fought until their ammunition was finished. Then they hanged themselves in the forests. . . .

One thousand men escaped in the fighting, crossed the Yangtze and rejoined their troops. About 4000, most of them wounded, were taken prisoner and herded into concentration camps where the majority died of sickness, disease, and maltreatment. After the United States entered the war, OWI workers in eastern China saw some few hundred survivors from a Kuomintang concentration camp. One OWI worker met two men who had escaped from the concentration camp. One, the brother of General Yeh Ting, had been crippled by torture.

Chiang Kai-shek, who tried to keep the Yangtze slaughter a secret, finally announced that he had taken "disciplinary action" against the New Fourth Army because it had refused to obey orders. The New Fourth was therefore declared outlawed and disbanded, he said. General Tang En-po, one of the most feudal-minded Kuomintang generals, was ordered to exterminate the "rebel remnants."

Immediately after the slaughter, the Nanking puppet government broadcast an order to its troops which stated:

"The destruction of the New Fourth Army has begun and it is our job to finish the remnants."

For a time it looked as if the New Fourth Army, of which General Chen Yi now took command, would be exterminated by the combined forces of Kuomintang, Japanese, and puppet armies. This failed, however. Kuomintang soldiers, however corrupted they might be, became confused and demoralized when told to fight their own countrymen instead of the Japanese.

When the true story of the Yangtze tragedy broke through Kuomintang censorship, the Chungking High Command charged that the New Fourth Army had been hatching a treacherous plot to occupy the Nanking-Shanghai-Hangchow triangle and to extend its sway along the entire China coast northward to Shantung.

This weird statement failed to divulge that the Nanking-Shanghai-Hangchow triangle was a Japanese bastion along the Yangtze River valley. If the New Fourth Army had indeed "plotted" to occupy this region, it had plotted to destroy powerful Japanese forces as well as the Nanking quisling government. The entire China coast was also held by the Japanese.

Again Mao Tse-tung and Chu Teh came forward. They were as careful as possible to prevent outright civil war, but nevertheless they exposed fully the facts of the tragedy and demanded that Chungking make amends by releasing and reinstating General Yeh Ting and other New Fourth Army men; they insisted that the men responsible for the tragedy be punished; that the families of the dead be compensated; and that assurances be publicly given that no such attack would ever occur again.

In addition, Chu and Mao charged categorically that fascist elements in the Chinese government were plotting with the Japanese to wipe out both the Eighth Route and New Fourth Armies, to turn north China over to the Japanese in return for a peace settlement, and to bring China within the Axis camp. To prevent civil war and surrender to Japan, they demanded that the basis of the Chungking government be broadened to include representatives of other parties and groups.

Chungking replied by discontinuing all money, food, and military supplies to the Eighth Route Army and ordering General Hu Tsung-nan to draw a tight blockade around the Yenan Border Region. A diligent effort to starve the Eighth Route Army was made, while the Japanese continued the work of extermination.

Two months after the New Fourth Army tragedy, two of Chiang Kai-shek's generals, who had been conducting operations against the New Fourth Army "remnants," led 50,000 Kuomintang troops into the Japanese camp. Generalissimo Chiang neither reprimanded them nor deprived them of their rank in the Kuomintang Army, nor did he send a punitive expedition against them.

From this time onward the Eighth Route and New Fourth Armies were dependent upon what they themselves and the people collectively produced. The Communists revived the Revolutionary Military Council of civil war days, and established the Yenan government whose directives guided all the Liberated Areas. General Chu appointed Chen Yi as commander in chief of the New Fourth Army and ordered him to regroup his troops for continued warfare on the Japanese and puppets in the lower Yangtze, and to defend himself if attacked by Kuomintang armies.

The two Communist-commanded armies and the people of north and central China had to take care of their stomachs and began what was recognized a few years later as a gigantic enterprise which amazed all who saw its results. After months of grisly suffering, the New Fourth

Army developed stable guerrilla bases like those in north China; introduced civil rights, with equal suffrage and free elections, in all areas which it controlled; developed civil administrative organs, small factories, arsenals, hospitals and educational and publicity institutions, on the same pattern as those of north China.

Chungking drew back from outright civil war. An armed truce was established until the Second World War ended in 1945. Communist representatives remained in Chungking as before, but were isolated, and their newspaper, the *New China Daily*, was allowed to appear only under the most ruthless censorship.

The Communists continued to state that they would maintain the united front wherever possible but would defend themselves if attacked, and that they would continue to carry out Dr. Sun Yat-sen's Three People's Principles and basic policies as before. They challenged the Kuomintang to do the same.

In a personal letter to me later, General Chu wrote:

Though cut off from all money and military supplies, our armies are now united under a centralized command to continue the anti-Japanese war. We began the intensive development of production in which our troops and all our party and other organs participated. Everyone worked either to bring land under cultivation, to increase livestock, to spin and weave, or do every variety of work to make ourselves and the people of north China self-sufficient. The first year was bitter, but after that things began to improve. Under the bitter hardships of that first year we intensified our new political-economic-military policy and developed our New Democracy which Comrade Mao has defined in his book of that title. We and the people are mutually dependent, but as our production movement progressively grows, our Army will be entirely self-supporting and we will not have to lean on the people.

It is not easy to keep a rendezvous with history.

Book XI

"We Have One Secret Weapon"

Chapter 36

Clouds of fighters and commanders
Are singing like a great wind.
Flashing guns force the Sun Empire to retreat.
Blood stains our rivers and mountains.
                                        —CHU TEH

THE years 1941 and 1942 tempered the spirit of the people and troops in the Liberated Areas in blood and suffering.

The lines were drawn so clearly that even the most obtuse could see them: while the Kuomintang cut the Communists off from all supplies and hemmed them in with a blockade of steel, the Japanese tried to exterminate them on the field of battle.

In the first six months of 1941 the Communists prepared for the attacks from the rear and battles at the front. Immediately after the establishment of the Kuomintang blockade, Mao Tse-tung officially announced the "Production Movement of Self-Sufficiency." This, with time, transformed the face of north China and made sustained military resistance possible. Of this movement Mao said:

Our policy is of resurgence through our own efforts. The reduction of rent and interest has raised the enthusiasm for mutual aid and raised the productive power of the peasants. Our experience shows that through mutual aid the productive capacity of one individual becomes four-fold. . . . Once mutual aid has become a habit, the productive output will not only be greatly increased, but all kinds of new creations will appear. Political standards will be raised and people will also improve culturally. Loafers will be reformed, customs changed and our rural society be led to new productive power. It will then be possible not only to carry on the war and cope with the famine years, but also to accumulate huge amounts of food and daily necessities for use in a counter-offensive. Not only peasants, but the army, party, and government institutions, must also organize to engage in production together.

The Production Movement began with planning conferences of every group of the population, including the armed forces, across the thousands of miles of the Liberated Areas. Tens of millions of people began working in Mutual Aid Teams, Labor Exchange Groups, in industrial, consumer, and transportation cooperatives, or in new small factories or other institutions. No one was exempt.

The Japanese offensive began in July 1941. In the eighteen months of fighting to the last day of 1942, the Eighth Route and New Fourth Armies suffered 82,456 casualties, of which 30,789 were killed outright. The number of civilian and local partisan dead and wounded could not be reckoned, but was much greater.

The Yenan press, for the next two years in particular, pictured General Chu Teh moving here, there, everywhere—writing, speaking, advising, laboring in his headquarters under candlelight until the small hours, and, early every morning, working in the fields like the peasants from whom he sprang.

Newspapers, pamphlets, and books put out by Yenan in those years are peppered with his writings, while reports of his speeches and interviews alone would fill volumes. His tenacious figure can be seen speaking before conferences of cooperatives, women, labor unions, youth, and at soldier-commander congresses; also at peasant gatherings on rural reconstruction, Labor Hero conferences, memorial meetings for the dead, in classrooms filled with Japanese prisoners of war, and at exhibitions on industrial and military achievements.

From Communist Party congresses where the strategy and tactics of the national revolutionary struggle were determined, he would go to such gatherings as the Production Conferences of the Women's Alliance of the Border Region, where, in the autumn of 1941, he sounded like Mayor LaGuardia talking to New York housewives on how to cook spaghetti and care for children:

We produce salt in this region, so we can put down large quantities of vegetables for the winter months. In Szechwan we always salted down vegetables. We did it in this manner: . . .

Now, let us talk about the soya bean, which should become a major crop in this region. Soya beans can be used in many forms—as green vegetables, as bean curd, sauce, or dried for winter use. They can also be pickled for winter use. Each Manchurian household puts down at least one large *kan* (vat) of salted soya beans for winter use, as well as another of sauce. They do it in this manner. . . .

After discussing crops with the women, he turned to the breeding and care of pigs, sheep, goats, cattle, rabbits, and bees. "Every bit of every animal—bones, meat, hoofs, and hides—should be used, while the care of bees and the increase in honey production should become one of the major industries of the Border Region," he told them, and went on to the care of children:

I sometimes find a woman sitting on her doorstep and weeping because her baby has just died. Why do we suffer such losses? One reason is because the people of north Shensi pay too little attention to sanitation. For ages our people have made very little progress in this respect. Poor sanitation can result in the extermination of a whole herd of swine, but when babies die as they do, the loss is infinitely greater. Our production propaganda must therefore go hand in hand with improved sanitation both on the farm and in the home. Cleanliness must be constantly stressed. We now have cooperatives which produce good, cheap soap. . . . Babies must be washed each day and children taught daily habits of cleanliness. Even under the most difficult conditions our soldiers try to keep themselves clean, and always wash their feet each night. If they can do this, people in the rear can do much more.

From the care of children he went on to the industrial cooperatives which, he said, should be developed on a large scale "to serve as a bridge between agriculture and industry and to activize commerce." Cooperatives should never become mere money-making organs, nor should their products be hoarded to raise prices and "propagate an economy of scarcity." The Yenan Border government, he reminded them, laid great emphasis on cooperatives and home industries, exempting some from taxation and imposing only a nominal tax on the others, and also honoring men and women who achieved high standards of production as Labor Heroes.

Some of our women production leaders tell me that they have a fund of two hundred dollars but don't know what to do with it. I should think you would use that money to make two twenty-spindle spinning machines. After two weeks practice, a woman can produce fourteen pounds of wool yarn a day on such a machine. From this yarn you can select five pounds of the best and spin it into good yarn for which our weaving factories will pay you thirty dollars. The inferior wool can be woven into blankets and carpets. . . . Hemp, which we produce in large quantities, can be mixed with wool and woven into strong, durable, warm cloth.

After such a meeting he would sometimes mount his big horse, captured from the Japanese, and ride down into the Nanniwan area. A brigade of the Eighth Route Army under Wang Chen garrisoned this zone to protect Yenan from the Japanese across the river and from Kuomintang troops blockading from the south.

The army production movement, which he called "the Nanniwan movement," was General Chu's pride and joy. When this powerful brigade was brought into the Nanniwan area, it found a wasteland. There were no buildings or caves and only the ruins of an occasional village or abandoned temple.

The Kuomintang blockade of the Border Region, General Chu told the troops, was intended to starve soldiers and civilians while the Japanese destroyed them in battle. Neither the army nor the people had any intention of allowing themselves to be starved or destroyed, nor could the army live off the people.

General Wang Chen's Nanniwan brigade looked about and found a two-thousand-pound bell in an ancient abandoned temple. From this they fashioned their first plow and hoes, the first picks and shovels to excavate living quarters in the hillsides, the first tools to make furniture and dig wells. The troops began transforming the wasteland into fields of grain and vegetables. From distant villages they bought a few draft animals, goats, sheep, and pigs, which produced and multiplied. They held frequent production conferences, founded their own spinning and weaving cooperatives and continued their education as well as even creating a dramatic group. When thousands of refugees from battle zones streamed into the Border Region, they helped settle them on the land, dug wells and made spinning wheels for them, and helped them found cooperatives, primary schools, night schools for adult illiterates, and Labor Exchange Groups.

The Production Movement was under way when, in early July 1941, General Yosuji Okamura, Japanese commander in north China, turned 300,000 Japanese troops loose on the Liberated Areas in what he called his "three-all" strategy—kill all, burn all, loot all.

The Okamura "three-all" offensive of 1941 was fought with one main aim: "Clean up north China to prepare for the great Pacific War." Japanese columns moved in, surrounded whole districts, and closed in for the kill. In one small southeastern Shansi district, typical of others, the Japanese slaughtered 13,000 civilians who had remained in their homes, sparing neither babies nor the aged. In one town which the Eighth Route Army recaptured, the troops found, and photographed, the naked corpses of hundreds of women and girls of all ages, lying in the public square.

Before, and during, this "three-all" offensive, the Japanese built 2400 miles of deep trenches, and 400 miles of protecting walls along the motor highways in central Hopei Province alone. High walls and protecting ditches also ran parallel with Japanese-controlled railways throughout the north and northwest. The Japanese constructed chains of blockhouses with underground chambers for food and ammunition.

The people on the northern plains also utilized the bosom of the earth. They dug underground air-raid shelters which they extended into long tunnels which often connected different villages. Inhabitants of a village under enemy attack could take shelter in another, while enemy troops entering a deserted village would find themselves suddenly surrounded by Eighth Route Army troops who arose out of the earth beneath them.

The people, who had been taught to make land mines of every kind, sought to protect their homes by sowing mines along all paths leading to them. Some of the "People's Heroes" produced by this struggle were little boys who wandered out to meet advancing enemy troops and reply innocently to requests:

"No, I cannot guide you to my village because that is forbidden, but it is along that path over there—" pointing to a mountain path sown with land mines where troops and partisans lay in ambush.

In his annual report on July 1, 1941, General Chu stated that Eighth Route and New Fourth Armies often went into battle with only five or ten rounds of ammunition and that the heavy losses suffered by the people and the troops of the north were the bitter fruit of the Kuomintang blockade.

By the first week of December 1941, Chu later reported, just when the Japanese thought they had crippled the people's forces in the north and could begin the Pacific War with a safe rear, "we launched a counter-offensive which prevented them from transferring troops to the south Pacific against the Allied armies."

This counter-offensive was accompanied by an upsurge of the Production Movement. As the people's forces recovered district after district, and the civilian population returned to rebuild their destroyed homes, Yenan transferred grain and livestock into these just recovered areas.

In his 1943 report, General Chu Teh was unable to estimate the amount of ammunition, food, and medicine captured during the counter-offensive, because, he said, all such supplies had been put to immediate use. The captured rifles, however, numbered 95,000; light and heavy machine guns over 2000; pistols, 4027; anti-tank guns, 29; field guns, 73; "quick-firing guns," 225; and two anti-aircraft guns. Other trophies included 272 radio transmission sets with generators; 939 field telephone sets; 112 cameras with films; 7201 gas masks; also bicycles, gramophones, parachutes, Japanese flags, and thousands of head of horses. One item on the New Fourth Army list of trophies read: "592 drums of American gasoline."

One of the most significant sections of General Chu's report dealt with the change that had come over Japanese troops during the preceding five years. By mid-1942, he said, the surrender and desertion of Japanese had become frequent.

These prisoners of war were never put in chains nor herded into concentration camps. They were given Chinese uniforms and placed in classrooms to study much the same subjects that the anti-Japanese armies studied, with special emphasis on the feudal structure of their own country, the history of the Japanese working class, and the principles of scientific socialism. Many graduates of the "Japanese Workers and Peasants Training School" at Yenan, in particular, later worked as special political propagandists with the Eighth Route Army at the front. By the end of 1944, thirty of them had been killed in action.

General Chu's 1943 report also gave considerable information on the underground activities of Japanese anti-fascist organizations within the Japanese army, one of which was the "Japanese Awakening Alliance."

By 1943 the Japanese Awakening Alliance had established contact with a number of Eighth Route Army units, which it kept informed of Japanese plans and moves. And in 1944 Susumu Okano (Tetsu Nosaka), one of the founders of the Japanese Communist Party and a veteran of Japanese underground work against Japanese militarism, made his way to Yenan to direct all educational work among Japanese prisoners of war and to work with Mao Tse-tung and Chu Teh in an advisory capacity.

The attitude of the Chinese Communists on other international problems was revealed in General Chu's 1943 report and in many of his other writings as well. Unlike some right-wing members of the Kuomintang, which for years had proclaimed fascism as the social system "best suited to China," the Communists were enemies of fascism, regarding it as the last stage in monopoly capitalism when the capitalist class, confronted with the people's growing power, destroys all parliamentary institutions and establishes its open dictatorship. In Germany and Italy this was done behind the smoke screen of anti-Communism, which was also thrown up in China by both the Japanese and the Kuomintang.

For these as well as for past historical reasons, neither General Chu nor the other Communists took at face value all the pronouncements of the Western powers about the democratic aims of the war. After all, they had sold strategic materials to Japan until 1940. Despite this, General Chu had for years been convinced that the Western powers would have to fight fascism whether they wished to or not.

He also believed that, in the course of this anti-fascist war, the people of the Allied powers would force their governments to live up to at least some of their democratic propaganda, and that the defeat of the Axis bloc would deal a mortal wound to fascism in every part of the world.

Neither General Chu nor the other Communists hid these ideas under a bushel. The Kuomintang proclaimed in and out of season that the "Red" or "Communist bandits," as they more and more called them, were merely using the war to extend their influence with the aim of establishing their power after the war.

The Communists most certainly aimed to extend their power and influence. But in this they were by no means unique. The Kuomintang tried to use the war to destroy all opponents with a view to establishing its dictatorship over the whole country. To this end, it adopted tactics of which the Communists were never guilty: whole Kuomintang armies began going over to the Japanese—with the toleration, and, General Chu believed, the support of the Chungking High Command. Even before Pearl Harbor, twelve Kuomintang generals led their armies into the Japanese camp. Fifteen others joined them in 1942. General Chu had formidable evidence proving that these defections had been undertaken with the aim of getting into north China with the Japanese and waging war on the Liberated Areas.

General Chu Teh's chief of staff, Yeh Chien-ying, once explained Kuomintang military defections to the enemy as due to corruption in the Chungking government, the denial of democracy to the people, and to the demoralization of Nationalist armies following Japanese victories. Instead of political education, he said, Kuomintang soldiers were told that the Eighth Route and New Fourth Armies were bandits and greater enemies of China than the Japanese. Illiterate, ignorant, half-starved and maltreated, Kuomintang soldiers were merely taught to obey and shoot.

Had the Eighth Route and New Fourth Armies not been so highly educated politically, they also would have been demoralized by the sweeping Japanese victories over the Allied armies in the first two years fol-

lowing Pearl Harbor. The Communists, however, had expected the Pacific
War and even anticipated initial enemy victories by reason of Japan's
geographical proximity to Asian battle fronts, and also because the
Western powers had for years helped strengthen the Japanese war machine. Despite these facts, however, the Chinese Communists were not
demoralized by Axis victories.

General Chu Teh's attitude toward all international issues was clearly
expressed in a lengthy paper which he read at a Conference of Eastern
Peoples held in Yenan just two weeks before the Japanese attack on Pearl
Harbor. This conference, attended by a few hundred delegates representing China, Japan, Korea, India and Mongolia, was one of those
small, obscure events which influence the course of history. General Chu
began his address by stating that Eastern peoples, constituting one billion
souls, or half the world's population, had carried on a revolutionary
struggle against imperialist conquerors for over a hundred years.

From this he went on to analyze China's revolutionary struggle from
the Taiping Rebellion onward, and to a concise historical review of the
independence movements of India, Burma, the Dutch East Indies, Indo-
China, the Philippines, and Korea. He included Japan also, recalling
the thousands of Japanese who had sacrificed their lives in the struggle
for democracy since the Meiji Restoration.

He next summarized the various stages leading up to a second
world war:

"Unable to conquer China," General Chu said, "Japanese imperialism
must now advance southward against other Asian countries."

As proof that this attack would come at any moment, he cited not only
Japanese documents captured in battle, but added:

Japan has reorganized her national defense, passed emergency war
measures, established a supreme air force, intensified domestic control,
and put its entire economy on a war footing. Large-scale air maneuvers
are taking place over Japan today. General Tojo's recent assumption of
power is an expression of the total militarization of Japan. All such
measures are unnecessary for war on China, but are essential for war on
Britain, America, and the Soviet Union.

He also cited the recall to Japan of thousands of overseas Japanese—
2700 from the Dutch East Indies, three boatloads from the United States,
and others from Hongkong.

From such information as he had gathered, he said, Japanese strategy
had divided Asia into four areas. The first embraced Japan, Korea, and
Formosa. The second included Japanese-occupied territory in China and

Indo-China. The Philippines, Thailand, Borneo, Malaya, Burma, and the Dutch East Indies—areas rich in oil, rubber, tin, iron, rice, quinine, and other raw materials essential for Japanese war industry—fell into the third area. India and Australia, with their cotton, wool, iron, and other resources, constituted the fourth, which also included Tibet, Chinghai and Sinkiang in central Asia.

Japanese war strategy, he continued, included the use of native traitors, spies, and Buddhists; the purchase and use of radio stations, movies, newspapers and magazines, and the bribing of editors, broadcasters, writers and lecturers of every nationality. Japan's chief and most effective propaganda in Asia lay in such slogans as "Asia for the Asians," "Japan and China must exist and prosper together," and "Liberate China from the yoke of Anglo-American imperialism."

Because of the slaughter of millions of Chinese, the burning of homes, and the seizure of China's natural resources, only Chinese traitors listened to such Japanese propaganda, he declared, and added:

We must not be taken in by Japan's anti-British and anti-American propaganda, nor by the Japanese-promoted independence movements in Eastern countries, because Japanese imperialism is no different from white imperialism. . . . We hope that Britain and America will adopt an enlightened policy toward Eastern races so the Japanese cannot disrupt unity between Eastern and Western peoples.

Two weeks later Japan attacked Pearl Harbor and the Pacific War began. Before an hour had passed, General Chu flashed orders to his troops, torn and bleeding from months of resisting Okamura's "three-all" extermination campaign, to launch a counter-offensive to prevent Japanese troops from being transferred to the south Pacific.

This same order instructed all armed forces and people of the north to give protection to any citizen of the Allied nations who escaped from Japanese-occupied territory.

A number of Allied refugees were already fleeing Peking into the Western Hills where Eighth Route Army guerrillas escorted them for weeks across north China, some to the Chin Cha Chi mountain base on the borders of Hopei, Shansi, and Chahar provinces, others on to Yenan. Of these, two were French, one was the American vice-president of the National City Bank of Peking, one was a Dutch businessman, and three were British educators.

Of the British citizens, one was Professor William Band, head of the physics department of Yenching University who, with his wife, remained in the Liberated Areas for two years, chiefly in the Chin Cha Chi regional base where he taught college physics and participated in the first Natural Science Congress in north China. Another Englishman, Michael Lindsay, also professor of economics at Yenching, remained as a teacher in Yenan until the war ended. With the Yenan Radio School, he constructed the broadcasting station on which China and the Western world depended for news of the north for a number of years.

Of the French refugees, one was Lieutenant George Uhlman who, after joining the Free French Forces in Europe, wrote of the Eighth Route Army:

Poor and deprived of everything, like the first armies of our French Revolution, without any help from the outside, the Eighth Route Army achieves the double task of driving back the invader and teaching liberty to the people.

The refugees who reached Yenan were present at a number of meetings addressed by General Chu Teh and other leaders. At one on July 7th, the fifth anniversary of the Sino-Japanese War, General Chu said:

On this occasion, and on behalf of the 570,000 fighters of the Eighth Route and New Fourth Armies, I send warm greetings of national liberation to all the people of China and to all fighters against fascism. We express our heartfelt sorrow at the loss of the finest sons and daughters of the Chinese nation, of the Soviet Union, and of Britain, America and other countries whose sons have given their lives for the sacred cause of national independence, human righteousness, and world peace.

Through month after month of sweeping Japanese victories in the south Pacific, General Chu Teh's speeches and articles resounded with calls to the troops and partisans under his command to "tighten your bonds with the Allied powers by attacking and containing enemy troops in China," and to destroy every Japanese stronghold in north and eastern China. He also called on the Kuomintang to adopt the same policy and to introduce democratic reforms which, he said, could mobilize China's manpower and natural resources on a voluntary basis and ensure Allied victory.

One of the most passionate appeals ever written by him was a proclamation to the people of Manchuria which began circulating through the Manchurian underground on September 18, 1942. It began:

For eleven bloodstained years Manchurian Volunteers have fought under icy skies and over snowy earth, without munitions and often without food. As men fell at the front, those behind stepped forward and continued the struggle under impossible conditions.

The proclamation then called on the Manchurian people to organize desertions and uprisings among Chinese conscripts in the Japanese army, to use every means to escape being drafted, and to organize their own local guerrillas to cooperate with the Volunteers and with the Eighth Route Army. Workers in mines and factories were called on to "carry on ceaseless and widespread propaganda and sabotage, to slow up work, make deliberate mistakes, and decrease production to cripple the Japanese army."

Villagers were called on to fight the enemy system of food control and distribution; to organize, feed, and protect local guerrillas; and not to allow themselves to be conscripted.

The proclamation ended:

Our Eighth Route Army's advance forces have penetrated Jehol and Chahar provinces, entered eastern Hopei, penetrated through the Great Wall into Manchuria, and contacted the Volunteers. All people, all Chinese troops, should cooperate with all our military activities.

The day of revenge and emancipation is nearing! We shall never forget your eleven years of anguish, your blood and tears, and the insults you have suffered. Mobilize! Unite! Prepare to welcome our attack!

As the year 1942 drew to a close, General Chu and his comrades continued using every possible occasion to encourage and strengthen their people by telling them that the people of the world were with them. At a memorial mass meeting on November 13th, third anniversary of the death of the Canadian physician, Dr. Norman Bethune, who died at his post in the service of the Eighth Route Army, General Chu spoke with deep emotion of the long years during which Canadians and Americans had helped China's war of resistance.

On December 30th, he also spoke in memory of Dr. D. N. Kotnis, a volunteer physician from India, who had died the year before in the service of the Eighth Route Army. After reviewing the history of India's long struggle for independence, General Chu said:

Dr. Kotnis understood that the emancipation of the Indian people was linked with the emancipation struggle of the Chinese people. He there-

fore regarded China's war of resistance as his own. He was the second
foreign friend to give his life for China.

Not all was sorrow and grief in those years, however, as was shown by
one of General Chu Teh's poems picturing the great achievements of
the Production Movement of Self-Sufficiency by mid-1942:

> On this seven-seven memorial day,
> Old people visit one another.
> Though fighting rages fiercely,
> Rest is treasured on this day.
> A light cart leaves Yenan,
> Carrying five old men.
> At Sanshihli village
> The heat grows wearisome.
> Winds bend the distant forests,
> White clouds drift over blue mountains,
> And yellow birds nest in green foliage.
> Climbing the crest of Million Flower Mountain,
> They gaze on the sea of hills below,
> The forests above sheltering them from the sun.
> Tigers and leopards, they say, prowl here.
>
> One year ago this was wasteland
> Without even a ruined cave as a sleeping place.
> New market towns now flourish,
> Cave homes burrow into the waists of hills.
> Good crops grow on the plains below
> And young rice gleams in water-fields.
> The wasteland blossoms.
> Fighters are warmly clad, their stomachs filled.
> Fat sheep and cattle browse on grassy meadows
> And Malan town makes beautiful paper.
>
> Resting at Taoshihkoo
> Near enough to a clear brook to embrace it,
> The old men enjoy themselves luxuriantly,
> Refreshed in body and soul.
> A warm breeze caressing their faces,
> They recall their homes in south China.
> Strolling in the evening cool they compose poetry,
> Gazing on the moon hanging in the treetops.

Chapter 37

THOSE Western powers that had so gloriously ruled generations of Asian peoples ate gall and wormwood in the first two years of the Pacific War when the peoples of Southeast Asia, believing the powerful Japanese propaganda against Western imperialism, welcomed the Japanese armies as liberators. After 118 years of British occupation, Singapore fell just two months after the Pearl Harbor attack. The Dutch debacle in Indonesia was complete by March, and by the early summer of 1942 the Allied armies in Burma were in full retreat, with Burmese burning the forests around them.

Chinese armies under General Joseph Stilwell's command were admitted to Burma after prolonged negotiations with the British. They feared the Chinese might recapture the country and stay, since it had been taken from the Manchus in 1885. At best they might give the Burmese "ideas." The Burmese who helped the Japanese, however, regarded the Chinese as traitors fighting for British imperialism.

By the end of 1942, Queen Wilhelmina of Holland, whose holdings in the Dutch East Indies had made her one of the richest women in the world, was promising the Indonesian people participation in a postwar commonwealth, with control of their own "internal affairs" but obligated to render "mutual assistance" to all branches of the union.

In early January 1943, the British and American governments also took steps to counteract Japanese propaganda. They abrogated their century-old unequal treaties and signed new equal treaties with China, and suggested that additional treaties covering trade and other matters be signed after the war ended.

All such developments served General Chu and other Communist leaders, as material to educate the troops and the people. On February 4th and 5th, General Chu published two articles, one on the old treaties which had reduced China to a semi-colonial position, and one on the new. The new treaties, he said, were "an important step forward," but "a paper treaty is not enough, and only a strong, democratic China and the development of national economy can achieve real equality with the Great Powers."

Yet there was not very much indication that the Chinese government intended to introduce democracy, and bring to an end the shameless hoarding and war profiteering which had long since replaced efforts at industrial development. Kuomintang armies were merely trying to avoid battle on the theory that "China has done its share of fighting; let the British and Americans do theirs." Instead of developing the national economy, Kuomintang officials and officers were hoarding and speculating, even selling rice to the Japanese in the midst of a famine in Kwangtung which killed one million people before it ended in 1944.

Another devastating famine in Honan Province in the north claimed three million lives during the same period. The army of General Tang En-po garrisoned Honan and, despite the drought, General Tang seized even the seed grain of the peasants as taxes or food for his troops. Much of this grain was put on sale at prices which only the rich could afford. A representative of the American Red Cross who went into Honan to carry on relief work had to buy wheat from General Tang En-po at a price higher than he would have had to pay on the American market. Thousands of starving peasants who tried to emigrate to the Liberated Areas were turned back by General Tang's machine gunners. A saying arose among the Honan peasants: "We suffer from four great calamities —floods, drought, locusts, and Tang En-po."

The great Nationalist daily of Chungking, the *Ta Kung Pao*, was even suspended by the censors for contrasting the starvation in Honan with the luxury and war profiteering in the capital.

General Joseph W. Stilwell, supreme American military representative in China and chief of staff to Chiang Kai-shek, began recording his private thoughts in a diary. Chungking he simply called the "manure pile," and Chiang Kai-shek "a grasping, bigoted, ungrateful little rattlesnake" whose aim was to hoard Lend Lease supplies for civil war instead of using them against the Japanese.

As the months passed, Stilwell became a thorn in the side of Generalissimo Chiang and other Kuomintang reactionaries. "Vinegar Joe" had no use for the reaction and corruption of Chiang's regime. For the Chinese people and the soldiers he had both pity and respect but his private diary, published in part later in *The Stilwell Papers*, became increasingly vitriolic as he wrote of Generalissimo Chiang, Minister of War Ho, and Kuomintang officers in the field.

Stilwell had one aim: to keep China in the war, to reform its armies so that they might play a role in the war, and to prevent civil war from splitting the nation open. In pursuit of this goal, General Stilwell repeatedly urged Generalissimo Chiang to withdraw his 200,000 blockade troops from the Yenan Border Region and use them instead against the Japanese. Such suggestions threw the Generalissimo into fits of rage. Yet these blockading troops, the best-fed and best-armed in China, had done no serious fighting for several years.

Kuomintang officials and officers, bankers and landlords seemed to use the war to build up private accounts in American banks. The people and armies of the Liberated Areas, however, continued to fight the Japanese and puppet troops and to beat off sporadic attacks of Kuomintang armies on their borders.

Until the battle of Stalingrad, which ended in early February 1943, powerful cliques in the Kuomintang seemed convinced that the Axis powers would win the war and that they were fighting on the wrong side. In not one speech or one article by Chu Teh or other leaders of the north, however, was there any indication that the Chinese Communists doubted eventual Allied victory. Instead, an article which General Chu Teh published on February 23, 1943—the twenty-sixth anniversary of the founding of the Russian Red Army—expressed the conviction that Chinese armies could play a decisive role in Allied victory:

In China we fought the Japanese for four years before the Nazis invaded the Soviet Union. China has double the population of the Soviet Union . . . yet we Chinese have not yet been victorious. Why? The main reason is because the government refuses to mobilize the country politically, economically, and militarily, for the war. . . .

The German Nazis have no comprehension of the special characteristics of revolutionary warfare, which calls for the mobilization and development of the people's forces to the highest degree. This explains why the Russian Red Army can overcome the superior equipment of the German Nazi army. It explains the great historic victory at Stalingrad, where 330,000 Axis troops were trapped, 91,000 taken prisoner, and the rest killed in fighting. China has everything to learn from the Russian Red Army. . . .

Nor must we forget that the Russian Red Army has a strong productive rear to support it. Another important point in the Red Army victory is unity among the Allies, and the material help to the Soviet Union from America and Britain. After Stalingrad, the last hope of Axis victory lies in splitting the Allied nations by raising the cry of

Communism. The Japanese have used this propaganda since the war began, and many Kuomintang officials and army officers have heeded it.

July 1st, the twenty-second anniversary of the Chinese Communist Party, and the sixth anniversary of the war of resistance a week later, were two of the many special days that General Chu used for speeches and writing to keep up the morale of the people and troops of the north.

Why, he asked on July 1st, had China produced a Communist Party strong enough to endure and grow and mobilize nearly a hundred million people to continue the war? He explained this as due to "the growth of the workers' movement and of the people's democratic movement, and the association of these two developments with scientific socialism." This combination, he said, had produced "a party guided by progressive theories, and with sufficient strength and vision to assume the responsibility of carrying the Chinese revolution to completion."

Developing this theme further, he declared that the Chinese Communist Party had "inherited the best traditions of thousands of years of Chinese culture"—hard labor, endurance, and respect for learning. It had also "enriched itself with experiences during the Great Revolution, the agrarian revolution, and the Anti-Japanese War." In the process of this "incomparably tense forging, our party has Sinicized Marxism-Leninism and adapted our historical heritage to the present needs of our society."

In reply to Kuomintang propaganda against democracy, he declared:

Our experience proves that people long for democracy as a thirsty man longs for water, or a hungry man for food, and we have never yet heard of one case of democracy being refused by the people. . . . We believe that the anti-Japanese forces of the nation could be surprisingly and freely developed if democracy were practiced on a national scale. . . . True, due to their low standing in the old society, the great majority of the Chinese people are illiterate. We have therefore given our greatest attention to educational work. This great study movement is unprecedented in history.

By July 7th, when General Chu made a special review of the entire six years of war with Japan, his records showed that the Eighth Route and New Fourth Armies had suffered 380,000 casualties, and had inflicted about the same number on the enemy. While these losses had been heavy, he said, "the party, the armies, and the people have transformed the face of north China, and influenced the thought of all progressive forces of the nation. We have erected anti-Japanese governments of the people which are democratic in character and which guarantee the protection and full enjoyment of civil liberties, and of human, property, and political rights by the people."

These achievements were possible because "we created a simpler and better army, a simpler and more efficient government . . . and because we prefer death to surrender."

"All our forces and power come from the people," he continued, "and all our ways and means are created by the people. Relying on the power of the people, we have defeated the enemy and overcome every difficulty. We have only one secret weapon—complete unity with the people. Had we been isolated from the masses, we would long since have failed."

And what, he asked, was the record of the Kuomintang since the fall of Hankow? Terror against all democratic forces; the most shameless corruption in Chinese history; secret negotiations with the enemy; and preparations for civil war.

That General Chu was not engaging in mere propaganda was revealed that autumn when representatives of the Allied powers intervened directly with the Chungking government to prevent civil war which most certainly would have resulted in a Kuomintang peace with the Japanese.

Chapter 38

A REPORT put out by the official Japanese Domei news agency on February 14, 1944, opened the new year with a summary of the Chinese national situation:

The only hindrance to the revival of China and defending Eastern Asia now existing is the Communist-bandits who have not yet been entirely annihilated. These bandits are agitating youth, destroying villages on the pretext of the war of resistance, and carrying on undisciplined activities which throw the Chinese people into the depths of sorrow and torture, and do harm to the progress of the New China and the construction of the New Order of Greater East Asia. This is the only hindrance now existing to the revival of China and the defense of East Asia, and we must combat it both spiritually and in actual action.

This statement, one of many of a similar nature published in the Japanese press, was made on the eve of the Allied counter-offensive in Asia.

By that time, the Liberated Areas of north China had been cut off from all outside aid for three years. As the Allied counter-offensive prepared to roll, General Stilwell applied to Generalissimo Chiang for permission to send an American Military Observer Group to the Liberated Areas to collect all possible military information about the enemy. Refused at first, his request was granted only months later.

At the same time, foreign correspondents in Chungking applied for permission to inspect the north to report facts of the anti-Japanese struggle in that area. They were also at first refused.

In May, Generalissimo Chiang permitted a group of foreign and carefully selected Chinese correspondents to visit the northwest, upon condition that they remain for three months. He was quoted as saying that they could not see behind the screen of Red propaganda by merely visiting headquarters for a short time. En route to the northwest, they were to visit General Hu Tsung-nan's troops in Sian, inspect one of the concentration camps for political prisoners at Sian, and pass through the southeastern corner of Shansi Province which was still held by the armies of the provincial warlord, General Yen Hsi-shan.

The Sian concentration camp was carefully prepared for them, and choice prisoners were trotted out to speak for the others. One of the men declared that he was an ex-Red who had voluntarily presented himself at the camp to be locked up and reformed! Until the group reached the Yenan Border Region, they were regularly presented with other men who declared themselves refugees from the hunger and terror in the Communist regions.

In late May the correspondents crossed the Yellow River into Communist territory. They were met by three or four young soldiers from the Eighth Route Army who conducted them to the headquarters of General Wang Chen, commander of the brigade which had been transferred from the front three years before to protect the Nanniwan area from Kuomintang and Japanese attacks.

The three books which came out of this trip of foreign correspondents —Harrison Forman's *Report from Red China,* Gunther Stein's *Challenge of Red China,* and Israel Epstein's *The Unfinished Revolution in China*— described the Nanniwan area in words approaching awe. Thirty-four thousand acres of former desolate wasteland were now fields of grain and vegetables. New cave dwellings dotted the hillsides, and thousands of peasant refugees from the Shansi war zones lived in new villages. Co-operatives, small factories, and schools flourished, and flocks of sheep and goats grazed on the mountains. For the first time since the war began, these veteran correspondents saw well-fed and well-clothed Chinese troops and peasants. For the first time they met and talked with literate common people and troops.

On June 6th, just as the party was starting out for Yenan, General Wang Chen ran from his headquarters and shouted to the troops gathered to bid the party farewell:

"Allied armies have landed in Normandy! The second front has been opened! Down with fascism! Down with Japanese imperialism!"

The foreign correspondents who talked with General Chu Teh in Yenan described him as a man sparing in words and with military precision in thinking, who spoke frankly about plans to aid the Allied counter-offensive.

American or other Allied military observers would be welcomed by Yenan, he said, and the Eighth Route and New Fourth Armies, the anti-Japanese war bases, and the entire anti-Japanese underground intelligence network throughout north China would be placed at their disposal. This intelligence network, he declared, reached into every center of Japanese occupation.

General Chu also expressed a hope that was never realized: that his armies would receive "certain simple military supplies" from the Allied powers, such as rifles, light automatic weapons, infantry guns, explosives, and ammunition. With these, and with occasional air support for specific operations, his armies could recover important strategic towns and paralyze all vital enemy communications. Either by fighting independently, or in regular units directly attached to Allied forces which would land on Chinese soil, he added, the Eighth Route and New Fourth Armies could contribute greatly to the Allied cause.

Nor, he said, could he see any objection to an Allied Supreme Command in China, which General Stilwell and President Roosevelt had suggested as a means of unifying all Chinese armies and preventing civil war. The British had been willing to accept an American commander in chief for the invasion of Europe and the final assault on Germany, and Chu believed that an Allied Supreme Command would indirectly lay the foundation of unity "because national unity on a democratic foundation is essential for China, and our troops are imbued with a spirit of unrestricted inter-Allied solidarity." He added that he would be willing to place the Eighth Route and New Fourth Armies under the command of General Stilwell, who had been proposed as supreme Allied commander.

General Chu's offer came to nothing, however. An American Military Observer Group set up headquarters in Yenan that autumn, but the struggle to bring all Chinese armies under an Allied Commander led to Generalissimo Chiang's charge that Stilwell was trying to make him "a slave." In October, at Chiang's demand, Stilwell was recalled from China and ordered by the United States War Department to make no public statement because the China problem was "dynamite."

After Stilwell's recall, when General Albert Wedemeyer took over, American policy toward China changed. Chiang Kai-shek and the right-wing Kuomintang clique were henceforth given the green light. As Brooks Atkinson, the *New York Times* correspondent, put it, the United States was henceforth committed to support a corrupt and moribund regime. From that moment onward, also, civil war became a certainty.

General Chu Teh expressed himself in no uncertain terms at a public meeting shortly after the American Military Observer Group's arrival, saying:

The Kuomintang is now so weak that some people abroad, mistaking it for China, ask: "Can China stand throughout the war?" . . . We have an old Chinese saying: "Don't start shedding tears till you've seen the coffin." . . . We have another which says that "three shoemakers make one Chu Kuo-liang." [Chu Kuo-liang was a great Chinese warrior-statesman of the Three Kingdoms Period.] Well, we in the north have three million shoemakers—our army and the people's militia—and we have elected representatives of the people in village, district, and regional governments. Count them up and see how many Chu Kuo-liangs they make. . . . The Kuomintang blockades us, so we work and produce for ourselves. People who have organized for joint work can also stand together against the Japanese even without supplies from the outside. That is the biggest historical lesson of all.

As for ourselves, we don't want to be added to the long list of the Empress Dowager, Yuan Shih-kai, Tuan Chi-jui, and other "leaders." If Chiang Kai-shek can't see why they failed, his name will soon be added to the list. The Manchus couldn't hold the people down with auto-cratic pressure and fine phrases, nor could Yuan and Tuan. I don't believe anyone can. We are merely warning the present dictator.

General Chu also stated that the Liberated Areas were now self-sufficient for food and clothing. The making of hand grenades and land mines had become a household occupation, but the small arsenals in the regional bases still could not manufacture enough ammunition for the troops. Life behind the enemy lines was often extremely bitter, and there were places where towns and villages had been ravaged dozens of times by enemy columns, while some areas on the fringes of liberated territory had been ravaged by Kuomintang troops sixty or seventy times. Despite this, by 1942 the Liberated Areas had begun to expand instead of shrink.

During the entire blockade period, Chu continued, the Kuomintang adopted a passive "avoid fight" policy with the Japanese, retreating when attacked and waiting for the Allied powers to win the war on the theory that "China had done its share of fighting." When the Japanese were forced by the Allied counter-offensive to complete their continental land route to south Asia and to destroy American air bases in south China, the starving and demoralized Kuomintang armies crumpled before them, and within six months the enemy achieved their aim. Within this same period, the Eighth Route and New Fourth Armies launched a counter-offensive and drove the Japanese from 80,000 square miles of territory and liberated new millions of Chinese.

When the war began in 1937, General Chu added, the Eighth Route Army had 80,000 effectives. By the end of 1944 they totaled 600,000 regulars, with over two million partisan auxiliaries. Within that period, the regulars had suffered a little under 400,000 casualties, of which about one third were killed outright.

Chapter 39

THE year of decision, 1945, began with Mao Tse-tung's announcement that the troops and people of the north henceforth had four main tasks:

(1) To strengthen anti-Japanese workers in the Liberated Areas.

(2) To organize the people in Japanese-occupied territory.

(3) To help the people in Kuomintang areas to form guerrillas and, with other forces, to fight the Japanese.

(4) To start a nationwide campaign for the establishment of a coalition democratic government to continue the war aggressively in cooperation with the Allied powers.

Supporting Mao's announcement, General Chu declared that China could play its proper role in the war only if Chungking introduced democratic measures, and whether Allied victory came early or late would depend substantially on China's war effort as well as on the Allied land and sea offensive.

After General Stilwell's recall, however, and particularly after Roosevelt's death in April, General Chu and Mao Tse-tung, as well as other

Chinese political elements, became suspicious of American motives. While Chu and Mao still fought and called for total support of the Allied cause, their armies received none of the Lend Lease supplies which poured into China over the Hump and the newly completed Burma Road. Hu Tsung-nan's 200,000 anti-Communist troops continued their blockade of the Yenan Border Region, and no more foreign correspondents were allowed to visit the Liberated Areas.

As the Japanese suffered defeat after defeat and their homeland began to suffer acute hunger, their troops in China turned into human locusts to plunder the harvests and feed themselves. Their attacks on the Liberated Areas were particularly desperate and ferocious, but with each Allied victory the Communist armies grew bolder.

Distant Shantung Province reported to Chu Teh's headquarters that 20,000 additional square miles of territory, some 20,000 villages, and a population of nine million had been added to that Liberated Area. An additional five hundred miles of the Shantung coastline had been recovered, and Eighth Route "sea guerrillas" were operating along the coast. A paragraph from this report is typical of many others:

SHANTUNG LIBERATED AREAS. Elected village governments have reduced rents, interest; increased wages. Productive efforts of army, people and Regional Government have overcome difficulties of food and material supplies. Vast areas of wasteland recovered; 13,031 wells dug; 290 miles of river bed dredged; 21 miles of new irrigation canals dug; 283,000 peasants organized in 62,000 Mutual Aid Corps; extensive loans given peasants and dependents of servicemen; 1012 Labor Heroes in three administrative zones. . . . Frequent enemy mopping-up drives failed to retard production and cultural reconstruction. Liberated Area now has 8134 primary schools with 471,158 pupils; seventeen middle schools with 4000 students; innumerable night schools for adult illiterates. Newspaper blackboards, village theater and folk dance groups in every village. Army has given extensive manpower in cultivation and harvests. Seventeen army medical stations treated over 22,000 civilians in past year. Temporary army hospital set up in village struck with epidemic. Army made spinning wheels and agricultural implements for people. One hundred public and private factories producing iron wire, soap, silk cloth, alcohol, medicine, cigarettes and sulphur. Prices have fallen twenty percent.

A report from the Shansi-Suiyuan Liberated Area on the Inner Mongolia border reported a conference of "People's Volunteer Heroes" and the existence of a thriving "demolition cooperative" which distributed dividends in war spoils.

An ironic intelligence report from a worker in the underground network in Nanking read:

Ma Yi-hsien, puppet magistrate in Soochow county, was arrested this week by the Japanese, charged with hampering military needs. Ma was beaten and sent to Nanking in a sack where he died of indignation. . . . Puppet Sung Yu-tsai, chief of puppet Kiangsu Provincial Reconstruction Department, entertained Japanese officers one night and during the party his guests raped his wife. . . . Yu Kung-cheng, chief of the puppet Labor Department accused of embezzling workers' wages, was ordered to commit hara-kiri to wash away his sins, but Puppet Yu is no Bushido warrior. Puppet Yu ran away, complaining that it's not easy to be a traitor.

Another underground intelligence source from Shanghai reported that after the American landing in the Philippines, the Japanese in Shanghai began arresting and imprisoning "unstable Japanese elements." From a number of fronts in north China came reports of a wave of suicides in the Japanese army.

In late 1944 and early 1945, General Chu was a proud visitor and speaker at the Reconstruction Exhibition of the Yenan Border Region where samples of crops and manufactured goods were displayed, together with photographs, posters, woodcuts, charts, and maps.

The economic section had charts listing the achievements of the Border Region since the blockade began. One million mu of land (1 mu = ⅙ acre) had been reclaimed and the Border Region now had a grain reserve of 730,000 tan (1 tan in the northwest = 400 lbs.). Three hundred thousand mu of land had been put into cotton, from which 14,500 bolts of cotton cloth had been produced. An effective serum against cattle plague had been manufactured and put to use. Over 200,000 people belonged to Labor Exchange or other mutual aid groups and the grain tax had been reduced until it was one-twentieth of that in bordering Kuomintang areas.

The manufactured goods section displayed various grades of paper, cotton, wool and silk; also towels, soap, dyes, matches and improved spinning and weaving machines.

There was also an exhibition of military supplies produced in the Border Region, which included smokeless powder, high explosives, grenades, grenade throwers and grenade-thrower shells, rifles, small arms ammunition, and land mines. A big map depicted the Kuomintang block-

ade system around the Border Region where there were three blockade lines with thousands of blockhouses. Speaking at the exhibition,
General Chu remarked that if Kuomintang troops had devoted as much
strength to fighting the Japanese and to reconstruction and helping the
people as in constructing this blockade system, the Japanese could have
been driven into the sea.

The exhibitions brought hundreds of thousands of people to Yenan,
where a big conference of Labor Heroes and Model Workers was also
held. In his speech of welcome, Mao Tse-tung told the delegates:

The respect paid you by the people is well deserved, but this can easily
lead to pride and conceit. If you become proud and conceited you will
no longer be Labor Heroes and Model Workers.

General Chu told the audience:

When we consider what we have achieved with no outside help, we
think of the 300 million [American] dollars in private fortunes which
rich Chinese have deposited in American banks. Not one person in our
Liberated Areas has made private profit from the war. Not one has a
bank account. We work and fight for the liberation of China and the
emancipation of our people. But Kuomintang officials and officers loot the
people and soldiers, black marketeer in Allied Lend Lease supplies, and
deposit their plunder in American banks.

Book XII

"The Great Road"

Chapter 40

SERIOUS changes took place in the thinking of General Chu Teh and his comrades in the last year of the war, when they became convinced that the Second World War would not end with the relaxation of the Kuomintang dictatorship.

The China situation had always been clear to them, and there had been more than enough "incidents" and danger signals to warrant their conviction that the Kuomintang would never give up the dictatorship without fighting. They had hoped, however, that the development of the democratic movement in the Liberated Areas and the consequent strengthening of the same movement in Kuomintang territory would be able to prevent civil war. They had also expected the proclaimed democratic aims of the Allied nations to loosen the Kuomintang grip on the Chinese people, and were convinced that the defeat of fascism would wash away the ideological ground from beneath the Kuomintang.

The replacement of General Joseph Stilwell's policies by those of General Albert Wedemeyer and Ambassador Patrick Hurley, who supported everything Chiang Kai-shek advocated, had aroused great fear among all the democratic forces of China. This fear had been offset to a certain extent by the re-election of Roosevelt as the President of the United States—an event which simultaneously cast gloom over the Kuomintang.

Another ray of hope penetrated the darkness when Roosevelt's influence forced the Kuomintang to include representatives of other parties in the Chinese delegation to the San Francisco United Nations Conference in the spring of 1945. Even then, however, Chiang Kai-shek insisted that he alone had the right to appoint such representatives. One Communist representative, Dr. Tung Pi-wu, was appointed by him, while two small parties in the Democratic League were allowed one representative each.

The news of Roosevelt's death on April 12th, before the San Francisco

Conference met, cast a dark shadow over all previously aroused hopes. Mao Tse-tung and Chu Teh wired condolences to President Truman and the Roosevelt family, and flags flew at half-mast over the Liberated Areas. The Yenan press described Roosevelt as "this great anti-fascist statesman, this good friend of China in her war of resistance, whose death is mourned by the entire Chinese nation." The *Emancipation Daily*, official organ of the Central Communist Party, wrote:

Roosevelt clearly understood that the interests of the United States were inextricably bound up with victory in the anti-fascist war, with peace and democracy in the postwar period, and that these were inseparable from cooperation with the Soviet Union. . . . Roosevelt has left his mark on diplomatic history with his Four Freedoms and the Atlantic Charter, by his leadership of the Dumbarton Oaks Conference and at the Yalta Conference. . . . He has altered the course of history. . . . We hope that the statesman who succeeds him will, in accordance with his fixed policy, lead the American people to carry out his will—the uprooting of fascism and the construction of a world based on peace and democracy.

Roosevelt's death revived the hope of reactionaries throughout the world that the anti-fascist war might be transformed into a war against Communism. On April 13th, for example, the *Tokyo Asahi Shimbun* again raised the cry of anti-Communism in China, declaring that the Chinese "Communist-bandits" maintained lines of communication along the entire Chinese coast from Chekiang Province to Manchuria, and that their Peasant Defense Corps "hamper the maintenance of peace and order by the Imperial and Nanking Armies."

These Communist-bandits and peasant marauders [the Japanese daily fumed] stop such essential commodities as rice, cotton, firewood, and coal from being exported from the interior, thus disturbing economy in the peaceful areas. Our garrison forces, together with the Nanking Peace Army and Peace Preservation Corps, have organized a Joint Special Corps and are launching daily punitive drives against the Communist-bandits in order to carry out the three great policies of peace, production, and the purification of thought.

In the months preceding Roosevelt's death, General Chu Teh repeatedly expressed belief that civil war in China could be prevented.

In talks with foreign correspondents in Yenan in the summer of 1944, he said:

We do not want to think of civil war, and we certainly shall never initiate such a war. But we, and other democratic forces in the country, are ready to defend the democratic gains of years of struggle, and to fight any reactionaries who may wish to destroy them. Should the Kuomintang wish to fight us, they must fight the entire Chinese people. Such a war would be a continuation of the present one—it would mean that the Second World War would not have ended with the defeat of the Axis powers.

A year later, however, General Chu warned that "victory on the battle-field will not be the end of the anti-fascist war," and that "the Japanese are trying to avert their doom by sowing seeds of discord among the Allied powers by fomenting civil war in China"—an effort in which they had "powerful Kuomintang support."

General Chu gave the same warning at the Seventh National Congress of the Chinese Communist Party, which convened in Yenan on April 24, 1945. His headquarters, he said, had thousands of documents as well as other evidence proving that Kuomintang armies had joined the enemy at Kuomintang direction, and fought the People's Armies under dual Kuomintang-Japanese command. The Kuomintang High Command, he charged, maintained radio contact with these puppet armies which were under orders, when the war ended, to replace their Japanese with Kuomintang badges, and to continue the war on the Liberated Areas.

The Seventh National Congress of the Communist Party met against a background of kaleidoscopic international changes. The session was repeatedly interrupted with world-shaking news: Mussolini and his mistress, together with seventeen other fascists, had just been killed by Italian partisans; Hitler, with many of his associates, had ended their gruesome careers in the flames of Berlin; Admiral Doenitz had made a last but futile attempt to split the Allies by offering to surrender to the Western powers while continuing resistance to the Russian Red Army.

On May 1st, when the congress ended, the Russians were fighting in the heart of Berlin and the Germans in Italy were surrendering to the Allies. One week later, the Germans in France surrendered and repre-sentatives of the Nazi army, naval and air forces signed the Allied document of unconditional surrender in Berlin.

It was against this vast international mosaic that Mao Tse-tung outlined plans for the establishment of a coalition government. This document, entitled *On Coalition Government*, began by calling for the total defeat of Japanese imperialism, the destruction of Chinese feudalism, and the abolition of the Kuomintang dictatorship, with none of which, Mao said, could there be any compromise.

He next outlined plans for the formation of a Chinese coalition democratic government representing all parties, organizations and groups, to replace the Kuomintang dictatorship. He demanded universal suffrage for the Chinese people, civil liberties, land reforms, the development of industry, mass education and culture, and the protection and development and education of the People's Armies.

Speaking directly to Communist Party members, Mao warned against dogmatism, factionalism, empiricism, "tailism" (or lagging behind), bureaucracy, warlordism, and arrogance, any of which, he said, would estrange them from the people. As in years past, he told Communists to listen to and merge with the people, and to raise the people's consciousness while giving necessary consideration to their level of understanding. Communists were told to teach the people "to organize themselves on voluntary principles" and to develop all necessary struggles compatible with the given circumstances. To prevent stagnation he urged serious self-criticism because "a running stream does not become putrid" and "a door pivot does not become worm-eaten."

Mao Tse-tung also warned that the tactics, methods, and policies which had proved effective in an environment of guerrilla warfare in rural areas would prove inadequate when, after the war with Japan, the great cities were liberated.

Susumu Okano (Tetsu Nosaka), representative of the Japanese Communist Party, who also addressed the Communist Congress, recounted the fourteen years of struggle carried on by his party against Japanese militarism. Despite heavy sacrifices, he said, "we have fought for the interests and well-being of the Japanese nation." Okano ended by expressing the hope that the new democratic Japanese government which "the Allies have pledged to assist, and for which they are fighting," would be established, and that it "should perhaps be of a republican nature."

General Chu Teh, who served on the presidium and was re-elected to the party's Central Committee, reviewed the eight years of war against Japan. Analyzing the various stages of the war, he stated that a part of the Kuomintang Army had fought gallantly on many fronts in the first stage of the war in particular. The government, however, had persisted in an "anti-popular political system" and had therefore failed militarily to capitalize on the strategic weaknesses of the widely dispersed Japanese armies, "thus enabling the enemy to capitalize on Kuomintang mistakes, and pocket large strategic areas of the country."

In nearly eight years of fighting, the Eighth Route and New Fourth Armies had penetrated into the enemy rear, launched counter-attacks, diverted large Japanese forces, set up many Liberated Areas and opened fronts in the enemy rear, shielded the Kuomintang battlefield, and won victories which had bolstered the war morale of the entire nation. Operating by the strategy of protracted warfare as formulated by Mao Tse-tung, the People's Armies had waged relentless struggles of the most sanguinary character.

He selected the two years following the autumn of 1940 as the most difficult for the Liberated Areas. Because of the "Hundred Regiment Campaign," and because the Japanese tried to transform north China into a military base for the great Pacific War, the enemy launched a succession of savage offensives, "correlating with Kuomintang troops in converging attacks on the Liberated Areas so that an unprecedentedly grave situation was created." From 1941 to 1943, "nearly half a million Kuomintang troops, led by sixty to seventy officers of general's rank, went over to the Japanese."

After the great Pacific War began, he continued, there were no important battles on the Kuomintang battlefront. But the Liberated Areas opposed the majority of Japanese troops in China and ninety-five percent of the puppets.

"Judging the situation reasonably," he added, "the Kuomintang might have devoted those same years to strengthening the forces of armed resistance and preparing for a counter-offensive. Instead, it continued secret dealings with the Japanese aiming at a compromise, and launched three anti-Communist drives."

General Chu advocated a number of military reforms in the nation. He envisaged a united High Command, in accordance with Sun Yat-sen's ideas, to replace the Kuomintang High Command; the dismissal of all defeatist and pro-Japanese elements; and the abolition of anti-popular and corrupt practices detrimental to the war of resistance and the people's interests. All friction between the various armies should cease, he declared. They were to be treated equally, and Allied war supplies should be equitably distributed among the front-line troops. He called for a democratic national army system with strengthened military training, drastic reform in the Kuomintang conscription system, and improvement in the treatment and remuneration of officers and men. Only thus, he declared, could Chinese troops develop their fighting capacity and China play an honorable role in bringing the war to a quick and victorious conclusion.

In that same month of June, Japanese armies in south China began withdrawing slowly toward the coast, looting and killing as they went. As they withdrew from a position, the bedraggled Kuomintang armies moved in and took over and Chungking propagandists proclaimed a "victory." The Japanese troops in the Liberated Regions, however, stayed put until blasted out by the People's Army.

When the Japanese along the Yellow River bend in the northwest began withdrawing eastward, General Hu Tsung-nan did not lift a finger. Instead, General Hu hurled nine divisions of his powerful army against the Yenan Border Region.

Weeks of savage fighting followed. General Chu Teh and Peng Teh-huai repeatedly wired Chiang Kai-shek, demanding that his troops return to their original positions. As public agitation mounted, the fighting simmered to a stop, and in early August, General Chu's chief of staff published a list of American Lend Lease weapons, with trade-marks and serial numbers, captured by the Eighth Route troops during the fighting.

The "American arsenal of democracy had been used by feudal fascists in China," thus "postponing and undermining victory in the war against Japan," charged the chief of staff, and he appealed to the American people and to "democratic elements in the American government" to end this reactionary policy. The Communist press in Yenan and Chungking chimed in and declared that American reactionaries were trying to destroy President Roosevelt's policy of promoting unity and democracy in China.

The Potsdam Declaration was announced while the Kuomintang offensive against the Yenan Border Region was on. It demanded the unconditional surrender of Japanese militarism and pledged the establishment of democracy in Japan, and again China's gloom dispersed slightly. If the Allied powers pledged democracy to Japan, they could surely not help the Kuomintang suppress it in China.

Chapter 41

ON THE first day of the portentous month of August 1945, while Japanese Pacific bastions fell under the shattering blows of the American Navy, General Chu again warned that the Japanese were trying to avert their doom by sowing discord among the Allied powers and by fomenting civil war in China—and that they had powerful Kuomintang support.

"We must act in unison with our Allies, and must not stop offensive operations until the enemy has laid down his arms," he wrote. "It is against the common interests of all the Allied nations to allow Japan any loophole of escape."

Suddenly the whole tempo of the war changed. On August 6th the city of Hiroshima, which was not a military objective, was laid waste by an atomic bomb dropped by an American plane, and two days later another devastated Nagasaki.

Of the entire press in Chungking, only one paper—the Communist *New China Daily*—seemed to realize the significance of these events. On August 7th this paper protested against the bombing of Hiroshima: "The aim of the war is the destruction of Japanese militarism, not the Japanese people. . . . The achievements of science should be devoted to the advancement, instead of the destruction, of the human race."

On August 9th, the Soviet Union, acting in accord with decisions reached at the Yalta Conference six months previously, declared war on Japan, and the Red Army began pounding down against the military bastion which the Japanese had constructed in Manchuria from 1931 onward.

Ignoring the censors, all but the official Kuomintang press in Chungking sang paeans of joy, crying that "the intrigues of the fascist bandits to alienate the Allies" had been shattered, and that the half million Japanese troops in Manchuria would now meet their doom. However, one telltale line appeared in the official Kuomintang press: "From this time on, we can count on a conflict between the Soviet Union on the one hand, and Britain and America on the other."

The Christian General, Feng Yu-hsiang, declared two years later in the United States that Chiang Kai-shek had boasted, in the presence of himself and a number of other Kuomintang leaders, that he had "forced the United States to fight Japan, and that he could force it to fight the Soviet Union." Chiang was also quoted as declaring that the Sino-Japanese War would now merge into a civil war, which in turn would merge into a Soviet-American war; and that the by-product of an American victory, which he took for granted, would leave him and his regime sitting on top of China.

The *New China Daily* of Chungking, however, expressed another attitude:

We will never forget the material aid and spiritual encouragement given us by the Soviet Union in the past eight years. . . . In the whole chronology of our movement for national emancipation, freedom and democracy, we have never had such favorable conditions as today. We must not waste a single minute in our efforts to unite the democratic forces of the whole country to oppose civil war, strengthen national unity, and increase the war effort to extirpate all fascism. The final victory will belong to the masses and to the free and democratic new China.

The Communists now began to think of the cleaning-up process. The press claimed the right of the Chinese people to list Japanese war criminals and to pass judgment upon them—a right which Chiang Kai-shek at once denounced. But the Communist press went full speed ahead publishing long lists of war criminals in China, giving a full record of their atrocities. First came General Yosuji Okamura, author of the gruesome "three-all" policy—kill all, burn all, loot all—in north China. General Okamura, now in Nanking, was supreme Japanese commander in China.

In Yenan, General Chu wrote:

Chinese puppets should not be allowed to change their designations and be considered absolved from sin. They should be treated as French collaborationists with the Nazis were treated by French patriots. We demand that all Japanese and puppet troops surrender to the local anti-Japanese units . . . as the Nazi armies in Europe surrendered to local Allied units. . . . Any who refuse should be liquidated by force.

To General Chu Teh's desk now came urgent coded warnings: a high Kuomintang official in Chungking had declared that the Japanese were surrendering at a propitious time.

"Two months later," this official had said, "we would have had to launch a counter-offensive against the Japanese and use our Lend Lease supplies. Now we have them for use against the Communist-bandits."

Another warning stated that Chiang Kai-shek had summoned three old generals, who had fled Manchuria in 1931, into secret conference and that they were to be sent back with Kuomintang officers to take control of the northeast.

Throughout that day of destiny, August 10, General Chu received other more serious messages: Chiang Kai-shek had ordered Japanese and puppet armies in north, eastern, and central China not to allow themselves to be disarmed, reorganized, or incorporated into any other army units "without specific orders" from himself. They were further ordered to "hold their positions" and to "maintain peace and order."

There were no Kuomintang armies in all north China. There were only Japanese and puppets, and most of the puppets were former Kuomintang troops. The pieces of a vast and treacherous conspiracy, already in its fourth year, were falling into place: the Kuomintang High Command was ordering the Japanese and puppet armies who had spilled rivers of blood in the Liberated Areas to fight if attacked by the Communists.

Reports from all the Liberated regions informed General Chu of one more move that fitted this game of chess: the puppet armies were reassuming Kuomintang designations and badges, lowering the Japanese flag and running up the Kuomintang banner.

Exactly at midnight on August 10th, General Chu issued the first of seven orders that changed the course of history. The first ordered all Eighth Route and New Fourth Army units, and all anti-Japanese forces in the Liberated Areas, to send orders to nearby Japanese and puppet troops, stationed in cities and along lines of communication, to surrender all their arms within a stated time limit. Those who refused were to be destroyed at once. The order stated that all places held by the Japanese or puppets were to be occupied and brought under emergency military control. Those who tried to disrupt these measures were to be treated as traitors.

At eight o'clock on August 11th, General Chu issued a second order, which began: "In order to collaborate with the Russian Red Army fighting in Chinese territory, and in preparation for accepting Japanese and puppet surrender in Manchuria, I order . . ."

The four-point order followed: three armies of the old Manchurian (Tungpei) Army under General Chu's command, and one army of the Eighth Route Army, were to leave their respective positions in Inner Mongolia, Hopei, and Shantung provinces, as well as the Liberation stronghold on the borders of Manchuria and Inner Mongolia, and drive into Manchuria against the Japanese at once.

Of the three Manchurian armies mentioned, one was commanded by Chang Hsueh-shih, younger brother of the Young Marshal, Chang Hsueh-liang, whom Chiang Kai-shek had held as his personal prisoner since January 1938.

One hour later General Chu Teh issued a third order to armies under General Ho Lung in Suiyuan, and to General Nieh Jung-chen in Inner Mongolia, to march northward and cooperate with the Army of the Outer Mongolian People's Republic, which had also entered the war and was driving down against the Japanese from the north. The order ended: "Smash and destroy all Japanese and puppet troops who refuse to surrender."

Order No. 4, issued one and a half hours later, placed General Ho Lung in command of all anti-Japanese forces in Shansi Province, and ordered him to disarm all Japanese and puppet troops and to "destroy all who resist."

Order No. 5, issued thirty minutes later, directed all anti-Japanese troops along all railways or near important communication points to attack Japanese and puppet forces "until they surrender unconditionally, and to destroy any who resist."

Order No. 6, issued at midnight on August 11th, ordered the Korean commander, Wu Ting, and his deputy commanders to lead the Eighth Route Army which he commanded into Manchuria, "to destroy the enemy, to organize the Koreans in Manchuria, and to emancipate Korea."

Order No. 7, dated the "18th hour, August 12th," ordered all Eighth Route and New Fourth Army troops to establish emergency military control over all cities or points seized from the enemy; to assign areas for prisoners of war; to arrest and register war criminals and national traitors; and to control and protect all institutions of a military or public nature, including arsenals, warehouses, factories, schools, barracks, and important strategic points, and strictly to prohibit freedom of movement in and out of such places. Likewise: to take over vessels, trains and military vehicles, wharves, post offices, telephone, telegraph, and wireless stations, and to carry out strict military inspection; to control all military and commercial airfields and their installations; to maintain order, protect the residents, be vigilant against reactionaries, remnant enemy spies and traitors, and to deal with such elements militarily; to bring all local anti-Japanese organizations and their armed groups under the local defense commander.

This last order also instructed all anti-Japanese forces to announce that anyone who hid enemy or puppet elements, scattered arms, etc., would be severely punished. "Treacherous merchants" were to be strictly forbidden "to hoard goods and manipulate the market" and the anti-Japanese forces were to control the food, water, coal, and electrical services.

While these orders were setting millions of men in motion, the Korean Independence League and the Japanese People's Emancipation League in Yenan wired to all their local branches to call on Korean and Japanese soldiers and residents to surrender to the anti-Japanese Chinese People's Armies.

On August 12th, news reached Yenan that American transport planes and ships were being assembled to transport 80,000 Kuomintang troops to battle stations in the Liberated Areas, and that the first of these would be the new Kuomintang armies armed and trained by American officers.

On that same day Generalissimo Chiang Kai-shek officially ordered Chu Teh to halt the advance of his troops and await orders about disarming the enemy, the terms for which, he declared, could be determined only by the Allied powers.

On the following day Chu Teh and his vice-commander, Peng Teh-huai, replied to Chiang, stating: "We consider that you have given us a mistaken order. We are compelled to . . . firmly refuse the order." And they went on to remind Chiang that he had just ordered the Japanese in south China to surrender to Kuomintang armies on the spot. Why, they asked, had Chiang ordered the hated puppets and Japanese to keep their arms and maintain law and order, and to refuse to surrender arms to anyone not designated by him?

Chu and Peng further informed Chiang that the Allied orders to German Nazi armies in Europe had been to surrender to the Allied armies on the spot. The Nazis had been given no right to choose where and to whom they should surrender. Their wire ended: "We have the fullest right to liquidate, with our own hands, those enemy and puppet troops who have caused us so much suffering."

The Japanese and puppet troops in the Liberated Areas obeyed Chiang's orders. Instead of surrendering, they launched a fierce counter-offensive. Preceded by bombers and tanks, they moved against the Communist troops in some of the most savage fighting of the war. American correspondents who later flew to Nanking with advance Kuomintang forces reported watching columns of fully equipped Japanese troops moving northward against the New Fourth Army.

In Shansi Province, the Japanese escorted the old warlord governor, Yen Hsi-shan, to the provincial capital, Taiyuanfu, in an armored train. The commanding Japanese general there became his adviser and placed 20,000 Japanese troops at his disposal. These Japanese troops, together with General Yen's, at once launched a counter-offensive against the Eighth Route Army. Three and a half years later the Chinese People's Liberation Army finally conquered Taiyuanfu and took thousands of Japanese troops, with their commanding general, prisoner. General Yen, however, escaped to Canton to become Premier of the shriveled Kuomintang regime.

On August 14th the Japanese formally accepted the Allied terms of surrender, which were conditional, not unconditional. The Emperor was allowed to retain his "prerogatives," a procedure which aroused energetic protests in China.

On that same day the China scene again suddenly shifted: the Chungking government—with American encouragement—signed a thirty-year treaty of friendship and alliance with the Soviet government.

This alliance established specific provisions against the revival of Japanese aggression, of which Manchuria had always been the focal point. After declaring Manchuria an inseparable part of China, these provisions included the following: joint Sino-Soviet operation of the Chinese Eastern and South Manchurian Railways; joint utilization of the Port Arthur naval base for thirty years, after which all installations, built at Russian expense, were to be delivered to China without cost; Dairen to be a free port under Chinese administrative control but with joint Chinese-Soviet port management. The agreement was to run for thirty years after which all the property of the two railways, like the Port Arthur installations, was to revert to China without cost. The two contracting powers pledged close and friendly cooperation following the peace, mutual respect for the sovereignty and territorial integrity of each, and noninterference in the internal affairs of each other's countries.

On the day this treaty was signed, Chiang Kai-shek, under pressure from the United States, wired the first of three invitations to Mao Tsetung to come to Chungking to discuss national affairs.

Mao replied that he would consider the question after Chiang replied to General Chu's previous demands concerning the disarming of Japanese and puppet troops.

It took Chiang two days to formulate a reply. In the interim General Chu telegraphed the hated Japanese general, Okamura, in Nanking. He ordered him to instruct all Japanese forces in the Liberated Areas to surrender to the Eighth Route and New Fourth Armies on the spot. Concerning south China, he wired, except for those forces surrounded by Kuomintang armies, the Japanese should be ordered to surrender to the South China Anti-Japanese Detachment.

General Chu further ordered that all installations and material in enemy-occupied territory should be preserved intact, all Japanese airplanes and warships in north and east China ports remain at their stations, and all warships anchored along the coast of the Yellow Sea concentrate at specified ports. The order warned Okamura that he and all Japanese officers under his command would be held strictly responsible for obeying these orders.

The Kuomintang immediately denounced the Chinese Communist Party as a "traitor party" and "Public Enemy No. 1." One Kuomintang daily quoted an editorial in the *New York Times* which attacked the Chinese Communist Party as "a conspiracy aimed at the usurpation of the Chinese government."

The Yenan press replied to the *New York Times* and the official Kuomintang press:

We have repeatedly announced our hostility to the corrupt and despotic rule of a small ruling clique, and together with the democratic forces of the entire nation demanded the end of this despotism and the creation of a coalition government representing all parties, groups, and classes.

Dr. Chang Lan, the venerable President of the Chinese Democratic League, also replied by calling for an inter-party conference to establish a coalition democratic government which alone, he said, could avert civil war.

General Chu Teh now entered the international diplomatic arena by addressing an official communiqué to the governments of the United States, Great Britain, and the Soviet Union, whom he asked "to recognize the realities of the Chinese battle areas."

In 1937, he informed these powers, the Liberated Areas were abandoned by the Kuomintang government and occupied by the enemy. By August 1945, the Eighth Route and New Fourth Armies had recovered nearly a million square miles of this same territory and liberated a hundred million people.

After summarizing the war record of the armed forces and people of the Liberated Areas, General Chu stated that the anti-Japanese armies and the people in the Liberated Areas "still engage and surround sixty-nine percent of the Japanese armed forces in China as well as ninety-five percent of the puppet armies," while the majority of Kuomintang armies not only gave them no support but "use 960,000 troops to surround and attack us."

The people of the Liberated Areas and the Chinese Communist Party, he informed the Allied powers, had repeatedly proposed a conference of all parties to establish a united coalition democratic government which alone could end internal conflict, mobilize the entire country for the anti-Japanese struggle, and guarantee victory and postwar peace. All such proposals had been rejected by the Kuomintang regime.

Declaring that "we have strong reasons to make specific demands on the Allied governments and peoples," he warned that the Kuomintang regime and its commander in chief did not represent the Chinese Liberated Areas, the Chinese people, nor the anti-Japanese armed forces in occupied areas, and that "we reserve the right to challenge anything in the terms of surrender or agreements which concern the Liberated Areas and the armed forces of the people in occupied areas to which our agreement has not been previously secured."

General Chu further declared that the Liberated Areas, and the anti-Japanese troops in these areas, had the right to accept the surrender of Japanese and puppet troops, to carry out Allied regulations following their surrender, and to be represented at the peace conference concerning the disposition of Japan, as well as to representation in the United Nations. His communiqué ended:

In order to avert the danger of civil war in China, we ask the American Government to consider the common interests of the people of the United States and China, and immediately to discontinue Lend Lease Aid to the Kuomintang Government. In case the Kuomintang initiates an anti-Chinese people's civil war on a national scale (a serious existing danger), we request that you [the American Government] give the Kuomintang Government no assistance.

None of the governments addressed took official cognizance of this communiqué. On August 23rd General Chu received the first reports that American military transport planes had begun transporting Kuomintang armies not only to Nanking and Shanghai, but to battle stations in north and eastern China—to Peking, Tientsin, and Tsingtao—and that Chiang Kai-shek had requested American troops to land in Tientsin and Tsingtao to support his troops "in the recovery of the Liberated Areas."

On that same day General Ho Ying-chin, Kuomintang Minister of War, ordered General Yosuji Okamura to take steps to ensure the safety of advance Kuomintang troops en route to Nanking, adding that Okamura would also be held responsible for the recovery of territory from the "bandits."

The next four years were comfortable, if not happy ones, for Okamura, who became one of Chiang Kai-shek's advisers in the civil war against the Communists. In 1949, when the Chinese People's Liberation Army approached Nanking, Chiang absolved him and a large group of other Japanese war criminals and sent them to Tokyo.

Chapter 42

THOUGH General Chu was a very down-to-earth soldier, he was imaginative enough to realize that he stood right in the center of one of the greatest struggles of human history.

Almost every document that reached Chu's desk, almost every development on the international stage, confirmed his conviction that class called to class across all national and racial boundaries.

On his desk lay copies of proclamations put out by Japanese troops in north China which stated categorically that they had "received orders from General Ho Ying-chin, Minister of War of the Chungking government, to attack the Chinese Communist-bandits." One from Shantung Province even stated that many Japanese troops "will be incorporated into the future Chinese National Army."

Among the papers lay a copy of the great nationalist Chinese daily, the *Ta Kung Pao*, crying out that Japanese surrender was only a "temporary truce" and that Chungking had taken "no action against Japanese war criminals or Chinese puppets or other traitors," but was "even using them in the civil war against Chinese in the Liberated Areas."

Susumu Okano, the Japanese Communist leader in Yenan, had, on August 24th, addressed a communiqué to the Allied powers warning that Emperor Hirohito's recent "imperial rescript" was couched in "obscure phrases which denied Japan's defeat, denied responsibility for the Sino-Japanese War, and even implied preparations for future revenge."

Warning against the new Japanese cabinet, Okano said:

Can anyone expect this band of war criminals and anti-democratic militarists to fulfill the Potsdam Declaration which demands strict punishment of war criminals, complete demilitarization of Japan, and the establishment of a democratic government? Never! Instead, Japanese militarism is using the Imperial household as a protecting screen behind which reactionary forces will collaborate with the Allied powers so as to preserve themselves.

This was Okano's last statement from China. Immediately after issuing it he, together with two hundred Japanese war prisoners who had been converted in Yenan, began marching across north China, picking up other groups in the Liberated Area strongholds, on their way to Japan which they hoped to persuade to their way of thinking.

A new stage was reached in mid-August by the return to Yenan of "The Big Wind." General Patrick Hurley, American ambassador to China, had first landed from a plane in Yenan in November 1944. He gave a war whoop as he strode forward to shake hands with Mao Tse-tung, Chu Teh, and other Communist dignitaries waiting to receive him.

Hurley had come to Yenan to urge Mao Tse-tung to negotiate with Chiang Kai-shek about national problems. Mao had proposed a five-point agreement:

(1) Kuomintang-Communist military unification to defeat Japan and reconstruct China.

(2) Formation of a coalition government and unified National Military Council.

(3) The coalition government to be democratic, espousing the aims of Sun Yat-sen.

(4) Anti-Japanese forces to obey the unified National Military Council and be supplied by it.

(5) All anti-Japanese parties to be legally recognized.

Hurley loudly proclaimed that the five points were so reasonable that he would sign them himself—which, according to rumor, he did with a flourish.

"The fellow's a clown," Mao told Chu Teh later, and thereafter "The Big Wind"—as Hurley was called in Chungking—became "The Clown" to Yenan.

Despite General Hurley's description of himself as "the Communists' best friend" and a friendly intermediary, the Communists themselves had detected increasing signs of America's decision to favor the Kuomintang. They had made preparations for a showdown. But the American-Soviet negotiations over China in 1944-1945 gave them pause. As Communists they could not be expected to run counter to the Soviet analysis of world developments. The Soviet signature to a treaty with the Chungking government and the assurances given by Stalin and Molotov to General Hurley in Moscow strongly suggested that Moscow did not want China to become an area of Soviet-American conflict at the time, and wanted the Chinese Communists to come to an agreement if they possibly could.

Toward the end of August 1945, General Hurley pressed Mao Tse-tung to negotiate in Chungking. On August 28th Hurley, accompanied by General Chang Chih-tung, to assure Mao that no trap was being laid

for him in Chungking, arrived in Yenan and took Mao, together with
General Wang Jo-fei, back with him.

Generalissimo Chiang's first demand on Mao was that the Eighth
Route and New Fourth Armies be reorganized into the Kuomintang
armies. Mao, who was not that much of a country bumpkin, replied that
his armies would surrender only to a coalition democratic government
representing the entire Chinese people, and that the Kuomintang Party
armies should do the same, so that a united national democratic army
might be organized.

Mao's demands were the same as those outlined in his book, *On
Coalition Government,* which were supported and even amplified by the
Chinese Democratic League which met in Chungking in its first national
congress during the negotiations.

Mao won the support of the non-official press when, on September 3rd,
he demanded from Chiang Kai-shek freedom of the press, the release of
all newspapermen imprisoned during the war for democratic activities,
severe punishment of all Chinese newspapermen who had collaborated
with the Japanese and their exclusion from the profession forever. Many
traitorous newspapermen, Mao informed Chiang—as if Chiang didn't
know!—had suddenly turned over to the Kuomintang.

In response to these demands, editors and owners of newspapers and
magazines throughout west and southwest China published notices that
they henceforth refused to submit to censorship. Acting upon their decision, they began warning that though fascism had been defeated in the
war, "its ghost still stalks China under many camouflages, perpetrating
all kinds of intrigues and dangerous activities." Japanese war criminals
and Chinese political and military traitors must be punished, they demanded, all Japanese and puppet armies disarmed, thought control termi-
nated, the secret police abolished, and the Kuomintang dictatorship
replaced by a coalition democratic government.

The stubborn Mao-Chiang negotiations lasted until early October.
When it became clear that the Kuomintang was on the defensive, the
secret police assassinated the editor of the *New China Daily,* apparently
in the belief that they were murdering Chou En-lai, one of Mao's two
advisers. Even this assassination, however, failed to prevent the signing
of the agreement on October 10th, by which Chiang agreed to call a
political consultative conference of all parties and groups to discuss the
establishment of a coalition government.

While these negotiations were under way, General Chu Teh was
hammering away in Yenan. In a public meeting on September 5th to
celebrate Allied victory in the war, he declared that only a democratic

China could unite the nation, and that the Liberated Areas must set an example to the entire country in the practice of democracy and in productive work.

"Victory in the war and victory in peace and reconstruction would have been impossible had there been no People's Armies which knew how to fight the enemy, engage in production in the midst of war, and truly serve the people," he declared. "We must never forget, however, that many Chinese traitors have not been punished, but have been appointed to high government positions instead."

Unofficial newspapers in Chungking quoted General Chu and asked the government: "Who are these traitors? Under whose orders are the Japanese still waging war on the Liberated Areas and massacring our people?"

When the government ignored the questions, foreign correspondents asked them of the Minister of War, who replied: "I have seen no such reports—I have been too busy!" to which General Chu Teh replied with an article on September 17th.

The Japanese gendarmerie in Tsinan, Shantung Province, he said, had just changed into Kuomintang uniform, changed its name to the "Chinese Gendarmerie," while its Japanese commander had taken a Chinese name.

The Japanese in Shansi, he said, still controlled all railways, motor vehicles, the post office, electric light plant, and factories in that province, and the Japanese commanding general in Taiyuanfu had just published an official proclamation which read:

In compliance with the request of the Shansi-Suiyuan Army commanded by General Yen Hsi-shan, the Japanese Expeditionary Forces in Shansi have agreed to keep part of its forces in Shansi to assist the Shansi-Suiyuan Army in its mopping-up of Chinese Communists. Those residents who had been planning to leave for Peking are advised to remain in Taiyuan for the time being.

In Taiyuanfu, General Chu further charged, Japanese and puppet troops operated under Kuomintang designations, while both old and new traitors and Chinese and Japanese commissioners "are behaving like members of one family."

He named them:

Li Hsien-liang, commander of the Japanese Imperial Collaborationist Army, has been appointed the new Kuomintang Mayor of Tsingtao. The official Central News Agency had already reported that the troops of this notorious traitor have taken over Tsingtao.

On September 4th, 1000 Japanese troops and several thousand puppets commanded by Lin Chao launched a furious attack on our South China Anti-Japanese Brigade, and fierce fighting is continuing. Also, Japanese troops in eastern Hopei Province, in cooperation with puppet Manchukuo troops, have started a combined campaign of plundering and killing in the Tsunhua region. . . .

Also, Wang Shih-ching, President of the puppet Central Bank in Peking during the war, was recently flown to Chungking for a secret conference. A Kuomintang plane flew him back after the conference. He has a special commission from the Kuomintang to continue operations as before.

Many traitors go unpunished while the officers and puppet soldiers who massacre our fellow countrymen are commissioned to high-ranking official position under the Kuomintang.

A few days later General Chu appeared in print again, this time to protest a list of Japanese war criminals which General Douglas MacArthur had just published in Tokyo. There were only thirty-eight names on the list—cabinet members at the time of the Pearl Harbor attack, and high officers responsible for atrocities in the Philippines, in Burma, and the Dutch East Indies. Not one Japanese responsible for atrocities in China was on the list.

General Chu also attacked a statement by General MacArthur on September 11th which declared that Japan would be permitted to retain some of her heavy industry and her leading position in Far Eastern trade. The Allies were making the same mistake as after the First World War, Chu warned, and MacArthur was "retaining a hotbed for Japanese fascists who are busily laying the dynamite for a third world war."

Many incidents soon indicated that the Chinese Communists had been called to Chungking for very different reasons than announced. On September 30th, while the negotiations were in progress, American Marines began landing, not in south China where there were also large numbers of Japanese troops, but in north China cities, allegedly just to disarm and repatriate the Japanese there.

On October 5th, five days before the Chungking agreement was signed, General Chu Teh again entered the international diplomatic arena by lodging a determined protest with the American military authorities in Chungking against American interference in China's internal affairs.

This protest was over American actions in the port city of Chefoo in north China, which the Eighth Route Army had liberated from the Japanese as early as August 2nd. On October 1st, an American naval vessel off Chefoo sent officers ashore who asked permission of the Eighth Route garrison to inspect American property in the city and to land Marines for recreational purposes on one of the islands in the bay.

Both requests were granted in the most friendly manner, whereupon the same naval officers appeared next day and asked permission to inspect Chinese coastal defenses. This request was also granted, Eighth Route officers aiding in the inspection.

At five o'clock on the morning of October 4th, however, an American destroyer landed officers who ordered the Eighth Route Army garrison to remove all coastal defenses from the Chefoo area and to withdraw all its armed forces, as well as the Chefoo Municipal Government, from the region, and to deliver the city in an orderly manner to the Americans!

In his protest to American military authorities, General Chu warned that the Americans would be held solely responsible for any serious incident should they try to land at Chefoo without previous agreement with his headquarters—which, of course, he would no more have granted than an American commander would have surrendered an American port city to a foreign naval force.

The Americans backed down on the Chefoo incident, but not on others. On October 18th, American troops surrounded and raided the Eighth Route Army office in Tientsin, arrested and brought its staff before the American military headquarters.

General Chu Teh also lodged protests at this incident and at two others. One incident involved a raid by ten American planes on Antze, a town in the Liberated Area, where a mass meeting was strafed and many people killed and wounded. The second incident also involved ten American planes which circled over Kuan in the Liberated Areas and dropped a letter ordering the Eighth Route garrison to withdraw within two days or be attacked!

After demanding an apology for these three violations of Chinese sovereignty, restitution of Eighth Route Army property in Tientsin, and compensation for the families of the dead and wounded at Antze, General Chu informed General Albert Wedemeyer:

I emphatically demand that you take proper steps and guarantee that no similar violations of Chinese sovereignty and interference in Chinese internal affairs will be repeated; and that no participation in Kuomintang military attacks on our Liberated Areas will be taken.

Ignoring General Chu's protest, General Wedemeyer was reported by American correspondents two days later to be speaking at a secret military conference where he informed Kuomintang generals of the number of Kuomintang troops and air personnel the United States intended to equip, as well as of American plans for supplying the Kuomintang with Lend Lease supplies.

At the same time, the Chinese press reported that American planes were transporting ammunition to Kuomintang blockading armies in the northwest and to Kuomintang troops in the Liberated Areas.

When the Kuomintang government did not even protest at the many cases of violence by American troops against Chinese, the hatred of Chinese of every class mounted against it.

This hatred grew after November 30, 1945, when members of the secret police hurled hand grenades in a mass meeting of students in Kunming to protest civil war and American occupation of Chinese soil, killing a number of students and wounding dozens. Student protest demonstrations flared up throughout the country. One in Chungking was addressed by two Democratic League leaders, Li Kung-po and Professor Lo Lung-chi, where Lo said:

Today it is easier to be dead than alive. We have heard of the horrors of hell, but so far we have not heard that there is thought control in hell, nor are there any secret police there. Today the living world is darker than hell.

Public anger mounted in late 1945 when a high school teacher, Fei Hsiao-chin, was shot dead in Tsingtao for refusing to answer questions about his thoughts and affiliations put to him by the mayor, the same traitor who had formerly commanded the Japanese Imperial Collaborationist Army.

In a mass meeting in Yenan to protest the killing of students in Kunming, General Chu Teh informed his audience that the Kuomintang authorities had "slaughtered from 400,000 to 500,000 progressive youth since 1927," and that the secret police continued to "kill people day in and day out."

"The Kuomintang pretends that it is more civilized than the old Peiyang (northern) warlords," he remarked contemptuously. "Let the people judge! Let the people realize what would become of our country if the Kuomintang should 'unify' it according to its desire! It would become a fascist dictatorship more malicious, more despotic, more cruel, more cunning than the Peiyang regime."

Cries of "Down with America! . . . Disarm Japanese troops! . . . Disarm puppet troops! . . . Stop the civil war! . . . Immediate evacuation of American troops!" soon resounded compellingly through the country.

The attitude of the Chinese Communists, at least, was not against Americans as a people, but against "American imperialism" or "American reactionaries." In the same manner they had campaigned against Japanese militarism but not against the Japanese people. As with the Japanese, they knew they had many American friends. When Brigadier General Evans F. Carlson died in the spring of 1947, they mourned as if he had been a Chinese patriot, and General Chu Teh, who had become Carlson's friend, wired Mrs. Carlson of his grief.

Similarly, the death of General Joseph W. Stilwell in October 1946 cast deep gloom over the Liberated Areas, and General Chu wired Mrs. Stilwell that "the Chinese people will remember forever General Stilwell's contributions to the war against Japan, and his struggle for a just American policy toward China."

A Yenan broadcast had stated:

If General Stilwell's advice last January to stop aiding Chiang Kai-shek had been followed, and if the American ambassador had adopted a really unselfish attitude like that of General Stilwell, the Chinese situation and Chinese-American relations would not be in the quandary they are today.

General Evans F. Carlson at least had one great consolation before he died. Mao Tse-tung, Chu Teh, Chou En-lai and Peng Teh-huai jointly signed a letter thanking him in the name of the Chinese people for his courageous struggle for Chinese democracy.

Chapter 43

OCTOBER and November passed and all north China became a battlefield between the forces of revolution and counter-revolution. American and Japanese soldiers jointly protected railways for the use of Kuomintang and puppet armies which were waging war on the Communists. American planes and Lend Lease supplies continued to pour into Shanghai and American-held port cities of the north for use of the Kuomintang armies.

The Soviet Red Army, which had completed the occupation of Manchuria on August 23rd, held the main cities and lines of communication in that region, while the Eighth Route Army and the Manchurian Volunteers operated in the countryside, avoiding all contact with the Russians who scrupulously held to the letter of the Sino-Soviet treaty of friendship and alliance.

Because of the presence of the People's Armies in Manchuria, Generalissimo Chiang Kai-shek had officially requested Moscow to postpone the evacuation of its troops until Kuomintang troops could take over. Moscow had complied with this request, and set January 3, 1946, as the date of its final evacuation.

In mid-December, however, Generalissimo Chiang's representatives again officially requested the Red Army to postpone its evacuation for another three months, and again Moscow complied. The Red Army, however, rejected the Kuomintang request that it disarm the Chinese "irregulars," stating that it could not interfere in China's internal affairs.

While the Kuomintang twice officially requested the Red Army to postpone its evacuation, Kuomintang propagandists, ably abetted by their American colleagues, carried on a violent anti-Soviet campaign, charging that the Red Army refused to evacuate Manchuria. In March 1946, when the Red Army began the final evacuation of the northeast according to schedule, Kuomintang propagandists charged that it was leaving in order to deliver Manchuria to the Chinese Communists!

For the previous months Kuomintang and puppet armies, transported by American planes, had been trying to fight their way into Manchuria against the Eighth Route Army and the Manchurian Volunteers. By the time the Russians evacuated, the Kuomintang could take over only the main south Manchurian cities. The Communist Armies moved in after the Russians in the north, even occupying the old Japanese puppet capital of Changchun—which they held until powerful Kuomintang armies converged on it.

The Americans, in particular, criticized the Russians for stripping Manchuria of its industrial machinery before leaving. There is no doubt that some of the charges were based on fact, but the reasons for the stripping were never explained honestly. I believe the facts to be the following:

The Russians undoubtedly stripped Manchuria of all war installations and industrial plants which Japan had constructed in Manchuria in the preceding fourteen years as the foundation of its military bastion against the Soviet Union. Until the Pacific War began, the Western capitalist powers had also regarded Manchuria as "the bastion against Communism in Asia." Manchuria, the "cockpit of Asia," had also been an objective of American financiers since the late nineteenth century; and, during the Russian Revolution, it had been a base of operation against the Soviets.

There seems no doubt whatever that some American supporters of the counter-revolutionary Kuomintang regime wanted Chiang Kai-shek to take over the Japanese military bastion in Manchuria as a base of operations for a possible third world war. When the Russians stripped this bastion, it weakened the foundations of a potential anti-Soviet base.

General Chu and other Chinese Communist leaders did not intend to allow their country to become a battlefield in a third world war during which, as General Chu expressed it more than once, "the Chinese people would be the meat and imperialists the butchers." They did not depend on the Soviet Union or its Red Army for anything, because the Soviet Union recognized the Kuomintang regime. There is no doubt, however, that the Soviet Union sympathized fundamentally with the Chinese Communists, though it is doubtful if they believed the Chinese Communists strong enough to come to power.

Such was the situation, or developing situation, at the end of November 1945, when two American correspondents flew into Yenan.

Mao Tse-tung, after returning to Yenan from Chungking in October, could not be interviewed, but General Chu talked frankly with the correspondents.

Yenan, the Communists' headquarters, was being evacuated. When the war ended, Eighth Route Army troops drove the Japanese from the industrial city of Kalgan, which was forty days' marching distance to the northeast. Along this entire distance rest-feeding stations had been established to care for the thousands of men and women who began moving out of Yenan for Kalgan and other regions. The famous Kangta —the Political-Military University—which had trained thousands of military and political cadres during the war, had been split up into several sections and distributed to the various Liberated regions. Most of the students of Yenan University had left, some for administrative jobs, others to continue their studies in the new Union University at Kalgan. The Lu Hsun Art Academy, which had produced some of the most vigorous art, music, and literature in modern China, had moved to Kalgan, as had the Bethune Medical College, which had graduated over a thousand medical workers from three-year courses during the war. The Medical College had taken with them most of the patients from the cave hospitals of Yenan.

Hundreds of party and army staff workers had also left, but Mao and

Chu, with their chief staff members, continued working and waiting in Yenan to see if Generalissimo Chiang intended to call the inter-party conference to which he had agreed on October 10th.

The first questions which the American correspondents put to General Chu Teh were about Manchuria and about the American and Kuomintang charges that the Chinese Communists were receiving help from the Soviet Union.

General Chu declared that neither the Communists at Yenan nor those in Manchuria had any contacts whatever with the Russians; and he was certain that the Russians had no intention of helping them in preference to the Kuomintang.

He became bitterly contemptuous when speaking of the Kuomintang policy toward Manchuria. During all the years following the Japanese occupation of Manchuria, he said, Kuomintang leaders had been willing to surrender the northeast to the Japanese, and had been content with the recovery of only such Chinese territory as the Japanese had occupied after the Sino-Japanese War began on July 7, 1937.

The Chinese Communists, he declared, had no objections to the Kuomintang pursuing activities in Manchuria, nor to sending officials there to carry out their duties, peacefully, in accordance with the Sino-Soviet treaty of friendship and alliance. Then he continued:

We must point out that for the past fourteen years the Chinese Communists have been associated with the people of the northeast in their struggle against the Japanese, while our Eighth Route Army, together with the Manchurian people, established the Hopei-Jehol-Liaoning (south Manchuria) Liberated Area during the war. We are therefore duty-bound to be concerned with the democratic reconstruction of the northeast, and to prevent the democratic rights which the people are already enjoying, from being destroyed. . . .

The real cause of the trouble is that the Kuomintang ignores the will of the people in the northeast and tries to impose its one-party dictatorship on that area. Kuomintang officials refuse to cooperate with the people but, instead, deny them their democratic rights. The Kuomintang depends on, and accompanies, American troops to intrude into the northeast. Certain reactionaries even intend to use the northeast as an anti-Soviet base and the battleground of a third world war. This is causing apprehension and resentment among the northeastern people. In fact, the presence of American troops in north China is absolutely unnecessary, nor have they any right whatever to enter the northeast. . . . If the Kuomintang does not relinquish its anti-people anti-democratic policy, the dispute between it and the northeastern people can never be eliminated. . . .

The northeastern people have proposed that local self-government be established and a local coalition democratic administration be set up, which would become a model region of democratic reconstruction. This is the best way to solve the Manchurian question, nor would its realization impair the integrity of a united China.

The Kuomintang should begin in the northeast to act upon its promises of returning rule to the people and of enforcing democracy. This would allay dissatisfaction of the northeastern people toward the Kuomintang and be a great help in the consolidation of the unity of the nation.

Throughout the preceding fourteen years, General Chu added, 100,000 underground workers in Manchuria, all of them under Communist leadership, had been killed in action. There were now 300,000 Communist-commanded troops in that area, under General Lin Piao's command.

Such were General Chu's ideas when the national scene again suddenly changed. On December 15, 1945, President Truman announced that the United States took cognizance of the fact that "the National Government of China is a one-party government" and that political unity could be worked out only by the Chinese themselves. Advocating a cease-fire order in the civil war, the President expressed the belief that peace, unity, and democratic reform could be furthered if the basis of the Chinese government were broadened to include other political elements. The United States would be willing to grant loans to such a broadened government.

This stated policy, and the appointment of General George Marshall to implement it, was received by the Chinese people with wild joy.

"Come out, you common people!" cried the *New China Daily* of Chungking, while the press of Shanghai rejoiced and the *Ta Kung Pao* published an appeal from Shanghai schools and universities to General Marshall:

(1) Help establish a democratic Chinese government.

(2) Help develop industrial, agricultural, commercial, medical and cultural work in China.

(3) Respect the interests of the Chinese nation and carry out the policy of the late President Roosevelt.

(4) Understand better the real sentiment of the Chinese people so Sino-American friendship can be strengthened.

(5) Arbitrate fairly in the civil war.

(6) Withdraw American troops from China within the shortest possible time and stop helping Chinese troops with arms under the Lend Lease agreement.

Both Mao Tse-tung and Chu Teh publicly welcomed the Truman statement and expressed the hope that George Marshall would "repair the damage done by General Patrick Hurley and General Albert Wedemeyer."

Despite this, however, American troops continued on Chinese soil, and American Lend Lease supplies continued to pour in. Subsequently General Wedemeyer complacently remarked to correspondents that the Chinese puppet armies had been "successfully absorbed" by Chiang Kai-shek's armies.

As if this were not warning enough, Mao Tse-tung and Chu Teh received copies of a new secret Kuomintang document, *Plan for National Revival*—a blueprint for the extermination of their armies. The juxtaposition of American actions and of this new plan must have made them speculate seriously about the purpose of the Truman statement and the dispatch of General Marshall as ambassador to China. Was it a delaying action to disintegrate and weaken them?

Despite such speculations, which were voiced only months later, the Communists at once dispatched a delegation to the Political Consultative Conference which Chiang Kai-shek finally called, on General Marshall's advice.

On January 31, 1946, representatives of the Kuomintang, the Communist Party, the Democratic League, and non-party delegates solemnly signed the historic Chungking agreement to establish a democratic coalition government. A committee immediately set to work to draft a new democratic constitution which, following general elections, was to be discussed and ratified by the assembly of a new Chinese democratic republic.

One of the most important points in this Chungking agreement, which the Kuomintang delegation fought without success, made the executive branch of the new government responsible to the National Assembly instead of to the President. This was a provision specifically made to prevent the government from becoming the tool of a dictator as had happened repeatedly since 1911.

Immediately after the Chungking agreement was signed, the Kuomintang and Communist Party representatives signed another, countersigned by General Marshall, agreeing to issue cease-fire orders to their troops, to reduce and reorganize their armies, and create a national army under a joint High Command.

The Communists were so confident that the agreements would be carried out that General Chu's headquarters at once began disbanding whole divisions of their People's Armies which, by the cease-fire agreement, were to be reduced to eighteen divisions, whereas the Kuomintang was to retain ninety. Within three months half a million men had been demobilized and sent back to their farms.

Chapter 44

In JANUARY, General Chu talked with a foreign correspondent, John Roderick, who pictured him as an "eager listener" with "old-world manners" who clasped his hands and made a slight bow when taking a proffered cigarette. General Chu, Roderick said, no longer played basketball with his troops, but walked a great deal and sometimes rode into the hills to hunt. Sitting in a winter-chilled cave five miles from Yenan—the town had been destroyed by Japanese bombers during the war—Chu was described as an "unpaid, ill-clothed revolutionary whose rank is equivalent to that of a five-star American General."

This much-wanted man [the correspondent wrote] goes about Yenan virtually unguarded, and never under arms. His soldiers idolize him—a rare thing in the Chinese Army. These days, when negotiations for unity in Chungking demand that he participate in important Party decisions as well as direct the 1,300,000 men under his command, he follows a full daily schedule. Up at 6 A.M., he eats breakfast, then plunges into a pile of dispatches from the front. He has a light lunch, then works all afternoon, conferring with other Party leaders, and often walking five miles into town to meet them. Both before breakfast and after supper he avidly reads books and newspapers and keeps up on the international situation through translations of foreign-language newscasts and papers. . . .

After spending a lifetime fighting for unity, freedom, and democracy, he says he is ready to lay down his arms the instant these are achieved. "I hope," he said, "that they will come in 1946."

General Chu spoke with eager enthusiasm of the Chungking conference. "With Japan defeated, Russia no problem, and the danger of civil war apparently past," he thought the next necessary step was to cut down and reorganize the armies to a level the country could afford. He thought both the Kuomintang armies and the Communist armies should be further scaled down. China should stand on her own feet as much as possible, and he saw no need for an American military mission for which Chiang Kai-shek had asked and on which General Albert Wedemeyer was already working.

Furthermore, foreign loans for military purposes would be difficult to repay, but loans to build up industry could be repaid from the proceeds of new factories, while living standards could be simultaneously raised.

When asked if a large well-trained Chinese army was not needed to preserve peace in the Far East, General Chu replied that the new Chinese democratic government would be the greatest safeguard for international peace. "That is why we believe in nationalizing the army. It is essential to eliminate power or profit as motivating factors in maintaining large armies in China." Speaking eagerly, he concluded:

I have helped carve out a territory here in north China where human beings may live secure from arrest and terror, free to practice democratic self-government. I have lived to see the democracy we established demanded by the rest of China which now lives in chaos and under oppression. For this I am grateful. My life has not been in vain.

At a mass meeting in Yenan on February 4th to celebrate the conclusion of the unity talks in Chungking, General Chu expressed the conviction that China would become a modern nation equal to any in the world if it could have thirty years of peace. Complimenting the Generalissimo for agreeing to a democratic government, he nevertheless called on Chiang to prove his sincerity by removing the military blockade around the Yenan Border Region—a challenge which Chiang ignored.

When General George Marshall visited Yenan on March 4th, General Chu told a welcoming mass meeting that within less than three months Marshall had helped the Chinese people bring fighting to an end, draft the army reorganization plan, and achieve the first steps toward democracy and peace. The People's Liberation Armies, he said, would faithfully carry out the direction of the truce teams and the Military Executive Headquarters established by Marshall.

General Marshall left for Washington in early March and asked for an American loan of $500 million which, according to President Truman's statement of December 15th, was to be granted to the new democratic government only.

However, there were more tricks in the arsenal of Kuomintang counter-revolution than were dreamt of in Marshall's philosophy. During Marshall's absence, the Central Executive Committee of the Kuomintang met behind closed doors and abrogated the decisions of the Chungking agreement. Repudiating the principle of executive responsibility to the National Assembly—which would have robbed Chiang Kai-shek of dictatorial power—the Kuomintang also claimed the right to appoint not only its own representatives, but the representatives of all the other parties, to the new coalition government.

The kind of government envisaged by the Kuomintang was revealed when it offered a Communist the Ministry of Forestry and Agriculture, a post which for years had been an asylum for retired warlords. The Ministry of Education was offered to a member of the Democratic League who replied: "It is more important for me to preserve my life!"

The Communist Party and the Democratic League rejected all offers of the Kuomintang and demanded that the January agreement be honored in full. The Kuomintang, however, had not only abrogated the decisions of the agreement, but began implementing its secret blueprint to wipe out the Communists.

Its plan was divided into three stages. In the first, or preparatory stage, the democratic movement led by the Chinese Democratic League in Kuomintang territory was to be silenced by bribery or destroyed by terrorism, and the "China problem" presented to the United States, not as a struggle of the Chinese people for democracy, but as an outright Kuomintang-Communist struggle for power. There was no doubt where all-powerful America would stand on such an issue.

The second stage—a war of extermination against the Communist Armies—was to begin in mid-July.

This second stage was expected to merge into the third: a Soviet-American war in which the Kuomintang was convinced that the United States would be victorious and the Communist menace to the propertied classes of China and the world finally and forever eliminated.

Chiang Kai-shek was quoted as saying that "we have three more months in which to prepare, and three more in which to finish the Communists."

That General Chu Teh knew the details of this conspiracy was made clear at an anniversary mass meeting of the great May 4th Movement of 1919, at which he said the Chungking agreement had been wrecked by it.

"The struggle has not yet been won, but we are convinced that the entire Chinese people can yet defeat the conspiracy," he said.

From March to July 1946, the first stage of the secret plan was carried out. While fighting continued throughout Manchuria and north China, a reign of secret police terror in Kuomintang areas was carried out. Opposition newspapers and magazines, particularly those of the Chinese Democratic League, were demolished by mobs of plainclothes secret police. Printers and newspaper staff workers were beaten up and many editors kidnapped or killed. In Sian the secret police destroyed the printing plant of the democratic daily, beat up the staff, and shot the editor. A lawyer, Wang Yen, who took the case to court, was seized and executed, after which the Kuomintang stated that he had been an opium smoker!

In Nantung, a city north of Shanghai, where a truce team went to investigate fighting between Kuomintang and New Fourth Army troops, the secret police warned the populace to remain indoors and give no testimony. The people turned out to welcome the truce team, instead, and twenty teachers, writers, and newspapermen testified. These twenty men disappeared the next day. The bodies of sixteen were never found, but the trussed-up corpses of four were discovered in a nearby river a few days later, their bodies mutilated and their eyes gouged out.

In Canton the secret police raided and closed down all bookstores and cultural organizations and demolished two liberal dailies which had exposed official corruption in UNRRA supplies. One shipload of relief rice had been traced by these papers to the local Fifty-fourth Kuomintang Army. A Chinese UNRRA official, when questioned by them about the disappearance of a few hundred sacks of rice of another shipment, replied:

"A strong wind came up and blew the sacks into the sea!"

In April, convinced that the Chungking agreement had been wrecked, eleven of the Communist leaders who had participated in it left Chungking by plane for Yenan. The plane crashed en route and every person in it was killed. The pilot and crew were Americans, but a little thing like that would never have deterred the Kuomintang secret police from sabotage. Among the dead were General Yeh Ting, former commander of the New Fourth Army—who had been released after five years in prison—together with his wife and two children.

The democratic forces of China fought. President Truman, the United States Congress, and General Marshall were inundated with protests from Chinese and organizations of all strata, even conservative businessmen and industrialists. America was asked to withdraw its troops from China and to stop all military supplies and loans to China until a democratic government was established.

In July, Madame Sun Yat-sen addressed an urgent appeal to Congress and the American people, urging them to withdraw all support from the Kuomintang and prevent another disastrous civil war which, she warned, would bring chaos, starvation, and death to new millions. The Kuomintang, she warned, could not win such a war.

Madame Sun's appeal, like thousands of others, met no response.

By July, the month set by the conspiracy for all-out civil war, there was still one democratic stronghold left in China. This was in Kunming in the southwest. There the Chinese Democratic League had its last organ: the *Democratic Weekly* edited by Li Kung-po. One of its editorial board was Professor Wen I-toh, a noted poet who for ten years had been professor of literature in Tsinghwa University.

On July 11th, the secret police shot Li Kung-po to death in the streets of Kunming. Next day, Professor Wen I-toh delivered an austere funeral oration over the body of his friend. "When I crossed my threshold today," he told the mourning thousands, "I knew I would never return." Challenging the secret police in the audience to come out in the open, he said:

"Oh infamy! Infamy! You destroy the living and defame the dead!"

A few hours later Professor Wen, with his eighteen-year-old student son, was also shot dead in the streets of Kunming.

Sixteen other Chinese democratic professors in Kunming, with their families, fled to the American consulate, and were flown to Hongkong and Shanghai. Thirteen leading professional men from other parts of China risked death by cabling the Human Rights Committee of the United Nations about the Kunming murders, stating that the pistols used were American weapons equipped with silencers.

The full exposure of the Kunming assassinations by the international press and the protests of intellectual leaders of many countries to Chiang Kai-shek called a halt to open assassinations, but not to the secret kidnappings and killings.

In the same week of the Kunming murders, Chou En-lai, chief Communist liaison officer in Nanking, delivered to General Marshall a copy of the final orders which Chiang Kai-shek had issued to his troops to begin the all-out civil war. The order set July 22nd as the day the assault on the People's Liberation Armies was to begin. And indeed, on July 22, 1946, Kuomintang armies moved in force into the Liberated Areas behind American-made bombers, tanks, and artillery.

Another six months passed before General Marshall returned to America and issued a report which condemned both the Kuomintang and the Communists for the civil war, yet honestly stated that a "dominant group of Kuomintang reactionaries" were "interested in the preser-

vation of their own feudal control of China and . . . counted on substantial American support regardless of their actions."

General Chu later stated that Marshall's failure was due to the policy
of the American government rather than to Marshall himself.

By October, when a group of American correspondents flew into
Yenan, Chiang Kai-shek had mobilized three-fourths of his forces, or
193 out of 253 divisions, for the civil war. The fundamental reasons for
the breakdown of the January cease-fire agreement, General Chu told
the correspondents, was Kuomintang determination to continue the dictatorship, and American encouragement and aid to Chiang. The Kuomintang, he said, hoped to establish a despotism like that of Hitler,
Franco, and Hirohito, which the Communists and the people were
determined to defeat.

Speaking of Kuomintang rumors about an impending Soviet-American
war, General Chu remarked that there was "a group of American
reactionaries who are manufacturing such a war, which Chinese reactionaries are hoping will come very soon."

> I don't think their ambitions can be realized [he added]. In case such
> a war begins, our attitude will hinge on the attitude of the two sides
> towards the Chinese people. . . .

There are two different polices which the United States could adopt.
One is to make China a bridge of friendship with the Soviet Union, the
other is to make China a battleground for attacking the Soviet Union.
The former policy is advocated by Mr. Henry Wallace, while the latter
is advocated by American reactionaries. We will prevent such a war
from developing! The formidable prospect of such a holocaust forces us
to strive for peace.

And how long could the People's Liberation Armies hold out against
such powerful Kuomintang armies?

General Chu smiled coldly:

> That depends entirely upon American reactionaries who send us
> weapons and ammunition through Chinese reactionaries! . . .
> Our people and troops know that this war was initiated by Chinese
> and American reactionaries, and that they would lose everything they
> have gained, and that millions would be exterminated, should we fail.
> The whole population therefore supports us as during the war against
> Japan. . . . Many of Chiang's subordinates do not want civil war either,
> but they must carry out his orders or break with him. This period of

obedience, however, will not last much longer. We have already exterminated twenty-five Kuomintang divisions in the past two and a half months, but the Kuomintang has been unable to exterminate even one single regiment of ours.

When asked if his armies would accept help from the Soviet Union should it be offered, General Chu said:

The great aid which we seek today is from the American people. We want the American people to call a halt to the inglorious policy of their government. I can say honestly that we are deeply grateful to all people and all nations which sympathize with Chinese independence, peace and democracy, and that we oppose all reactionaries who interfere in our internal affairs and encourage civil strife.

American imperialism is as hateful as Japanese imperialism [he declared bitterly]. The American government is a reactionary government! The aid which these reactionaries have already given Chiang Kai-shek exceeds three billion American dollars. All of this, except for the part pocketed by officials and the warlords, is used to kill Chinese. There are now tens of thousands of victims of American guns in China who, one year ago, were wildly happy over President Truman's policy statement and General Marshall's arrival in China. While Marshall talked peace, the Kuomintang and the American government prepared for war!

As the year 1946 drew to a close, north China and Manchuria ran with the blood of the people of China, but for every man who fell at the front many sprang forward to take his place. The People's Liberation Army had given up great cities and withdrawn to the countryside to whittle down and exhaust the enemy. Kuomintang morale sagged lower and lower until whole divisions began going over to the Communists.

With iron discipline, tempered in thousands of battles, and clad in an armor of conviction that only death could shatter, the Chinese People's Liberation Armies were swiftly arming themselves with the best of American weapons, approaching the moment when they could advance from guerrilla and mobile fighting into regular warfare.

General Chu Teh, son of a poor peasant of Szechwan Province, had now finished his sixtieth year. On November 30th, in the midst of battle, the people and the troops of the north celebrated and sent him messages of love and encouragement. From distant Manchurian battle-fields Lin Piao's staff wired him:

"To celebrate your sixtieth birthday we present you with another victory. Another regiment of Kuomintang troops has just come over to us."

The editorial staff of the *Chun Chung* magazine, published in Shanghai, sent a letter to General Chu in time for his birthday. It read:

HONORABLE ELDER,

You have saved the Chinese people from the iron hoof of the enemy. You led the Chinese people to emancipate themselves from a thousand years of slavery, you have helped them clothe and feed themselves. You drive trespassers from their fields. You are a great son of the Chinese race, the parent of the Chinese people's rebirth. . . . Today, on your sixtieth birthday, we burn incense to you in our hearts.

From early morning until evening on November 30th, people streamed to General Chu's Yenan headquarters. A group of four peasants, one a woman, walked twenty miles to present him with birthday tarts, two bottles of wine, and a basket of birthday noodles. Troops from the Yenan garrison made sandals and shoes for him, sang revolutionary songs, and danced the *yang-ko* before his headquarters.

But the tribute which Chu Teh perhaps treasured most was a scroll from the Central Committee of the Communist Party which recounted his work for the overthrow of the Manchu dynasty, for the overthrow of Yuan Shih-kai, his role in the Great Revolution, his joint founding, with Mao Tse-tung, of the Chinese Red Army, his command of the armies during the Long March, and his great achievements in the Anti-Japanese War. This document ended:

You symbolize the great struggle of the Chinese people for freedom for the last sixty years. You are a good son and brother of the oppressed Chinese people. . . .

Today, when Kuomintang reactionaries, together with American imperialism, are attempting to rob the Chinese people of the fruits of victory over Japan, you and Comrade Mao Tse-tung stand at the front of the struggle in defense of our country and the interests of our people.

General Chu published one article on his sixtieth birthday—the story of his mother, daughter of an outcast wandering theatrical family, a

woman so humble that she did not even have a name, a peasant woman
who labored until death claimed her in her eightieth year.

Two weeks after this sixtieth birthday, General Chu was again tramping the paths and roads of China. Chiang Kai-shek's blockading army
under General Hu Tsung-nan was converging on Yenan. The little city
was empty as the enemy advanced.

To the farmers who came out with blanched faces to bid him farewell,
General Chu said:

"We will not be gone long!"

To Mao Tse-tung, now fifty-three, who walked by his side, General
Chu said:

"I have lived sixty years. From now on, every year of my life is just
so much gain!"

So he went forward on the great road of human liberation, this time
to lead his country and people to the victory which three years later
shook Chiang Kai-shek and set the reactionaries of the world a-tremble.

Chronology

(The following chronology is based on that in the Japanese edition of this book.)

1886 December 12 (or November 30), Chu Teh born in village of Linglungtsai, near Ilunghsien, Szechwan Province.

1892 Goes to small neighboring school of seventeen pupils.

1893 Goes to landlord Ting's private family school.

1895 Moves with uncle to town of Ta Wan, enters school of Hsi Ping-an; China defeated in Sino-Japanese War, Shimonoseki Treaty.

1898 Reform Movement (Wu Hsu Cheng Pien).

1900 Boxer (I Ho Chuan) Rebellion, imposition of foreign indemnities.

1905 Russo-Japanese War, Russian Revolution of 1905; Chu Teh enters modern school at Shunching.

1906 Autumn, passes State Examinations in Ilunghsien, receives title of *Hsiu Tsai;* studies physical training in Higher Normal School at Chengtu.

1907 Teaches physical training in new school in Ilunghsien.

1909 Enters Yunnan Military Academy, Yunnanfu, Yunnan Province; studies under Brigadier General Tsai Ao; secretly joins republican Tung Meng Hui and peasant organization Ko Lao Hui; assigned to Szechwan Regiment.

1911 July, graduated from Academy, second lieutenant; October, Yunnanfu republican uprising under Tsai Ao, Chu Teh commissioned captain, joins revolutionary expedition into Szechwan; Chinese Revolution, declaration of Republic.

1912 February, Sun Yat-sen, first provisional President, replaced by Yuan Shih-kai; May, Chu Teh promoted to major; begins teaching at Military Academy; autumn, marries Hsiao Chu-fen; transfers membership from old Tung Meng Hui to new Kuomintang.

1913 Serves for two years in south Yunnan in border guards against French-instigated raids from Indo-China.

1915   December, promoted to colonel, commanding 10th Yunnan Regiment; joins Tsai Ao's Szechwan expedition in campaign against Yuan Shih-kai regime.

1916   Szechwan campaign successful, Chu Teh promoted to brigadier general, Tsai Ao becomes Governor General of Szechwan; death of Yuan Shih-kai; "new tide" cultural renaissance centering in Peking; deaths of Tsai Ao and of Chu Teh's wife; Chu Teh stationed in Luchow, with Yunnan Protection Army.

1917   Marries Chen Yu-chen; during this period takes up opium, gradually becomes involved in warlordism.

1919   May 4th Movement stimulates political and cultural awakening.

1921   Chu Teh tries to resign from Protection Army, remains as police commissioner in Yunnanfu.

1922   August, takes opium cure in French Hospital, Shanghai; meets Sun Yat-sen; applies for membership in Communist Party, is rejected; September, sails for Europe; October, meets Chou En-lai in Berlin, shortly afterward secretly accepted into Chinese Communist Party.

1923   Enrolls in political science faculty at Göttingen.

1924   Returns to Berlin, organizes branch of Kuomintang.

1925   Studies with German Marxists; March, death of Sun Yat-sen.

1926   June, Chu Teh arrested by German police, released; returns to China, goes to Szechwan via Shanghai, Hankow.

1927   Appointed director of Nanchang Military Training School and police commissioner; March, Nanking incident; April, Shanghai massacre; July, Chu Teh attends Communist Party conference near Nanchang, vote taken to arm the people and begin agrarian revolution; Nanchang uprising, revolutionaries take city, Chu Teh placed in command of Ironsides new 9th Division; September, Ironsides defeated at Swatow; Chu Teh retreats to south Hunan, elected commander in chief of renamed Workers and Peasants Revolutionary Army.

1928   January, Chu Teh establishes Soviet at Ichang, Hunan; Soviets next established at Chenhsien, Leiyang; at Leiyang Chu Teh marries Wu Yu-lan; May, meeting between Chu Teh and Mao Tse-tung at Linghsien, they withdraw to Chingkanshan mountain base; Communist Party conference at Chingkanshan adopts four-point military program, reorganizes into Fourth Red Army, Chu Teh commander in chief, Mao Tse-tung political commissar; Chingkanshan blockaded by Kuomintang.

1929   January, Fourth Army defeats enemy at Tapoti, occupies Ningtu,

Tungku, Hsingkuo, establishes Tungku-Hsingkuo Regional Soviet; Chu Teh's wife Wu Yu-lan captured and beheaded; spring, Chu Teh harasses enemy, occupies Tingchow; Juikin, conference between Chu Teh, Mao Tse-tung, and Peng Teh-huai; Chu Teh campaigns in south Kiangsi, retakes Ningtu, occupies Lungyen; September, withdraws to west Fukien, takes Shanghang; defeated in East River Regions, Kwangtung; marries Kang Keh-chin.

1930   January, Red Army conference, Kutien; Chu Teh harasses enemy throughout Kiangsi, destroys Yunnan Army; June, Tingchow Red Army conference, reorganization of army, partial acceptance of Li Li-san line; Changsha occupied by Peng Teh-huai, bombarded by U.S. gunboat *Palos*, evacuated by Red Army; Chu Teh besieges Nanchang, withdraws; September, besieges Changsha, withdraws, with Mao Tse-tung repudiates Li Li-san line; October, takes Kian; Chiang Kai-shek begins first of series of Red Extermination Campaigns; December, Chu Teh defeats enemy at Lungkang.

1931   March, Shanghai Communist Party Congress affirms Chu-Mao line, repudiates Li Li-san line; May-June, Chu Teh and Peng Teh-huai defeat enemy in south Kiangsi, Second Extermination Campaign; September, Mukden incident, Japan begins occupation of Manchuria.

1934   September-October, Red Army begins Long March.

1935   January, Central Red Army occupies Tsunyi; Chu Teh learns of death of his wife Yu-chen and his son at Nanchi; May, Central Red Army crosses Ta Tu River; July, at Moukung Central Red Army meets Fourth Red Army under Chang Kuo-tao, Politburo conference reorganizes Red Armies; August, at Maoehrkai Chang Kuo-tao takes Chu Teh and staff prisoner, with subsequent division of command during march in Sikang; October, Mao Tse-tung reaches north Shensi.

1936   October, Chu Teh makes first contact with Central Red Army at Huihsien; December, meeting of Chu Teh and Mao Tse-tung at Paoan; Sian incident, Young Marshal "kidnaps" Chiang Kai-shek.

1937   January, Communist headquarters established at Yenan, Agnes Smedley arrives in Yenan, meets Chu Teh; February, Mao Tse-tung and Chu Teh appeal to Kuomintang to form national anti-Japanese united front; March, Chu Teh and Agnes Smedley begin working together on this book; July, Japanese attack

Peking, beginning of Sino-Japanese War; August, Chu Teh
and Chou En-lai attend National Military Defense Council
meeting at Nanking, Kuomintang in principle accepts formation of united front; September, Eighth Route Army formed,
Chu Teh commander in chief, Peng Teh-huai vice-commander;
October, Chu Teh begins campaign against Japanese throughout Shansi, Agnes Smedley at his headquarters, Wutai mountains; December, Nanking captured and sacked by Japanese.

1938   Chu Teh continues Shansi campaign; summer, Kuomintang raids
Communist Liberated Areas, sometimes in conjunction with
Japanese; autumn, Chu Teh reports at Yenan on first year of
war; October, Chu Teh pleads with National Military Defense
Council for implementation of united front, introduction of
democratic reforms.

1939   March, Mao Tse-tung and Chu Teh publicly protest Kuomintang
armed attacks on Red Army; September, World War II begins
in Europe; December, Kuomintang armies in south Shansi
join Japanese in attacking Eighth Route Army, Chu Teh leaves
front for Yenan.

1940   August, Chu Teh and Peng Teh-huai begin hundred-regiment
campaign against Japanese; December, successful conclusion
of campaign, virtual collapse of Kuomintang-Communist
united front, Chungking orders Fourth Army to evacuate
fighting zone.

1941   January, Kuomintang armies slaughter part of Fourth Army,
Mao Tse-tung and Chu Teh protest, Chiang Kai-shek takes no
action; Mao Tse-tung announces policy of economic self-
sufficiency in Liberated Areas to counter Kuomintang-Japanese
blockade and attacks; June, Germany invades Soviet Union;
July, Japanese begin attack on Liberated Areas with "three-
all" strategy; November, Conference of Eastern Peoples at
Yenan; December, Japanese attack Pearl Harbor.

1944   May-August, foreign correspondents permitted by Chiang Kai-
shek to visit Yenan Liberated Area; autumn, American Military Observer Group established in Yenan; October, Stilwell
recalled, Wedemeyer appointed; Mao Tse-tung and Chu Teh
open Reconstruction Exhibition of Yenan Border Region.

1945   April, Communist Party representative on Chinese delegation to
San Francisco United Nations conference; Seventh Communist
Party Congress meets at Yenan, Mao Tse-tung publishes *On
Coalition Government*, Chu Teh warns of danger of civil war;

May, World War II ends in Europe; July, Potsdam Declaration on unconditional surrender of Japan; August, atomic bombing of Hiroshima, protested by Communist *New China Daily*; Chu Teh, to counter Chiang Kai-shek's cooperation with Japanese, orders Red Armies to accept Japanese surrender; Japanese surrender, qualifying Allied terms, retaining Emperor; Chu Teh urges Allied powers to support Communist efforts to avert civil war and form coalition government; September, Mao Tse-tung at Chungking, negotiates with Chiang Kai-shek; October, Chu Teh protests American military interference in Chinese internal affairs; Chiang Kai-shek agrees in principle to conference for establishment of coalition government; November, Communists begin to move headquarters from Yenan to Kalgan; December, Truman declaration supporting establishment of coalition government in China, appointment of General Marshall as American representative in China.

1946   January, at Chungking representatives of Kuomintang, Communist Party, Democratic League, and other delegates sign agreement to establish democratic coalition government; March, Marshall visits Yenan; Kuomintang begins secretly subverting Chungking agreement; July, Kunming assassinations; Kuomintang armies invade Liberated Areas; November 30, Chu Teh celebrates his sixtieth birthday.

Index